FROM RONNIE RADFORD
TO ROGER OSBORNE

FROM RONNIE
RADFORD
TO ROGER OSBORNE
WHEN THE FA CUP *REALLY* MATTERED
VOLUME 2 - THE 1970s

Matthew Eastley

First published by Pitch Publishing, 2014
Pitch Publishing
A2 Yeoman Gate
Yeoman Way
Durrington
BN13 3QZ
www.pitchpublishing.co.uk

A CIP catalogue record is available for this book
from the British Library

ISBN 978 1 90962 645 4

Typesetting and origination by Pitch Publishing

Printed by Latimer Trend Ltd, Plymouth

Contents

This book is dedicated to the
memory of
Derek Hamersley

25 June 1958 to 22 April 1975

Acknowledgements

HUNDREDS of people were kind enough to share their memories with me during the research of this book. I would like to say how grateful I am to everyone who responded with such enthusiasm to my requests for help. I would like to extend special thanks to the following people – the brackets indicate which team they support: Ray Ashworth (Leeds), Ian Brunton (Manchester United), Bernie Butt (Arsenal), John Cross (Ipswich), George Forster (Sunderland), Dean Goodman (Arsenal), Mick Gorman RIP (Manchester United), Rosemary Gorman, Peter Hamersley (West Ham), Mick Kelly (Arsenal), Ray Leonard (Sunderland), Carole Parkhouse (Leeds), Mike Paxton (Newcastle), Tony Ryan (Manchester United), Jeanette Sutton (Sunderland), Derek Thornton (Newcastle), Jeff Van Doorn (Chelsea), Steve Van Doorn (Chelsea), Les Wake (Leeds), Chris Wood (Liverpool), Emilio Zorlakki (Arsenal).

Big thanks also go to Dave Barber at the Football Association, the brilliant football reporter Ken Jones, formerly of the *Daily Mirror*, the *Sunday Mirror* and the *Independent* newspapers, as well as the following fans: George Ackinlose (Newcastle), Malcolm Adams (Millwall), Colin Appleby (Newcastle), Kevin Appleby (Newcastle), John Archer (Newcastle), Roy Arrigon (Arsenal), Ken Banham (Arsenal), Di Betts (Arsenal), Joe Blake (Newcastle), Stephen Blank (Manchester United), Peter Boyle (Manchester United), Dave Bowman (Sunderland), Alan Brabon (Newcastle), Geoff Buffey (Newcastle), Phil Carmichael (Newcastle), John Carrick (Newcastle), Frank Cozens (Newcastle), Peter Darby (Manchester United),

Richard Davis (Arsenal), Paul Devine (Ipswich), David Dickie (Newcastle), John Doyle (Newcastle), Ken Dyer (Ipswich), Chris Eaton (Arsenal), Wendy Edgar (Kilmarnock), Stu Eglon (Newcastle), Alan Findley (Newcastle), John Foley (Chelsea), John Gateshill (Newcastle), Brian Gleghorn (Newcastle), Peggy Goulding (Arsenal), Andy Griffin (Newcastle), Paul Griffin (Manchester United), Dennis Guildford (Newcastle), Geoff Hall (Arsenal), Tom Hall (Arsenal), Peter Harris (Southampton), Barry Hatch (Arsenal), Michael Hoban (Manchester United), Peter Hollingworth (Arsenal), Keith Hudson (Newcastle), Gary Humphrey (Arsenal), Mick Hush (Newcastle), Rob Innis (Southampton), Damian Inwood (Chelsea), Colin Johnson (Newcastle), Colin Kriedewolf (Ipswich), Dale Lang (Newcastle), Peter Lawson (Newcastle), David Lewis (West Ham), Steve Lillico (Newcastle), Bill Lisgo (Newcastle), Paul Lockett (Manchester United), Tony Mallon (Newcastle), Niall McKenzie (Newcastle), Mick McNeill (Newcastle), Andrew McTernan (Newcastle), Alan Millen (Newcastle), Alan Mitchell (Sunderland), Jonathan Morley (Ipswich), Richard Morris (Arsenal), Layne Morrison (Newcastle), Ian Morton (Newcastle), Pauline Nicholas (Liverpool), Alan Oliver (Newcastle), Steve Oliver (Newcastle), Terry Paddison (Newcastle), Ken Parkin (Newcastle), Don Richards (Arsenal), Clive Risbridger (Southampton), Alex Royffe (Spurs), Ian Ruddick (Newcastle), Ronnie Rutter (Newcastle), Andrew Sanderson (Newcastle), Pete Sanderson (Newcastle), David Schofield (Manchester United), Liam Shannon (Newcastle), John Shelley (Newcastle), Ian Short (Manchester United), Ken Smith (Arsenal), Ian Snelling (Arsenal), Jonathan Stott (Newcastle), Graham Stubbins (Arsenal), Phil Stubbs (Leeds), Bill Tebay (Newcastle), Keith Udale (Manchester United), John Whiteoak (Newcastle), Brian Wood (Manchester United), Pete Woods (Southampton).

Thanks also to the following journalists, website owners and press officers who provided me with valuable assistance and publicity: Steve Parish, Andy Exley, Paul Chronnell, Chris Hall,

ACKNOWLEDGEMENTS

Andy Philip, Brad Jones, 'Biffa' at www.nufc.com, Barney at *Red News*, Philip Ham at www.twtd.co.uk, Simon Walter, Peter Blythe and Susan Swinney.

Thanks also to the staff in the central libraries at Leeds, Liverpool, Sunderland (Phil Hall), Southampton (Vicky Green), Manchester and Newcastle.

Introduction

THE FA Cup is a shadow of its former self and especially so the FA Cup Final. It used to be a showpiece, a truly glamorous event that transcended football and stopped the nation in its tracks. It wasn't just another game. It was the biggest occasion of the domestic sporting calendar.

This book articulates this magic through the eyes of fans who were lucky to attend these famous matches which are etched in the memories of football supporters all over the globe.

It begins with the epic 1970 Chelsea v Leeds FA Cup Final, two matches which encapsulated the true drama of the competition. This book is about the 1970s, which was a particularly magical decade for the cup when the wonderful 'David and Goliath' stories that were part of the fabric of the competition at last spread to the final itself.

Though the First Division at that time was usually fought out between Liverpool, Derby County, Nottingham Forest, Leeds United and Arsenal, for some reasons none of these top clubs were able to assert a stranglehold on the FA Cup, allowing less fashionable teams like Sunderland, Southampton, West Ham United and Ipswich Town their moment in the limelight and their fans a journey of unimaginable joy.

The stories of these successes are known by most football fans everywhere. For instance, they know that, in 1973, Sunderland produced one of the greatest shocks in FA Cup football when a goal from Ian Porterfield was enough to beat Don Revie's mighty Leeds side, or that, three years on, a late goal from Bobby Stokes gave Southampton victory over Manchester United.

But, what aren't known are the stories of the fans who were at these games. Fans who went to extraordinary lengths to get tickets for the greatest match on football's calendar, fans who defied the Football Association's unfair ticket allocation policy to watch their team at Wembley.

Mixed with news reports of the day, the television programmes that people were watching and the pop songs they were humming, this book portrays the sights and sounds of a time when the FA Cup Final was a truly unique and momentous event, watched on television not just by football fans but even by millions of people professing no love of the beautiful game. A time when the nation really did stop for a football match.

Hundreds of fans from the clubs who played in the FA Cup Final during this golden period have recounted their personal stories for this book.

They share their reaction to victory or defeat. What *did* those Sunderland or Southampton fans actually feel like when those goals went in?

What *were* Arsenal fans thinking when Charlie George's 1971 screamer hit the back of the net to clinch the double?

Because, after all, the FA Cup was, ultimately, not about the players, the managers or the dignitaries who attended, it was about the ordinary fan. The fan who followed his or her club through the good times and bad times and everything in between. For many of those fans, a Wembley FA Cup Final was the pinnacle of their football-supporting life. And many of them are able to recall it as if it were yesterday.

As Tottenham legend Danny Blanchflower once said of the FA Cup Final, 'The dream is not for the player, it is for the fan... the lover of the game who doesn't really know what it is like out there and never will know. It is the fan's day.'

In the 1980s and 1990s three factors conspired to change the complexion of the FA Cup. In the early 1980s, terrestrial television companies began tentatively screening live league and cup football matches at weekends. Then the arrival of satellite television resulted in several live matches a week, removing much of the gloss and glamour from those extremely rare matches broadcast live during the 1960s and 70s, of which the FA Cup Final was the jewel in the crown.

Then came the Premier League, which made the rich clubs richer. Winning the Premier League became the ultimate achievement and, for the big clubs, eroded their interest in winning the FA Cup, rendering it a 'nice-to-have' rather than a 'must-have'.

Before long, the top clubs were resting players for FA Cup matches, blooding youngsters or giving disgruntled reserves a run. This pattern reached its peak in 1999/2000 when Manchester United did not take part in the competition at all. It was the clearest signal yet that the cup was not what it was.

This book takes us back to a period of tight shorts, mutton-chop sideburns and giant-killing, played out against a backdrop of economic gloom, industrial turmoil and some great (and not so great) music and television.

A MOST DESERVING CAUSE

Chelsea v Leeds United
Saturday 11 April 1970

EVERY morning at 4.30am, an alarm sounds in a terraced house in Hemsworth, West Yorkshire, and a young man rouses himself from his slumber, rubs his eyes, and prepares to go to work. While the rest of his neighbourhood sleeps, he slaps some tepid water on his face before leaving his home to catch a bus to South Kirkby Colliery, part of the Barnsley Area of the National Coal Board. He arrives at the pit at 5.25am, at the same time as hundreds of miners and support workers, and clocks on, ready for his 5.30am shift. It is March 1970. Les Wake is 17 years old and an apprentice electrician. These facts are incidental. The most important thing in this young man's life is Leeds United Football Club.

Les is the kind of person who forms the bedrock of any club's support. Fiercely loyal, unwavering and prepared to go to extraordinary lengths to watch the team they love. He has seen Leeds play an impressive 49 times during 1969/70, 28 at Elland Road and 21 away. This takes some doing. Midweek away games all over the country mean Les has to call in regular favours from his boss at the pit to let him go. But, wherever he goes – Derby, Ipswich, Southampton, or London – he has to be back in time to report for his shift at 5.30am the next morning. This is a young man who, more than most, deserves to see his team on the biggest stage of them all. He is not alone. Les sees hundreds of other similar devotees on the coaches that leave Elland Road. This Leeds side – unpopular elsewhere – inspire utter devotion from their hardcore fans, but such is the FA's absurd ticket allocation policy, many of these fans are set to miss the biggest match of the season. However, Les is different. He is a determined young man and adamant that he is not going to be one of them when his team meet Chelsea in the upcoming 1970 FA Cup Final.

Carole Parkhouse comes from a very different background to Les. She is a 15-year-old pupil at a private convent school, St Philomena's, in Carshalton, Surrey, her Welsh father being a successful small businessman. Like Les though, she is a Leeds nut. Carole got the Leeds bug in 1965. Then, knowing nothing whatsoever about football previously, she went on a day trip to London. It just happened to be FA Cup Final day as well, with Leeds playing Liverpool.

She recalls, 'I was ten at the time and totally oblivious to football, I knew nothing about it. But I remember I was agog watching all the cars and buses going past with scarves and banners on them. It really fascinated me and my dad had to explain what it was all about.'

Carole remembers being particularly struck by a Mini passing them with a life-size model of the hugely popular, hard and talented Leeds and Scotland midfielder Bobby Collins on top of it. All this razzmatazz and colour intrigued young Carole. She says, 'I asked my dad about all of the fans and came to the conclusion that, well, we must be Leeds fans too, because we come from Leeds. But dad was Welsh and rugby mad. He later became chairman of Wakefield Rugby Union Club and he wasn't interested in football at all.' There was no turning back for Carole. She had 'got it'.

Back at her convent, while other girls read *Bunty* or *Jackie*, or pored over pictures of the Small Faces, Love Affair, the Herd or Scott Walker, Carole spent hours reading *Charles Buchan's Football Monthly* or *Goal!* from cover to cover. This newly-found obsession could only be fed by a visit to Elland Road. Though Mr Parkhouse was more interested in fly-halves than centre-halves and lock-forwards than inside-forwards, Carole nagged, pleaded and cajoled in her quest to get there.

'At last, he relented,' she recalls, 'and so, for Christmas 1968, he finally took me. I think he thought I would hate it. Unfortunately for him, we beat Burnley 6-1 and I was even more hooked than ever. Plus, now I knew my way to the ground and so would be able to make my own way there from now on.'

Once there, Carole found a team that was about to reach their full potential. Managed by Middlesbrough-born Don Revie, who took over a struggling side in 1961, they were now vying with the two Manchester and two Liverpool clubs to be the dominant force in English football.

But while United, City, Everton and Liverpool had plenty of friends throughout football, Leeds did not. Come 1970 they are unloved by the footballing public for their perceived win-at-all-costs attitude and an approach to games which opposing teams and supporters view as ruthless and intimidating. Yet they are unquestionably a great side, masterminded by the tough-tackling, creative genius Johnny Giles and the inspirational captaincy of the pint-sized, fiery Scot, Billy Bremner. They mix muscle with skill and a streetwise know-how, which can infuriate, but is undeniably effective. For fans like Carole and Les Wake they are qualities that inspire complete and utter devotion.

By comparison, Chelsea are seen as flamboyant artisans. They are the club that became most closely associated with the 1960s cultural revolution, which, in England, had London as its epicentre. Just a stone's throw from Stamford Bridge is the King's Road, the hangout of dandies, aesthetes and luvvies, a clutch of whom inevitably find themselves drawn to Stamford Bridge.

They are there for the big games: United, Liverpool, Spurs and Arsenal. Most true Chelsea fans, the working-class hardcore that gathers in the Shed, despise these fans. Fans like 15-year-old skinhead John Foley. Originally from Mile End, East London, John lives in Chingford and attends the Sir George Monoux School in Walthamstow. He is Chelsea through and through and a Shed regular. Each home game he jostles for a spot to watch his heroes: Osgood, Hudson, Cooke and Harris, sporting the famous blue shorts and shirts with the white lion clutching the staff of the Abbot of Westminster on the left breast.

John recalls, 'I used to wear a checked Ben Sherman shirt, white Sta-Prest trousers covered in Chelsea graffiti and, my pride and joy, which were my Dr Martens. I was very much into the skinhead clothes and music. As well as Ben Shermans, I liked Brutus shirts and Levis, with the regulation quarter of an inch turn-ups. When I wasn't wearing my Dr Martens I wore a classy pair of brogues and a Crombie overcoat with matching top pocket handkerchief and socks, often of a very garish colour.'

When John was getting ready to go to Stamford Bridge for the third round of the FA Cup against Birmingham City, the weather was cold and wet and, instead of his smart Crombie, he wore an old, dark raincoat. After Chelsea brushed the Blues aside 3-0, John decided the raincoat was lucky and pledged to wear it to every FA Cup game until Chelsea lost.

Except they didn't lose. In the fourth round they beat Burnley 3-1 at Turf Moor, after a 2-2 draw at Stamford Bridge. John wore the raincoat again to Selhurst Park, where Chelsea really turned it on to beat Crystal Palace 4-1. Then it was another London derby in the sixth round, when Chelsea made the short trip to Queens Park Rangers and, in a brilliant game, won 4-2. The raincoat is working its magic. Chelsea are in the semi-final.

Meanwhile the draw has worked in Leeds's favour. A 2-1 victory at Elland Road over Swansea City in the third round then saw them travel south to Surrey and earn a 6-0 victory at Isthmian League side Sutton United, at the delightfully named Gander Green Lane, in front of a record 14,000 crowd. Naturally Les Wake was there and so too was Carole Parkhouse. It was almost like a home game for her.

She recalls, 'The nuns at my convent were very sweet and trusting. I told them my dad had got me a ticket, although he hadn't. Luckily they didn't ask to see it. But I went down to the ground and managed to get one.'

Then, Mansfield Town were seen off 2-0 at Elland Road in the fifth round before a trip to Wiltshire at the quarter-final stage saw Leeds beat Swindon Town 2-0 at the County Ground.

So to the semi-finals, which brought together two giants of the game. Leeds against their hated rivals Manchester United. Fifty-five thousand watched a goalless draw at Hillsborough and then almost 8,000 extra fans crammed into Villa Park for the replay, which was also goalless.

Just two days later the sides – now thoroughly sick of the sight of one another – reconvened at Bolton Wanderers' Burnden Park, where a solitary goal from Billy Bremner finally separated them and meant Leeds were going to Wembley.

Chelsea's task was comparatively simple. They beat Watford – conquerors of Liverpool in the sixth round – 5-1 at Tottenham. The die has been cast – it is to be Chelsea v Leeds at Wembley stadium. And now the scramble for tickets will begin in earnest.

Most games at Elland Road during 1969/70 have attracted around 40,000 fans. So when the FA allocates Leeds a total of just 16,000 tickets, of which 12,000 automatically go to season ticket holders, it means there will be less than 4,000 for the so-called 'ordinary' fans. This includes hundreds, possibly thousands of hard-working fans, like Les Wake, who have followed the club the length and breadth of the country.

The unfair allocation process means thousands of fans are going to be bitterly disappointed. But Les, who has spent a considerable chunk of his apprentice's wages following the team, is determined not to be one of them. He says, 'As soon as we'd beaten United in the semis, tickets went on sale to season ticket holders who, at that time, were just limited to people in the main stand seats. Next in line were token holders and, finally, any remaining tickets would be made available to the general public.'

The crucial token system, which would be Les's passport to Wembley, worked like this: every Leeds home match programme during the season carried a token, which fans had to cut out and paste on to a special sheet provided by the club. This, coupled with the front of any away match programme, made up the necessary number of tokens needed to qualify for a Wembley ticket.

Les and his mates were relaxed and confident they would be going to Wembley. 'We were all happy as we fell easily into this category and had all the necessary tokens,' he says. 'It was just a case of waiting for the season ticket holders to buy theirs and then we could get ours.' So Leeds put the tickets on sale and before anyone can say 'Peter Lorimer' 12,000 of them are snapped up by season ticket holders. 'At least that's what the club told us,' says Les, wryly.

News then leaks out that a hefty 3,500 have been distributed among players, club officials and staff. Les was aghast, as were thousands like him. He says, 'What this meant is that there were a mere 500 or so left for the token holders, who could prove that they were the "real" fans.' Suddenly panic set in among the Leeds hardcore. Thousands of regular away-travelling fans, previously convinced they easily qualified to get a ticket, were now horrified they were going to miss out on seeing a match they had every right to attend.

It was the talk of the city. Who was going to get the remaining 500 tickets? Les says, 'My mates and I decided we needed to queue all through the night if we were going to stand any chance at all of getting a Wembley ticket. Again I had to skip off work early so that we could get in the queue by around mid-afternoon. When we got there we were devastated to see that the queues were already building and, within an hour, the queue stretched from the ticket windows through the car park and into Elland Road itself.'

The mood was tense and threatened to turn nasty as more and more people turned up. Les recalls, 'There was a lot of pushing and shoving as late arrivals tried to jump the queue.'

With the situation threatening to boil over, the police decided to lock the car park gates with the queuing fans inside. Then, at last, came some official news, which brought huge smiles to the faces of Les and his mates. 'We were told that there were about 300 of us in the car park and that there were about 500 tickets left,' he says. 'It was going to be tight, but at least we were in. I felt for those people who had been locked out.'

There was a party atmosphere in the car park as the fans started planning their trips to Wembley. Les remembers that night as if it were yesterday, 'The footballs came out and we played in that car park for most of the night to really get us in the mood.'

Dawn breaks over Leeds and, at Elland Road, the expectant fans, who have waited all night, look forward to their prize and some blissful kip back home. They smile and give the thumbs-up sign to the TV cameras and photographers who have arrived. Several are wearing Celtic scarves, which have been swapped after the first leg of the European Cup semi-final the week before. In the ticket office, the staff take a deep breath and get ready to dispense the last of the tickets. There is a cheer from the crowd as the shutters are pulled up. It is 9am.

Cheering as loudly as anyone is Les, who can barely contain himself. One of the 500 tickets will shortly be his. He says, 'When the office opened I was really excited because I was near the front of the queue and I was going to watch Leeds in the FA Cup Final.'

The first lucky recipients get their tickets and pose for the cameras. Les quite fancies his picture in the paper or his face on the TV. But then something happens. There are groans, then swearing, and then anger. The ticket windows, open for less than ten minutes, are starting to close.

'Then the truth came out,' says Les. 'It turns out there were less than 100 tickets left. People began throwing things at the windows and the police had to move in.' It is like a bad dream, but soon the reality dawns. All the tickets have gone. Les feels sick. Les thinks back upon the season. Week-in, week-out at Elland Road, the away trips to Sutton, Southampton and

Ipswich, the midweek away trips to Highbury, Turf Moor, the Baseball Ground and Upton Park. The late nights, the early starts down the colliery. It all seemed grossly unfair.

'We were totally devastated and angry,' Les continues, 'especially after seeing every game and queuing all through the night. We had been lied to and shunned by our own club.'

Sniffing a good story, the press move in. Les appears on national television explaining what the club has told them. 'Everyone else backed up what I said,' Les remembers. 'This meant that the truth was now on national television, which would bring to light the plight of true fans to the FA and the clubs themselves.'

Les can still remember the utter devastation and sense of injustice he felt on that cold April morning. He recalls looking around the car park. Most of the distraught faces were familiar. Many of them, like him, have spent their hard-earned cash following the club around the country. Many of them have become friends. Les says, 'There was one girl called Christine who could not stop crying when she was interviewed. I tried my best to console her, but she broke down uncontrollably in front of the cameras.'

Carole Parkhouse has not queued through the night – perhaps understandably she hasn't been allowed to but her best friend Margaret did so on her behalf. She says, 'Margaret was quite near the front of the queue and she didn't get one either. Word spread like wildfire that only a couple of hundred tickets were actually sold to Leeds fans at the ticket office that day. There was lots of controversy. Everyone was asking where all the tickets had gone.'

Then the scandal took a somewhat sinister turn. It may have been sour grapes or it may have been anger, but soon rumours were circulating around West Yorkshire that some of the Leeds players have been spotted in and around the city doing business with ticket touts. Chairman Percy Woodward promises an inquiry if any evidence is produced to show that any of his players are profiteering.

Les, meanwhile, is inconsolable. The 17-year-old trudges home, his eyes welling up with tears, feeling cheated and robbed. Maybe as he makes his way back home the 18 miles to his house at Hemsworth he can hear a Stevie Wonder song that is in the charts, 'Never Had a Dream Come True'. In the song, from the *Signed, Sealed and Delivered* album, Stevie Wonder sings, 'I never, never had a dream come true. Without you, the world out there is painted shades of blue.'

Other songs dominating the charts at that time may also reflect Les's mood. The first is 'Wandrin' Star', from the hit movie *Paint Your Wagon*, and features the almost comical, gravelly tones of Lee Marvin. It has been displaced at the summit by Simon and Garfunkel's epic 'Bridge Over Troubled Water'. For Les, Simon's words and Garfunkel's superb delivery are extremely poignant, 'When you're weary, feelin' small. When tears are in your eyes, I will dry them all.'

'I just went home totally gutted and went straight to bed,' Les says. 'When my dad, Ken, came home from work he couldn't believe it when I told him I didn't get a ticket. We were both so angry.' One of Leeds United's most loyal and devoted fans was going to miss the FA Cup Final. The ticket that by rights should have been his, has been allocated to someone surely less deserving.

How many times have we heard about the 'hallowed' Wembley turf? Players would wax lyrical about its 'bowling green-like' quality and eulogise about the lush, smooth surface, which afforded wonderful, free-flowing football. Such pitches need a bit of tender, loving care. Probably the absolute last thing it needs is dozens of agile horses cantering all over it, jumping and landing, rooting their hooves in the turf as they change direction. But, amazingly, this was precisely what happened at Wembley stadium in the summers of 1968 and 1969, when the Royal International Horse Show was staged there.

To the dismay of football lovers everywhere, a huge tent was erected in the middle of the pitch, fences were built and the galloping horses proceeded to tear the Wembley pitch to shreds.

The damage to the pitch greatly affected the 1969 League Cup Final between Arsenal and Swindon and, to a lesser extent, the same year's FA Cup Final between Manchester City and Leicester. It will now have an enormous influence on the 1970 FA Cup Final.

In the week leading up to the final, both sides have injury worries. Chelsea's midfield wonder-kid Alan Hudson is sweating on a place after tearing ankle ligaments against West Bromwich Albion. The highly rated 18-year-old schemer joins Ron Harris (hamstring) on the treatment table. Chelsea trainer Harry Medhurst says of Hudson, 'The trouble with these injuries is that they sometimes take a long time to mend. If there is no swelling when the plaster comes off he may well be able to start a little training.'

Compared with Leeds right-back Paul Reaney, both Hudson and Harris are lucky. Reaney, 25, lies in a London hospital, with a broken leg, after colliding with West Ham's Keith Miller at Upton Park nine days before the final.

Remembering the tackle, Reaney says, 'There was just one thought in my head. Bang…there goes everything.' The injury means the classy and bang-in-form man has no chance of playing in the cup final, and, perhaps worst of all, no chance of going to the forthcoming World Cup in Mexico.

Reaney says, 'Every footballer's dream is to play in an FA Cup Final. And Mexico – well, that is out of this world. Now, after being virtually about to run on to the field for both, it's all gone.' But he adds, charitably, 'But Keith must feel no blame. It was a complete accident.' Striker Mick Jones and hard-man stopper Norman Hunter are also injury worries for the Yorkshire side.

The tabloids are full of stories about the match and the players. In a regular slot in the *Daily Mirror*, charmingly called 'The Wembley Birds', Frances Bonetti, wife of Chelsea keeper Peter, tells a reporter who asks if she is looking forward to the final, 'I'd much sooner just walk around the local shops. But I can't very well do that, can I? But I am terribly nervous.

'I've become superstitious and always wear a charm bracelet Peter gave me. I never leave it off on cup days. The only time I did, we were half way to White Hart Lane for the semi-final against Watford. Peter made me turn back and get it.'

On the Saturday before Wembley, Alan Hudson says the next 48 hours will be crucial if he is to play, telling reporters he will do anything to be running out against Leeds in a week's time. The countdown is on. Fans and players alike are getting nervous. But thousands of fans still don't have a ticket.

On the Thursday before the final, the newspapers are full of a ticketing scandal which doubtless holds the answer as to where the tickets that should have been claimed by people like Les Wake and his mates have gone.

'BIG PROBE INTO CUP TICKETS RACKET', screams the front page of one of that morning's newspapers. The story reads, 'Cup Final tickets stamped in the name of Leeds United were being sold by touts on London's black market yesterday. Last night Leeds promised a full-scale probe into how the touts got their tickets.'

Chairman Percy Woodward said, 'If we find out that a player is involved he will be in very serious trouble indeed. If we discover it is a season ticket holder who sold these tickets, he will immediately cease to be a season ticket holder at our Elland Road ground and he will never again be allowed to have one.'

Back in Hemsworth, Les and his mates read the papers with growing anger, seething at the unfairness of it all. They just want to watch their team at Wembley. That evening they make a decision. By hook or by crook, they are going to make it to the final. This means travelling to Wembley and paying over the odds for a ticket, if they can find one that is. That night Les looks at his bedroom wall: the poster of the 1968/69 championship-winning team, the rosette and scarf. Nothing is going to stop him from seeing his side in the most famous domestic football match in the world.

The preparations continue and Leeds stage a behind-closed-doors practice match as they push Norman Hunter and Mick

Jones through final fitness tests. For Chelsea, Harris and Hudson are both looking likely starters.

Hudson's 19-year-old squeeze Maureen O'Doherty is the latest girl to be featured in 'The Wembley Birds'. She says, 'I just know Alan will be fit in time. I have thought so ever since he was injured.' Maureen, a model, spends endless days filling up hot- and cold-water baths to treat her loved one's ankle. Asked about 'sharing' the heart-throb with his legions of female admirers, Maureen says, 'It's hard to accept. I must admit I get jealous sometimes. You should see some of the letters he gets!'

Meanwhile, Don Revie's wife Elsie says she is hoping to see more of her husband once the cup final is safely secured and tells the papers, 'It will be nice to make his acquaintance again. I have almost forgotten what he looks like as he has been so busy with football.'

However Elsie, a schoolteacher, knows all about a footballer's life. Her father and uncle were both professionals. Now she admits she is looking forward to relaxing with her husband with a trip to Mexico to watch England in that summer's World Cup, with the FA Cup under their belts.

But that was later. For now, Elsie is hunting for a new car. So she heads for the Regent Street area of Leeds, where there are several dealerships to choose from. On such things fate is decided. Mrs Revie finds herself at Arnold G. Wilson, which sells upmarket British Leyland vehicles, as well as Aston Martins. She scans the cars on the forecourt. The showroom manager hovers, but respectfully keeps his distance.

Like Les, Carole Parkhouse is just one of thousands of Leeds fans plunged into the depths of depression. She has resigned herself to watching the FA Cup Final at home and is deciding which TV channel is likely to provide the better coverage. She is in her bedroom silently bemoaning the fact that she won't be there in person when she hears the shrill, mechanical ring of the family telephone. It is her dad. She gets to the phone and she and her father make small talk. But Carole thinks he sounds odd, as though he is concealing something.

She takes up the story, 'Suddenly, dad asked – as a joke I thought – if I wanted to go to the cup final. I told him not to mess around but then he told me he wasn't joking.' It turns out the man loitering dutifully at the car showroom was Carole's dad and he has managed to sell Elsie Revie a brand new car. Perhaps because of the excellent service he's provided, he has been rewarded with a cup final ticket.

'Unfortunately, I don't know what car Mrs Revie bought, but I imagine it was an upmarket Rover, rather than an Aston Martin,' remembers Carole. No matter. She is going to Wembley. Her eyes well up with tears of joy.

On the day before the final, Chelsea also get dragged into the ticketing scandal with tickets issued to followers of the London side freely available on London's black market at an astronomical £15 for a 25 shilling seat. FA secretary Denis Follows orders an inquiry, while Chelsea club secretary John Battersby says, 'We go to a lot of time and trouble to stop the tickets from reaching the touts.'

For skinhead John Foley, our 15-year-old Chelsea fan, getting tickets has been routine. 'I got my ticket through the post,' he says. 'I sent in all the vouchers from every home game programme. They used to cancel the vouchers later so that you couldn't just buy a programme weeks after to try and get one.'

John, like Carole, can now start preparing for Wembley. It is only poor Les Wake who doesn't have a ticket, but he isn't giving up. Every possible avenue is being explored and, suddenly, a chink of light appears.

Les's colliery has an FA-affiliated football team, which means they automatically receive two cup final tickets. The committee decides the fairest way to allocate them is to raffle them off. The trouble is there are 2,500 men at the pit.

Les says, 'I was running out of time and I realised my chances of getting a ticket were incredibly slim. However, countless men at the colliery knew my plight and how much I wanted to be at Wembley. Many of them had been coming up to me to tap me on the shoulder to promise me the tickets should they win the raffle, which gave me hope. I also had another possibility. My dad was a member of a local club team and they also had two tickets to raffle. Where there was hope, I was not giving up.'

The wife of Chelsea midfielder John Hollins is interviewed in the papers. 'Lovely' Linda Hollins hasn't had much time to think about the cup final because she and John are in the process of moving house. Linda says she will make sure John will spot her in the 100,000 crowd because she will wear something bright.

The last time hubby played in an FA Cup Final three years ago, Linda watched the game on television. She tells reporters, 'I didn't know John then and I can't say I even noticed him during the game. I knew nothing about football at the time…and only a little bit now. But at least I will know which team are Chelsea.'

Meanwhile there is a blow for Chelsea as Alan Hudson loses his race for fitness. He fails a 15-minute fitness test at Stamford Bridge and his ankle won't be ready. He walks once around the dog track at the stadium and then tries to jog, but can't manage it and tells Blues manager Dave Sexton, 'Sorry boss, I can't keep you waiting any longer. I'm out of the Wembley running.'

Life goes on. The Beatles have been in turmoil for some time now, the cracks showing in the warts-and-all documentary *Let It Be*, which was fraught with tension from start to finish. But now it is over. The day before the cup final, Paul McCartney announces he is quitting. In a no-holds-barred statement the 28-year-old star says, 'I have no future plans to record or appear with the Beatles again. Or to write any more music with John.'

The final straw appears to be the appointment of 'business adviser' Allen Klein, a move supported by the three other Beatles. McCartney wanted the gig to go to his father-in-law, Lee Eastman.

Chelsea announce they are treating Saturday's final as 'just another match'. The players will spend Friday night in their own beds and will report for duty only four hours before the kick-off. Manager Sexton believes the team should stick rigidly to the timetable that has taken them to Wembley.

All over the country football fans are preparing to go to the match – as many as 50,000 of them may not be fans of either Chelsea or Leeds. The clock is ticking. That Friday evening millions of Britons will be glued to the box. At 6.25pm spotty, bespectacled teenagers battle it out in *Top of the Form* with its distinctive 'Marching Strings' signature tune. This is followed by the latest episode from the Shiloh Ranch, in Medicine Bow, Wyoming Territory, policed by a foreman known simply as *The Virginian* and played by actor James Drury.

Next up it is Galton and Simpson's brilliant sitcom *Steptoe and Son*, which precedes the *Dick Emery Show*, which has people all over the country adopting a silly, effeminate voice, playfully slapping their mates and saying, 'Ooh you are awful, but I like you.'

Then it is *Miss England 1970*. Meanwhile, ITV viewers can watch *Peyton Place*, *Wheel of Fortune* with Michael Miles and *Doctor in the House*. Plenty to stay in for then.

Back in Yorkshire, there is tension in the air in the works canteen at South Kirkby Colliery as the raffle for FA Cup tickets is about to take place. Young Les Wake sits, heart pounding, praying, wishing, hoping that somehow, just somehow, his number might come up. Next best is the hope that one of the many colleagues who have promised him their ticket will win the raffle.

'The draw takes place,' recalls Les. 'The winner is announced. Not surprisingly, it's not me. Then surprise, surprise, the bloke who wins it wants to keep the tickets and sell them for a profit. Once more I was angry and devastated. Although I was very young I shouted at him across the canteen with a couple of swear words thrown in. Just about everyone in that canteen agreed with me and had a go at him as well. I was still going to Wembley to try and get a ticket from a tout, but that was no guarantee at all and I could have really done with getting a ticket through work. I was gutted again.'

It is yet another kick in the teeth for Les and there is less than 24 hours before kick-off.

As Les trudges home he thinks about his weekly wage from the pit and how much he is prepared to sacrifice if a ticket does become available. Five pounds, ten pounds, 20 pounds, surely not 25? Back home, he lays out his football clothes and prepares to go to Wembley.

He remembers, 'I always dressed the same when following Leeds, home or away – Wrangler jeans, Wrangler jacket and my favourite scarf. It's amazing how many Leeds supporters recognised me that way. After tea, my dad asked me to go to the clubrooms with him. This was very strange and unusual as I wasn't yet old enough to drink.' Les shrugs his shoulders and thinks 'why not?'

Mr Wake and his son walk to the clubroom and, when they arrive, the committee is seated around a big table. Big, bluff, imposing, red-faced Yorkshiremen, of the Fred Trueman ilk. Their expressions give nothing away. Les looks at them curiously. He thinks of trips to Portman Road, The Dell and Anfield. Nothing is said.

Then the chairman speaks, 'Are you going to Wembley, Leslie?' 'Yes, definitely, I couldn't miss this,' Les replies. The chairman looks at him. Les notices the slightest hint of a smile on his face. Is he being mocked? 'I feel for you son,' says the chairman finally. 'I know what you've been through. I take it you haven't got a ticket yet?' 'I haven't, but I will try and get one in London. That's my only hope.' Les remembers Goodison Park, Highfield Road and The Hawthorns.

There is silence, some shuffling of feet, a nervous cough from one of the other committee members. The chairman's face shows a further trace of a smile. Les looks confused. Then he says it, 'The committee has decided that, instead of raffling the cup final tickets this year, we have decided to give them to the most deserving cause.' Les gulps, wondering what is coming next.

The chairman continues, now with a full smile breaking out on his face. His next words are simply magical, 'You are that cause. Here are two tickets, young lad. Now, go and bring back that bloody cup!'

Les says, 'I was gobsmacked, speechless and dumbfounded. I looked at my dad, who was smiling at me. I just couldn't believe it.'

Les tears home with the delirious weightlessness that only such happy news can bring. No longer is it Stevie Wonder singing 'Never Had a Dream Come True'. It isn't 'Wandrin' Star' or 'Bridge Over Troubled Water'. Now it is Norman Greenbaum's 'Spirit in the Sky'. It is Elvis Presley's 'The Wonder of You'. It is Free's 'Alright Now'. Perhaps, most of all, it is Ray Stevens's 'Everything is Beautiful'.

Les remembers, vividly, 'I got home, rushed in, went up to my younger brother, Eric, who was 15 at the time and had seen most of the away games as well, shook him, and screamed, 'Eric! We've got tickets!'

Les and his brother have already booked their coach to Wembley, which leaves Leeds at midnight. Wallace Arnold is the coach operator and they are universally known, in the city and surrounding area, as 'Wally's Trolleys'. There are hundreds of them setting off from Leeds to Wembley.

'When I met my mates in Leeds I did feel a bit guilty that I had a ticket and they still hadn't,' says Les, 'but they were really happy for me and they were confident that they would get tickets in London.'

The coaches lurch into life. Les sits back, closes his eyes and fingers the ticket in his breast pocket. It's his. The convoy heads for the M1 and a date with destiny.

The big day dawns. Yvonne Ormes, a 21-year-old photographic model from Nantwich, Cheshire, was crowned Miss England the previous night, beating 28 other girls for the title at the Lyceum Ballroom in London. Three hundred rioting soccer fans are thrown off a football special train at Walsall. They are thought to be Coventry City supporters returning from a match at Wolverhampton Wanderers, where their team have won 1-0 and gained entry into next season's Inter-Cities Fairs Cup. Turned off at quiet Bescot Junction the fans headed towards Walsall town centre, where terrified locals dialled 999, after which police made dozens of arrests.

A landlord in Cambridgeshire announces he will only open his pub for an hour every day and keep it secret to stop a group of 'caravan dwellers' from coming in. He says, 'Business has gone down the drain since they arrived. Many of my customers refuse to come in any more. They have been frightened off by the unruly behaviour of the newcomers. I am fed up with the whole business.'

Back at Wembley the shifty-eyed, chain-smoking touts are preparing for a decent earner. One says out of the corner of his mouth, 'We can't lose. Leeds are the team of the moment and every football fan in London is willing to pay to see Chelsea win the cup for the first time.'

But the touts will have their work cut out evading the attentions of the police. More than 700 uniformed officers will be on duty in and around Wembley, as well as scores of plain-clothed colleagues looking out for pickpockets and hooligans.

Influential right-back Ron Harris is fit to play, but it takes two crunching tackles from assistant manager Ron Suart to prove it. Suart thunders into 'Chopper' twice during a late fitness test to see if his hamstring will stand up. It does, and Harris says, 'I'm as fit as I'll ever be and looking forward to the final.'

Meanwhile Chelsea will be gobbling down rice pudding as their lunchtime dessert, not daring to break with the ritual that has served them so well, thus far. They will arrive at their Gloucester Road hotel at 11am and then sit down for a lunch of beef fillet and toast, followed by rice pudding. Hotel proprietor Edgar Bonvin says, 'It is what I call the Chelsea Special.'

Leeds manager Don Revie says, 'It will be a hard game, but I don't think it will be as close as most people think.' But Revie – a reluctant tipster at the best of times – declines to say which team will win the cup, though everyone *knows* he thinks it will be heading north. Chelsea are also quietly confident. Left back Eddie McCreadie says, 'We have the right kind of confidence, the best kind, the quiet kind.'

It is expected to be a tough game and referee Eric Jennings of Stourbridge has the unenviable task of keeping the sides at bay.

Fans are now descending on the famous old stadium. Back in Chingford, Chelsea fan John Foley carefully puts on his lucky raincoat over his Ben Sherman shirt and Sta-Prest trousers.

Leeds supporter Carole Parkhouse is travelling down to London with Gordon Hirst, the parts department manager at Arnold G. Wilson, where Elsie Revie has bought her car, and his son. Carole is probably the only person heading to Wembley also carrying a tennis racquet.

'As my school term started the following week I had to also travel with my suitcase and tennis racquet, so that they could drop me off at the station after the game and I could make my way back to the convent at Carshalton,' she explains.

On the journey down, Carole cannot stop looking at her ticket, feeling almost sick with anticipation. They park at Golders Green and catch the Tube. The tension is rising.

The 'Wally's Trolleys' have trundled down the M1, full of expectant Leeds fans, and arrived at King's Cross station at around 6am. Les Wake's mates scamper off in search of tickets, while Les and his brother Eric catch a train to visit their aunt and uncle, who live in Elstree. They feel great. The relief of having a ticket is overwhelming. Their aunt cooks Les and Eric a huge fried breakfast and then they retire for a quick, well-earned kip, safe in the knowledge that in just a few hours' time they will be there in person at one of the world's great sporting occasions.

The teams are also making their way to Wembley. Peering out of the Leeds coach windows are Billy Bremner, Johnny Giles and Jack Charlton. They look hard, determined. Chelsea appear more jovial, laughing and waving to their fans. Perhaps, as underdogs, they're more relaxed.

John Foley has made the short trip from east to north-west London and arrived early to soak up the atmosphere. His ticket is for the lower tier behind the goal, at the tunnel end. At first, the spot is not to his liking. 'I tried to get into the top tier where there was more singing going on and, being a Shed boy through and through, I felt as if most of the Shed regulars would be there. But my mates and I were turned back,' he says.

Suitably fed and watered, and still grinning like Cheshire cats, Les and Eric are taken to Stanmore Tube station by their uncle, from where they catch a train to Wembley Park. Les says, 'We had arranged to meet my mates near the Tube station. When we met them they had already managed to get tickets which was great, so we headed up Wembley Way feeling fantastic and full of anticipation.'

Carole Parkhouse is also within touching distance of the famous old stadium and says, 'I remember being so excited walking up Wembley Way that I was literally almost sick. I held on to my ticket so hard that it was creased right across.'

The players are now at Wembley and in their respective dressing rooms. The anticipation around this final is immense. There hasn't been a really good final since Everton v Sheffield Wednesday in 1966 and the public is expectant.

Now the moment Les has dreamed of is here. With his younger brother in tow, he gleefully hears the 'click/clack' of the old, cast-iron turnstile, feels the lightness of his feet as he goes up the steps and on to the big open concourse and then, taking a deep breath, walks through the aperture and on to the top of the Wembley terraces, from where he can see the pitch. The 17-year-old apprentice looks around him, breathes in the atmosphere, saying nothing. But he puffs out his chest, reflects on the last couple of weeks, exhales and murmurs two words to himself: 'Made it.'

The teams emerge; both are wearing specially commissioned Wembley tracksuit tops – Chelsea's bright red and Leeds's light blue. Leeds are also wearing slightly girlie red socks. The reception is rapturous and, on ITV, commentator Brian Moore says, 'And what a tremendous welcome for them – two of the greatest sides in modern British football, deserving every cheer that they get.'

After being introduced to Her Royal Highness Princess Margaret and standing to attention during the national anthem the two teams break away. Most of Chelsea's support is massed at the tunnel end, opposite their Yorkshire counterparts. The pitch looks ominously patchy, barren and sandy in places – there is a lack of grass. It is a far cry from the lush, green turf that most football people associate with the home of English football.

Les remembers, 'The atmosphere at the start of that match was absolutely unbelievable. We just soaked up every minute.' At the Chelsea end, John Foley agrees, 'It was absolutely brilliant. There were hard men all over the pitch. For us, "Chopper" Harris, Webby, Eddie Mac and Ossie. For them Bremner, Giles and Hunter.'

From the outset it is clear that the pitch is going to be an important factor. The ball is bobbling about, the bounce uneven. The mix of mud and sand will quickly sap the players' energy. In short, the pitch is a disgrace. What also quickly becomes clear is that there is no love lost between the sides. After some tentative opening exchanges, Peter Osgood and Jack Charlton have a 'coming together' and square up to one another. Leeds appear to be trying to intimidate Chelsea. The Londoners are determined to give as good as they get.

Then, a quite absurd opening goal. Eddie Gray prepares to take a corner with his left foot. In the six-yard box Jackie Charlton is, as usual, making a nuisance of himself. Gray takes and Bonetti comes, but is beaten to it by Charlton, who looks like he nudges the Chelsea keeper as he does so, throwing him off balance.

Charlton's header plops down. On the line, full-backs Harris and Eddie McCreadie both go to clear, but each take an air shot and the ball, killed by the pudding-like pitch, trickles between them and just crosses the line. Harris waves his arms back and forth as though he is trying to attract the attention of a helicopter, and cries foul, but referee Jennings gives the goal. It is first blood to the Yorkshire side. High up in the stands, the Wake brothers dance with delight and Carole Parkhouse beams with joy.

Meanwhile, behind the goal, John Foley shakes his head in disbelief. The Chelsea fans are livid. It is a goal that, in their view, reinforces all the old Leeds stereotypes. John says, 'Bonetti was definitely fouled and then "Chopper" and Eddie Mac were both beaten on the line by the header, because of the terrible uneven bounce of the disgraceful pitch.'

The young skinhead looks at his lucky raincoat and wills it to work its magic. And it appears to, with more help from the bumpy pitch. A speculative left-footed shot from 20 yards by Peter Houseman squirms under the body of the error-prone Gary Sprake, whose late dive looks shockingly amateur. Houseman stands stock-still, raises his right arm to the sky, revealing a huge patch of armpit sweat, and then punches the air before being submerged by team-mates. Now it is John Foley's turn to celebrate.

'Mick Jones falls to his knees in despair,' says Brian Moore in the commentary box. 'What a tragedy for Sprake.'

On the stroke of half-time, Hollins scythes down Gray, who is the one player whose skills are showing despite the awful surface. It is 1-1. The pitch is cutting up ominously. The ranks of Chelsea fans massed at the tunnel end wave their scarves frantically as the teams head for the tunnel. They think they have the beating of this fearsome Leeds side. At half-time, fags are puffed frantically; a few brave souls battle to the bar and get some more ale down them. It is tight and tense, low on quality, but high on drama.

The second half begins with a Dempsey foul on Mick Jones. 'During half-time Mick Jones had a ten-minute rest from Dempsey, but straight away he's letting him know that he's here again,' says Moore. Chelsea start better and nearly score after a terrific goalmouth scramble, but Sprake keeps them at bay. Then two of the hardest men in the British game – Ron Harris and Billy Bremner – contest a 50-50. Boy, is it an ugly confrontation.

Harris goes miles over the top, Bremner leaps to avoid the tackle and, in doing so, grabs Harris round the neck, tries to pull him down, fails and then takes a swing at him. 'Oh, Harris and Bremner getting into a tangle there,' says Moore, charitably.

The play moves on and the brilliant Gray mesmerises the outclassed Webb on the edge of the box, firing a great shot goalwards which Bonetti tips on to the crossbar. Leeds are getting on top. The camera stays on Gray and Moore says, 'What a tremendous afternoon this man's having. There can't be any doubt who the man of the match is, whatever the result is. It's got to be Gray.'

At the other end Houseman drags a weak shot wide, with Hutchinson screaming for the ball behind him. 'F**k me,' Hutchinson appears to say in anger after Houseman's cock-up. 'Hutchinson not at all happy with what Houseman did there,' says lip-reader Moore.

Then Bremner shows the other side of his game and creates the third goal of the final. He flights a beautiful pass over McCreadie, which frees Giles, tearing down the right. He crosses first-time, Clarke heads superbly, but the ball strikes a post with Bonetti beaten. It rebounds out and perfectly into the path of Mick Jones, who rifles in a low shot which nestles in the back of the net.

The Leeds fans go bonkers. Jones skips and jumps in delight before being caught by Charlton and Madeley. They indulge in a rather dodgy-looking *ménage à trois*. Jones escapes, blows a kiss to the Leeds fans on the Royal Box side and then claps his hands repeatedly like a seal demanding fish. There are just 12 minutes to go.

The Wake brothers, plus the thousands of other Yorkshiremen and women, now believe the cup is theirs. Few would bet against this Leeds side not lifting the cup now. It is the closing stages and the pitch resembles something between Passchendaele, the Somme and the Gobi desert – mud, sand and a little bit of grass.

The players look knackered, but Leeds are convinced the cup is theirs. Les and Eric Wake are getting ready to celebrate, Les feeling this is just reward for a season of travelling all over the country. Carole Parkhouse can't stop smiling and thanking Elsie Revie for buying that car.

Leeds hold on for another ten minutes or so. The white ribbons to adorn the cup are being prepared.

The camera pans in on a serious Don Revie, chewing gum violently. He checks his watch. There are less than three minutes to go. 'Every minute must seem like an hour to him,' says Moore. He will soon have reason to chew even harder.

Chelsea are awarded a fortuitous free kick 30 yards out, but near the far touchline. They need to make this count. Behind the goal something has come over John Foley. He feels strange, in a good way. It is something to do with that raincoat. He is already bouncing up and down as his team prepare to take the kick.

He can still recall the moment vividly, 'As soon as we won that free kick I absolutely – 100 per cent – knew that we were going to score. In fact I swear I was almost jumping up as if we had already scored because I simply *knew* it was going to be a goal. I have never had a feeling like that, before or since.'

Jennings blows his whistle. The ball is rolled to Hollins. The little schemer flights in a dangerous cross. It is a straight contest between Ian Hutchinson and Jack Charlton as to what happens next. And it's Hutchinson who steals a precious few inches to reach the ball first. He strains every sinew in his neck to direct a marvellous header past Sprake. It is a belter.

The Yorkshire side cannot believe it while, behind the goal, the Chelsea fans wave their blue and white scarves delightedly. John now lets himself go completely while, at the other end, the Leeds fans, including Les and Eric, are frozen with shattered disbelief. 'Leeds United prostrate on the deck!' screams Moore. 'Lorimer is down. Bremner is down. Jones is down.' Hutchinson isn't cursing any more. He looks delighted, but exhausted, and punches the air in delight.

Two minutes later, referee Jennings blows his whistle for the end of normal time. Leeds dominate extra time, with Gray continuing to torture the Chelsea defenders, in particular Webb, but the players are so tired that no one seems to have the energy to get a winner.

The pitch continues to cut up. Cooper goes down with cramp. Osgood sportingly does that odd thing where you grab the stricken player's boot, stretch their leg and press down. But the sides can't be separated and so, for the first time since 1912, a replay is needed. The Leeds fans feel hard done by.

Carole Parkhouse says, 'We should have won about 20-4. The pitch was appalling because of the showjumping event and the great heaps of sand everywhere slowed everyone down, except Eddie Gray. We were not happy with the 2-2 result as we completely played Chelsea off the park.'

John Foley agrees with Carole, but only up to a point. 'Yes, we were out-played, but not out-fought,' he says.

At times, this cup final was more like a war than a football match and the battles will continue long after the final whistle as the fans head home with the Chelsea fans – by virtue of their late equaliser – goading their Leeds counterparts.

John says, 'There was quite a bit of trouble, but we ran Leeds everywhere. I was on an underground train when a legendary Chelsea fan called Danny Harkins, known as "Eccles", who was our leader, punched a Leeds fan in the face and then made the Leeds fan say "thank you" for it. I have to admit that "Eccles" was almost as much of a hero to me then as Peter Osgood. There was a lot of trouble at football in those days, but when "Eccles" turned up for a game, somehow you just got a big lift and we all thought that whoever we were playing that day were the ones who were going to be on their toes.'

Convent-educated 15-year-old Carole Parkhouse steers well clear of any trouble, but extra time and the age it takes to leave Wembley means it is 8pm by the time they get back to their car. Carole then has to struggle with her suitcase and tennis racquet across London, spotting numerous fans of both clubs as she does so. What sticks in her mind is the somewhat incongruous sight of a group of fellow Leeds fans, very carefully painting a mural at Charing Cross. 'I always wondered what happened to that,' she says now. By the time she reaches Victoria station it is 9pm. 'I was already running late and then I managed to get on the wrong train – the one to Carshalton Beeches, not Carshalton,' she says. 'Then I didn't know how to get back from Carshalton Beeches to my school, so by the time I eventually made it to my school, with my Leeds scarf and my tennis racquet, it was around 10pm. It turns out the school had notified the police in Surrey and Middlesex.'

Late back for school, Carole is packed off to bed and deprived of the opportunity of watching the game again on *Match of the Day*. 'I wasn't actually allowed to watch it anyway,' she remembers, 'but I had devised a neat little system of sneaking into a classroom where they had a telly, sitting with the lights out and watching it after everyone else had gone to bed. I lived in constant fear of being caught by the caretaker but thankfully never was.'

By this time, the 'Wally's Trolleys' are already on their way back up north. The mood on the coaches is somewhat flat because victory was so nearly theirs. Les and Eric Wake get some sleep, at least sound in the knowledge that they have scored a victory for the true fan.

Four decades on, Les now firmly believes the scandal surrounding the allocation of 1970 FA Cup Final tickets was instrumental in finally bringing the situation to the public's attention. He says, 'I am convinced that what happened had a big influence on the FA reviewing its policy and increasing the allocation of cup final tickets to the participating clubs.'

The coaches continue their journey. The talk is of the terrible pitch, how lucky Chelsea were and how superbly Eddie Gray played. From the back of the coach, a single Yorkshire voice can be heard, 'We'll do the southern bastards in the replay,' it says. There are loud cheers and a deep, almost primeval chant of 'United! [clap, clap, clap] United!'

That night, all three major channels broadcast live pictures of the take-off of Apollo 13. It has been less than a year since the momentous Apollo 11 expedition involving Armstrong, Aldrin and Collins. The success of the two previous missions has made the public comfortable, possibly slightly blasé, but still fascinated, about the whole concept of space travel.

Millions tune in to see astronauts Lovell, Haise and Swigert blast off. All is well until, on 14 April, comes news from NASA that the mission has run into trouble – real trouble. A major technical hitch has left the astronauts effectively stranded in outer space, nearly 260,000 miles from the safety of earth. The newspapers describe it as 'the greatest cliff-hanger the world has ever known'.

For Carole Parkhouse, the plight of the mission matches the plight of her own beloved Leeds. She says, 'It was very odd, but I always felt some strange affinity to the astronauts, because it was all happening at the same time as the cup final. When their mission went pear-shaped I felt as though somehow it was Leeds United up there in space. Does that make sense?'

The world is gripped by a drama that even Hollywood couldn't conceive. In the end the ingenuity of NASA technicians gets the astronauts home in one piece. An astonishing 42 million people watch them splash down on Thursday 16 April.

For a few days, the real, life-or-death drama has made everything else seem irrelevant. Then, in Britain at least, the dust settles and people remember that there is still the small matter of the 1970 FA Cup to sort out. The replay is rather inconvenient for the FA. With all minds focused on England's summer trip to Mexico to defend the World Cup, a replay is not very desirable for anyone. Then there is *that* pitch, which has been slaughtered by all and sundry and labelled a disgrace.

Other factors also come into the equation. Leeds have a midweek return leg against Celtic to play. The England v Northern Ireland home international match is scheduled to be played at Wembley on 22 April. There is only one real option – to move the game elsewhere. The replay is scheduled for Wednesday 29 April and the whole shooting match is heading north to Old Trafford.

GETTING CANED
Chelsea v Leeds United
1970 FA Cup Final Replay, Wednesday 29 April

IT is 1pm on Wednesday 29 April 1970 and London's Euston station is abuzz with Chelsea fans preparing to head north. Blue and white scarves, rosettes and dozens of homemade banners, one of which reads, 'Webby's boot will kick Gray's a***.'

There are thousands of them. School kids playing hookey, office workers attending a spurious meeting, fake dental appointments, others who have thrown a tactical 'sickie' and bosses who have pulled rank and simply taken the day off.

These fans are not going to miss this, whatever the consequences – a rap over the knuckles from the boss, a summons to the headmaster's office – they are going to be there.

This time it hasn't been a question of tickets. The FA Cup Final waifs and strays, the hangers-on, the non-supporters only ever wanted to experience the 'occasion'. That meant 3pm, on Saturday, at Wembley, watched by royalty, with all the accompanying pomp and pageantry. A midweek evening game at far-off Old Trafford is another matter. But to the real fans, this is an even bigger game.

Among the Chelsea fans is John Foley, the 15-year-old skinhead from East London. Naturally, he is wearing his lucky raincoat, Sta-Prest trousers and DMs. Of course, he is supposed to be at school in Walthamstow. Fat chance. He is not missing this for anything. 'I bunked off,' John says, matter-of-factly, as if to demonstrate that any other course of action would be unthinkable. So, instead of catching the bus to the Sir George Monoux School, John has made his way to Euston to join the throng of Chelsea fans, many of them already sinking a few pints in readiness for the journey north.

On platform six their carriage awaits, a football special, and soon it is on its way. John says, 'I was with two mates. Ian Hastie from my school and a black guy called Julian, who I only knew from supporting Chelsea and who I think was also a regular at Highbury. There were quite a few fans who just used to go for the "buzz" and a ruck! Danny Harkins – "Eccles" – spent about half an hour in our carriage on the way up chatting about this and that. He told us that it was his 23rd trip to Manchester and I was very impressed. I didn't mention to him that it was my first!'

As the trains surge north, thousands of other Chelsea fans are heading up the M1 towards the Midlands before – in these pre-M6 days – taking a series of A-roads up to Lancashire.

Among them is a white Mk II Ford Cortina, festooned with blue and white, containing five Chelsea fanatics, including brothers Jeff and Steve Van Doorn, veterans of the 1967 cup final defeat at the hands of Spurs and both Chelsea to the core.

Steve, then 16, remembers, 'I'd had to do an exam that morning so I'd been in to school and Jeff, who was a clerical officer at New Scotland Yard, couldn't get the morning off work. So, after the exam was over, Jeff picked me up from school in the Cortina we'd hired and we set off to Manchester.'

Perhaps it was a sign of the times that Jeff did not tell the hire car company why he needed it for two days.

He says, 'I told them I was taking my grandparents down to Dorset for a family anniversary bash. While I was doing this, the rest of our crowd had gathered at our house and had been out buying rolls and beer. We set off at about 1pm full of high hopes with our blue scarves trailing out of the back windows.'

A copy of that day's *Daily Mirror* is passed around the Cortina. In it, reporter Ken Jones says he expects tonight's final to be, 'Hard, perhaps bitter, and possibly violent.'

Jones believes it will be another tight affair, but thinks it may rest on a crucial decision by Chelsea boss Dave Sexton. Should he play David Webb, who was given the run-around at Wembley by the silky skills of Eddie Gray, or not? Even at this stage, no one is sure who will be wearing the blue number six shirt.

There can't have been many Chelsea fans living in the north-eastern railway town of Darlington in 1970, but one who did find himself there was trainee journalist Damian Inwood, who was attending a block release course at the town's college and living in digs.

He recalls, 'On the day of the replay I decided not to risk taking my ticket with me to morning lectures in case anything happened to it, so I left it at home.'

Displaying the nervous paranoia concerning big match tickets that all football fans can relate to, Damian checked and then checked again with his landlady that she would be at home to let him in so he could change and collect his ticket. 'She assured me she'd be there,' he says.

In the wider world, the Beatles continue to dominate the news. Young people under 18 will not be allowed in to see John Lennon's 'erotic drawings', which are being displayed at the London Art Gallery in Mayfair.

The prints show Lennon and his wife Yoko Ono in various sexual poses. They have caused an outcry, but a magistrate dismisses an indecency summons against the gallery.

Design experts slam the 'Wee Mannie' mascot, which has been created for the forthcoming Commonwealth Games to be held in Edinburgh. Mathew Wylie, chairman of the Council of Industrial Design's Scottish Committee, says that 'Wee Mannie' is, 'A gimmick which lacks any form of elegance or design.'

And the latest kitchen gadget goes on sale. Morphy Richards introduce the Easimix, which is described as, 'An electric three-speed mixer, made in shake and rinse stainless steel.'

'It's a serious kitchen machine,' states the advertising blurb. 'If you want something more serious you must be running a restaurant.'

While mum gets to grips with Easimix, dad can lounge in front of the box watching the football. And in April 1970 the TV to have is the Hi-Vantage. Its press ad reads, 'Move to Hi-Vantage – the TV of the 70s. The 70s will be the most exciting decade of the century. That's why you need the TV designed for the 70s – Radio Rentals Hi-Vantage TV. It's the set with every new feature to bring you the sights and sounds of the 70s in brilliant detail from around the world on all three channels.'

That day's viewing on the BBC includes *The Woodentops*, *Playschool*, *Jackanory*, *Vision On* and *The Adventures of Parsley*. At midday there has been a programme called *Apna Hi Ghar Samajhiye*, which the TV listings helpfully describes as 'for immigrants'.

But the FA Cup Final replay is without doubt the highlight of the day. There is massive interest in the match, which will be screened live on both ITV and BBC1.

In the newspapers, coverage of the replay jostles for space with Arsenal's triumph in the Inter-Cities Fairs Cup. A brilliant night at Highbury sees the Gunners overturn a 3-1 first leg deficit to defeat Belgian side Anderlecht 3-0 with goals by Eddie Kelly, John Radford and Jon Sammels. It is their first major trophy for 17 years and now some people are starting to sit up and take notice of Bertie Mee's side.

And, all the time, the football special trains are powering northwards, almost swaying with the deafening chants of the Chelsea faithful who, after getting lucky in the first game, now feel this is going to be their day.

Back in Darlington, student Damian Inwood's morning lectures are over so he speeds back to his digs to collect his prized ticket. He doesn't have a lot of time. Breathlessly he knocks on his landlady's front door. There's no answer. To Damian's absolute horror, his landlady has gone out.

In West Riding, the Leeds coaches are preparing to make the 40-mile journey across the Pennines on the A62. Standing among a group of fellow Leeds fans is Les Wake, wearing his trademark denim jacket, jeans and scarf. This time – because the hangers-on don't view a midweek replay in Manchester as anything remotely like a cup final – tickets to true fans have been relatively easy to come by. Each club is allocated 25,000 tickets for the Old Trafford shindig. Les and his brother Eric still had to queue all night but, while the queues for the Wembley game were fraught and tense, this time the atmosphere was far more relaxed.

Les recalls, 'There was loads of banter throughout the night and everyone seemed in really high spirits. We played football in the Elland Road car park. I remember there was a biscuit warehouse next door with loads of vans parked up. Some idiots managed to get into a couple of the vans, which were full of biscuits. Before long, there were Jaffa Cakes, Chocolate Home Wheat and Ginger Nuts being passed around. By the morning, everyone had begun to throw them at each other. It got very silly. We formed gangs in the name of the biscuits. So we had Jaffa Cakes trying to beat up Ginger Nuts, who were trying to fend off Chocolate Home Wheat. You just had to see the funny side of it.'

Tickets safely secured, Les and Eric prepare to board their coach. 'We set off for Old Trafford,' says Les. 'As usual, "Wally's Trolleys" were the method of travel. But the thought of going to Manchester and back on a bone-shaker was not my ideal choice.'

The Leeds fans travelling across the Pennines are supremely confident. This is not a side that loses many matches or gives a second chance, as Chelsea have been granted. 'We're going to win the cup! We're going to win the cup! Ee-aye-addio, we're going to win the cup!' sing the fans as the coaches travel west through Marsden, Slaithwaite, Linthwaite and Huddersfield and head towards the Pennines.

Back in Darlington, thousands of options are racing through Damian Inwood's head. Should he smash a downstairs window and incur his landlady's wrath, although surely she would understand that, in these circumstances, such a course of action would be more than justified? Perhaps he should force a lock, or shin a drainpipe? He has to think fast as he has a lift waiting.

Then he gets lucky. He has remembered he has left his bedroom window open upstairs. He looks at the drainpipe, but decides against it. Then, by amazing coincidence, 200 yards up the road, he spots a wonderful sight – a kind of knight in shining armour – in actual fact, it is a window cleaner.

The Chelsea trains have now reached Stoke. John Foley's train is packed. Fans are everywhere, lying in the corridors, hanging on to luggage racks, swigging booze from cans or bottles. They are in fine voice, singing songs about Osgood, Charlie Cooke or John Hollins or a new song which has only recently been adapted to gravel-voiced Lee Marvin's 'Wandrin' Star' from the 1969 film *Paint Your Wagon*, top of the charts only two months earlier:

'I was born under a Chelsea Shed,
'I was born under a Chelsea Shed,
'Knives are made for stabbin'
'Guns are made to shoot,
'If you come under the Chelsea Shed,
'We'll all stick in the boot!
'I was born under a Chelsea Shed,
'A Chelsea, Chelsea Shed.'

And, with thanks to Mary Hopkin:

'Those were the days my friend,
'We took the Stretford End,
'We took the Kop, we took the f*****g lot.
'We'd fight and never lose,
'Then we'd sing "Up the Blues",
'Those were the days,
'Oh yes those were the days.
'La la la la la.'

John Foley takes another swig of ale. He shouldn't really, but this is the FA Cup Final. He is in his element and, as the Long Life slides down his throat, is supremely confident that his lucky raincoat will ensure that the Blues return to London with the cup.

Decades on, Steve Van Doorn can still recall the excitement and anticipation of that journey north in the hired white Mk II Cortina. He remembers the hundreds of cars with blue and white scarves fluttering from windows, the car horns sounding, the smiling, excited faces of fans from London suburbs like Mitcham and Surrey towns such as Epsom, Leatherhead and Banstead. The feeling is that Ian Hutchinson's late equaliser at Wembley has given Chelsea the advantage and now the cup will be theirs.

There is a minor inconvenience just north of Birmingham for the lads to contend with when a lorry pulls out and scrapes down the wing of their pristine hire car. Jeff Van Doorn says, 'The lorry driver claimed it was our fault and was prepared to call the police if need be. With time ticking away, we couldn't afford to wait around and my cousin Pat was convinced that with some T-Cut we would be able to remove all trace of the collision and so on we went.'

Back in Darlington, the window cleaner finds himself confronted with one of the most excited, fast-talking individuals he has ever encountered, spewing forth a stream of consciousness that James Joyce would have been proud of.

Between the babbling, the startled window cleaner deduces something about the wide-eyed young man in front of him being a mad keen Chelsea fan. FA Cup Final replay tonight in Manchester. Against Leeds. Was at Wembley in 1967 when they lost. Now a chance to put that behind me. Have a ticket but left in digs. Landlady buggered off out. Lift to Manchester waiting. Upstairs window open. Need ladder.

By this time the window cleaner – a regular at Darlington's Feethams as it turns out – is smiling broadly and, fully appreciating Damian's predicament, lends him one of his wooden ladders. Scurrying as fast as someone carrying a long ladder can, Damian races round the back of his landlady's house, puts the ladder up, climbs through the open window and there, concealed between a copy of *Abbey Road* and *Piper at the Gates of Dawn* is one FA Cup Final ticket. The simple word 'relief' does not even begin to describe how Damian feels.

Damian remembers, 'I'd arranged to get a lift from some guys who worked at the *Evening Gazette* in Middlesbrough, where I was training. All three were from Yorkshire and all three were massive Leeds fans. All the way to Manchester I had to endure their smug comments about how Leeds were going to massacre Chelsea.'

'Massacre' was an apposite word to use. The first match at Wembley had been likened to a war and the replay was expected to pick up where it had left off.

Both teams are staying at the same hotel in Manchester. Leeds's injury fears have centred on their highly influential and combative skipper Billy Bremner and goalkeeper Gary Sprake. Reserve keeper David Harvey is on standby.

For Chelsea, Alan Hudson has again lost his battle for fitness and must watch from the stands. To compensate for Hudson's absence, the West Londoners have re-arranged their formation to give themselves more attacking options than they had at Wembley. Charlie Cooke moves into midfield to allow Peter Houseman the chance to operate on the left wing. The time for talking is now over though and the teams start making their way to Old Trafford.

The London trains slide into Manchester Piccadilly station and the boozy, good-natured Chelsea fans spill on to the platforms, dozens jumping off before the trains have actually come to a halt, flinging doors open dramatically and twirling blue and white scarves out of windows to let everyone know who they are and why they are here. John Foley remembers, 'The atmosphere was absolutely incredible at Manchester Piccadilly station. We caught a connecting train to Old Trafford and we were there.'

The streets around the ground are packed with Chelsea and Leeds supporters. There are a few minor scuffles for the police to deal with as there is some bad blood lingering from the Wembley match. Chelsea fans have been allocated the Stretford End, which gives them a psychological advantage.

'This was great,' says John Foley. 'However, when I got into the ground I was horrified to find that a small fence separated us from the Shed, which had completely taken over the rest of the Stretford End. We weren't having this so we promptly climbed over the fence and joined our main mob. Leeds had been given the other end, which really surprised everyone because their fans didn't have half as far to travel as we did. In truth, we had three sides of the ground and the Chelsea noise was just incredible. This was going to be our night.'

Les Wake well recalls the convoy of Leeds coaches arriving at Old Trafford and the tinge of disappointment felt when they realised they were in the open terracing at the Scoreboard End behind the goal opposite one of the most famous 'ends' in British football. 'We had definitely hoped that we'd get the Stretford End, but we didn't,' he says. The Leeds fans quickly fill the terrace. A banner reads, 'Eddie will make it a GRAY day for Chelsea.'

The Van Doorn brothers and their travelling companions have also arrived in their hired white Cortina. Jeff recalls, 'We parked about a mile from Old Trafford. It was less than an hour before kick-off. We hurried to the ground and made our way inside. We found ourselves on the side of the players' tunnel. The Stretford End, packed with Chelsea fans, was to the left. We thought about climbing over to join them but with five of us, it was going to be difficult, so instead we found a spot midway between our goal and the halfway line from where we could all see.'

Now all our friends are in the ground and the atmosphere is building to a crescendo. One person not present is schoolgirl and Leeds fan Carole Parkhouse. An evening midweek replay 200 miles from school is a bridge too far and her dad has made it clear that she cannot be there.

So, as the teams enter the fray, she finds herself at school watching the game live on a black and white TV. Amazingly, the nuns at St Philomena's have allowed the girls to watch. Everyone else in the room supports Chelsea. Carole smiles with quiet satisfaction as she sees Billy Bremner leading her beloved team out. Somehow, Leeds are not Leeds without him.

Some 62,000 fans greet the sides into the early evening, late spring sunshine. Alongside Bremner is 'Chopper' Harris. The hard men avoid eye contact as the sides filter out. The Stretford End is, unusually, a sea of blue and white. Steve Van Doorn still gets a shiver down his spine when he remembers the atmosphere in the ground that night.

The players line up for the national anthem. Behind the famous old dirge, you can hear the Chelsea fans singing, 'We shall not, we shall not be moved. We shall not, we shall not be moved. Until we come back with the FA Cup, we shall not be moved!'

The camera moves slowly down the line of Leeds players: Bremner, who looks right up for it; the largely untried goalkeeper David Harvey, in for the injured Sprake, tapping his fingers on a ball in time to the anthem; Madeley, looking deadly serious; Giles, chewing gum, with a 'come and have a go if you think you're hard enough' look on his face; Hunter; Cooper, looking uncharacteristically tense; Jones looking a bit like the vicar in *Dad's Army*; Lorimer puffing his chest out; Gray and Clarke, expressionless; Charlton, looking like the tallest boy in the year in borrowed PE kit; and full-time substitute Mick Bates.

The teams break. This time it is Chelsea's turn to wear slightly girlie socks – yellow to match the trim and numbers on the famous all-blue strip. They run towards their supporters, the streamers come down, billowing in the wind and Brian Moore comments on how breezy it is. Chelsea have made a tactical switch. Ron Harris is given the job of looking after the dangerous Gray with Webb, run ragged at Wembley, moving away from right-back to central defence alongside John Dempsey. Eric Jennings gives a blast of his whistle and we are off again.

Eighteen days earlier, Gray did his damage on the left wing but, with a mere five minutes on the clock, he breaks dangerously down the middle after a probing ball from Bremner. Gray hares goalwards past Webb who then, rather viciously, takes his legs away. It has 'that's for making a mug of me at Wembley' written all over it.

It is an ugly tackle, cynically executed to stop attacking play and, unfortunately, sets the tone for the rest of the match. Webb, marching back, his first task completed, looks distinctly Neanderthal, a bit like prehistoric man. Maybe it is the slightly simian features, craggy face and unkempt hair. Harris, lining up alongside him for the free kick, almost looks angelic.

The ensuing free kick – lobbed forward by Bremner – is gathered safely by Bonetti. Six weeks later, in far-off Mexico he won't do so well but, for now, he is looking in good nick.

Shortly afterwards, Bremner gets chopped down by fellow Scot Charlie Cooke. It is spicy. Bremner has a little whisper in referee Eric Jennings's ear. What he says is anyone's guess. Not long afterwards Houseman clatters into the little Scotsman, bundling him into touch. Are they targeting him by any chance? Bremner has another word with Jennings. It is a brutal opening.

Chelsea fan Jeff Van Doorn says, 'It was the most vicious and bruising encounter that English football had ever seen and if the game was played today I think the referee would have to abandon it, due to lack of players being on the pitch.'

It is tense and tight. The camera pans to three nervous-looking female Chelsea fans in the stand. One is wearing a *Daily Express* blue and white paper hat. Conscious that the lens is upon them, they decide to leave their allegiance in no doubt whatsoever and bellow, 'Come on Chelsea!' But their team are proving second best and time and again Leeds threaten the Chelsea goal, causing frayed nerves for the thousands of Londoners massed behind Bonetti's goal in the Stretford End.

The sun falls lower in the sky and the shadows of the players lengthen across the Old Trafford pitch. The game is being played at a breathtaking pace with Bremner running the show. And, now, a moment of real significance. As Peter Bonetti goes to collect a ball in his area, Mick Jones clatters into him. It looks nasty and Bonetti is left lying in a crumpled heap in the six-yard box. Though he climbs gingerly to his feet, he is still feeling the effects. In short, he is in agony.

It is a turning point, as Jeff recalls, 'The clash between Jones and Bonetti was a crucial moment. We were all incensed, convinced it was a foul.' The chants of 'We want a ref, we want a ref, ee-aye-addio, we want a ref!' echo from the Stretford End.

Bonetti's injury fires up the Leeds fans, hitherto somewhat quiet. From the open end, a passionate, deep chant begins from the Yorkshire followers, 'We're going to win the cup, we're going to win the cup – and now you're gonna believe us, and now you're gonna believe us – and now you're gonna be-lieeeee-ve uuuuuuuus. We're going to win the cup!' And, before long, we are starting to believe them, after what will prove to be the best goal of both matches by far.

Leeds break from defence. Some deft footwork from Allan Clarke evades another agricultural lunge by Webb and a despairing tackle by Houseman. Suddenly, play has opened up. Dempsey senses danger and moves forward from the centre-half position, but Clarke is too good, beats him to the ball and touches it beautifully into the path of the advancing Jones, who is still a good 45 yards from goal. The speed of Clarke's break has left Chelsea at sixes and sevens and Hollins and McCreadie arrow in on Jones, who is going at full pelt towards the penalty area. But neither player can stop him.

He is now in the box and unleashes a powerful, perfectly placed, angled shot across Bonetti into the net. It is a quality goal. Jones wheels away while Lorimer tries to pull him back by his shirt to congratulate him. The Leeds fans at the open end celebrate.

Two hundred miles away, in her convent school in Carshalton, Surrey, Carole Parkhouse jumps up and down with delight, while her classmates boo and hiss.

Jones is delighted. The Leeds fans start singing that old classic "'ere we go, 'ere we go, 'ere we go'. Chelsea fans are stunned into silence and – noticing Bonetti hobbling in the area – feel hard done by, especially as Bonetti's injury has been caused by Jones.

John Foley recalls, 'Bonetti would definitely have saved the shot had he been fit, but he was so badly hurt that he was hobbling terribly and couldn't even take his own goal kicks. We were now behind for the third time in the two matches and I admit that at this stage I feared the worst.' But, while John continues to wear his lucky raincoat, he still has hope.

The war continues. Chelsea are narked about the goal and, shortly after, Harris scythes down Gray, who is left clutching his left leg. Clarke has a word with Harris, whose face is a picture of innocence. Commentator Brian Moore says something telling, 'And by whatever means, there's no doubt about it, Gray has not been as effective in this game as he was at Wembley. Thanks in no small measure to the work of Ron Harris.'

Gray looks in genuine pain. He recovers and carries on, but a couple of minutes later he is fouled again by Hutchinson. They are well and truly after him. The half-time whistle blows. It is 1-0 to the Yorkshiremen. On the concourse behind the Stretford End, all the talk is about Jones's foul on Bonetti and how this could cost them the game. There is disgruntlement when the thirsty Chelsea fans can't get a proper drink, as Steve Van Doorn recalls, 'All they had was one tap with cold water running out of it and they were just filling up plastic cups.'

At the other end of the ground, Les and Eric Wake are quietly satisfied. They have got their noses in front. They know their side are made of stern stuff and surely they won't relinquish a lead again like they did at Wembley? In the dressing room, Don Revie hammers this home to his men. Leeds desperately want the cup. Watching in the darkening classroom in Surrey, Carole Parkhouse prays that they get it.

As the second half starts, the night is drawing in. It doesn't take long for the fun and games to start again.

Charlton nips the ball off Osgood's toe and Osgood scythes Charlton down in response. Charlton leaps to his feet and then aggressively barges Osgood to the ground. In the modern game it would be a sure-fire sending-off. In those different days it actually induces laughter in commentator Moore, who chuckles, 'Oh my goodness. Surely there's going to be a booking now.'

Jennings speaks to both players but, amazingly, takes no further action. Shortly after, Osgood is involved again when he and team-mate Hutchinson tussle with Bremner, leaving the red-haired Scot in a heap on the ground. At last Jennings takes his book out and enters Osgood's name into it. It is a niggly, messy game but, at the same time, utterly captivating. And Chelsea are more than holding their own. The fans crammed into the Stretford End roar their support and urge their team forward. And now the men in blue respond.

With 12 minutes to go, the gifted Scottish winger, Charlie Cooke, finds himself with a rare bit of space and charges forward towards the massed ranks of blue supporters. At the same time Osgood begins a run from the edge of the penalty area. Cooke flights a perfectly judged ball into his path which, from eight yards out, Osgood meets with a brilliant diving header past Harvey.

'A wonderful goal!' screams Moore. And it is a great goal. Behind the net the swarms of Chelsea fans are in raptures and tumble down the terracing. Osgood turns to them and raises both arms in triumph. For thousands of Chelsea fans of that generation, it's a particularly special goal.

John Foley says, 'I have a print of that goal on the wall in my front room signed by the great man himself about six months before he passed away. It says simply, "To John, best wishes Peter Osgood".' It is among John's most prized possessions.

It is not just the Stretford End that is cavorting. There are Chelsea fans on three sides of the ground, leaping around, dancing and hugging. Jeff Van Doorn says, 'We just went wild. We must have tumbled down five or six terrace steps as we jumped for joy and hugged one another. From that moment I knew we were going to win.'

There are ten minutes left on the clock. The fouls and niggles continue during the nervy closing stages but no further goals are scored. We are going into extra time.

Now the Chelsea support seems to go up a notch and Old Trafford shakes with the roars of the Londoners. John says, 'We sang our hearts out, "Chelsea, Chelsea, Chelsea" non-stop for what seemed like an age. We were just willing the team to score. I am sure it inspired them.'

By contrast, Leeds are looking rattled and their fans at the open end seem nervous. They can see the FA Cup – which should have been won on 11 April – slipping away. They will Eddie Gray to weave a bit of magic, but the combined efforts of Harris, Webb, Dempsey and McCreadie have neutered him.

The players look exhausted and, as the first period of extra time draws to a close, Hunter, following a nasty-looking tackle from Houseman, goes down with cramp. The players are running on empty. Who has got the will, the desire to win it? We are just about to find out.

McCreadie takes a throw-in in his own half, which he fires up the left flank. It is headed out. Now Hutchinson takes over. Hutchinson has the longest throw in the English game and has developed a distinctive 'windmill' style delivery. He arrows one further down the line. Charlton heads it out.

The consecutive throws have had the desired effect and stolen crucial ground to create an opportunity. Now Hutchinson is gearing up for the big one. He gives the ball a good wipe on his shirt, takes a couple of steps back and then moves forward. He unleashes a monster of a throw which causes utter havoc in the Leeds box, to the alarm of the Yorkshiremen and women behind the goal. Harvey comes for it but doesn't get there. Osgood goes up with Charlton, who only succeeds in heading the ball backwards and upwards.

Loitering on the far post – like a caveman stalking his prey – is Webb. There is an unsightly bundle at the post consisting of Gray, Hunter, Baldwin and Webb. But it is Webb, face grim with determination, who gets there first, forcing the ball into the back of the net with what looks like his face. Pretty it isn't (the goal, not Webb's face). Webb goes mad, punching the air and leaping with delight, as do the Chelsea fans. For the first time in the two games, Chelsea are ahead. The Londoners in the crowd are ecstatic. John Foley says, 'Finally we were ahead and I knew we were going to do it now.'

For the last few minutes, the Chelsea fans sing incessantly while their Leeds counterparts are mute, seemingly conceding that the 1970 FA Cup is not to be theirs.

Webb's messy effort is the final goal of an epic FA Cup Final. Referee Jennings – who has certainly been kept busy over the course of the two matches – blows his whistle for the last time. Chelsea have won the cup. And they have beaten arguably the best team in the country in doing so.

Most neutrals think the key to Chelsea's win is the way they contained – by fair or foul means – the brilliant Eddie Gray, who was a marginal figure in Manchester. Ironic then, that the deciding goal has been scored by David Webb, who was made to look a clown by Gray at Wembley. Theirs has been the major battle over the two matches. And both players know it.

The camera pans in on match-winner Webb, who lip-readers can see shouting 'Eddie, Eddie!' in Gray's direction. Webb wants Gray's shirt. Gray magnanimously obliges and the two players swap and embrace.

Now it is time for Chelsea to get the cup. The knackered winning team, climbing the steps at Wembley, is one of football's most famous images. So it looks somewhat odd to see the ritual being fulfilled elsewhere when 'Chopper' Harris raises the cup aloft in the Old Trafford directors' box, in an area of the stadium now so familiar to us as roughly the spot occupied for so many years by Sir Alex Ferguson.

At first, the Chelsea players look strangely subdued. But now they let all their inhibitions go and race down towards the Stretford End, holding the cup aloft. Hollins, Harris and

McCreadie run, pursued by cameramen, with the cup, blue ribbons streaming off it, towards their ecstatic fans. 'Just fantastic,' recalls Jeff Van Doorn. Damian Inwood remembers dancing on the terraces and randomly hugging total strangers at the final whistle.

'It was just pure exhilaration,' says John Foley. 'I had never seen Chelsea win a competition before and now my Tottenham acquaintances back in London were going to hear all about this! The sight of Ronnie Harris holding up the cup to us from the stand on the right was the stuff of dreams for me. And when they paraded it round the pitch and then right in front of us, it was blue heaven!'

For Leeds, it is yet another kick in the teeth. They are so upset that they cannot bear to take their place at the presentation of the losers' medals and slink off quietly to the dressing room where, later, FA chairman Dr Andrew Stephen will finally present them with the unwanted medals.

The TV cameras keep picking out Webb, now wearing Gray's white number 11 shirt. The Stratford-born defender suddenly jumps up and swings on the crossbar, which does nothing at all to detract from the primate, monkey-like image. He bends over slightly and turns his back to his adoring fans, pointing to Gray's shirt. The noise from the Chelsea fans is deafening. Osgood, wearing Bremner's shirt, poses for the photographers, cup aloft.

In stark contrast to the delirium on the pitch and terraces, the post-match interview between David Coleman and Chelsea boss Dave Sexton is surely one of the lowest key in cup final history. It is akin to a local news reporter interviewing someone who has just been newly appointed to the position of assistant branch manager at a local bank, with his first question the slightly obtuse, 'Growing ulcers down there were you, Dave?'

Leeds fans are glum and distinctly bitter, believing they were given inadequate protection by the referee. The defeat still rankles with Les Wake. He says, 'Chelsea altered their game plan from Wembley and opted for dirty and rough tactics to stop us playing football. History shows that it worked, but I doubt if any referee would allow it today. The game in my mind was robbery with violence.

'After the game I felt numb, as I'm sure many others were too. In the space of four or five weeks we had had to play two FA Cup Finals, three FA Cup semi-finals, two European Cup semi-finals plus a load of league games as well. It would have been too much for any team.'

In Surrey, 200 miles away, Carole Parkhouse shares Les's bitterness. She says, 'Once again we'd outplayed Chelsea, but lost. One of the joys of being a girl is being able to behave badly on occasion and I had the satisfaction of having extremely noisy hysterics, which kept everyone up most of the night.' But Carole and Les won't have to wait long for cup glory.

Not that Chelsea had too much sympathy with the miserable Leeds fans. As they streamed out into the night, they were trying to come to terms with winning the most famous domestic cup competition in the world.

The Van Doorn brothers and their companions were in heaven. Jeff remembers, 'We had some membership card that got us into a working men's club close to Old Trafford and so we went in to celebrate with a few beers.'

His younger brother Steve, just 16 at the time, says, 'I remember that the elation made me slightly tipsy. We then stopped at a fish and chip shop on the way out of Manchester. I can still see the lady who was serving asking if the whole of London was stopping for food tonight because she had never seen so many Cockneys in her life.'

Damian Inwood's return journey back to Darlington was vastly different from the inward one. He recalls, 'It was with three very glum Yorkshiremen who were a lot quieter now. They barely said a word as I laughed and sang Chelsea songs all the way back across the Pennines. I was gasping for a drink, but the miserable sods wouldn't even stop for a coffee and they very grudgingly dropped me off back in Darlington. But what a day!'

As the Leeds coaches headed back to Yorkshire, the fans were shell-shocked and though they had nothing like as far as Chelsea to travel, the journey seemed like an eternity, as Les Wake remembers, 'What made it worse was that, due to extra time, we arrived in Leeds too late to get any form of transport home. As it turned out, we had a chat to our driver, who was local. He dropped us off at the depot and we walked the three miles home. I had to be at work at 5.30am so I got little, if any, sleep.'

Fifteen-year-old John Foley, due back at school in East London the next morning, finally made his way out of the ground and headed towards Manchester Piccadilly. There were even more Chelsea fans there than there were at Euston earlier in the day. 'The crush was almost unbearable,' says John. 'Looking back, it's a miracle that there were not more crowd disasters in those days.

'The songs were non-stop. "Ee-aye-addio, we've won the cup!" "We shall not be moved!" The noise was deafening. I didn't see any trouble whatsoever after the game. I guess the Leeds fans were gutted and just couldn't wait to get home.'

That day's edition of the *Daily Mirror* is already rolling off the presses. It is dominated by a remarkable picture, taken by photographer Alfred Markey, of a distraught young man. It is Billy Bremner in the dressing room at Old Trafford, naked, head in hand, looking down at the floor.

'IT'S THE FINAL AGONY', reads the headline. The article says, 'Leeds United skipper Billy Bremner weeps in the Old Trafford dressing rooms last night after his side's final disappointment in a season of bitter frustration. The team that came so near to winning everything finished up with nothing after Chelsea beat them 2-1 in the replayed FA Cup Final. It was the final blow in a season which has already seen the league championship and the European Cup snatched from their grasp.'

Even Chelsea players express some sympathy with Leeds. Centre-half Dempsey says, 'We feel very sorry for them and hope they do better next season.'

Such sentiments, if they are genuine, are confined to the players. The cars, coaches and trains heading back south crammed with Chelsea fans are filled with the excited babble of cup victory.

Despite the lateness of the hour and the exhaustion of the fans, the train ride back to London was like a huge, travelling party. At around 2am, the trains started pulling back into Euston and spilling out the fans, who were now ready for bed. But, as all train-travelling football fans know, when you arrive at your station, you give it one last chant.

'When we got off at Euston,' says John Foley, 'the noise was thunderous and our chants were bouncing off the roof. I seem to remember they kept the Underground open for us to get home.' It was nearly 3am when John arrived back home in Chingford, feeling knackered, but fantastic.

The white Cortina carrying the Van Doorn brothers and their friends made its way southwards, with songs of victory resounding. Jeff says, 'By around 3am we had got as far as Birmingham and I suddenly found that I couldn't keep my eyes open and found myself drifting across the road. My cousin said he felt fine so he took over the driving and drove back the rest of the way and we arrived home at 6am and crashed out to get some sleep.'

Les Wake, vanquished and distraught, but a loyal, steadfast young man, was up and reporting for duty at his colliery at 5.30am the next day. He had less than three hours' sleep. As usual, he gathered with all the other electricians at the mine, waiting to be deployed. He was the only apprentice there. He felt utterly desolate.

Les recalls, 'I wasn't saying much because I was just totally gutted. I had just turned 17 and I didn't want to show people how upset I really was. In my view, we had totally outclassed Chelsea in both games and ended up with nothing. The supervisor looked at me and called out my name. He could see how upset I was. He said, "I'm saying nowt young 'un" and asked me if I was at the game. I just gave him a slight nod. All the blokes looked at me and I thought to myself "here it comes". But no one said a word and I got the feeling that they were showing me some respect, or sympathy, as a die-hard football fan.'

While Les was hard at work down the pit, feeling sick at the memory of last night's defeat, the Chelsea boys were getting ready to party. After a few hours' kip, Jeff and Steve Van Doorn got up and made their way from South London to Euston to welcome their conquering heroes back home. Off the train they got: Houseman, Hollins, Cooke and McCreadie, holding the cup for the fans to see. They received a rapturous ovation. The TV cameras were also there and Steve remembers that one of his teachers spotted him in the throng of jubilant Chelsea supporters, blowing that oldest excuse in the book – a dentist's appointment – out of the water. He didn't care. 'It was just a great, great couple of days,' he says.

While this was going on John Foley, who had grabbed a couple of hours' shut-eye, dragged himself out of bed and made his bleary-eyed way to the Sir George Monoux School, where he was treated like a bit of a hero. Even though most of the lads in his year supported West Ham or Tottenham Hotspur, he earned big respect for travelling to Manchester and back. Just about everyone had watched the game on television and they all wanted to know his story.

John was in full flow when he heard the less-than-mellifluous tones of his form master, 'Foley. A word, please. NOW!' in that peculiar fashion which only teachers seem able to achieve. 'Good night last night was it, Foley?' 'Yes sir, brilliant,' said John. 'Well, the headmaster wants to know all about it. He doesn't like football very much of course, but I'm sure he'd be very interested in hearing all about your experience. Off you go.'

'I knew what was coming,' says John. 'I wanted so much to be at the victory parade but the only parade I was making was to the head's office.' The head didn't even bother with any small talk.

'Bend over, Foley,' he said wearily, as he reached into a cupboard in the corner of the office. It was over in a flash. 'I got the cane,' says John, 'but I didn't mind. It was so worth it!'

To this day, the 1970 FA Cup Final remains a classic. An utterly absorbing 210 minutes of football, with twists and turns, controversy and drama. Few dispute that Leeds were the better side and probably deserved the trophy, but the beauty of football is that the most superior side does not always triumph. Chelsea, urged on by their adoring thousands, fought like dogs in both games.

The matches are now best remembered for the sheer brutality of the clashes – perhaps hardly surprising when some of the hardest players to have played the game were involved. But there were moments of great football too. Gray's silky skills in the first leg, Jones's opener at Old Trafford and Osgood's memorable equaliser. But maybe it was fitting that the final was decided by that famous goal from Webb, which owed everything to guts, determination and the desire to win.

The final was to prove a watershed for Les Wake and, in the days and weeks that followed the crushing defeat, he became increasingly reflective. Now living in Adelaide, South Australia, he says, 'After the Old Trafford replay, it was somehow never the same. Even though I had made many friends travelling to matches, the buzz of getting on the coach to grounds all over the country had gone. I got to know many, many people. There was one particular guy called Pete, who always kept himself to himself. I later found out that this guy was none other than Peter Ridsdale, who would become chairman. Whatever happened with his subsequent dealings I, for one, can vouch that he was a true fan of Leeds United.'

For Les it was suddenly a case of 'been there, done that' and he decided he simply did not want to do it any more. 'For that reason I rarely went to an away game again,' he says.

Les continued to work as a colliery electrician for several years before becoming a contractor, which took him all over the north and Midlands. He married and had a young family, but became increasingly dissatisfied with life in the UK. In 1982, aged 29, he decided to move his family to Australia. He is unequivocal about his reasons for doing so.

'To escape Thatcherism and to get a better life,' he says. More than 30 years later, Les still feels as though he is on some kind of extended working holiday. 'To be honest, I've never looked back and I currently work as a construction manager for one of the largest electrical contractors in Australia. Work has taken me to all parts of Australia.'

Les remains a die-hard follower of Leeds and is currently secretary of the official Leeds United Supporters' Club, Adelaide branch. He says, 'After we were relegated to League 1, the televised games were very sparse but, when we get together for a game, it's usually at one of the major pubs in Adelaide and we currently have a membership of 50-plus.'

At heart, there's still some of that hard-working, early-rising 17-year-old who fought for the FA Cup Final ticket he so richly deserved. 'As any fan will realise, the passion for your team never really dies, regardless of who you follow. We all have the same connection and that can never be taken away.'

Steve Van Doorn – 16 in 1970 – also emigrated. In 1981, aged 27, he went to live in Johannesburg with his wife and, in 1990, he and his family moved to Cape Town. A brief return to the UK did not work out because the family had become 'Africanised' and they returned to Cape Town before upping sticks again and moving to Perth in Western Australia in 2002.

There, Steve kick-started the Chelsea Supporters' Club. He says, 'We have a good following but, since the introduction of daylight saving, the mid-season is a tale of seven or eight of us meeting at various houses in the northern suburbs to watch matches at very awkward times. For instance, a 3pm kick-off is midnight, a Saturday 5.15pm kick-off is 2.15am Sunday morning and the 4pm Sunday matches are a 1am kick-off on a Monday morning, when we all have to go to work at 7/8am!'

Strange kick-off times are also a way of life for John Foley, who has lived in Thailand for nearly 25 years. He is married to a Thai woman and has two children, Harry, and Catherine Chelsea. But his continuing Chelsea addiction is well fed. He says, 'We get almost every Chelsea game televised live and I stay up until the early hours if Chelsea are playing midweek – I never miss a game. My wife thinks I'm mad. I guess it must be the noise coming from the front room at 4am when she's asleep and Chelsea have just scored!'

Jeff Van Doorn has stayed in the UK. He lives in Thatcham, Berkshire. Now retired he has a part-time job, two days a week, delivering commercial vehicles. He still has a season ticket at Stamford Bridge and attends the occasional away game too. In 2014 he celebrated 41 years of marriage to his wife, Barbara. They have two children (Cressida and Chris) and three grandchildren, Harry, Ariana and Tilly-Rose. 'They are all encouraged to support Chelsea,' says Jeff.

In recent years, Jeff has travelled to Amsterdam to watch Chelsea play Benfica in the 2013 Europa League Final and the year before, he was in Munich to see Chelsea beat Bayern Munich after penalties in the Champions League Final. 'That was just fabulous,' he says.

However, like thousands of Chelsea fans of his generation, the events of April 1970 will never be forgotten: 'It was just brilliant,' he says. 'I shall never forget that night at Old Trafford. The Chelsea supporters were absolutely amazing and totally silenced the Leeds fans who, I think, deep down, knew they were going to lose. It's a wonderful memory for all Chelsea fans. And being there was magical. Back in 1970, Chelsea had won the FA Cup at last – and we were there to witness it.'

'TIL DEATH US DO PART
Arsenal v Liverpool
Saturday 8 May 1971

THERE is an old truism among football fans, which is this, 'We can change our car, our job, our wife or husband, our house. Hell, we can even change our sex. But we can't change our football team.'

Through the good times and bad times, we are saddled with the damn outfit. For richer for poorer – and mostly poorer – 'til death us do part. Once a man has decided which team he will follow, nothing can make him switch allegiance. Least of all a girl. Ridiculous suggestion. It just couldn't happen. Not in a million years. Could it?

Derek Butt was born in 1954 in Liverpool, where his mother hailed from. However, Derek's father, a train driver, was a Mancunian and a devout fan of United. So Derek grew up with tales of the great Busby Babes side and his passion intensified when he was old enough to understand the significance of the Munich plane crash in February 1958, which wiped out a young team on the verge of greatness.

The year before the Munich tragedy, Derek's family had moved down to London when Mr Butt secured a much sought-after job driving trains out of Euston station.

All through the 1960s, Derek followed United from afar – the FA Cup win over Leicester in 1963, the league championships of 1965 and 1967. By the time United thrashed Benfica 4-1 at Wembley to win the 1968 European Cup, Derek's allegiance to United was cemented forever. Or so he thought. He hadn't reckoned on the impact a young girl of Irish parentage was about to have on his life.

Bernadette Nalty – Bernie – grew up on a housing estate in the small North London district of Mornington Crescent. When Bernie's dad arrived in London from Ireland he took digs in Putney and began going to nearby Fulham with Bernie's mum. Mr and Mrs Nalty both had season tickets at Craven Cottage and Bernie started going with them at a young age.

But Bernie wasn't a South Londoner. She was a North London girl and the nearest club was Arsenal. As soon as she was old enough to make up her own mind, Bernie decided there was only one place she wanted to watch her football – and that place was Highbury. Fate and an extraordinary season in London, N1 were going to bring Bernie and Derek together.

%, %, %,

To this day, Dean Goodman gets a shiver down his spine when he sees the season number 1970/71 written down in print. As do thousands of Gooners.

For Dean, the adoption of Arsenal as his club was a straightforward matter. It was in 1963, on the way to Monkfrith Junior and Mixed Primary School in Southgate, when a friend called Stevie 'K' King asked ten-year-old Dean which team he supported. Not knowing what to say, Dean threw the question back at Steve and got the answer, 'Arsenal, of course.'

Dean says, 'Coming from Wood Green, the "other" North London team had been my local club, but as Steve was more important to me than them I replied quickly, "me too"!'

Shortly afterwards, Dean saw his first game at Highbury and it made a huge impression on him. 'What a corker it turned out to be,' he says. 'I stood on the corner of the North Bank in a "friendly" against Glasgow Rangers. Is this what football is like, I thought? The atmosphere was electric, but the intimidation for an 11-year-old unbearable. But I quickly became fanatical about the club.

'Our goalkeeper Jim Furnell lived locally and I passed his house on my way to school every day, so it became important to take that route each morning and evening just in case he was at the door. Defender Bob McNab lived round the corner from my house, so round the corner" was an important place to be on a regular basis.'

Except all was not well in the famous marble halls. For Arsenal fans, the 1960s was a lean period, spent constantly, it seems, in the shadow of their bitter rivals Spurs who, much to Arsenal's annoyance, won the double in 1960/61 and the FA Cup in 1962 and 1967.

Yet, Arsenal had a wonderful tradition of success and their older fans could still recall the glory days of the 1930s. Arsenal did reach two League Cup finals at the end of the 1960s, but lost them both, 1-0 to Leeds in 1968 and then, the following March, losing humiliatingly 3-1 to Swindon Town on a Wembley quagmire.

When the 1960s ended you could almost hear the sighs of relief emanating from those marble halls and the bust of Herbert Chapman. Whereas British society changed dramatically during the decade, football was slow to catch up, especially so considering the World Cup glory of 1966.

However, by 1970 things were changing. Teams became better organised and fitter – some might say more cynical and professional. A win-at-all-costs attitude started to prevail, and Arsenal were definitely one of those teams starting to get their act together. Under the stewardship of Bertie Mee and Don Howe, they were beginning to look useful.

Dean Goodman was 17 when the 1970s began, and a pupil at Ashmole School in Southgate. He recalls this period vividly. 'What was the meaning of life at that time?' he says. 'Well, there were girls, and don't get me wrong they were important. But what was *really* important was that girls did not get in the way of football. It was the lifeblood of all teenagers who loved sport. England had won the World Cup for goodness sake, so the nation was at the pinnacle of footballing success. Gordon Banks, Bobby Moore, Geoff Hurst…at the time even my mum could list the names of those magical footballers. But to my mind, there was something missing.'

That 'something' was domestic success for Arsenal and Dean was thinking big, 'We needed to win a domestic trophy and one that represented the accolade of being the top club. Not just in London, but in England.'

The first inkling that something truly special might be around the corner was the stunning triumph in the Inter-Cities Fairs Cup, the club's first major achievement in almost two decades. It is an occasion still remembered fondly by thousands of Gooners of a certain age.

Dean recalls, 'We lost the first leg of the final against Anderlecht 3-1 and no one thought that we would come back. But, on that dull April evening in 1970, we did the impossible and won 3-0 to steal from "that other North London club" the achievement of being top London side. I was there that night, in the West Stand, and then on the pitch. Great! Fantastic!'

The Fairs Cup triumph proved a pivotal moment in the development of Arsenal's success and demonstrated to the players – and fans – that the approach and tactics Bertie Mee and Don Howe were espousing had real merit. At last, they were ready to challenge for domestic honours again. It was going to be a great time to follow the Arsenal.

※ ※ ※

It is May 1970 and every night after tea, Derek Butt and his mates meet on a stretch of waste ground near their estate and play football until sunset. Chelsea have just won the FA Cup, Everton the league championship and the England squad are preparing to fly off to faraway Mexico for that summer's World Cup, desperate to retain the Jules Rimet trophy, won so magically four years earlier.

They do so with the song 'Back Home' being played, sung and hummed throughout the nation. Written by Bill Martin (a Scot) and Phil Coulter (an Ulsterman), it is a strident tub-thumper with an attention-grabbing brass section, a walking bassline and sing-a-long vocals, which perfectly capture the sense of a team doing battle on the other side of the globe for the benefit of the millions cheering them on back in England.

At first, Derek barely noticed the two girls who had started hanging around on the sidelines, watching him and his mates play. He was too busy pretending to be Brian Kidd, George Best or Carlo Sartori. The girls hung around, frequently giggling, sometimes clapping, occasionally cheering until the lads gradually became conscious of their presence and started trying clever flicks, nutmegs and volleys to impress them. Derek especially liked the girl who one of his mates said was called Bernie. 'She's Arsenal-mad,' said his mate Tom, 'North Bank regular. Likes Peter Marinello.'

'Do you mean that girly-looking, Scottish bloke they bought from Hibs? She with anyone?' said Derek. 'Don't think so,' said Tom. 'Only has eyes for Marinello, and after that John Radford. I wouldn't bother mate.'

The next time the boys turned up to play, the girls were already there wearing plimsolls. They were both pushing each other forward. Eventually Bernie advanced, 'Do you mind if Sue and I join in? We can play.' The lads looked at each other and shrugged their shoulders. 'S'pose not,' said Tom. Bernie remembers, 'The lads were quite surprised when we said we wanted to play, but I was a good netball player and could catch a ball, so I became the goalkeeper.'

From that point on, the girls became regulars and soon the lads embraced them as their own. Derek started to really look forward to the games and realised he couldn't wait to see Bernie flinging herself around in goal, trying her utmost to keep his shots out. And similarly, Bernie found herself thinking a bit less about Peter Marinello, who was struggling to live up to his £100,000 price tag and 'the new George Best' label, and a bit more about the young lad who, she suspected, was holding back just a tad when he took a shot in her direction.

The ball always seemed a bit too close to her, struck at a nice height, yet she still took great delight in saving his shots. But there was a far bigger problem.

One hot day, just as the World Cup was beginning in Mexico, Derek finally got Bernie on his own. Hands in his pockets, looking down, shuffling his feet, he started to talk. 'Excuse me, Bernie. I was just wondering if you would, um, like to come with me to the, err, pictures.'

'Sorry Derek, but I can't,' said Bernie smiling sweetly.

'Oh, okay, err, fine,' said Derek, rather taken aback by the immediate rejection. 'Any particular reason why?'

'Because I've heard you support Manchester United,' replied Bernie.

'Oh, I see,' says Derek. 'But...'

'Sorry Derek. I'm Arsenal. Always. Bye for now.'

Clearly, there was no room for compromise.

The 1970 World Cup is a belter. Though it ends in abject despair for England, who throw away a 2-0 quarter-final lead to old rivals West Germany, the public thrill to the sublime skills of the Brazilians who, for the first time, are projected on to television screens in glorious Technicolour.

It has football fans all over Britain champing at the bit for the new football season to begin. Derek is among them, but he's seriously distracted. He can't get Bernie out of his mind. One night he is lying in his room playing 'air harmonica' to 'Groovin' with Mr Bloe', which lies at number two in the charts behind Mungo Jerry's 'In the Summertime', when there is a knock at the door. It is Tom and he is out of breath. 'Just seen Sue,' he gasps, 'guess what? Bernie really fancies you and wants to go out with you.'

'Brilliant!' says Derek. 'I'll go and ask her.' But he can tell by Tom's face that there is a catch.

There is. 'She'll only go out with you if you start supporting Arsenal.'

'B******s to that,' is roughly the thought that flashes through Derek's mind.

The new season approaches. There is a buzz of anticipation. The estate football games continue. Bernie continues to shine in goal and the joke doing the rounds is that she is a better goalkeeper than Felix, the only dodgy member of the fabulous Brazilian side which contains Pele, Gerson, Tostao and Carlos Alberto.

Bernie is still playing hard to get, but she admits she likes Derek. Once when he does manage to get one past her he slides to his knees and does the sign of cross in imitation of the brilliant Jairzinho, which makes Bernie laugh. 'He's not as good as Geordie Armstrong,' she shouts at him, happily. 'But he's ten times better than George Best!'

Arsenal begin the 1970/71 season with high hopes and, as the players disembark from the team coach outside Goodison Park before the opening league match, the players are feeling quietly confident. But not one of the clutch of Gunners fans who have travelled to Merseyside could even remotely predict just how memorable and special the season would be for them. Undeniably, though, something in their make-up has changed, as Dean Goodman remembers.

He says, 'The team was a mixture of players who, individually, had limitations, but collectively were masterful. This had to be down to the skills of the manager and his back-room team. Dear old Bertie Mee was a physiotherapist by trade, who had taken on the manager's mantle with few credentials, but he was Arsenal through and through. His discipline was renowned and he had the respect and commitment of the players.

'The coach, Don Howe, was at his peak. There was a feeling of something special in the air. The red machine was purring away and Arsenal supporters knew that either this season, or one close by, was going to explode.'

The first home game of the season is approaching. Ironically, it is against Manchester United. Derek is at home deep in thought. So is Bernie, with her friend Sue, who thinks Bernie is being a bit harsh on Derek.

Bernie thinks of the North Bank, the marble halls and the art deco Highbury stands. She thinks of Ray Kennedy and

George Graham. Her mind is made up. Simultaneously, Derek is thinking of Best, Law and Charlton, the roar of the Stretford End, the Busby Babes.

He thinks of that wonderful night two years earlier when, wearing blue, they won the European Cup. He pictures Best dribbling the ball round the Benfica goalkeeper Jose Henrique, and sliding it masterfully into the empty net. He pictures Bobby Charlton crying, Nobby Stiles, and Pat Crerand. His mind is also made up. No girl is going to come between him and his team.

The next time he sees Bernie he resolves to tell her that he was sorry he asked her out and hopes that they can still be friends, but he is really not prepared to stop supporting Manchester United just for the privilege of going out with her. In fact, the more he thinks about it, the more preposterous it seems.

'How could I even have considered it?' he wonders. At the end of a match, he walks up to her. 'Bernie. I, um, just wanted to tell you something.' She looks gorgeous, slightly out of breath, wearing a hair clip. She looks him straight in the eye. 'Yes,' she says, softly. Derek thinks of Sir Matt Busby, Alex Stepney and John Aston.

'Well, I've decided something.' An image of Denis Law scoring with a bullet header flashes through his mind. Bernie says nothing, but nods quickly several times, encouraging him to go on. Derek notices how beautiful her eyes are. Then he thinks about Ian Ure. Now his mind is definitely made up. It is no contest. He fancies her too much. 'Do go on, Derek,' she says sweetly. Derek has now melted. 'I'm an Arsenal fan now, Bernie.'

'And I'm your girlfriend now, Derek,' she says, pecking him lightly on the cheek, before running off home.

'We went to every home game that season,' says Bernie, more than 40 years later. 'At that time, it was really scary being a young girl at a football match. We used to watch from the North Bank, which was always absolutely packed. When anything exciting happened, the crowd surged and you had no control where you ended up. When we came out after games, there were always fights going on all over the place.'

※ ※ ※

It is Christmas 1970. Clive Dunn is at number one in the charts with 'Grandad', pretending to be 76, when he is actually only about 27. In round three of the FA Cup, scheduled for Saturday 2 January, Arsenal have been drawn away at Southern League side Yeovil Town, conquerors of Bournemouth in the previous round.

They play at Huish Park, famous for its sloping pitch. The new year starts with snow and ice, delighting Yeovil as they think it will even things up. However, referee Bill Gow, of Swansea, decides the conditions make it too dangerous to play. It is a decision that angers the Somerset side who claim they will lose money. Treasurer Brian Moore says, 'We had taken £12,500 from ticket sales and there were a lot of fringe benefits.' The game will be replayed on the Wednesday afternoon. The Glovers' chairman Norman Burfield claims Gow's decision to postpone the match delighted Arsenal.

'Bertie Mee was the first to pat him on the back,' he says. While club captain Cliff Myers moaned, 'Bertie Mee wants to wrap his players in cotton wool.'

The cancellation of the match pales into insignificance with events at Glasgow. Sixty-six people – 32 of them teenagers – are crushed as crowd barriers at Ibrox, home of Rangers, collapse just before the end of the Auld Firm derby. Seconds before the disaster, the home fans had been ecstatic after their team's late equaliser against Celtic. Fans leaving the ground tried to get back in, one person slipped, chaos ensued and steel railings buckled under the weight of people.

On the Monday, the *Daily Mirror* asks, 'How could it happen? Are other grounds vulnerable? Are spectators' lives being put at risk unnecessarily? These are the questions a horrified nation is asking after the Ibrox Park disaster. Questions that the official inquiry, announced yesterday, must pursue with rigour and answer with frankness.'

With the nation in shock over the terrible events at Glasgow, the Yeovil–Arsenal match is rearranged for the following Wednesday. If Yeovil were worried about a midweek afternoon match being less attractive than a Saturday match, they were wrong. If anything, there is even more interest in the rescheduled match than the original fixture. It is another sell-out and many of the town's employees are given the afternoon off, as long as they make the time up. This time referee Gow gives the all-clear.

Making his way to the West Country by train is Dean Goodman. A thousand or so Arsenal fans gather at Paddington station in the morning, smoking and laughing. Cans of beer are already being fizzed open. On platform three, a football special awaits. If ever the word 'special' was misplaced, this is it. As Dean recalls, 'British Rail reserved their crummiest, oldest and most decrepit railway carriages for football fans, but as long as it had a card table, we were okay. You could bring along cans or bottles with no restrictions, so a good drink, a pack of cards and a sing-song when we neared our destination were the order of the day.'

The Arsenal fans, now well oiled, pile off at Yeovil station and make their way to Huish Park under heavy police escort. The ground is packed with people crammed into every nook and cranny. All the talk has been of an upset with the crazy incline expected to knock the Gunners off their stride.

The snow and ice has turned to claggy, energy-sapping mud. In the build-up to the game chairman Burfield has been talking Yeovil up, and says, 'Arsenal won't know what has hit them on our pitch.' He is made to eat his words by an ultra-efficient performance by the Londoners. In the 36th minute a cross by Jon Sammels is met by John Radford who, in acres of space, nods the ball over Yeovil keeper Tony Clark. Just before half-time Ray Kennedy adds another from close range and, in the second half, another headed goal by Radford makes the game safe. A potentially tricky tie is negotiated.

Arsenal manager Mee says, 'We came here to do a job and we did it well.' On the way back to Paddington, the Arsenal fans sing

'We're Going To Wembley' and 'one Johnny Radford, there's only one Johnny Radford'. They are on their way.

But there are a number of other teams who think they've got a chance of winning the 1971 FA Cup. Holders Chelsea, Tottenham, Everton and Leeds are all quietly confident. But, one team with a growing reputation are Liverpool and, on the eve of the team's home third-round tie against Aldershot, their mercurial manager Bill Shankly tells reporters, 'With our players' ability and our crowd there is nothing Liverpool can't achieve.'

One goal is enough to see off the Shots – a 28th-minute effort by teenager John McLaughlin, after a mistake by skipper Jimmy Melia, a former Liverpool player.

Watching his team's narrow win over Aldershot from the Kop is 18-year-old Liverpool obsessive Chris Wood, who has become a virtual ever-present. In 1970/71, apart from one end-of-season game at Nottingham Forest, he sees every Saturday league match between August and May, 34 of the 42 fixtures and 11 cup ties as well. Yet despite all the trips to the City Ground, Upton Park and Bloomfield Road, something is missing. 'What I really wanted to do,' says Chris, 'was to watch Liverpool at Wembley.'

It has been hard for Derek Butt. When he first took his place on the North Bank it felt like the ultimate betrayal and, at first, his mind frequently wandered to Old Trafford or wherever United were playing. How could he spurn a team containing the likes of Best, Law and Charlton? But then he sees Bernie shouting 'go on Ray' or 'saved Bob!' and he slowly, ever so slowly, starts to forget, especially as Arsenal are playing superbly.

The FA Cup fourth round ties take place on 23 January and Arsenal have a tricky-looking trip to Second Division Portsmouth. Down go their fans – Dean Goodman, Ken Banham and Peter Hollingworth among them. And it *is* tricky – only the brilliance of goalkeeper Bob Wilson keeps Arsenal in the cup.

Playing on another mud bath, Arsenal go in front with a 35th-minute penalty by Peter Storey, but are then battered by Pompey, who are denied time and time again by Wilson. But then, in the last minute, up pops 1966 FA Cup Final hero Mike Trebilcock to secure a replay for the South Coast side, sending the Fratton Park faithful bananas in the process, as Trebilcock somersaults in front of them.

However, the big story from round four is about more crowd safety problems. Just three weeks after the Ibrox tragedy, six people are hospitalised and 24 others slightly injured after a wall collapses at Oxford United's Manor Ground during a cup tie against Watford. Following a goalmouth melee, the crowd behind the goal pushes forward and then there is a terrifying noise – like a rifle crack – as 35 yards of wall give way.

In an article in Monday's *Daily Mirror*, reporter Frank Taylor writes, 'How many more walls have to collapse and how many more soccer fans have to risk their lives before we get some positive action on our archaic soccer grounds?'

The replay against Pompey takes place in the midst of a mini-crisis for the Gunners, which has rocked their title challenge. On the Saturday they lose 2-0 at Anfield. It is their second successive league defeat and leaves them five points behind Leeds. Mee calls the players in on the Sunday for a heart-to-heart to chew over what's going wrong. Pompey have been buoyed by a surprise 1-0 win at Hull, the Second Division leaders. The replay is something of an unwanted distraction for the Gunners.

It is a classic, feisty match, only decided by a late Peter Storey penalty which gives Arsenal a 3-2 win and takes them through to the last 16. They are awarded a third successive away tie. And this one will be a real test. They must travel to Manchester City.

The UK is preparing to go decimal. Former Beatle George Harrison is at number one with 'My Sweet Lord'. Shortly afterwards a court rules that his simple major-minor chord sequence and accompanying melody 'unconsciously plagiarises' the Chiffons' 1964 hit 'He's So Fine'. Neil Diamond is in a rich vein of form. He quickly follows up 'Cracklin' Rosie' with 'Sweet Caroline'. And 1971 will be a massive year for T-Rex and they are in the charts with 'Ride a White Swan'. Although to most serious lovers of music, the charts are starting to make people cringe. It is a year dominated by 'bubblegum' like Middle of the Road and Dawn, or 'nudge/nudge, wink/wink' novelty records like Benny Hill's 'Ernie' or 'Johnny Reggae' by the Piglets (aka Jonathan King).

Every Thursday night, Bernie goes to Derek's house, where they watch *Top of the Pops* together on the black and white TV in the Butt living room. They are not really watching Ashton, Gardner and Dyke, the Mixtures or the Jackson Five though; they are too busy talking about Arsenal. The season is getting better and better, and their relationship is growing with it.

During the week the huge potential being displayed by Charlie George is recognised by England boss Sir Alf Ramsey, who includes him in a 14-strong under-23 squad to face Scotland in Glasgow. Arsenal manager Bertie Mee says, 'I have always believed that Charlie has the ability to go right to the top.'

As if buoyed by the news, George plays brilliantly in the rearranged tie against City, which takes place the following Wednesday night on a heavy pitch at Maine Road, in front of 45,000 people. On 17 minutes he scores with a great free kick. His second is even better. A left-flank move involving Bob McNab and Geordie Armstrong leaves the long-haired striker in the clear and homing in on goal. Avoiding a challenge from Tony Book he drives the ball low, past the advancing Joe Corrigan in the City goal.

A Colin Bell goal six minutes from time is too little, too late for City and Arsenal are through to the quarter-finals. It is a terrific win for the Londoners. Can anyone stop them? What makes it even more exciting for the Gunners' fans is that the previous Saturday, in one of the most sensational results in FA Cup history, mighty Leeds crashed out of the competition after losing 3-2 to Colchester United at Layer Road.

Arriving back at Euston station the following day, Arsenal receive glowing praise from an unlikely source. Leeds boss Don Revie, still licking his wounds after his team's defeat in the garrison town, says generously, 'Arsenal are a fine side on the crest of a wave and it's not out of the question that they could win the lot.'

By which Revie means the league, the FA Cup and the Inter-Cities Fairs Cup, which Arsenal are still in. Charlie George meanwhile, with his rock star looks, is becoming a favourite with tabloid photographers and in many of Friday's papers he is pictured being greeted at Euston by his glamorous girlfriend, Susan Farge.

Life goes on. Prime Minister Edward Heath sacks the Government's top arbitrator in pay disputes, Professor Hugh Clegg, believing he is too friendly with the unions, who see the move as evidence of a tougher-than-ever pay policy by the Conservatives. The latest must-have car is the new Vauxhall Victor which is selling for £1,042. The accompanying PR blurb says, 'At Punishment Park – our 700-acre proving ground in Bedfordshire – we test drive the Victor to make them all they're worth. We call it test proving. A programme of drastic action that compresses months and thousands of miles of hard usage into weeks of continuous scientific testing. We know it's worth it, so will you.'

Arsenal travel to Filbert Street to meet Leicester for a place in the semi-final. All the talk beforehand is of whether Arsenal's deadly strike duo John Radford and Ray Kennedy – 41 goals between them this season – can get past Leicester's brilliant young goalkeeper Peter Shilton, who says, 'We have a lot of respect for Radford and Kennedy, but we are not frightened of them.' And Shilton keeps them out in a goalless draw.

Over 57,000 are at Highbury for the replay on Monday 15 March and, once again, it is Arsenal's talisman Charlie George who settles it. Watched by the entire Stoke City squad, who will play the victors, George heads the winner in the 45th minute of the game. It is enough to take Arsenal to the semi-finals. And they did it the hard way, being drawn away in every round.

Liverpool, by comparison, have enjoyed a more sedate tournament, never having to travel away from Anfield, where they have only conceded seven times all season and are gaining a reputation as a really tough nut to crack. The victory over Aldershot in round three was followed by 3-0 and 1-0 wins over Swansea and Southampton, respectively.

Chris Wood was there for each game and is there again when Tottenham are the visitors in round six. There is a minor blip for the Reds when the game ends goalless, but they clinch a semi-final place with a 1-0 win in the replay, courtesy of a Steve Heighway goal. It sets up a mouth-watering all-Merseyside semi-final against Everton.

It is Monday 22 March and Arsenal enter a critical week. Their players will reportedly earn a staggering £15,000 *each* if they win the treble. In classic football parlance, Bertie Mee says the team are 'taking one match at a time' and their fans are agog with excitement. Something is happening in North London. It all seems to be coming together. As the Arsenal fans prepare to head to Hillsborough for the semi-final against Stoke, there is even talk of, whisper it, the double.

On Saturday 27 March 1971 young lovers Bernie Nalty and Derek Butt are at St Pancras station along with thousands of other Arsenal fans. 'Bet you're glad you became an Arsenal fan now, aren't you Derek?' says Bernie, as they pile on to a football special bound for Sheffield. The trip north is noisy and boisterous. The card schools are in full swing, the booze is flowing and the singing is incessant. They go through virtually the whole team. Pat Rice, Peter Simpson, Eddie Kelly, they all get a mention.

Derek feels very protective towards his girlfriend, who is in her element, even though it gets increasingly rowdy as the train powers north. Bernie says, 'At one point a policeman's hat got thrown out of a window, then there was a massive punch-up and I ended up beneath a pile of men!'

While Arsenal are hot favourites to progress to Wembley, they are wary of the team from the Potteries who inflicted their heaviest defeat of the season, thrashing them 5-0 at the Victoria Ground in September, in a match which had commentator Alan Weeks drooling.

Both teams are wearing their change colours for the clash: Arsenal in yellow and blue and Stoke in all white. It is yet another dramatic game. At half-time Arsenal are staring at a cup exit and their dreams of the double are in tatters – they trail 2-0 after goals from Denis Smith and John Ritchie. The Stoke fans, gathered at the Leppings Lane end, are in dreamland.

One fan who hasn't made the journey to Hillsborough is Dean Goodman. His desperate quest for tickets failed and he is forced to tune in to live coverage on Radio Two, while revising for his A Levels in his front room. Still, the unrivalled brilliance of commentator Peter Jones to paint vivid pictures with words makes it seem as if he is there. At half-time, Dean is distraught.

Two hundred miles north Bernie and Derek stand glumly on the terraces, silently sharing a bag of crisps. Neither can see the Gunners clawing back the deficit. It is going to be a long journey home. Yet, unbeknown to Dean, Bernie and Derek and the thousands of other browned-off Arsenal fans in the ground, down in the dressing room, coach Don Howe and manager Bertie Mee are imparting a newly-hatched plan to their charges.

As soon as the second half starts, it is clear that Arsenal have changed their shape. They have pushed Charlie George right forward, creating a highly attacking formation. They are effectively playing with four strikers in a win-or-bust 4-2-4 formation as they seek a quick goal to get them back into the match. And it works. Peter Storey drives in a great shot from the edge of the box. Derek turns to Bernie and says, 'We can do this.' He no longer feels conscious saying 'we' – he is as Arsenal as the next man now.

The Gunners pour forward. Back home in North London, Dean casts aside his A Level textbooks and stares daggers at the radio, clenching his fist, willing his team on. Across the airwaves he can hear the chants of the Stoke fans. They still think they are going to Wembley. 'Come on Arsenal,' he says to himself. 'Come on!' But time is running out. It looks like Stoke City are going to make the FA Cup Final for the first time in their long and proud history.

But with seconds remaining, there is high drama – the kind only the FA Cup seems capable of dishing up. Frank McLintock floats a ball over into the danger area. It should really be meat and drink to a keeper of Gordon Banks's quality. But, as he rises to claim the ball, he appears to get a nudge from a yellow shirt behind him. The blue-shirted Banks loses the ball and it eventually goes for a corner.

Banks – looking alarmingly like Japanese Emperor Showa Hirohito – is usually a calm man but now, possibly with good reason, he is apoplectic and races to confront referee Pat Partridge. 'And I've never seen Gordon Banks like this,' says commentator Brian Moore. Banks's protests are to no avail and Arsenal have a corner. It is almost a minute into stoppage time. Back home in Southgate, Dean has his face in the carpet praying. On the Hillsborough Kop, Derek clutches Bernie tightly. It is do or die for Arsenal.

George Armstrong takes the corner. It is perfect. Nicely flighted and wonderfully inviting. McLintock accepts and bullets a header, which flashes past Banks and towards the net. But standing on the goal line is Welsh midfielder John Mahoney who flings himself to his right and, in a fashion which even the great Banks might have admired, pushes the ball round the post with his hand. It has happened like lightning but Partridge has seen it and points to the spot. The Stoke fans packed behind the goal are stunned, motionless and aghast.

Back at home, Dean hears commentator Peter Jones say, 'It's a penalty. The referee has pointed to the spot.' The 90 minutes is up. This is make or break time. The double hangs by a thread.

Storey steps up, chewing gum aggressively, his eyebrows smeared with Vaseline. Arsenal's season depends on him putting the ball past a goalkeeper still considered by many to be the greatest in the world.

At the other end of the ground, Derek holds Bernie to him as tightly as possible. Not a word is spoken except for a half-whispered 'please Peter' by Bernie. Back home, Dean crouches on the floor, hands clasped in prayer, pleading with Storey to equalise.

Banks sways like a monkey on the goal line. Storey advances and simply passes the ball low past him. It is 2-2.

As the ball hits the back of the net, Bernie screams with delight and she and Derek hug and dance as the delirious Arsenal fans cavort on the Kop.

Listening to the drama, Dean forgets all about his A Levels. 'When Peter Storey scored from the spot, I jumped so high that I recall hitting the lamp shade – books went everywhere,' he says. 'The whole street knew we'd scored – we'd been rescued from the brink.'

Arsenal are still in the competition – by the skin of their teeth. Maybe their name is on the FA Cup?

Whoever wins the replay will meet Liverpool at Wembley. At Old Trafford, watched by ardent Reds fan Chris Wood, they have seen off Everton 2-1 with goals from Alun Evans and Brian Hall cancelling out Alan Ball's opener.

The general feeling was that Storey's last-minute penalty shifted the momentum firmly in Arsenal's favour for the replay. Dean certainly thought so. 'I felt this match was a foregone conclusion, as the team were on such a high and there was no doubt that the trip to Wembley was going to happen,' he says. 'I could hardly contain myself.'

A whopping 62,500 people are at Villa Park on the Wednesday night for the replay. The atmosphere is incredible and Arsenal line up the way they finished on Saturday, with four up front. It takes them just 15 minutes to edge ahead for the first time in the two games. A George Armstrong corner floats across the crowded six-yard box, where it is met beautifully by the head of George Graham, who makes no mistake.

Two minutes after half-time, Ray Kennedy tucks home John Radford's low centre to make the game safe. Arsenal are going to Wembley. The Arsenal fans head back to London knowing that the dream of the double is still on. The Stoke fans head back to Staffordshire wondering what might have been. So near, and yet so far.

So the 1971 FA Cup Final will be between Arsenal and Liverpool. Bernie and Derek are on cloud nine. As Arsenal's fabulous season has progressed, so their relationship has blossomed. They have been to the pictures, bowling and ice skating together. They are now going on their best date yet – Wembley, on 8 May.

At least, that is the plan. Those tokens on the back of match programmes, barely noticed before, are now the most important things in the entire universe.

Bernie says, 'When we got to the final, we realised we had one complete set, but another set which was two tokens short.' With the optimism of youth, they are still convinced they will both be at Wembley, that somehow their voucher submission will be sufficient to get two tickets. When they discover it is not, they are devastated.

Dean can still see the blue-uniformed postman delivering his ticket. He says, 'I had collected all the vouchers, carefully stuck them into the final match-day centrefold and sent them recorded delivery to Avenell Road, in the hope of success. I kept my fingers crossed all week. Then, the gold dust hit the letterbox – a standing ticket in the Arsenal end. It had arrived!'

On Monday 3 May 1971, Arsenal Football Club began what surely still remains the most exciting week in the club's long and rich history. Not only did they have an FA Cup Final to play but also, that night, they had to make the short journey to their bitter rivals Tottenham Hotspur in an attempt to win the league championship.

It is a game that remains legendary in Arsenal lore. There was so much symbolism, so much significance attached to it. It was Arsenal's chance to win the league for the first time since

1952/53, on the ground of their most loathed enemy. More than that, even, Spurs' double of ten years earlier was still sticking in the craws of Arsenal fans everywhere. This was a chance to achieve the first part of that triumph and, once and for all, shove that accolade back down Spurs' throats.

Nobody knows quite how many people turned up at the Lane that night. Some people claim there could have been as many as 100,000 people in the vicinity, possibly more.

Derek and Bernie were among them. Bernie remembers, 'We went to White Hart Lane along with thousands and thousands of other people. In fact, it was actually very scary because there were so many people there. In the mayhem, a police horse trod on Derek's foot and I was nearly crushed against some wire fencing. We finally managed to get into a queue ready to pay at the turnstile. We were four from the front when they locked the gates! We ended up in the Corner Pin pub. We were too young to have a drink, of course, but the place absolutely rocked that night.'

Dean Goodman was luckier. He says, 'I was desperate to go. No matter what, I was going to watch that match at White Hart Lane. I had no ticket so I decided to arrive several hours before the kick-off, as we all knew there would be problems getting in. So it proved! The place was packed by 4pm, but thankfully I managed to get in. My mates were lost in the crowd, so there was no option but to stand where I was, on the corner of the Shelf and the Park Lane end. It was mostly Arsenal. There was no violence as the Reds had the upper hand in those days with the majority of young support.'

Another Arsenal fan who manages to get in is Don Richards, and he and the tens of thousands of other Arsenal fans see the Gunners make sure of the title courtesy of a late, late goal from the head of Ray Kennedy. Don recalls, 'At the end, all of us Arsenal supporters went on to the pitch, completely filling it and all dancing around with joy. This must have gone on for about an hour.'

Dean says, 'There is little I can honestly recall about that famous match, except the end when I went on the pitch, singing loudly, getting to the players, jumping up and down and getting on TV. I think it's me I can see when I watch the DVD nowadays – anyway, I like to think so... Brilliant!'

So, with the First Division title secure, Arsenal now start planning for Wembley. Bernie and Derek are on tenterhooks. They still only have one ticket and can't bear the thought of watching potentially the greatest match in Arsenal's history without each other.

Dean recounts the tension felt by every Arsenal supporter during this momentous week in May 1971. He says, 'True football fans all know that sleeping in the build-up to big matches is difficult, especially the closer you get to the day. But this game was massive! What sort of sleep do you honestly expect a 17-year-old fanatic to get? No one outside the realms of football fanaticism can understand what excitement is created in such circumstances.'

The Liverpool squad travel down to London by train on the Thursday before the final and a photographer takes a picture of John Toshack, Tommy Smith, Chris Lawler and Emlyn Hughes playing travel scrabble. Seventeen players are in the squad but boss Bill Shankly pledges to keep faith with the same side that beat Everton in the semi-final.

'It would have been an injustice not to play the same side,' he says. It means Alun Evans will start and left-winger Peter Thompson will be on the bench. Arsenal's main injury worry is their semi-final saviour Peter Storey, who still only has a 50-50 chance of playing.

While the Liverpool players grapple with triple word scores, double letters and blanks, Arsenal take it easy as well and Frank McLintock, Bob Wilson, George Graham and George Armstrong are pictured, somewhat randomly it has to be said, riding on a tractor. There are too many of them aboard it and they are not wearing protective clothing or footwear. Luckily, health and safety was less of an issue then.

A toss of the coin has decided that Liverpool will wear their traditional red shirts. It is a surprise move by the FA. Where the colours of the two competing clubs clash or are similar, traditionally, both clubs must change – like 1968 for instance – unless they can agree on alternative arrangements. But, for the 1971 FA Cup Final, FA secretary Denis Follows holds a private toss of a coin, which Liverpool win, giving them the right to wear their usual strip. Arsenal will wear yellow.

In Liverpool, thousands of fans preparing to head south by train are tearing their hair out after drivers decide to stage a 24-hour strike because rail bosses turn down their demand that Liverpool men only drive 12 FA Cup special trains. Just three of the drivers from the city have been given the plum jobs, which will earn drivers the equivalent of 14 hours' pay for an eight-hour shift.

Meanwhile tickets for the game have soared to £80 on the black market for a good seat. Police fear trouble between rival fans unable to get in with one officer quoted as saying, 'If the rival factions get at each other – and both lots are bitter that they can't get in – there could be a lot of trouble.'

One Liverpool fan gets lucky. Fourteen-year-old Stephen Lancashire, of Hooton, Cheshire, writes the word 'please' 1,010 times in a begging letter to Bill Shankly and is rewarded with a £1 ground ticket.

Life in the UK ticks over. In Mansfield, Nottinghamshire, a row erupts over the town's newly-crowned 'Coal Queen'. Rosemary Wray, 20, wins the contest but, three days later, is stripped of her crown when it is discovered she is not married to a sailor or a miner as the rules specify. Furious Rosemary storms into the committee room at the town's miners' club then tosses her sash, £20 prize and bouquet on to the table before flouncing out.

A new advert appears for Moussec wine and it is aimed at 'girls with expensive tastes'. It says, 'You deserve the best – make sure you get it. Don't let him palm you off with half a pint of shandy and a bag of crisps when, with a little feminine guile, you can get Moussec. Light, sparkling, cool Moussec for girls who are going places. It costs a little more but the effect is worth it. He'll see you in a new light, and he'll like what he sees, and forget what it costs him.'

Quite how many girls convinced their fellas to splash out on a glass of Moussec is unclear, but the drink is barely remembered today.

The Friday night before the match, TV viewers are treated to *On the Buses*, *The Dick Emery Show* and *Budgie*, which stars Adam Faith as a lovable rogue dreaming up schemes to make his fortune. Arsenal fans go to bed that night frantic with anticipation. Can they win the double? The Liverpool fans already heading south don't care. They just want to win the FA Cup.

A tight game is expected. Many experts think, like 12 months before, a replay might be needed. At an Internationals' Club Lunch in London the previous day, Cardiff City manager and Newcastle's 1955 cup-winning captain Jimmy Scoular says, 'Both teams have such tremendous strength that it may take more than one match to sort it out. It smells like a draw and I expect it to finish that way.'

The day of destiny arrives and it is a beautiful, warm, sunny morning. Arsenal fans everywhere are preparing for a quite extraordinary day, including 44-year-old supporters' club member Rose Douglas, who first started supporting Arsenal in 1950. She wakes early. In 2010, still an avid Gooner, she recalled, 'I can still remember thinking "THIS IS IT! The day we do the double." I was literally shaking with anticipation.'

At 9.30am, Dean Goodman and his mates Steve King, Andrew Silver and Johnny Beslali meet up and head off on the Tube to Wembley. It is an early start in anyone's book. 'We wanted to get a great position in the ground,' explains Dean. 'Standing up meant it was important to get your place sorted and then enjoy the singing and banter.'

Ken Banham, who first went to Highbury in 1953 aged five, and a group of about 20 fellow supporters meet up near Highbury Quadrant and begin the short walk to Arsenal Tube station, which is buzzing. Ken says, 'I had on white trousers and a red top with two rosettes pinned to it. The first said "FA Cup Final 71" and the other said, simply, "Champions". When we went past Highbury we all kissed the stairs leading to the main entrance and said, "We'll be back with the cup".'

Derek knocks on Bernie's door. Both of them have worried looks on their faces. Despite their best efforts, they still only have one ticket between them. They are both desperate to see the game but their relationship has grown to such an extent that neither wants to deny the other the privilege. They are considering both missing the game. They look at each other. 'Let's go along and see what happens,' says Derek. 'We might be able to pick one up outside the ground.'

The day gets hotter. Dean Goodman and his mates are now nearing Wembley and pose for a picture. 'We didn't bother with a real drink beforehand,' recalls Dean. 'We'd made some cardboard hats about nine inches tall and plastered lots of yellow and blue all over them. I also got a *Daily Express* "I support Arsenal" freebie hat for my head, which came flat-packed in the newspaper.

'Yellow tape was stuck to the side of my trousers and we all had the obligatory football scarf. In 1971, these were either worn round the neck – which wasn't fashionable – or, preferably, around the wrist or tied to the trouser belt.' They enter Wembley. It is only 11.30am.

Already a special atmosphere is developing in the sunshine. Rose Douglas remembers arriving and being taken aback by the colour. She says, 'There were so many hats, scarves and flags it took our breath away. People were sitting on the steps eating and drinking, others were singing and dancing and with all the decorated food stalls it was like a huge carnival. I remember thousands of fans all having a wonderful time. A few policemen even joined in a dance or two.'

Derek and Bernie have also arrived at Wembley. The two teenagers are frantically trying to get another ticket, forgetting all their shyness and approaching anyone and everyone to see if there is one going spare. There is no joy. This is not a game people are prepared to miss. Even outside the ground, you can cut the atmosphere with a knife.

The temperature keeps rising. Dean and his mates tour the stadium to try to kill some time, but it is hard work. 'There is only so much you can do outside Wembley, even on cup final day,' says Dean. 'We walked around our end a couple of times and then we took a stroll around the "away" end. We knew that Scousers were of course renowned for their humour, wit and friendly nature, but I seem to remember we had to beat a hasty retreat to safety.'

The clock is ticking down. Both sides are approaching Wembley. The Arsenal coach arrives and their manager Bertie Mee is first off, smiling like a travel rep greeting holidaymakers arriving at a foreign airport. His team follow him. The square-jawed McLintock; Peter Simpson who looks like he would be equally at home, crook in hand, rounding up sheep in Devon; and the long-haired superstar from Holloway, Charlie George, whose appearance sparks a couple of shy shrieks from some long-haired teenage girls wearing hotpants.

Bernie and Derek are still without tickets and starting to get frantic. Derek knows his girlfriend really has more right to claim the single ticket than he does. After all, this time last year, he was a United fan. 'I want you to have it,' he says to Bernie, quietly. 'No,' she says firmly. 'I'm not going in without you.'

Making his way to Wembley, Liverpool fan Chris Wood is trying to imagine what cup final victory or cup final defeat will feel like. 'Both scenarios were extremely difficult to envisage,' he says,' but it mattered, it mattered so much. I could deal with victory of course, but I knew that defeat would place me in the depths of utter despair.'

His team's coach arrives at Wembley and the Liverpool players are stunned at the crowds milling about. 'Hell's bells,' proclaims degree-owning Brian Hall. It's not an expression you can imagine today's players uttering. Imagine Wayne Rooney, John Terry or Craig Bellamy uttering 'Hell's bells' or 'Gosh'. The modern equivalent might feasibly be 'F**k me!'

The coach inches its way through and off steps Bill Shankly. He looks deadly serious, but you feel you are never far off a wisecrack when he is around. Tommy Smith, a player who could make buying a pint of milk seem scary, follows him.

Bored of circling the stadium, Dean Goodman and his mates decide it is time to enter the ground. The satisfying clack of the turnstile means they are in, and they find their spot. He recalls, 'We were halfway back in the upper tier. Great view and centrally placed behind the goal. The terracing at Wembley was steep and even if you were really short it was still possible to see the turf, but only if the blokes in front didn't have a large flag... which they did.'

The sides are confirmed. Arsenal line up as Wilson, Rice, McNab, Storey, McLintock, Simpson, Armstrong, Graham, Radford, Kennedy and George, with Kelly as their substitute. Liverpool's team is Clemence, Lawler, Lindsay, Smith, Lloyd, Hughes, Callaghan, Evans, Heighway, Toshack and Hall, with Thompson on the bench.

Derek and Bernie still have just the one ticket and the young couple start an agonising conversation – if push comes to shove, who watches the match? Touchingly, both insist that the other should have the ticket.

The players stride on to the pitch, wearing wide-collared suits and platform shoes. They walk around, waving to loved ones. Kick-off is getting ever closer. In the May sunshine, the famous pitch looks a glorious shade of brilliant green, like a billiard table. It is time for the community singing. The clock is ticking down. The Liverpool fans are massed at the tunnel end. Their banners are flying. 'Tommy Smith eats Cockneys', says one. At the other end the Arsenal fans seem oddly subdued, perhaps exhausted by Monday's triumph at Tottenham, although a banner saying 'Charlie's gunning for you' is waved and scoffed at by the Scousers.

In 2010, Rose Douglas could still recall the emotion she felt when 'Abide With Me' was sung. 'It sent shivers down my spine,' she remembered.

But Rose's view is not held by all present. Many of the people in the crowd are into T-Rex or Motown. Nearly all of them would swap 'Abide With Me' for Chairman of the Board's 'Everything's Tuesday', or the Stones' 'Brown Sugar', which is just about to hit the charts.

Dean Goodman was one such fan and recalled, 'The one thing a 17-year-old will NEVER do, is sing "Abide With Me". I have no idea why the FA insisted on this ridiculous fiasco for so many years. I would be surprised if more than 25 per cent of the crowd took any notice, let alone tried to sing with words that no one knew.'

Now the moment of truth. Led by Bill Shankly and Bertie Mee, the players come out, squinting in the sunshine. Fitness and stamina is going to be important today.

The teams line up for the national anthem. The fans wait expectantly. But, outside Wembley, our two teenage lovebirds are distraught. They are both sobbing.

'It was five minutes before kick-off and we were just sitting on the steps outside, crying, with our one ticket,' says Bernie. 'I was saying to Derek "You go in". And he was saying to me "No, you go in"'.'

And then, rather like the shopkeeper in *Mr Benn*, a man appeared. To this day, Bernie has no idea who he was or where he came from. Suddenly he was just there, standing above the pair of stricken youngsters, smiling slightly. Then he said the magic words, 'Would you like a ticket for the game?'

Bernie and Derek looked up at him disbelievingly with tear-stained eyes. Was this some sick wind-up? Apparently not. The man said, 'get up' and beckoned them to follow him, saying, 'I know someone.' Bernie recalls, 'We followed him and then saw this bloke who simply handed over a ticket.'

Seemingly, miracles *do* happen. The two men then disappeared, their identities a mystery. 'We didn't care,' says Bernie. 'We were in. I sat in the "posh" seats with all the people in suits while Derek went into the stands with the "real" supporters.'

Bernie takes her seat just as referee Norman Burtenshaw, a newsagent from Great Yarmouth, blows his whistle and Steve Heighway touches the ball to Alun Evans. The 1971 FA Cup Final and Arsenal's date with destiny is under way.

It is a game that has promised so much with both sides in a rich vein of form. Liverpool have lost only twice in their last 15 matches and Arsenal have won nine of their last 11. But, in truth, in pure footballing terms, it is a disappointment and, these days, most people remember little of the first 90 minutes.

It is a tense, cagey affair, though Arsenal do have enough chances to win comfortably. University graduate Brian Hall doesn't look too brainy when a sloppy back-pass almost lets in Ray Kennedy, but Ray Clemence does just enough to force Monday's goal hero wide. The mistake earns Hall a rollicking from Liverpool skipper Tommy Smith and Larry Lloyd, a scenario you wouldn't wish upon anyone. The likelihood is neither Smith nor Lloyd are saying, 'Hell's bells, Brian, you might have performed rather better just then.' The half-chance sparks a concerted, confident chant from the North Bank crowd. Clap, Clap! Clap, Clap, Clap! Clap, Clap, Clap, Clap! 'Arsenal!'

Next John Radford, playing wide on the left, skilfully eludes a nasty-looking challenge from Tommy Smith, and crosses deep. At the far post Peter Storey is closing in, but he is just beaten to it by Liverpool's popular beak-nosed left-back Alec Lindsay – a man looking at least ten years older than he actually is and rather like a former pro turning out for one last game in a testimonial.

Then we get a glimpse of Charlie George's powerful right-footed shot. McLintock brilliantly wins a header near the halfway line, which falls to George Graham, who lays it off to George, 40 yards from goal. He moves forward ten yards or so then unleashes a howitzer which fizzes just over the bar.

Unfortunately, the heat prevents too much flowing football. Many years on, the late and much-missed Emlyn Hughes will say that Liverpool's brand new FA Cup Final shirts were made of thick, heavy cotton and the Merseyside players were sweltering.

Arsenal's short-sleeved jobs look cooler in both senses of the word.

The half-time whistle blows and Bernie vainly tries to spot her boyfriend in the mass of Arsenal fans. She can't, but she hasn't stopped smiling since the man handed them the extra ticket. Of course, it would have been wonderful if she and Derek could have sat together, but beggars can't be choosers.

The second half follows the pattern of the first. Kennedy misses a golden opportunity when played in by Radford, scuffing his shot from six yards with the goal at his mercy. Then George tries another long-ranger, this time with his left foot, which trickles wide.

Yet another Radford cross is met by Kennedy, who prods it wide. The 20-year-old isn't having one of his best afternoons. Soon, Radford is again the supplier, this time with a long throw which causes havoc in the Liverpool defence. It is met by George Graham, who somehow gets above Lloyd and nods the ball against the bar. After 90 minutes the game is goalless. It goes to extra time.

Chris Wood recalls that he and his fellow Liverpool fans around him were not fazed at all by the prospect of extra time, remembering that Liverpool's only other FA Cup win six years earlier had also required it. But, worryingly, Liverpool have been completely anonymous as an attacking force. The much-vaunted Toshack has barely had a sniff and wide-men Callaghan and Heighway are almost passengers. All of which makes what happens three minutes after the start of extra time quite astonishing for everyone at Wembley and millions watching the game around the world.

Lloyd wins a header on the edge of the Liverpool area, Hughes plays a simple ball to substitute Peter Thompson, who gets his head down and moves quickly forward. The move is picking up momentum and Arsenal suddenly find themselves stretched and back-pedalling for the first time in the match.

Out on the left Heighway is lurking and Thompson finds him. Both Pat Rice and George Armstrong move towards the moustachioed number nine, but he teases them. He is now in the area and looking to cross as Toshack waits. Except he doesn't cross. Instead, he quickly takes a couple of paces forward and, from an extremely acute angle, surprises the entire stadium and opts to shoot. Before anyone can blink, the ball is in the back of the net.

It looks like an error of judgement from the normally ultra-reliable Bob Wilson who, anticipating a cross and probably with half an eye on Toshack, has left too much space between himself and the upright, allowing Heighway to squeeze the ball in.

On ITV, Brian Moore is as shocked as anyone. 'Oh! A goal. That's the goal,' suggesting what many are thinking – that one goal might be enough to win it.

The look on the Liverpool players' faces is a mixture of shock and delight. Thompson hugs Heighway like two long-lost brothers being reunited. Heighway looks to the heavens disbelievingly. Hughes, Hall, Callaghan and Toshack join the love-in. In the excitement, the ITV caption writer mis-spells Heighway's name and 'Heigway' flashes up on the screen.

At the tunnel end, a party has started. A throng of Liverpudlians who look like Jimmy Tarbuck, Stan Boardman and the three members of Scaffold are performing a frenzied, impromptu jig. A man with buck teeth and crazy hair, who, viewed after several pints of strong ale, might look a tad like Ken Dodd, leaps up and down. They know they don't deserve it, but they couldn't care less. They are now visualising Tommy Smith lifting the FA Cup and wrecking Arsenal's double dreams in one fell swoop.

The Arsenal fans don't know what has hit them. Don Richards was standing behind the goal, looking through the net which Heighway's shot had just entered. 'To say that we were stunned would be an understatement. Liverpool had done nothing all game but were now one up,' he recalls.

Dean Goodman thinks it's all over. He says, 'We all thought that was that. No one beats Liverpool once they go ahead late on was the general consensus.'

While the Arsenal fans stand in stunned silence at the tunnel end the Liverpool fans continue to cavort, watched by dozens of police officers who seem to be fearing a possible pitch invasion. After all, Merseyside fans have previous in FA Cup finals. Well, most of the fans were going wild anyway. Chris Wood didn't know how to react.

Remembering the moment, he says, 'For some reason, I found myself frozen to the spot, unable to move or speak. It was almost as if such a euphoric moment was too much for my emotions to deal with. I guess I thought the goal would only be worth celebrating if it was the winning goal. I remember thinking as the players lined up for the restart, "Why didn't you do that a minute earlier, Steve?!"'

Within minutes, Wilson makes amends for his error with a fine point-blank stop to keep out a Brian Hall snapshot. It is a save which changes the mood among the Arsenal fans, as Don Richards recalls, 'There had been complete silence all around me, but Wilson made that save and then suddenly a man behind me shouted, "Come on let's get behind the lads!" and the entire Arsenal end came alive again with "Good Old Arsenal" ringing out with real vigour.'

The mood on the terraces appears to be transmitting to the Arsenal players and they dig deep and begin pouring forward. This is a team with real guts and they want this double desperately. But the Liverpool fans are basking in their position of dominance. They break into a rousing rendition of 'We're gonna win the cup, we're gonna win the cup. And now you're gonna believe us, and now you're gonna believe us. And now, you're gonna belieeeeve uusssss! We're gonna win the cup.' They are woefully premature. Arsenal are about to equalise with one of the scrappiest, messiest goals ever seen in a Wembley final.

Mr Consistency Peter Simpson takes a throw-in. Kennedy and George exchange passes before Kennedy makes a right-footed pass to Radford, who has his back to goal, 30 yards out. It is a neat build-up.

A decision by Radford then alters the course of events. The Yorkshireman flicks the ball up and then, on the full, kicks it back over his head towards the penalty area. It causes mayhem. There is a scramble with Eddie Kelly tussling for the ball with Hughes, but the ball is in no-man's-land. Kelly's persistence causes Hughes and Smith to dither. It is a real mess but Kelly gets a touch on the ball and prods it goalwards. Somehow it eludes Clemence – who may be distracted by the onrushing Graham. Graham appears to get the slightest touch.

The next thing it is rolling gently into the net and Graham wheels away, left arm raised to the sky, claiming the goal. It is a horrible, messy goal but its significance is massive. As ITV co-commentator Jimmy Hill says, 'An untidy goal but at this stage of a cup final they're just as effective, untidy or not.'

Watching from the other end of the ground, Don Richards says, 'I only saw the ball being put into the penalty area by Radford's overhead kick and the ball pushed goalwards by Eddie Kelly. I did not know it had gone into the net until George Graham ran wildly across the area, from our left to right, with his arm above his head.'

Dean Goodman says, 'George Graham claimed the goal, but as we all know it was Kelly who got the last touch and he became the first substitute to score in a cup final.'

For Chris Wood, it is the moment he had been dreading, 'We were still singing "and now you're gonna believe us", as the ball dropped into the penalty area in front of us. The moment of sickness and panic I had feared was about to happen and the ball dribbled slowly past Ray Clemence into the corner of the net. That was the moment that really hurt me. The momentum is with the team that has equalised.'

Dean and his still-dancing mates sense this. 'The force was now with us. We had the upper hand,' he says. The first period of extra time ends with the score at 1-1. Up in the 'posh' seats Bernie is a nervous wreck praying that someone in yellow can find that flash of inspiration to win the match, the cup and the double.

Now Arsenal are attacking the goal behind which their own fans are massed. They are being urged on to glory by the fans from the North Bank, who are now in full voice. From where she is sitting, Bernie can see the 'Charlie's gunning for you' banner. She looks down at the pitch and looks at George; cocksure, insouciant, surly. Has he got anything in his locker? He has. In a few minutes he is going to produce one of the great cup final moments and one of Wembley's most enduring images.

There are nine minutes of extra time left when Clemence takes a tired, left-footed goal kick. It just about reaches the halfway line but has gone straight to George Graham, who heads it back into Liverpool territory. It goes to Radford then George who, first-time, gives it back to the Pontefract-born striker.

Right-back Chris Lawler is covering the flank, so Radford cuts inside. He draws Smith towards him and, at the last minute, plays a clever ball back to George, who is just over 20 yards out. It looks like Radford is expecting a one-two and indeed, that would have played Radford in. But George has only one thing on his mind. 'Oh Charlie George who can hit 'em,' says Brian Moore, anticipating what is going to happen. With textbook technique, George takes aim and lets fly.

Don Richards recalls the moment, 'I was right behind the shot, watching it through the goal net. The ball was coming towards me but, out of the corner of my eye, to my left, I could see Ray Clemence diving, and in that split second it was whether he got to the ball before it hit the net.'

George has only had inches to aim at, but the shot is perfectly positioned and struck with the necessary power to beat Clemence. The net bulges and Arsenal are in fantasyland.

The Arsenal fans are delirious. Ken Banham sinks to his knees and looks to the heavens, uttering a single word, 'Yeeeessssss!' Bernie is shouting and screaming, looking to her right at the sprawling mass of Arsenal fans leaping around. How she would love to be with Derek at this moment.

There is utter bedlam behind the goal. Dean recalls, 'You would have thought that, given the steep terracing and the strategically-placed barriers to prevent crowd surges, it would be impossible for a teenager to end up 50 feet down the terrace from where he started, but it is [possible] and I did.'

George starts to run back but then does something that makes this one of the most famous goal celebrations of all time. He slides to his feet, lies flat on his back with his arms outstretched and, raising his head slightly, waits for his adoring team-mates to arrive, which they do. They haul him to his feet and, to a man, embrace him tightly. Eventually George breaks free and then performs his own personal salute to the North Bank and then simply does a series of double-fisted air punches.

While George was on his back, so was Tommy Smith, though Smith was lying utterly despondent on the turf, spread-eagled with his arms outstretched. The Liverpool fans are now stunned into solemn silence. Just 20 minutes earlier they had thought the cup was theirs. Chris Wood says, 'The moment George's missile flashed past Clemence, I knew the game was up and I tried to resign myself to that sad fact.'

When the game kicks off again, the Arsenal fans are bouncing up and down. They have witnessed an astonishing comeback and they are ecstatic. They are less than ten minutes away from doing the double. 'We shall not, we shall not be moved,' they sing as Liverpool kick off again.

Liverpool throw everything at them and, with the clock ticking down, the unlikely figure of Chris Lawler turns up in the centre-forward position and volleys over after Toshack wins a header. Lawler goes down with cramp and is sportingly assisted by Bob McNab and Peter Simpson. The camera pans to the crowd, which is bouncing up and down, red and white bar scarves waving, a Union Jack flag swaying. 'They come from North London,' says Brian Moore.

We then see the other end, the tunnel end. The Liverpool fans are silent and still. 'The Kop, for once, very quiet indeed,' says Moore. With a couple of minutes left, Heighway tries to make something happen, but Kelly cynically scythes him down.

Liverpool's final chance comes when they win a corner, but Wilson comfortably claims it. He takes an age to punt the ball out and, when he does, referee Burtenshaw raises his left arm and blows his whistle for the end of the game. Arsenal have won the double.

George looks across at the bench, runs towards it and then performs an impromptu somersault, while Liverpool substitute Peter Thompson looks on forlornly.

Photographers are sprinting towards George. They know it is his picture that all their editors are going to want. He then continues to the bench and hugs the Gunners' trainer and physio, George Wright. McLintock, looking totally knackered, raises both arms aloft and embraces Radford tightly. 'We did it Raddy, we f*****g did it,' he seems to be saying.

In the seats, Bernie is crying with joy. Behind the goal, Derek has forgotten all about the Stretford End and he is singing 'We shall not be moved' with all his might, alongside the rest of the North Bank.

The Liverpool fans are distraught but they recognise they have been beaten by the better side. Their scarves wave slowly from side to side. A banner saying 'Heighway did it my way' waves defiantly. 'That's the kind of fair-minded crowd that comes from Liverpool,' says Brian Moore.

The electronic scoreboard flashes up a message, 'CONGRATULATIONS ARSENAL – A MAGNIFICENT 'DOUBLE' it reads. 'HARD LUCK LIVERPOOL'.

McLintock seems so tired he can barely climb the famous steps. Arsenal fans wearing jackets and ties stretch over to congratulate him. When he reaches the top, he beams broadly and approaches His Royal Highness The Duke of Kent and the cup, adorned with one yellow ribbon and one blue one, is presented.

He turns to his left and looks to the Arsenal fans behind the goal. Charlie George is crying like a baby and, by the time he reaches the bottom of the steps, somebody has placed a blue and yellow *Daily Express* paper hat on his head, which he puts the trophy's lid on top of.

The national anthem is played again. The Arsenal fans don't want to hear it and probably can't hear it as they are belting out a rendition of 'Ee-aye-addio, we won the cup!'

It was all too much for Rose Douglas, who was overcome with emotion. 'I cried with pride, then laughed with happiness as I watched our team dance on the pitch with the cup,' she says.

Nowadays, Bernie and Derek would be excitedly chattering away on a mobile phone, but not in 1971. Both were wondering what the other was doing and wishing they could share this wonderful moment.

By way of contrast, the Liverpool fans are inconsolable and are starting to leave. Chris says, 'I remember thinking it was strange that people would leave before the presentations but, as I got older, I discovered that it *is* hard to hang around watching someone else picking up the cup you dreamed your players would be holding.'

Chris stayed and was proud of the way the Liverpool fans warmly applauded the Arsenal players. This is something that has also stayed with Don Richards, who says, 'One great memory from the occasion was the amazing sportsmanship of the Liverpool fans, who gave the Arsenal team a great ovation as the cup was taken to the Liverpool end of the ground.'

But the Merseysiders are distraught.

Chris says, 'I noticed some of my travelling companions from a long and eventful season. A couple of them were weeping openly. I stayed to talk and try and console them for a couple of minutes before I made my way out of the stadium and went straight home.'

Finally, Bernie and Derek meet up again. They embrace like the lovers they have become and they pledge undying love to one another. 'Bet you're glad you became an Arsenal fan now, aren't you?' Bernie whispers into Derek's ear. 'Cor, you bet,' says Derek. 'Anyway, I had no choice. I was not going to miss the chance of going out with you.' The two hug even tighter. No further words are necessary.

A party to end all parties is beginning. On Rose's coach, members of the supporters' club sing Arsenal songs all the way home. All the way down to Wembley Park Tube station, the Arsenal fans are singing and chanting. The Tube trains rock to the sound of the North Londoners' victory tunes.

Dean Goodman and his pals head back to the Osidge Arms in Southgate for a night on the beer. Ken Banham and his mates go straight back to Highbury to kiss the steps of the stadium, just as they had done eight hours earlier. Then it was off to the Gunners pub on Blackstock Road, just around the corner from the ground, to begin the party proper. It's a riotous night. While the rest of the nation settles down to watch *The Two Ronnies*, *Ironside* or *The Val Doonican Show*, North London is awash with Gunners, singing, drinking and dancing.

Ken says, 'By 11 o'clock, the whole of the Blackstock Road was doing the conga, police as well. I was on the shoulders of my pal Dave Pooley. There was a guy called Johnnie Hoy who, in those days, was known as the king of the North Bank. He was going mad and everyone followed him. You could say that the Highbury boys partied.'

Hangovers or not – and there can't have been too many Arsenal fans in the 'not' category – thousands gathered in Islington the next day for the victory parade. The pubs of Highbury, Finsbury Park and Islington were full of delirious Arsenal fans singing 'Charlie is my darling'.

The bus leaves Highbury to the strains of 'Good old Arsenal, we're proud to say that name. While we sing this song, we'll win the game', to the tune of 'Rule Britannia'.

The scenes are amazing as the bus makes its way slowly to Islington Town Hall, where the mayor, dressed in all his robes and finery, greets them. 'Up the Gunners, I love you Gunners!' cries a long-haired teenage girl. A man in his 50s wearing a huge yellow and blue top hat approaches the camera and says simply, 'Yeeeeeeeessssssss!'

Then Frank McLintock, wearing a very '1971' sky-blue roll-neck top, gives a speech and gets a huge cheer when he says he never thought he would see the Kop outsung, but that it was yesterday.

As McLintock holds aloft the cup to give the fans another look, Bernie looks across at her boyfriend and notices his eyes are wet with emotion.

Reflecting on the events of May 1971, Liverpool fan Chris Wood says, 'We all experience setbacks in our lives and it's how you deal with them that matters. It had been a privilege to attend an FA Cup Final, but I was devastated by the result and it would take another 30 years and a different stadium to properly heal the pain I felt in 1971 at watching Arsenal clinch the double at Liverpool's expense.'

Rose Douglas says, 'What a glorious memory and what a glorious time May 1971 was. I've never forgotten a minute of that wonderful time, even though I'm now 83 and just starting my 59th year as a Gooner. You know the old saying, "Once a Gooner, always a Gooner".'

For Dean Goodman, the events of 1971 are pivotal in his memory. He says, 'Nearly half a century of watching a fantastic team, that has probably been the single most important influence in keeping me sane. Through the "ups" and the "downs", from Brussels to Wrexham, to infinity and beyond.' Now 58, Dean has been going to games since 1985 with his son, Jon, and with his good friend Dave since 1987.

Dean belongs to an exclusive club, one with just a handful of privileged members. He says, 'I've seen Arsenal win the title at White Hart Lane in 1971, at Anfield in 1989, at Old Trafford in 2002 and at White Hart Lane again in 2004. Not bad!'

Dean is now partially retired after working 35 years for a large organisation. He set up his own one-man business in 2009, and also trades part-time in football shirts. Dean has never held a season ticket, but has managed to see about 90 per cent of home games over the last 42 years and, using his ingenuity, countless important away games too.

For Bernie and Derek Butt the 1970/71 season will always be extra special. The pair, who met on a North London council estate and forged their relationship on the North Bank, married on 10 May 1975. In 1980 they celebrated the birth of their first child, James. Their second child, Lindsay, was born three years later. Today, they live in Cheshunt, Hertfordshire. Derek is a builder, Bernie works for Enfield Council and they have five grandchildren.

They are still Arsenal to the core, season ticket holders at the Emirates and watch as many away games, both in this country and abroad, as they can get to. Bernie says, 'These days, watching Arsenal is much more civilised and women and children can go to the Emirates without any worries, but Derek has a different view. He would prefer to go back to the 'good old days!'

Once in a while, on a quiet Sunday perhaps, Bernie will think back to the magical summers of 1970 and 1971. But, she'll think beyond *Here Come the Double Deckers, Scooby Doo* and *Animal Magic*, beyond Simon and Garfunkel and *Hunky Dory* to a patch of waste ground, which a group of girls and lads turned into their own Wembley and where she met her future husband. Theirs was a relationship that developed on Saturday afternoons on the famous Highbury North Bank during a magical season, and reached its glorious climax on a never-to-be-forgotten sunny day in May.

BEHIND ENEMY LINES

Leeds United v Arsenal
Saturday 6 May 1972

IT is the early hours of the morning on Saturday 6 May 1972 and a young local newspaper reporter called Mick Kelly is sitting – somewhat the worse for wear – with the secretary of Walthamstow Avenue FC. The two are sharing a bottle of Scotch in the secretary's cramped and cluttered office, underneath what passes as the main stand at Green Pond Road 'stadium', London E17.

In just over 12 hours' time the FA Cup Final between Arsenal and Leeds United is due to kick off. Mick, 19, a massive Arsenal fan, is planning at some point to head home, get some kip, sleep off the effects of the 'gold watch' and then try to find a colour TV somewhere to watch the game.

He says, 'I had spent the football season as a junior reporter on the *Walthamstow Guardian* covering Walthamstow Avenue in the Isthmian League. For the most part, it was a miserable season watching what was then still called "amateur football".'

Mick and the secretary work their way through the whisky and reflect on Avenue's disappointing campaign. Mick, notebook in hand, has followed the team on long, fruitless trips to Wycombe Wanderers, Hitchin Town and Bishop's Stortford. He has penned reports of hard-fought local derbies with Ilford and Barking.

Some 40 games have been played, 12 games won, eight drawn and 20 lost. Mick has seen them all. Goals for 58, against 71. Total points 32. Final position 16th out of 21, with only Leytonstone, Tooting and Mitcham, Clapton, Dulwich Hamlet and Corinthian Casuals below them.

The FA Cup has been equally inauspicious with Avenue knocked out back in September in the qualifying rounds against Dover.

'The trip back from the Kent coast on the team coach, with an unscheduled stop for a comfort break (12 pissed players all relieving themselves beside the A2), was one of the highlights of a very poor season,' recalls Mick.

By becoming a football reporter Mick has fulfilled a dream but, just occasionally, when he sits in the stands at places like Hendon, Woking and Walton and Hersham, his mind wanders and he imagines he is reporting on the exploits of George Armstrong, John Radford or Charlie George at Highbury, Old Trafford or the Baseball Ground.

It was a Walthamstow Avenue tradition to hold their end-of-season club disco on FA Cup Final eve. After Mick had sat through the formalities of the Player of the Season awards, he was approached by 'Big' George Whiting, the club secretary, who came over and whispered that he had something for the young newspaperman in his office.

Mick says, 'George was the type of East End character it was wise not to mess with. Legend has it that it was George who stepped in and disarmed a player who allegedly pulled a knife on the team captain in the dressing room during a heated half-time team-talk earlier in the season.'

Mick and George start talking about the following day's cup final and what a great game it should be. Mick says he is nervous about the game and knows that it will be tough for Arsenal, especially without Bob Wilson in goal. How Mick wishes he could be there.

'Like most clubs, Arsenal printed a ticket voucher in their programmes for fans to collect just in case they should make it to a Wembley final,' he says. 'Because of my reporting commitments, I had a measly half-a-dozen tokens by the end of the season, so I stood no chance of being allocated a ticket.'

As Mick explained his predicament, the big, hard Londoner opposite nodded sympathetically. Mick recalls, 'Then, George simply reached into the inside pocket of his crumpled, mohair suit and pulled out a cup final ticket. Even now, I remember the sense of shock and sheer joy when he handed me it. He wouldn't take any money for it. He muttered something about me deserving to see Arsenal at Wembley after spending the season on the exploits of the Avenue in the Isthmian League.' Quite out of the blue, Mick Kelly is going to Wembley.

※ ※ ※

In 1972, Carole Parkhouse was going through a sartorial transformation. The convent schoolgirl, who was so devastated after Leeds lost in 1970, had discovered fashion. She says, 'By 1972 I was going through a Crombie coat phase and I dressed head-to-toe in black, except for my new, white silk Leeds scarf, which I thought was the last word in chic.'

Perhaps oddly for a club so closely associated with the colour white, Carole had decided black was her lucky colour, 'I remember I had to talk my mum into letting me buy the Crombie coat,' she says. 'She thought it was going to be like the one my dad had, which was made of camel hair and very posh. But, of course, it was like the ones worn by skinheads, with a little hanky in the top pocket. Shoes were platforms of course, trousers were plain black, but not too wide and I also wore a black jumper.'

The cruel cup final defeat of 1970 had been consigned to history. Don Revie's side had come of age and, though still not popular, even their harshest critics struggled to deny that they were playing some sublime football. Late 1971 and early 1972 was, quite simply, a fabulous time to be a Leeds supporter and there were few people prepared to bet against them emulating Arsenal's recent double-winning achievement.

For long-standing fans like Phil Stubbs and Ray Ashworth it was dreamland and rich reward for years of support. Phil remembers, 'My dad was actually a huge Leeds rugby league fan and he followed them home and away. After much persuasion he took me to Elland Road in August 1963 to see Leeds v Rotherham United in the old Second Division. We won 1-0 and that was it. I was hooked on Leeds and started going more and more each season as I got older and then, in 1969, I began going to every single game, home and away.'

Ray's first match at Elland Road was on 16 November 1963, when Leeds drew 1-1 with Preston North End. Ray hailed from the West Yorkshire town of Normanton. 'Why did I pick Leeds?' he says. 'Well my father, who wasn't actually a football fan, took me around lots of Yorkshire grounds like Barnsley, Bradford City, Bradford Park Avenue, Halifax and Huddersfield, but I just felt most at home at Leeds. I was also very impressed with the West Stand at the time, which bore the City of Leeds crest, although that has since been covered by a soulless banqueting suite. Anyway, there was only one team for me from that point on.'

By the time the early 1970s comes around, Ray is a regular. One of his clearest memories of this period is of the fashions that prevailed among football fans.

He explains, 'Essential wear around this time were silk scarves, which had replaced the old woollen bar and college style ones, and were either tied round your wrist or secured through the belt loop in your trousers. Also, very surprisingly – because I wouldn't be seen dead in red now – red v-neck jumpers were in vogue. They had Yorkshire Rose badges sewn on them (round in shape, black with the rose in white) along with the name of the area you were from – so ours naturally sported Normanton.

'The trouser wear was Levi's Sta-Prest, although around Leeds at the time there were trousers similar to Rupert the Bear's that were also popular. Footwear had moved away from Doc Martens on to brogues and loafers and I remember well that my brogues were original Church's, purchased at great expense from Schofield's department store, on the Headrow, in Leeds.'

%% %% %%

Third round day falls on Saturday 15 January. The weather has been appalling during the week and a number of ties face being washed out. At St James' Park, where Newcastle are preparing to face Southern League side Hereford United, an early morning pitch inspection is planned to save the 3,500 Hereford fans a wasted journey to the north-east.

Leeds, at 5/1, are already the bookies' favourites to lift the cup and they kick off their campaign with a home tie against Bristol Rovers.

Holders Arsenal, meanwhile, are failing to live up to the stellar heights of the previous campaign, and are installed at 12/1. They must travel to Wiltshire to play Swindon Town, player-managed by 1967 FA Cup-winning captain Dave Mackay, who says before the game that Arsenal are the more worried side.

The County Ground pitch is notoriously heavy and the incessant rain during the week is considered by some to improve Swindon's chances. Arsenal, of course, have bitter memories of Swindon and mud. But in the event, they never look remotely like losing their grip on the cup, winning 2-0 with goals from George Armstrong and Alan Ball. Their only concern is a nagging injury to left-back Bob McNab, which keeps him out of the game, replaced by Irish international Sammy Nelson.

Leeds make no mistake in seeing off Bristol Rovers 4-1 in front of 33,565 fans at Elland Road, with two goals each for Johnny Giles and Peter Lorimer. The following Monday the Leeds players gather in their dressing room after training to listen to the draw for the fourth round. When it is announced, there is a sharp intake of breath. Leeds have got the hardest tie possible. In what is easily the tie of the round, they must travel to Liverpool, whose Anfield home is rapidly gaining a reputation as a fortress.

Following their win at Swindon in round three, Arsenal have another trip along the M4. This time they go to Elm Park, home of Fourth Division side Reading, managed by Sunderland legend Charlie Hurley.

In early 1972 the UK is facing huge problems. Conflict in Ulster is causing grave concern and fear. It reaches a nadir on Sunday 30 January when British paratroopers open fire on participants in a civil rights march in Derry/Londonderry's Bogside area, killing 13 men and youths and wounding a further 17. The killings are described as 'Bloody Sunday'.

On 22 February six civilians and a priest are killed when a bomb explodes on the 16th Parachute Brigade at Aldershot. The IRA claims responsibility, saying the bomb is in response to the 'Bloody Sunday' killings. On 25th March Conservative Prime Minister Edward Heath takes the decision to impose direct rule on the province, with governance now administered from Whitehall.

Elsewhere industrial relations are dire. Total electricity blackouts lasting nine hours are imposed as the crisis over a pay row between the Government and the miners intensifies. Unemployment in the UK rises above a million and the film *Clockwork Orange* is blamed for a number of violent attacks on members of the public by gangs imitating Alex and his 'droogs'.

At times like these, people look to sport and entertainment for some light among the gloom and few neutrals can fail to have been cheered by events at Hereford. After gaining a brilliant 2-2 draw at St James' Park, Hereford take Newcastle back to their Edgar Street ground. The game is postponed several times and can't be played until Saturday 5 February, when the fourth round is being played elsewhere.

Newcastle take a late lead from a powerful Malcolm Macdonald header but then, out of nowhere, Ronnie Radford equalises with one of the greatest and most famous goals ever scored in the history of the competition. Then, Ricky George, an 82nd minute substitute, scores the winner in extra time. Both Hereford goals spark wild celebrations and memorable pitch invasions by what looks like a colony of alien, khaki-clad aardvarks, which actually turn out to be young boys dressed in parkas.

At Elm Park, Reading call up Arsenal reject Will Dixon in a bid to stifle the threat of Alan Ball. Dixon has a fine game and Reading play well, but an 83rd-minute left-footed shot from 30 yards by right-back Pat Rice, which takes a slight deflection on its way past Royals keeper Steve Death, is the decider in a 2-1 win for the Londoners.

At Anfield, a 56,598 crowd witnesses a titanic struggle between Liverpool and Leeds played in a cauldron of noise. The home side create five clear-cut chances, but spurn them all with Steve Heighway and John Toshack the main culprits. A defiant, backs-to-the-wall effort from Leeds earns them a replay.

The industrial climate continues to affect football. Due to an ongoing dispute, the FA holds the fifth round draw just two hours after the conclusion of the fourth round ties to help pools companies with their printing deadlines. The power crisis also means that all replays must be played in daylight as energy companies are unable to guarantee sufficient power to illuminate floodlights.

At least car manufacturers are still managing to knock out the occasional new vehicle and the latest must-have model is British Leyland's Morris Marina. Adverts running in that week's national newspapers say, 'It's possible some people only have a blurred idea of what the new Morris Marinas look like. The following may explain why. The 1.3 litre saloon, the gentlest powered model in the range, does 0-50mph in a mere 11.8 seconds. The 1.8 Coupe does it in 8.5. And the 1.8 TC in an incredible 8.3 seconds. The new Morris Marina. Beauty with brains behind it.'

The weather is still awful, cold and wet. As Don McLean is singing on 'American Pie', which is riding high in the charts, 'February made me shiver'. So, with the UK a pretty gloomy place to be, many a head will no doubt be turned by a concerted advertising push by Australia's Migration Office, which sets about enticing Britons with the promise of not just wall-to-wall sunshine and beautiful beaches, but also a high standard of living, excellent wages for skilled men, low interest rates and a progressive education system based on equality and fairness.

It concludes, 'If you've got a skill and really want to get on, you can be better off in Australia. Your money goes further too, on things like big rump steaks.'

There is massive interest around the midweek replay between Leeds and Liverpool on Wednesday afternoon with an estimated 10,000 fans locked out of Elland Road. The 45,821 who do manage to get in, including Carole Parkhouse, who has had to bunk off school, are treated to a brilliant display by a Leeds side who are running into a superb vein of form.

Two great goals from Allan Clarke settle the tie, which is so good that even popular, progressive referee Gordon Hill, who also officiated at Anfield, applauds the teams off the field at the end. 'It was my way of saying thank you for two of the greatest games a referee could wish to control,' he says. The Liverpool win is the advent of a superb period for Leeds who start producing some of the best football ever seen in this country.

Carole, now back at school in Leeds, says, 'In 1972, Don Revie's dream machine was running to perfection. I think the football I saw that season was probably the best I have ever seen.'

Even the side's fiercest critics can only sit back and admire a series of performances between February and April which border on footballing perfection. One game at Elland Road on 4 March, where Leeds beat Southampton 7-0, will pass into legend, primarily for a famous sequence at the end of the match where the team showboats and toys with the Saints players, who are tormented and teased by the sheer skill, not to mention audacious arrogance, of Giles, Bremner, Lorimer et al. The *Match of the Day* cameras have preserved this for posterity.

Only two weeks earlier, *Match of the Day* viewers also witnessed another Elland Road demolition – this time with Manchester United the sacrificial lambs, being trounced 5-1. Cardiff are no match for Leeds in round five and two goals from Johnny Giles – again in front of the *Match of the Day* cameras

– are enough to beat them at Ninian Park. They are red-hot favourites for the cup.

Yet this time it is Arsenal who are involved in the tie of the round. It takes three matches to separate them from Brian Clough's high-flying Derby County. A 2-2 draw at the Baseball Ground is followed by a dull 0-0 draw in the replay at Highbury. However, this game is remembered for a terrifying incident in which a crush barrier on the North Bank collapses after 30 minutes, causing slight injuries to 50 fans. Later angry fans in the capacity 63,077 crowd say they warned police that the barrier was loose an hour before kick-off.

Fred Rose, a 42-year-old chauffeur, of Muswell Hill, was on the North Bank and said, 'I noticed before kick-off that the barrier was loose. Half an hour after the match started, the crowd came tumbling down on top of me. I thought I was going to be killed.' With memories of Ibrox still fresh in people's minds, a full safety investigation will now be held.

Arsenal finally edge the tie in the second replay at Leicester City's Filbert Street courtesy of a fifth-minute goal by Ray Kennedy. But it is Charlie George who is continuing to steal the headlines. The hero of Wembley in 1971 grabs both goals in the first tie but finds himself in hot water after a double-handed v-sign incident and a booking following a sending-off against Oxford reserves. There is growing concern among Arsenal officials about George's temperament, although a perceptive piece by Ken Jones in the *Daily Mirror* says, 'Charlie George is a product of his environment. A largely unschooled young man who, in moments of stress and elation, displays the extravagance of those with whom he grew up – those who can now be found on the North Bank at Highbury.'

※ ※ ※

FA Cup sixth round day is on 18 March. All eight remaining teams have their sights set firmly on Wembley. Leeds are at home to Bill Nicholson's Tottenham, while Arsenal have a short trip to East London to play Orient at Brisbane Road.

Yet again, *Match of the Day* trains its cameras on Leeds and, yet again, the home side serves up a treat for the watching nation and the 44,000 spectators in the ground.

Before the game, Leeds have a surprise for their adoring fans. These days, both teams have a pre-match warm-up on the pitch. But in 1972, it rarely, if ever, happened. So Don Revie announces that before the quarter-final tie his players will perform warm-up exercises.

Other new features include brand new white tracksuit tops with the players' names on the back and, even more revolutionary and unique, special numbered stocking tags. Though one of Gary Sprake's worryingly regular howlers gifts Spurs the lead – a speculative long-range cross from a John Pratt free kick eludes him – goals from Allan Clarke and Jack Charlton take Leeds through to the final four. Carole Parkhouse, Ray Ashworth, Phil Stubbs and the hordes of Leeds fans can scent cup glory.

At Brisbane Road, a stuttering performance from Arsenal is just enough to scrape a 1-0 victory thanks to a goal from Alan Ball. But something is not right with the Gunners and Orient count themselves unlucky to be out of the cup.

One week before the semi-final, Leeds left-back Terry Cooper breaks his left leg following an innocuous-looking tackle with Stoke City right-back John Marsh. It rules him out for the rest of the season. But Leeds have a superb replacement in Paul Madeley, who can play virtually anywhere on the park.

Leeds are drawn against Birmingham City in the semis and, much to the chagrin of the Blues manager Freddie Goodwin, the game will be played at Hillsborough. Goodwin believes playing the game in Sheffield benefits Leeds. The Yorkshire side are hot favourites, even though City are riding high in the Second Division and will eventually win promotion, claiming the runners-up spot behind Norwich City.

Revie springs a surprise and keeps faith with goalkeeper David Harvey, who had an excellent game at Stoke in Gary Sprake's absence. Leeds's pre-match training routine and salutes to the crowd have been the talk of football. Cheekily, Birmingham try to imitate it before the semi, but it is under-rehearsed and amateurish and the Midlands team end up looking a bit silly.

Two goals from Mick Jones and one from Peter Lorimer give Leeds a routine 3-0 victory. They are going to Wembley – and looking in excellent shape in the process.

However, the real story of the two semi-finals happens at a blustery Villa Park with a serious injury to Arsenal keeper Bob Wilson in his side's 1-1 draw with Stoke. With 22 minutes to play, and Arsenal a goal to the good courtesy of George Armstrong, Wilson rises to catch a free kick by Potters defender Alan Bloor. But he falls awkwardly and twists his knee before adopting, according to press reports, 'a grotesque posture'. He later tells reporters, 'I was leaping at full stretch and something seemed to explode in my knee like a bomb. It was sheer hell.'

John Radford is forced to go in goal for the remainder of the match. It gives Stoke – toothless up to that point – a chance to get back in the game. They take it.

The following day, Wilson has a cartilage removed from his left knee and is out for the rest of the season.

Wilson's injury is a massive blow to Arsenal, as much from a psychological perspective as anything else. Wilson's calm authority was a vital ingredient in the team's double success and his absence causes genuine consternation among Gunners supporters. The injury also raises a discussion about whether teams should be allowed to carry extra substitutes to replace injured goalkeepers – a call which Arsenal manager Bertie Mee rejects, saying, 'The one substitute rule has worked well and nothing which happened on Saturday can persuade me to change that opinion.'

Suddenly, Arsenal's reserve keeper Geoff Barnett is thrust into the limelight. 'Rusty Geoff gets into trim' is the headline on the back page of the *Daily Mirror* on Monday 17 April. Barnett has been playing reserve team football and admits he has been getting stale. Now he will wear the green number one jersey in Wednesday's replay at Goodison Park.

'It's a big jump from reserve team football to a semi-final tie,' he says. Barnett says on Saturday he went out for a walk after hearing that Arsenal were 1-0 up. He adds, 'Then a chap suddenly came rushing out of a shop to tell me that Stoke had equalised and Bob had been carried off. What it all meant didn't really hit me until later.'

The replay takes place at Goodison Park on the Wednesday in front of almost 40,000 spectators, most of whom seem to be followers of Stoke, who are hungry for more success after beating Chelsea in the League Cup Final six weeks earlier. And, with 14 minutes on the clock, Jimmy Greenhoff scores from the spot to put the Staffordshire side in the driving seat.

Arsenal dig deep and a half-time rollicking brings them out with renewed vigour. But the goals, when they come, owe more to good fortune than anything else. In the 55th minute a hopeful centre from Peter Storey is contested in the box by George Armstrong and Stoke's Peter Dobing. The latter jumps clumsily – but not maliciously – and the Potters are aghast when referee Keith Walker points to the spot. Charlie George executes the kick with power and style.

The Gunners in the crowd can now scent victory and urge the team in yellow on. But the winner again has Stoke protesting vehemently. Walker allows George to run on from an offside position to create the winning goal for Radford.

So it is an Arsenal v Leeds final, two of the biggest rivals in the late 1960s and early 1970s. There is history between the sides going back as far as the 1968 League Cup Final when Arsenal were convinced Jack Charlton fouled keeper Jim Furnell before the solitary goal which won Leeds the match.

Leeds bring out the obligatory FA Cup Final record called simply 'Leeds United'. Its lyrics do not bear too much scrutiny. Here is a short sample:

'There's a red headed tiger known as Billy,
'And he goes like a human dynamo.
'Mick the Mover of course, he can work like a horse,
'And Top Cat Cooper's always on the go.'

Chorus:
'And we play all the way for Leeds United,
'Elland Road is the only place for us.
'With heart and soul for the goal that's clearly sighted,
'We're out to toast each other from that silver cup.'

The B-side 'Leeds, Leeds, Leeds' is not as good, unfortunately. The players also get measured for their cup final suits which are a delightful shade of green, officially described as 'pear'. You could get away with such sartorial crimes in 1972.

It is April. The cinema world is going mad for Francis Ford Coppola's epic *The Godfather,* with its marvellous cinematography by Gordon Willis and haunting theme tune composed by Nino Rota.

On the final Saturday of the month, England crash 3-1 at Wembley to a green-shirted West Germany side, inspired by a great performance from Gunter Netzer, in the European Nations Cup quarter-final first leg. Almost immediately, the recriminations begin and, unthinkably, there are even mumblings of criticism in the direction of the hitherto untouchable manager, Sir Alf Ramsey.

FA Cup Final fever grips Leeds. The fans are convinced that this will be their year and demand for the final is massive. Ray Ashworth recalls the trauma of acquiring tickets. He says, 'I can still see myself carefully cutting my tokens out and pasting them on to the sheet provided, knocking pounds off the value of the home programmes which I had collected week after week.'

Leeds have also printed reserve team fixture programmes for that season and tokens from these are also accepted, as are the front page of first-team away match programmes. Ray says, 'Being from Normanton, friendships had been developed around our love for Leeds United and all of us from the area were successful in our ticket applications.'

Carole Parkhouse went to every home and away game during the season and so was virtually assured of a ticket, but she still remembers the relief she felt when her postman delivered it. Phil Stubbs and four or five mates from the Harrogate area were all season ticket holders and regular travellers to away games, so a Wembley ticket was virtually guaranteed for them too.

On the Monday before the final the *Daily Mirror* carries an extraordinary photograph of Charlie George. Alongside the headline 'King George' the hero of 1971 is pictured sitting on a throne dressed in full regalia, holding the FA Cup. The accompanying caption reads, 'Behold the King of Highbury, His Majesty Charlie George. Note the regal splendour of his throne, crown, sceptre and ermine cloak. Observe too, that golden trophy the FA Cup, which Charlie, the darling of Arsenal, is determined his club will retain after the big match against Leeds at Wembley on Saturday.'

On the Wednesday before the game, Scottish Judge Lord Wheatley publishes his findings following the Ibrox disaster of January 1971 in which 66 people died. The report recommends that fewer people be allowed on to terraces and that structural alterations are made at virtually every ground in Britain. For teams attracting big crowds on to large terracing – like Arsenal, Aston Villa, Manchester United and Liverpool – it could mean revenue losses of up to £50,000 a year.

The Government has already accepted one post-Ibrox recommendation – that big sporting venues should be licensed annually by local authorities to ensure that safety standards are met.

With the inquest into England's Wembley defeat still raging, Sir Alf Ramsey takes action and dramatically announces that 1966 World Cup Final hero Geoff Hurst is dropped and will not play in the second leg of the European Nations Cup quarter-final against West Germany in Berlin.

Cup fever is growing. James Loudon, who runs a pub in London's Bloomsbury area, creates a new cocktail in honour of his beloved Arsenal. It has a Dubonnet base to give an Arsenal shade of red and is called The Gunners.

As Saturday's match edges closer there is much speculation about whether reserve goalkeeper Geoff Barnett will be able to stand the pressure that Leeds will doubtless apply to him. Many view him as a weak link, who could hand Leeds the cup, but Arsenal fans are rallying around him.

Andy Locker of Winchmore Hill, London, says, 'We have been incensed at some of the treatment Barnett has received. He needs encouragement, not criticism.'

Leeds travel down on the Thursday, check in to the Hendon Hall Hotel and train lightly in a local park. They have no major injury worries and relax with bingo and carpet bowls before watching a re-run of their 7-0 demolition of Southampton two months earlier.

In an interview in the *Daily Mirror*, Arsenal captain Frank McLintock talks of his respect for Don Revie and his desire that Leeds win the First Division title. He then tempts fate by saying, 'Don't overlook the part our full-backs have played in our success. When was the last time you saw Pat Rice or Bob McNab get a chasing? If they allow players to get in behind them, I am in trouble, because there is no way then that I can keep attackers out of the area.'

It won't be long before McLintock's words will come back to haunt him.

On the day before the final, stories of industrial unrest and rising prices continue to dominate the newspapers. It is a grim time. So when two teenage 'revolutionaries' called Christopher Herman and Garry Knighton come up with an idea to get Britons smiling again, the papers immediately latch on to it. Herman and Knighton want people to smile and wave at complete strangers on the street. 'The rest will follow naturally,' they claim. 'We would like motorists to put National Waving Week stickers on their cars and others to wear "I'm a Waver" badges.'

The idea came to the lads when they were on a lengthy car journey. Chris said, 'We were bored and so started waving and smiling at people. We found that 79 per cent of people waved back.' The lads hope that National Waving Week will become an established event.

Arsenal have spent the days leading up to the final at a training camp near Bournemouth. They are feeling good, as manager Bertie Mee tells reporters, 'I have never known us to be so relaxed, there has almost been a holiday atmosphere at our training camp. There is not going to be any team talk tomorrow, we don't need one. Every player knows exactly what he has got to do. I am not going to make any rash forecasts, but we are in confident mood and we expect to see the trophy back on the sideboard on Monday.'

Back in Leeds, late on Friday night, the coach travellers are preparing to head south on the convoy of Wallace Arnold buses. On board there is supreme confidence that this time Leeds will not miss out. Carole Parkhouse travels with her three best friends, Margaret, 'Creamy' and Sharon, who have each been to every game this season. The coaches leave Leeds at midnight.

'These midnight coach trips were very popular at the time,' Carole says. 'The lads liked them because they could get plenty of drink down them and us girls could do some sightseeing if we wanted to.'

Ray Ashworth is also on one of the 'Wally's Trolleys'. 'Wallace Arnold used to run coaches to all Leeds home and away games and had collection points at Normanton town centre, Castleford bus station, Kippax and Leeds depending on the demand. Needless to say, for this game the coach was full after Normanton, Castleford and Kippax,' he says.

The coaches make the long trip down the M1 with the radio blaring out. In the charts are Gilbert O'Sullivan with 'Alone Again (Naturally)', Lindisfarne with 'Meet me on the Corner' and Neil Young with 'Heart of Gold'. But the number one is not something you would describe as especially radio friendly, or at least on the stations of choice of most of the fans travelling to Wembley. The Pipes and Drums and Military Band of the Royal Scots Dragoon Guards are entering their third week at the summit with 'Amazing Grace', notable for its prominent use of bagpipes.

Ray recalls, 'I remember thinking on the coach trip down that this had to be our year, there was a kind of symmetry about it.' Applying the kind of logic which only football fans can understand, Ray explains, 'Our first ever cup final was in 1965 against Liverpool – that was their third final and they'd lost the previous two. Our second was in 1970 and that was Chelsea's third final, having lost the previous two. This was now our third final, having lost the previous two – and on those facts alone this had to be our year!'

Phil Stubbs travels to Wembley on a football special from Leeds with his mate Bill. He says, 'We both wore scarves. Mine was a double length scarf, which had been stitched together by my mum. We were both armed with plenty of tinnies and travelled on the train to London.'

Arsenal fan Mick Kelly wakes with a thick head and a vague taste of Scotch in his mouth after his late-night drink-up in Walthamstow, but he springs up the moment he remembers he is going to Wembley.

Mick recalls, 'I rang my Arsenal mates and told them I had blagged a ticket and arranged to meet them at Seven Sisters Tube for the journey to Wembley. This was my first FA Cup Final. What's more, it was the centenary cup final. The FA had planned a parade of football legends before kick-off and now, totally out of the blue, I had a ticket to see it all.

'I was determined to enjoy the day – despite the fact that the omens for Arsenal did not look great. Geoff Barnett did not inspire much confidence and, although it was virtually the same team that had won the double the previous season, the Gunners were not playing at the same tempo. I blamed Alan Ball and his infamous white boots. He was bought to strengthen the side, but he never really won the fans over at Highbury.'

Arsenal fan Don Richards, who was at Wembley in 1971, expresses the unease that most Gunners fans are feeling, 'I was not very confident before this game. Arsenal had not been playing well and the injury to Bob Wilson was playing on our minds.'

The papers make great play of the fact that, between them, the Leeds team has 178 international caps, compared with Arsenal's 97. 'Never before has an FA Cup Final side had so much international talent to draw on,' the report says.

With fuel prices rising, police report a spate of petrol thefts. Thieves are also targeting petrol caps and the latest wheeze to wind somebody up is to put sand in their tank. So, locking petrol caps, costing between £1.35 and £1.60, are selling fast.

The Leeds side takes a stroll around the grounds of Hendon Hall Hotel before returning for a pre-match meal and then watching some *Cup Final Grandstand*. Then Don Revie gives his main team talk, discussing each Arsenal player and going through the tactics, before announcing the side. The team are ready for business and set off.

Tens of thousands of Londoners and Yorkshiremen and women are now descending on Wembley. Mick Kelly is walking on air. This time yesterday he was wondering where to find a colour TV to watch the game. Now he is actually here, at Wembley, with all its wonderful sights and sounds.

He says, 'We reached Wembley Park and headed for Wembley Way. I wasn't one for wearing team colours but, as it was the cup final, I splashed out 30p on a red and white rosette. I wasn't prepared to pin it and spoil the look of my black, leather safari jacket. Instead I pinned it to my shirt, underneath the jacket. It proved to be a smart move on my part.'

Inside Wembley, the Band of the Royal Marines is in full flow. From outside, Mick hears the distant strains of Henry Mancini's 'Moon River' from *Breakfast at Tiffany's* and knows he will shortly be in.

The convoy of coaches carrying Leeds fans starts pulling into the Wembley car park. Normanton lad Ray Ashworth can remember his first view of the famous old stadium 'in the flesh'. He says, 'My initial thoughts were that the pitch did not appear as large as I had expected, but apart from that I was very impressed. We were in the lower tier at the tunnel end, with the actual tunnel just to our right.

'The stewards forced us to the front, which we didn't want, so we went back out again until the ground had filled up enough for us to stand at the height we wanted. There was also a fair amount of trading of tickets on the concourse to enable people to get into the same area as their friends.'

Both teams have now arrived at Wembley and have made it to the sanctuary of the dressing room.

Mick is still lapping up the atmosphere outside the ground, smiling like the cat that has got the cream. He mingles proudly with the Arsenal fans. Among them, somewhere, are Dean Goodman, Ken Smith, Ken Banham and Peter Hollingworth, all veterans of 1971 and hoping for, but maybe not expecting, a repeat of that outcome.

Mick says, 'We continued to move along Wembley Way, a sea of red and white, separated by mounted police from the white, yellow and blue of the Leeds fans.'

The atmosphere is terrific. He hears the band playing Jimmy Webb's 'Up, Up and Away'. Soon Mick will be in, part of the North Bank that has transferred to Wembley for the day.

He says, 'We came to the stadium, one end Leeds, the other Arsenal. I checked the block and row numbers on my ticket. That was when I discovered I was in the block behind the goal, at the tunnel end.'

To his horror and dismay, Arsenal fanatic Mick must stand smack bang in the middle of the most ardent and boisterous Leeds supporters.

Ray Ashworth and Carole Parkhouse are somewhere in that heaving throng of Leeds fans. 'Our end seemed fuller than Arsenal's,' remembers Ray.

There are quite a lot of pre-match festivities to celebrate the centenary final including a parade of all the previous cup winners. The players come out to inspect the pitch. Allan Clarke checks the penalty area for divots. Both sides look relaxed and are happy to be interviewed by the waiting TV reporters as they head back to the dressing rooms to get changed. Maybe it is a relief for the Leeds players to get out of those pear-coloured suits.

Now it is time for the community singing and this year the job of leading this oddly quaint – not to mention outdated – ritual falls to Cockney entertainer Tommy Steele, thought to be an Arsenal fan. Which makes it slightly strange that he decides to dress from head to toe in white. The Leeds fans quickly start a chorus of 'Tommy's wearing white, Tommy's wearing white, ee-aye-addio, Tommy's wearing white!'

Outside Wembley, Mick Kelly swallows hard, keeps his lips firmly sealed, joins the throng of slightly scary Yorkshiremen and women and enters the turnstile. He says, 'Suddenly, there was no red and white around me. Just white. Self-preservation demanded I button up my leather jacket, thus ensuring my "true colours" were no longer on display. But there was no turning back. I had to complete my mission – even if it meant paying the ultimate price – watching the final surrounded by 20,000 Yorkshiremen chanting obscenities at anything and all things Cockney.'

Though cloudy, it is a humid day and the temperature is rising at the tunnel end, which looks dangerously packed. Leeds fan Phil Stubbs remembers, 'With only ten minutes until kick-off, my mate Bill said he felt faint. I summoned the St John Ambulance people who decided to take poor Bill away to recover. They were quite shocked when I refused to accompany him, because I was adamant there was no way I was going to miss the match!'

The atmosphere on the terraces is amazing. It is the Leeds fans you can hear. They are singing at the tops of their voices to the tune of 'When The Saints Go Marching In', except they are singing, 'When the whites go marching in.'

It is beery and boisterous. The Leeds fans are crammed in. They have come from all over the Leeds area. Not just the city itself, but from Bramhope, Otley, Rothwell, Garforth and Yeadon. These fans are an essential part of the Leeds experience. They are mostly men – passionate, proud and noisy. Absolutely no place for a Londoner to be. But it is where Mick Kelly is. He can smell the odour of freshly drunk ale. He has reached the terraces and his eyes are darting round for a place that might offer if not a haven, then at least survival.

Mick recalls, 'I spotted a group of dads with their kids. Though they were Leeds, they looked harmless enough. I went and stood alongside them, my north-London lips sealed so as not to reveal my identity.'

Mick keeps quiet as he sees the flags of previous winners pass by: Bradford City, Huddersfield Town, Charlton Athletic, and others. The stewards are shepherding more and more fans in. The terrace is filling up and, as it does, Mick feels less and less secure. He says, 'As kick-off drew closer and the parade passed we were packed in like sardines.'

With his main team talk delivered at the hotel, Revie doesn't have a lot to say, but he does give his players one final reminder of the Chelsea final and replay of two years ago when Leeds let victory slip from their grasp. Then, finally, as he does before every game, Revie says two words to his players: 'confidence' and 'concentration'.

The centenary parade forms a guard of honour outside the tunnel and awaits the arrival of the teams. Arsenal emerge from the northern dressing room into the tunnel and, gentleman that he is, Bertie Mee strides out beaming and warmly shakes the hand of his opposite number Revie, who returns the smile.

As the Leeds players gather in the tunnel, all that can be heard from the crowd is a constant, monotonous chant of 'Leeds, Leeds, Leeds, Leeds'. When the Yorkshire hordes tire of that, they start singing in a slowly descending dirge, 'U-Ni-ted.' 'U-Ni-ted.'

Ray Ashworth remembers, 'In those days, the songs were mainly in support of your team – there were no anti-Man U songs around at this time, and indeed Arsenal and Liverpool were bigger rivals in this period than our erstwhile friends from somewhere west of Bradford.'

Nothing can be heard of the Arsenal fans. Arsenal skipper Frank McLintock waits at the doorway of his dressing room, grinning widely and sharing a joke with some of the Leeds players. He seems remarkably relaxed. Not all of the Arsenal players are so jovial. Peter Simpson appears to be trying to psych out Allan Clarke. Peter Storey, trademark Vaseline on his eyebrows and chewing gum almost threateningly, looks as mean and moody as ever.

Londoner Mick Kelly continues to shuffle uncomfortably on the terraces among the Leeds faithful. Then a possible ally appears.

'With just minutes to go to the opening whistle, I felt a tug on my arm from a guy who had wriggled his way through the crowd to stand directly in front of me,' he says. 'His London accent cut through the Leeds chanting like a Charlie George 30-yard screamer. He had spotted the slightest glint of red poking out from the top of my jacket, which must have come open during the hustle and bustle as the stewards packed us in.' Mick's secret is out.

Finally, the teams emerge and, as they enter the fray, the Leeds players throw footballs into the crowd and then pass through the guard of honour. As usual, both clubs are wearing natty new tracksuit tops. Arsenal's red Umbro top has a little white FA Cup with 1972 alongside it, stitched above the famous cannon. Each Leeds player has his name emblazoned in blue on the back of his white top.

Bremner and McLintock exchange Caledonian pleasantries all the way to the halfway line. Now the Arsenal end is as jam-packed as the Leeds end and finally the Londoners find their voices. It's their early 1970s anthem, sung to the tune of 'Rule Britannia', 'Good old Arsenal, we're proud to say that name. While we sing this song, you'll win the game!' which rings out.

The players are then introduced to Her Majesty The Queen, who is attending her first FA Cup Final since 1965, when she saw Liverpool beat Leeds. Now the Arsenal fans have really found their voice and they sing a version of the Christmas carol 'The First Noel'. Instead it is about Charlie George and it goes, 'Charlie, Charlie, Charlie, Charlie. Born is the King of Highbury'. And, when the national anthem is played, it is largely drowned out by the North Bank chanting simply, 'Charlie! [clap, clap, clap]. Charlie! [clap, clap, clap].'

Both sets of fans then start singing a version of 'Son of my Father'. The song, by Maidstone four-piece Chicory Tip, was top of the charts from 19 February to 11 March and has been assimilated remarkably quickly into terrace culture. The song – co-written by Italian producer and songwriter Giorgio Moroder – will still be sung today. It is up there with 'Guantanamara', 'Knees Up Mother Brown' and – ironically – 'Amazing Grace' as a durable terrace anthem.

It is all set up for a great match. There are great players on both sides, intense rivalry between them and two sets of passionate fans. Don Revie has said in the build-up that Leeds are going to attack from the off.

Yet, once again, the game itself disappoints. The first half is tense and cagey and dominated by stoppages and fouls. In fact, in the first 36 minutes of the match, there are 24 fouls committed – one for every 90 seconds played – and, apart from an early free kick by McLintock which Harvey does well to save, it is not until just after the half-hour mark that anything of real note happens.

Arsenal win a corner which George Armstrong floats to the edge of the penalty area. There, wearing his distinctive white boots, waits the flame-haired, all-action Alan Ball. He catches it perfectly on the volley, keeps it low. It is past Harvey in the Leeds goal but is cleared off the line by the perfectly positioned Reaney.

Mick Kelly winces, but just manages to stay quiet. His new-found Arsenal 'mate' has no such concerns. 'Unlucky Bally!' he bellows at the top of his voice. 'F**k off Cockneys,' says a gruff Yorkshire voice from somewhere. Mick is very, very uncomfortable.

Leeds then go close themselves when Arsenal's left-back McNab makes a hash of a clearance, skies it, and allows Lorimer to volley a cross to the far post where, stretching, Clarke gets his head to the ball which, with Barnett beaten, scrapes the bar.

The Leeds fans around Mick surge forward. It is mightily close. 'What a let-off for Arsenal,' says Brian Moore. 'They were all over the place.' 'Keep 'em out Gunners!' bawls Mick's mate.

At half-time it is goalless, but Mick is starting to get concerned for his safety. His North London companion is being less than coy about his allegiance to the Gunners. Mick says, 'He'd been getting increasingly hot under the collar about some of the Leeds tackling. Of course, he completely ignored the agricultural efforts of our own Peter Storey. Having engaged in a heated debate with the Leeds fans surrounding us, he looked to me for verbal support. Once again, survival instinct kicked in as I did my best to come across as the "voice of reason".

'It was a pathetic effort on my part and it didn't impress my new Arsenal buddy. So much so (and to great relief on my part) he abandoned me and looked for somewhere else to stand for the rest of the match.'

Shortly after the restart, Charlie George is booked following a tussle with Bremner, who has himself been booked at the end of the first half. Referee David Smith has previously booked Hunter and McNab too.

In 1972 four bookings in one match is considered a lot and, in these pre-yellow card days, will lead to weak terrace jokes about officials developing writer's cramp in the course of a match.

At different places behind the goal Carole Parkhouse, Phil Stubbs and Ray Ashworth are all confident that a goal for Leeds must be on its way, such is their side's dominance. They are right. Mick Kelly, too, is sensing that his beloved Arsenal cannot hold on for much longer. Aside from a header into the side-netting from Bob McNab – when both John Radford and Charlie George were well-placed to score – the men in red and white have barely turned up.

The game's decisive moment comes after 53 minutes and stems from an Arsenal attack that breaks down. In trademark fashion, Alan Ball surges forward trying to make something happen and passes to George. But the hero of 1971 loses control, enabling Jack Charlton to nick the ball and play it into the path of Paul Madeley who, with a look of grim determination on his face, carries it forward.

Leeds, ruthless exploiters of opponents' errors, scent an opportunity. Madeley plays the ball to Lorimer, who has moved inside, and he in turn lays it off to Mick Jones, who is in the right-wing position. From this point the action bears a remarkable similarity to Neil Young's winning goal in the 1969 final but with Jones in the Mike Summerbee role and Bob McNab doing a bit of an 'Alan Woollett'.

It is precisely what McLintock has been fearing, but said hardly ever happens.

Jones takes on McNab who, just like Woollett, goes to ground after only making a half-tackle. Just like Summerbee, Jones manages to keep his feet and gets to the byline. But, unlike Summerbee who laid the ball back low, Jones gets his toe beneath it and produces something akin to a golf chip and lofts a perfectly weighted ball tantalisingly towards the penalty spot.

It is on a plate for Clarke, but 'Sniffer' still has to choose his spot. He does so, expertly launching himself with a diving header and masterfully placing the ball into the far corner beyond Barnett's full length, arms-stretched-out dive.

It is scored at the Leeds end and the fans go wild. Ray says, 'I remember the move very well – and to me time seemed to slow – from the cross coming over to Allan Clarke connecting with the header. I knew it was going in from the moment the ball was crossed.' Carole recalls, 'It was a lovely sight to see the whole of our end go up in ecstasy.'

In the midst of the seething, writhing mass of ecstatic Yorkshiremen and women is Mick Kelly, who is being buffeted around like a pinball and now has to suffer endless taunting and sarcastic hair ruffling. He has no answer either because Arsenal look devoid of inspiration.

Leeds are well on top and a short spell of keep-ball from them sparks memories of the famous Southampton rout two months earlier and earns cheers from their fans. On the rare occasions that Arsenal do venture forward, they are thwarted by the redoubtable Charlton and – in the form of his life – the brilliant Norman Hunter.

Arsenal are not at the races, which makes it all the more surprising that, out of nothing, they are inches away from equalising. Ball tries a speculative effort from 30 yards. It stays low and is going wide, but clips the heels of Bremner and tees up perfectly for George. Though Paul Reaney is sticking to George like glue, he gets in a great first-time shot which flashes past Harvey. It looks like a certain goal, but it slams against the crossbar and rebounds out. Following up, Peter Simpson balloons it over.

Mick can't help himself and lets out an anguished cry, which evokes great derision from the Leeds fans and more barging, hair ruffling and anti-London comments. It is the same end – and almost exactly 12 months on – as George's glorious winner against Liverpool. George holds his head in his hands and then looks to the ground. It is Arsenal's only real chance in the second half. They have not done themselves justice. Ray Kennedy replaces John Radford and ITV co-commentator Jimmy Hill notes, 'Charlie George is kept on for that fantastic shot that he keeps somewhere in his locker.'

It now looks simply a case of Leeds playing out time. But things rarely go smoothly in football, as Ray Ashworth explains, 'It would not be Leeds without further drama, which was duly provided by the unselfish Mick Jones.'

In injury time, Hunter breaks out of defence and passes to Jones in the right wing position. Jones beats McLintock and is in on goal, but he pushes the ball slightly too far forward and Barnett bravely knocks the ball away from him. Jones's momentum carries him forward and he falls awkwardly and painfully over Barnett's body and lies in a crumpled heap on the turf clutching his shoulder. He stays down.

Arsenal try to attack again, but it is too late and referee Smith signals the end of the game. Jones writhes in agony. Revie stays seated but simply clenches both fists in triumph at Leeds winning the FA Cup for the first time. The Leeds fans go wild. At last, the FA Cup is theirs. 'Hard luck Cockney,' says an unsympathetic Leeds fan to Mick. The cameras pan in on the fans gathered at the tunnel end, scarves and flags waving in delight. Still Jones is down.

Carole and her girlfriends are all worried about poor Jones. 'It really took the edge off the moment when the ref blew the final whistle,' she says. 'Of course, we were delighted that we had won, but we were all so worried about Mick, especially as we had to play the title decider on the following Monday. Modern managers please take note; this is what teams used to have to do!'

For Mick, the final whistle is the signal for him to get out – and fast. He recalls, 'All I wanted to do was get out of there – hopefully in one piece. The entire stand was jumping as the Leeds fans celebrated their win. I somehow managed to get to the gangway and started to make my way up to the exit. Halfway up, a Leeds fan spotted my rosette, shoved me, and growled something to the effect that I should stop and watch Billy collect the cup. I pulled away, head down, and did my best to bulldoze my way out of the ground.'

On ITV, Brian Moore says, 'The Leeds fans are going crazy. And Harvey has collapsed on the floor. No, it's Barnett!'

Leeds trainer Les Cocker is tending to Mick Jones, who looks in genuine pain and as though he might pass out. Cocker appears to be making a makeshift bandage for the stricken centre-forward. He's surrounded by cameramen and photographers, who sense a story. 'He really is quite badly hurt,' says Moore.

Bremner leads the victors up, receives the trophy from Her Majesty and salutes the adoring thousands. But the attention keeps going back to Jones. Carole says, 'I had waited years to see

Billy Bremner lift the FA Cup and I actually missed the magic moment as I was still looking at the physio with Mick. I have seen it re-run a million times since, of course, but I always feel a bit robbed of the actual moment. Oh well, that's the drama of being a Leeds fan!'

Finally, Jones gets to his feet and edges his way over to the Royal Box. Arsenal have now collected their losers' medals. 'Jimmy, what do you think that is?' says Brian Moore as Jones moves into focus. 'Well the bandages that were put on him,' says Hill, 'are bandages for a broken arm, not for a dislocation. You would tend to put the arm in a different position for a dislocation.'

Jones has now reached the foot of the famous steps. Just as it looks like he might struggle up alone, Hunter rushes over and comes to his assistance. Then Jones goes up. The eyes of the whole ground and millions watching on television at home, are on him. Though he is in agony he has, without wishing to for one moment, completely stolen the show. Everybody seems to remember Jones's cameo role.

He climbs the stairs. A group of well-dressed young women – early 1970s WAGs perhaps – gather by them. A couple of them seem to be shedding tears of sympathy.

As Carole says, 'It was a very special moment. Mick was helped up the steps by Norman Hunter so that he could meet the Queen and get his medal from her. It was very dramatic and very moving.'

As Jones reaches the summit he receives a tremendous cheer from the Leeds end and smiles shyly through the obvious pain as the Queen presents him with his winner's medal. As Jones descends the stairs, the Leeds fans break into a chorus of, 'M-I. M-I-C. M-I-C-K. Mick Jones!'

Even Arsenal fan Mick Kelly says many years later, 'The image of Jones making his way gingerly up to the Royal Box, his arm in a makeshift sling, to collect his winner's medal from the Queen, is probably the thing most people remember about a very forgettable final.'

Except Mick was not there to see it as he made a sharp exit from the ground. 'The sense of getting out was palpable,' he says, 'but then came that sense of frustration and bitter disappointment that every football fan knows all too well when your team fail to perform on the big occasion. It had been my first FA Cup Final and, without doubt, the worst day I've ever had following Arsenal for nearly 40 years.'

The teams stand through another rendition of the national anthem and then the Arsenal players slink off while Leeds embark on a lap of honour. First they take the cup to the Arsenal end where they receive some polite – if rather grudging – applause. Then they trot down to the tunnel end where they are received by their hordes of supporters, waving scarves and banners.

The TV cameras switch between the lap of honour and Mick Jones who is being carried away on a stretcher. He manages a weak wave of acknowledgement to the fans, who are continuing to chant his name. Now the Leeds fans are pouring out of the stadium safe in the knowledge that the cup is theirs. It is completely appropriate that the Leeds side of 1971/72 win a major domestic trophy because they are, on their day, the best side in the country at the time.

Carole says, 'After the game we headed back into town and there were some running battles around the Trafalgar Square area. Some Arsenal fans tried to kidnap Margaret and me and we were rescued by one of our own fans called Mouse (don't ask why!).'

Arsenal fan Ken Banham agrees that a small element of Arsenal fans did try to hunt down some Leeds fans to exact some kind of revenge for losing the match. Ken says, 'It's important to remember that at that time the two clubs had become sworn enemies, which may have started with that goal in the 1968 League Cup Final, after which Frank McLintock and the players chased the ref. That was when the hate started. Additionally, there were rumours that Don Revie had been calling us things like "southern softies" and "London dandies" so, as far as we were concerned, the battle lines were drawn.'

Ken continues, 'Before and after the cup final there was trouble all around the station, on Wembley Way, in the car park and the back streets around the ground. Fights were breaking out and there were running battles with as many as 100 or so fans from each club. Arsenal had a bit of a reputation at that time but, unlike Leeds, Chelsea or West Ham, we did not start trouble but could look after ourselves if it did go off.'

Carole and the girls steer well clear of any aggravation and end their wonderful day in the Rising Sun pub near King's Cross station where they watch the game's highlights on *Match of the Day*. 'Finally, we were collected by our bus to go home,' says Carole. 'I remember being dropped off in Leeds City Square at about 5am, buying all the Sunday papers and waiting for the first bus back home.'

While the Leeds fans begin to do some real celebrating, there is no such luxury for the players who have the small matter of a championship decider at Wolves to think about – and they have just 48 hours to prepare for it. Mick Jones is obviously out. Allan Clarke and Johnny Giles played at Wembley with the lingering effects of groin strains and, along with Eddie Gray, will need pain-killing injections before they can take the field at Molineux.

The title race has gone to the wire and can still go three ways. On the Monday night Liverpool play at Arsenal knowing they must win and Leeds lose at Wolves for the title to go to Merseyside.

If both teams lose then the title will go to Derby, who have already played all their games and are already sunning themselves in Majorca. Though Wolves are no mean side, it still looks like Leeds's title.

Both games are massively controversial. The match at Highbury ends goalless, but Liverpool are bitter. Two minutes from time, John Toshack turns a mis-hit Kevin Keegan shot into the net, but a linesman flags and referee Roger Kirkpatrick disallows the goal. Bill Shankly is furious and says later, 'That man Kirkpatrick has deprived us of the championship.'

More than 53,000 fans pack Molineux for the vital game and again it is the officials who steal the headlines. Wolves show absolutely no compassion towards Leeds and tear into them, but the Yorkshire side hold firm. But then Leeds are denied a blatant penalty when Wolves full-back Bernard Shaw handles in the area.

Goals from Munro and Dougan then give Wolves a 2-0 lead. Bremner replies for Leeds, but try as they might they cannot score again. A draw would have been enough for Leeds to take a richly deserved title but, unexpectedly, the title goes to Derby.

The front page of Tuesday's *Daily Mirror* sums it up perfectly. Alongside stories about Arab guerrillas hijacking an Israeli plane bound for Tel Aviv and impending strike action by railwaymen are two pictures of Leeds captain Billy Bremner. One shows him with both arms raised in triumph and a smile as wide as the Yorkshire Dales, taken immediately after Saturday's final. It is, perhaps, the definitive Bremner picture and will form the basis of the sculpture of the great man erected many years later outside Elland Road.

The other picture, taken at around 9.30pm at Molineux, shows abject despair on Bremner's face as, head bowed, he trudges off the field as the realisation that Leeds have been pipped for the title hits home.

Looking back now, Carole Parkhouse is bitter about the way Leeds had to play the final on Saturday and then a championship decider on the Monday. 'We looked all set to do the league and cup double but, as usual, the fixtures had been shoehorned,' she says. 'Needless to say, we lost the league game and the title was handed to Derby. It left a sour taste.'

Missing out on the championship certainly takes the edge off the cup win for Leeds fans. When Phil Stubbs returned to work at the Ministry of Defence on Monday morning, everybody stood up and applauded when he entered the office. Winning the FA Cup in those days made everyone sit up and take notice. Losing the league, which their football throughout the season deserved, was a bitter pill to swallow.

Today, Stubbs, Parkhouse and Ray Ashworth are able to remember the events of May 1972 with pride and affection. He now lives in Cambridgeshire, where he was moved by his employers, the Ministry of Defence, in 1995.

He took early retirement in 2007 and, after a few years without one, decided to get a season ticket again.

He has now attended over 2,000 Leeds games and, despite the club's fluctuating fortunes, has only missed two matches home and away in the past five years.

Looking back to 1972 he says, 'The FA Cup Final in those days was the most treasured event any football fan could dream about. A hundred thousand people in attendance and the match beamed to countless countries made it the ideal climax to end the football season. Walking down Wembley Way with thousands of fans draped in the white of Leeds and the red of Arsenal, with the twin towers on either side, was one of those occasions in life you never forget.'

Having been at two previous finals when Leeds lost, Phil knew the utter despondency of Wembley defeat. But now, at last, he could bask in the glow of victory, 'The euphoria of winning the centenary cup final was very special. Having shouted yourself hoarse until the final whistle when all hell broke loose, jumping up and down, hugging everyone in sight and then seeing Billy lead the team up those famous steps and proudly lifting the trophy to the skies – they are treasured moments that live with you forever.'

Ray lived in Bramley and Churwell, where he could see Elland Road from his lounge window. He now lives in Guiseley and is an accountant by profession, working in IT for a major financial company.

He still follows Leeds home and away.

He says, 'For me, that Leeds team was the greatest and, even now, the names of the cup-winning side roll off the tongue. I thought then that the 1972 success would be the first of many cup final victories. The fact that more than 40 years later it is still our only FA Cup success is testament to the ineptitude of the various boards that have been given or have taken control of this great football club.'

Carole's school, St Philomena's in Carshalton, Surrey, is still there, but no longer a boarding school. Carole has been a season ticket holder at Leeds since 1971/72. She worked in stage management until 2000, since when she has done a variety of jobs, including writing and project management. Her partner, Ashley, is also a Leeds fanatic.

Carole's best all-time Leeds team is, perhaps, not too difficult to guess. It is Sprake, Reaney, Cooper, Bremner, Charlton, Lorimer, Clarke, Jones, Giles and Gray with Madeley as the substitute. 'Virtually every Leeds fan I know can reel those names off, in that order, at the drop of a hat,' she says.

Carole never saw the great John Charles, but admires relatively modern players like Gordon Strachan, though her own personal favourite is the versatile 1970s defender Trevor Cherry. She adds, 'These days it's quite rare for players to stay more than a few years at a club, so modern supporters can't really imagine it but, at Leeds, once a player came to the club, they stayed. The likes of Norman Hunter, Paul Reaney and Billy Bremner came to the club as youth players, got in the team at 17, and just got better and better.

'The continuity also bound the players and fans together. I quite often see Paul Reaney and Norman Hunter at Elland Road and they always stop and say hello. They knew the fans then and remember them, which is sadly not the case with modern players.

'Sadly, the FA Cup doesn't have the magic it used to have; 1972 was a golden year for us and the actual day was fantastic. For me, winning the FA Cup was probably what people now feel about winning the Champions League. It was wonderful.'

Twelve months later, though, Leeds would once again be on the receiving end of defeat in one of the most sensational results in FA Cup history. And, once again, Carole would be there to witness it.

FROM BOVRIL TO CHAMPAGNE

Sunderland v Leeds United
Saturday 5 May 1973

'I DIDN'T bring the magic. It's always been here... I just came back to find it.' – Bob Stokoe.

It is 2 December 1972 and a herd of grumbling, cursing football fans are making their way home through the late autumn gloom. They have just seen their team – Sunderland – lose again, this time 1-0 at home to Burnley. It leaves them in 19th place in the Second Division and in a perilous position.

Among them is a 19-year-old girl called Jeanette Coyle, who is close to tears, as Sunderland Football Club is the love of her life. She is steeped in the club's history. Her devoted father Bill, who is alongside her, his father before that and *his* father before that were Roker Park regulars, and now Jeanette rarely misses a game.

Bill puts a comforting arm on the young girl's shoulder and they make their silent way home.

Also in the miserable pack trudging away from Roker is a young man called Ray Leonard, with his wife Barbara. The talk among the Sunderland faithful is about the club's new manager and whether he can turn around what is becoming an increasingly dire predicament. In the club shop, business is non-existent. Supporters' club stalwart George Forster looks forlornly at the unsold stock and watches sadly as the uninterested, disgruntled Mackems pass by without a second glance.

This is a town and a club which deserves better. BBC's *Man Alive* documentary series has just broadcast a programme called 'Out of School, Out of Work'. It is a report on unemployment amongst the young in Sunderland, where unemployment is twice the national average. The programme, presented by Desmond Wilcox, includes a studio discussion involving unemployed youngsters, their parents, councillors, industrialists and union leaders.

As the rain starts to fall, the fans go their separate ways, their weekends ruined by their under-achieving team. A home defeat on a wet, dark miserable Saturday – it is about as bad as it gets. That night, if you had told any of these Sunderland fans that, in six months' time, their side would produce one of the most astonishing achievements in the long, rich history of the FA Cup, they would probably have thumped you.

Throughout the game, the north-east is respected for its proud footballing tradition with, in particular, Newcastle United and Sunderland arousing deep loyalty and passion among their followers. Jeanette was born into this hot-bed, as she explains, 'Where I come from, you are born either "red and white" or "black and white" and my parents, grandparents and great grandparents all supported Sunderland, so the die was cast. I have been around football all my life.'

Indeed, her dad Bill was a professional footballer himself and played for Darlington and West Auckland and, in the early 1950s, the young Jeanette used to watch from her pushchair at the side of the pitch. In 1959, when she was six, Bill first took his daughter to Roker Park, where she and her sisters stood in Block 13 of the Roker End, at the back of the children's enclosure with their watchful parents directly behind them in the main Roker stand. 'Sunderland has always been a great family club,' says Jeanette, 'with everyone looking out for each other.'

Before long, Jeanette had fallen for the charms of the club and, lured by the likes of great players such as Brian Clough and Charlie Hurley, spent her weeks counting the days until Saturday home games came around.

As the 1960s progressed, Jeanette and her dad began travelling all over the country in support of the team. One series of games in March 1967 would leave a particularly bitter taste. Sunderland were paired against high-flying Leeds in the fifth round of the FA Cup. Both the first tie, at Roker Park, and the replay, at Elland Road, finished 1-1. The Elland Road match will be remembered for a 15-minute delay after the capacity crowd spilled on to the pitch. It needed a decider at Hull City to prise the sides apart. Jeanette and her father made the trip to Boothferry Park for what proved to be one of the most explosive games of the latter part of the decade.

With the score at 1-1, referee Ken Stokes awarded Leeds a penalty after a foul on Jimmy Greenhoff. Sunderland fans say it was outside the box, Greenhoff was offside *and* he dived. After Johnny Giles slammed the spot-kick home, some furious Sunderland fans invaded the pitch and caused a delay of several minutes. Then Sunderland's George Herd was sent off and was pelted with a scarf by a young Leeds fan at the tunnel's entrance.

By this time referee Stokes had completely lost the plot and sent off Sunderland's George Mulhall, prompting another pitch invasion. In the chaos, a bottle struck Leeds trainer Les Cocker. The game will stick in the memory of Sunderland fans for many years to come.

In the following season, 1967/68, Jeanette, now 14, landed a job at Roker Park, selling pies and Bovril in the stands. After displaying enthusiasm and aptitude for the task, at 16, she was promoted to a dream job in the players' tea room, where she became friendly with many of the players' wives and girlfriends. It cemented her love affair with Sunderland AFC.

As Ray Leonard and his fiancée Barbara shuffle home disconsolately after the home defeat to Burnley, Ray has one of those moments which all football fans experience at some time or another, 'Is this all worth it?'

At 25, and just starting a career in the teaching profession, he begins thinking back through his years of devoted support. As he does so, a distant image enters his mind. It is the 1960/61 season and, at his family home not far from Roker Park, 12-year-old Ray, a pupil at Bede Grammar School, watches with growing fascination as his mother, Joyce, works at the dining table, using red and white ribbons and a piece of card to make a rosette.

The town is gearing up for a huge match – an FA Cup sixth round tie against the mighty Tottenham Hotspur, the best team in the land at the time, nine points clear at the top of the First Division.

Ray's mum works at a famous Sunderland department store in the High Street called Blacketts and all the staff there have decided to wear red and white rosettes in support of the team.

In fact, the whole town is being festooned with red and white. This display of allegiance to their local club intrigues Ray. 'I was becoming aware that Sunderland, then in the old Second Division, were on something of a cup run,' he says. 'My dad, originally from Somerset, had been to a few games and had seen Len Shackleton play, but had never developed a real passion for the club. He had taken me to one game but I can remember very little about it, apart from being fascinated by the empty Bovril cups swirling around the terraces.'

Ray's interest in the team was being fuelled by the forthcoming Spurs match, but he still only felt like an outsider looking in, as he explains, 'The thought of actually being allowed to attend the Spurs game never entered my head. I don't even remember any radio commentary, but I'll swear I heard the roar of the 61,000 crowd through my open window, three miles from the ground, when Willie McPheat equalised Jones's first-half goal.' The game finished 1-1.

Although Spurs went on to thrash Sunderland 5-0 in the replay back at White Hart Lane, something in Ray had changed. He was hooked. 'It was then that my passion for Sunderland started to burn, the flame had been ignited,' he recalls. 'I started doing the classic schoolboy thing of collecting football cards and newspaper clippings. I went to some reserve games and, at one, even overcame my shyness sufficiently to approach the already legendary Charlie Hurley and ask him for his autograph as he watched from the stands. I still remember the thrill as he smiled and signed with some warm words in his Cockney accent.'

By 1962/63, Ray was a regular at Roker Park and the end of that season brought the first of many heartbreaking moments as he watched Tommy Harmer of Chelsea score a last-minute winner, when a draw would have seen Sunderland promoted. But he didn't have to wait long.

Twelve months later they were promoted with – ironically – Leeds. The season also saw a memorable FA Cup run which included crushing victories over Northampton Town and Bristol City before First Division side Everton came to Roker. A fabulous 3-1 win for the Black Cats was soured somewhat for Ray by a frightening incident with alarming portents.

'Roker Park was a big ground,' recalls Ray, 'with massive crowds, mostly standing. Considerable surges of people often took place when they all leaned in the same direction to follow the ball. My joy at our win over Everton was tempered by my experience in the Clock Stand upper standing area. Foolishly standing behind a barrier, instead of in front of one, I became squashed up against it for what seemed like several minutes, and I passed out.

'People were trying to give me breathing space, but no one could move. Only when the ball went up the other end were they able to find enough space to get me to an aisle and some fresh air. Looking back to those times, something like the Hillsborough disaster was inevitable.'

The warning signs were there and indeed tragedy was just around the corner. The quarter-final meant a trip to Old Trafford and an FA Cup classic. Sunderland led 3-1 with four minutes to go but last-gasp goals from Best and Charlton meant a return to Roker Park. Interest in the game, played on Wednesday 4 March 1964, was huge. Ray remembers, 'I went to the ground straight from school for the replay to get a good place in the queue at the Fulwell End. By the time the turnstiles opened, all the queues had merged into a seething mass of people. I somehow stayed in line with the gate, as opposed to being squashed against the wall, and was "squeezed" into it after some scary moments.'

The game finished 2-2, but the only real story of the night was at the Roker End, where the sheer pressure of people trying to get in before the turnstiles closed broke down an exit gate. Two people died in the crush, 47 people were taken to hospital and hundreds more were treated for minor injuries. Once again, the signs were there, but they weren't heeded. Sunderland lost the second replay 5-1.

Sunderland were relegated in 1970 and, the following year, Ray married Barbara. The newlyweds rented a flat in Gateshead while Ray did his teaching practice at the Royal Grammar School in Newcastle. He then got a job teaching chemistry at Lord Lawson of Beamish School, Birtley, Chester-le-Street, where the kids' football allegiances were split evenly between Sunderland and Newcastle.

Under manager Alan Brown, Sunderland finished the 1971/72 season in an encouraging fifth place and, during the summer of 1972, there was optimism around the club and among the supporters. As the Sunderland fans made the short journey down the A19 to Middlesbrough, in brilliant sunshine, for the first game of the 1972/73 season, there was talk that they might be able to make a push for promotion.

Stewarding one of the coaches making its way to Ayresome Park is George Forster. Sunderland through and through, George is one of those people who comprise the backbone of any club's grass roots support. Seven years earlier, in June 1965, the club's first ever supporters' association had been founded with the backing of the football club. At first, it was something of a closed shop, with the committee consisting of 12 successful businessmen from the town, who were effectively hand-picked.

But, after pulling off a modest business deal, which involved the sale of two boxes of a 'gross' of pens at his workplace, George was approached by the committee chairman on the way to an away game and invited to join. In doing so, he became the first 'working-class' man to join the committee.

'I was given the title of sales manager,' recalls George. 'The association ran a shop, transport to away games and a social club, the Black Cat Club. In 1966 the World Cup came along and some games were held at Roker Park. We did very well selling items to the Italians and the Russians. Most of the profits we made went to the football club to purchase items for the ground staff.'

George never missed a single game. He can still remember, as an 11-year-old, the elation he felt when the FA Cup came home to Sunderland in 1937. Apart from that and the promotion to the First Division in 1964, the good times were few and far between.

There was no joy at Ayresome Park either. Despite a goal by local lad John Lathan, the side went down 2-1. Results improved briefly, but during autumn 1972 the side slumped completely and hit rock bottom, with a 5-1 drubbing at Oxford. This was the start of a nine-match winless run and, after the seventh game of that run, a home draw with Hull City, manager Alan Brown was axed.

Ray Leonard remembers, 'Suddenly, we were in danger of dropping into the relegation zone, so Alan Brown had to go. He had been in charge when we were relegated in 1958 and I can recall the Newcastle fans in late 1972 singing, 'You're going down again, with Alan Brown again' to the tune of "Those Were The Days".'

In Brown's place comes a man who will earn himself a place in footballing folklore. Step forward Bob Stokoe. Ray says, 'There was a bit of scepticism at first. First of all he was a former Magpie and no one really knew what to expect.'

Stokoe's first match ends in a 1-0 defeat to Bristol City and this is followed by the depressing Burnley game. Then, something extraordinary happens. Whether it is the Stokoe effect or not, the team stop losing. A 3-2 win at Portsmouth is quickly followed by a goalless draw with Preston and then a 4-0 thumping of Brighton.

Stokoe seems to have stopped the rot. League form is picking up. The FA Cup, when it comes, is suddenly almost a distraction, and a third-round trip to Meadow Lane, home of Notts County, on the first Saturday of January 1973, is one for the die-hards only.

In many ways, 1973 was the grimmest year in what history largely views as a grim decade. Food and energy shortages, dire industrial relations, spiralling inflation and grey clouds have all come to define this year. At the start of the year, the papers are full of stories about stark rises in the cost of living. Beef up to 74p a pound, mince up 3p to 42p a pound, cod fillets up 2p a pound and, shock horror, the tabloid press warns housewives (just housewives, by the way) that the 5p egg is on its way.

In football, a debate is raging about why attendances are plummeting. Three factors are being blamed: too many games, too much television coverage and hooliganism. A flu epidemic is sweeping the country and causes the cancellation of four English games.

Among all the gloom, a few hundred Sunderland fans gather on Dundas Street, just a stone's throw away from Roker Park, waiting to board the coaches that will take them to Nottingham to begin their team's cup campaign. None of them could possibly imagine in their wildest dreams that they were embarking on an extraordinary journey which will stun and delight the footballing world.

Jeanette Coyle and her father are among the fans travelling to County by car. Jeanette says, 'By this time dad had got a season ticket, so was eligible for cup tickets. The players were always very generous with any complimentary tickets that were going, so I could also go to away matches with dad and we always filled any spare seats with youth or reserve players who wanted to go. Mam would make us breakfast and then off we'd all go.'

The Sunderland team that sprints out at Meadow Lane is, of course, familiar to their followers but players like Billy

Hughes, Bobby Kerr and Ian Porterfield are barely known outside Wearside. That is also going to change in spectacular fashion. Yet Sunderland are woeful in the first half and trail at the interval to a goal from the Magpies' front-man Les Bradd. Unless they improve, they are going out at the first attempt.

A rollicking from Stokoe sees an improvement in the second half and a late equaliser from Dave Watson keeps them in the cup. 'We were very, very lucky to come away with a draw,' recalls Jeanette.

Just over 30,000 are at Roker Park on Monday to see the replay when Jeanette is back on tea-making duty in the players' lounge. 'I managed to see most of the replay,' she says. 'They used to let me stand at the back of the press box and I'd come back into the lounge shortly before half-time to brew the tea. We played much better this time and goals from Dave Watson and Dennis Tueart secured a 2-0 victory.'

Slowly but surely, the team are starting to climb the league. Stokoe gives the players freedom to express themselves and the team respond by playing more positive football. A draw at Swindon is followed by a comfortable 2-0 home win over Millwall.

Next up in the cup is a home match against Reading. On paper it is an unspectacular tie but is rendered more significant by the fact that the Berkshire side are managed by Roker legend Charlie Hurley. 'He got a great welcome from the crowd when he came out,' remembers Jeanette. 'Everyone was singing "Charlie, Charlie". He was all smiles and really seemed to enjoy the moment. To this day he is still "The King" in Sunderland.'

A 1-1 draw with a goal by Dennis Tueart is followed by an excellent 3-1 victory for Sunderland in the replay at Elm Park, with goals from Watson, Tueart and the 'Little General', Bobby Kerr. For this game Stokoe had played Watson up front but now he has a new man to fill the number nine shirt – Vic Halom.

The win at Reading takes Sunderland into the last 16 and now comes the draw that looks likely to end their interest in the competition. They must travel to Maine Road to face Manchester City, who have just won 3-2 at Spurs to go eighth in the First Division. More importantly, City have disposed of cup favourites Liverpool in the fourth round and many people are backing them to lift the trophy. Ray Leonard still gets shivers down his spine when he remembers the game.

He, wife Barbara and a friend called Alan are among 10,000 Sunderland fans who make the trip to Manchester. 'The atmosphere in Maine Road that day was electric,' remembers Ray. 'City were all over us and could easily have been four up in the first half hour. The fact they only scored once was due to a combination of great goalkeeping by Jim Montgomery and a large slice of luck.'

With City 1-0 up, their usually faultless, giant goalkeeper Joe Corrigan inexplicably kicks the ball straight to the feet of flame-haired Sunderland midfielder Micky Horswill, who advances and smashes it back into the goal, sending the travelling Mackems into raptures. Ray says, 'My friend Alan later said he had never seen me so red in the face and he was afraid I was having a heart attack. From nowhere, we were back in the game.'

Then, unbelievably, Sunderland find themselves ahead after a mazy run and fantastic finish from Billy Hughes. Only a late equaliser, credited as a Montgomery own goal, saves City from a shock exit.

'We left the ground emotionally drained,' remembers Ray, 'but we were still in the cup. It was announced that tickets for the replay would go on sale next morning and, as we were staying in Lancashire, we were back at dawn, somewhat hungover, to queue up outside Maine Road.'

Sunderland supporters recently voted the Tuesday night replay as the greatest game ever seen at Roker Park. By all accounts it was an electrifying night. Ray and Barbara crammed themselves into the ground alongside more than 50,000 other supporters. And, quite simply, Sunderland were superb, with the opening goal a belter. Vic Halom scored with a brilliant diagonal screamer from the edge of the box which, straight as an arrow, rocketed into the roof of the net at the Fulwell End to send the home fans bonkers.

Ray says, 'I've never heard a noise like it. This was the famous "Roker Roar" at its loudest. I've tried to analyse the noise that comes out of my mouth at such moments. Do we shout "GOAL"? No, I think it's the word "YES!" and there's no greater feeling. We jumped up and down and hugged each other and total strangers.'

Soon after, Hughes, who is flourishing under Stokoe, scores a quality second goal from a similar angle to Halom. Francis Lee pulls one back for City, but Hughes secures a place in the quarter-finals with his close-range second, right in front of the packed Roker End.

It is a game that no Sunderland fan who was there will ever forget and is pivotal in the 1973 cup run. Jeanette Coyle remembers the drama as if it were yesterday. She says, 'The atmosphere was just amazing that night. We played brilliantly and were well-deserved winners. The crowd raised the roof.'

Ray says, 'We made our way through the traffic to Alan's girlfriend's house to enjoy the highlights on local TV with a beer or six. Halom's wonder goal will always be etched in my mind.'

Something is stirring in the north-east. The dramatic win over City has given the Sunderland faithful a taste of cup glory and they are hungry for more. But a quick glance at the clubs left in the cup does not bode well for further progress: Arsenal, Leeds, Derby, Chelsea, Wolves and Coventry from the First Division and Luton Town and Sunderland from the Second Division.

At this point, Sunderland are probably the seventh least likely side to win the cup. Now it really is about the luck of the draw. And when the sixth round draw is made at Lancaster Gate, Sunderland *do* get lucky. Luton at home. It is now game on.

Looking back, George Forster believes the win over Manchester City and the fortunate home draw against Luton was the turning point for Sunderland. He says, 'It was at this point that we started to dream and could almost see the famous Wembley towers.'

Interest in the club was growing by the day. Now the club shop, so sad and empty after the Burnley defeat in December, was getting busier and busier. George says, 'I remember around this time that the chairman of our London and South East branch, Ian Todd, showed us a Brentford FC scarf. We liked it, so instead of the traditional red and white bar scarf, which we'd had for many years, we created a new scarf, which had an inch of black woven into the white. It was a winner and we sold hundreds and also had the black incorporated into our bobble hats and other clothing items.'

As the Luton game approached, merchandise was flying off the shelves. Home wins against Middlesbrough and Oxford see the side continue its climb up the league. Winning is becoming a habit.

Away from football, things in the UK remain dire. Gas workers begin a nationwide strike over pay. Tens of thousands of car and engineering workers are laid off as the dispute paralyses factories. Embattled Prime Minister Edward Heath tells the gas men and the nation that the Government won't budge and that there will be no exceptions to the Government's pay ceiling. The nation is in turmoil.

But it is an ill wind that blows no good, as science teacher Ray Leonard recalls, 'Our school was heated by natural gas. I'd only been teaching for a few months, and now I had to endure an enforced three-week break away from my little batch of enquiring minds. YES! Tickets for the quarter-final match went on sale on a weekday, on what would have been a schoolday, and I could actually go down and get a couple. Thank you, gas men!'

Cup fever is growing on Wearside. Lapsed supporters are emerging from the proverbial woodwork. People who had never previously set foot in Roker Park start to swear their undying allegiance to the team in the famous red and white stripes. Everybody is getting caught up in the excitement. The old cup is working its magic again.

Jeanette remembers, 'Everybody was getting really excited now. We had started the season badly, but with the cup run came a winning formula, which transferred itself to the league. Suddenly we were winning every match.'

Club officials, sensing something special might be in the air, take the decision to issue various lettered and numbered vouchers to fans entering the turnstiles at the Luton game. It is not an ideal system by any stretch of the imagination. The official supporters' association, which usually spends time and energy drumming up new membership, now finds itself inundated with requests to join. It decides not to register any new members before the game.

And Luton, the club of choice of everyone's favourite comedian Eric Morecambe, still have to be dealt with. Though unquestionably the best possible draw for Sunderland, the Hatters are not a bad outfit and will win promotion to the First Division in just over a year's time.

They had won 2-0 at Sunderland's arch-rivals Newcastle in the previous round and have some decent players in John Aston, Jim Ryan and Barry Butlin. But they have sold their best player, Vic Halom – to Sunderland. By a quirk of fate, the Saturday before the sixth round tie Sunderland have to travel to Kenilworth Road for a league game, which the Hatters win 1-0, courtesy of a rare Don Shanks goal.

There are just over 53,000 in Roker Park for the quarter-final tie. Before the game, fans' favourite Jim Montgomery – Sunderland born and bred and a loyal one-club man – is presented with a gold watch for setting a club record of 453 appearances. That night, *Match of the Day* viewers watch a game in which Montgomery has virtually nothing to do thanks to a brilliant collective performance by Sunderland's back four of Malone, Guthrie, Pitt and Watson.

At the other end, Sunderland score two goals from corners, the first a header by Watson and the second a hooked shot by Guthrie, to earn a deserved 2-0 win. Unbelievably, they are in the semi-final of the FA Cup, where they will play Wolves, Arsenal or Leeds. Surely now, their number is up?

The reputations of Leeds and Arsenal go before them. Wolves are also an extremely strong side, good enough to finish fifth in the First Division that year. They boast a wonderful centre-forward in John Richards, who will score 35 times in all competitions this season, the feisty Ulsterman Derek Dougan, as well as Steve Kindon, David Wagstaffe and FA Cup perennial Jim McCalliog. Sunderland are, by some distance, the least likely team to lift the FA Cup.

It is Monday 19 March 1973. Britain is at loggerheads with, of all nations, Iceland, in a fishing dispute which is dubbed 'The Cod War'. An Icelandic gunboat fires the first live shots in the increasingly bitter row over fishing rights.

Slade are at the top of the charts with a brilliant barnstorming number called 'Cum on Feel The Noize', featuring a ball-breaking vocal performance by lead singer Noddy Holder. It is a superb pop song and the first single since the Beatles' 'Get Back' to enter the charts at number one. But all this is immaterial to Sunderland fans, who have their ears pressed against their radios straining to hear that lunchtime's semi-final draw. Out of the three other sides, it is Wolves they want.

It doesn't happen. Leeds, conquerors of Derby in the quarter-finals, will play the men from Molineux. The sigh of relief from Arsenal fans in North London can almost be heard in the north-east. It means their team will play Sunderland.

This is an Arsenal team who are pushing hard for the championship. They have recently won 2-0 on a mud bath away at champions-elect Liverpool. The core of the double team remains. If anything, on paper, they are even stronger with Alan Ball bolstering their ranks. The match will be played on Saturday 7 April, at Hillsborough. Arsenal are firm favourites. With Leeds expected to see off Wolves it is looking increasingly like a repeat of the 1972 FA Cup Final.

Ray Leonard was finding it increasingly difficult to concentrate while teaching chemistry lessons and remembers the almost surreal feeling that fans had after the semi-final draw was made.

'Surely we had no chance?' he says. 'But, then, at the same time, people were starting to believe in this team. Maybe, just maybe, we could get to Wembley for the first time in 36 years.'

As is their wont, fans begin looking for omens. Sunderland had won the FA Cup in 1937, so reverse the last two numbers and you get 1973. Ray has a 1937 *Sunderland Echo* FA Cup Final special, handed down to him from his granddad, and thinks it would be wonderful to put a 1973 one beside it.

Sunderland is now agog with cup fever. The media, previously only interested in Sunderland when seeking a story about industrial decline and economic bleakness, starts to become obsessed with the town. The players give endless interviews. During one radio interview, they bump into Rod Stewart, who takes a great interest in the side and becomes friendly with some of the players. Billy Hughes is given a special disc of 'Little Willy' by the band The Sweet. Then the team record a song called 'Sunderland All The Way' with local comedian Bobby Knoxall and some Sunderland schoolchildren. Players are given sponsored cars to drive. Suddenly everyone is interested in Messrs Kerr, Malone, Pitt, Horswill et al.

Despite their newly-found national fame, Jeanette remembers that the players retained their modesty and handled the attention impeccably. 'This was a completely new world for a set of Second Division, down-to-earth people,' she says. 'But I remember they embraced it and enjoyed the moment for what it was, while at the same time, remaining the same friendly lads in tune with the Sunderland fans. They were always accessible, not like the footballers of today. They were one of us.'

Two more league away wins at Preston and Fulham up the ante even more. The club decide that, for the home match against Carlisle on Tuesday 27 March, fans will be issued with vouchers, which will then go into a draw to see who will get tickets for the semi-final at Hillsborough. Thankfully George, Jeanette and Ray will all be there. Another 2-1 win keeps the momentum going.

And so to Hillsborough. It is pouring with rain. George Forster is in charge of one of the coaches that leaves Roker Park. What was a sprinkling of fans at the start of the cup run at Notts County has now turned into an army, which heads down the A1 in fine spirits. 'I remember stopping at a service station,' says George, 'and the atmosphere was simply incredible. I sold out of all the scarves and hats that I was able to carry.'

Jeanette and her dad arrive in Sheffield where the rain continues to fall and father and daughter are soaked by the time they arrive at Hillsborough, where they join the rest of the Sunderland fans on The Kop. 'The ground was lifting with the sound of the Sunderland supporters,' remembers Jeanette. 'We listened to a girls' piped band and laughed as some of the fans tried to join in.'

Ray Leonard wedges himself in with the Sunderland 'crazy guys' on the Kop who are in buoyant mood and, says Ray, singing this song:

'We are the Sunderland,
'The Sunderland boot boys,
'We are mental and we are mad,
'We are the loyalest football supporters the world has ever had.'

'The noise was awesome,' remembers George. 'We outnumbered the Arsenal fans and the atmosphere was electric.'

Arsenal come to the game in second place in the First Division, but have suffered a blip the previous Saturday when losing 1-0 at home to Derby County, only their second home defeat of the season. Sunderland's confidence is high with Hughes, Tueart and Halom all in good goalscoring form.

Sunderland, wearing all white, fly into the yellow-shirted Londoners, who are without their influential skipper Frank McLintock. In his place is Jeff Blockley, a £200,000 autumn signing from Coventry, yet to win over the North Bank. And it is a horrible error by Blockley which gifts Sunderland a goal after 20 minutes.

His underhit and miscued back-pass allows Halom to steal in and score right in front of the euphoric Sunderland fans. You would think Arsenal would storm back but they are woefully out of sorts and it is the Second Division side who continue to press with Halom a constant threat. At half-time they lead 1-0.

Then, just after the hour, the Arsenal defence fails to deal with a long throw, which is met by Billy Hughes, who loops a header over Bob Wilson and into the net. Hughes and Horswill dance a jig of joy in front of the Sunderland fans.

'And now the task for Arsenal is enormous!' cries commentator Brian Moore. They are not equal to it and can only manage a late consolation goal from Charlie George, the ball trickling across the line after a valiant effort by Montgomery to keep it out.

And, suddenly, it is all over. Astonishingly, wonderfully, Sunderland are going to Wembley. Every member of the team runs to Stokoe, who is rapidly becoming a cult figure. From the terraces comes a constant one word chant, 'Stokoe! Stokoe! Stokoe!'

On the Kop, the Sunderland fans are going absolutely bananas with many of them waving the specially commissioned new scarf. Jeanette can scarcely believe her eyes.

'We played brilliantly,' she says. 'Halom and Hughes ran rings around the Arsenal defence and they quickly became known as the "H Force". When the final whistle went Stokoe ran on to the pitch hugging the players and waving to the fans behind the goal. There were tears in his eyes as he turned back to leave the field.'

Commentating on *The Big Match*, Brian Moore can scarcely believe it either. He has a delighted, disbelieving tone. 'The side that has lived of late on the rising passions of north-east football has given the north-east what they so dearly wanted,' he says. 'The photographers in their hundreds are surrounding Bob Stokoe on that Sunderland bench. The man that has revitalised and transformed football in the north-east.'

Ray Leonard can't stop grinning and punching the air. 'We fully deserved our win,' he says, 'We wouldn't leave until our new "Messiah", Bob Stokoe, had come out to take a bow. He eventually took the salute and then headed back to the dressing room with tears running down his cheeks.'

When the Sunderland players eventually slump down in the dressing room, exhausted but delighted, they learn that at Wembley they will meet the most feared team in the land, Leeds United, who have beaten Wolves 1-0. They've no chance. But then again, they had no chance against Manchester City or Arsenal. It seems with this group of players and Bob Stokoe at the helm, anything is possible.

Now, quite simply, Wearside goes cup mad. Red and white adorns houses, shops, offices and pubs. Everywhere. Not just in Sunderland but all over the surrounding area too. Places like Seaham, Houghton-le-Spring, Hetton-le-Hole, Ryhope and Murton have never known anything like it. For nigh on a month, a single subject dominates conversation. Local businesses start reporting reduced absenteeism and sick levels attributing this to the positive influence the astonishing cup run has had on the town.

Tickets are like gold dust and, as ever, there is genuine resentment about how some bandwagon-jumpers get tickets while some fans of many years' loyal support miss out.

Vouchers are issued at the next two home games against Huddersfield and Portsmouth, which are both won.

Between them Ray and Barbara Leonard acquire four vouchers, but their names are not drawn out of the hat. And they are bitter. 'I know people who picked up a winning voucher attending what was their first match for years,' recalls Ray. 'Where were they last year when I was standing at Roker Park in the rain in an 8,000 crowd watching Portsmouth? One of these people had my ticket!'

Because of his position in the supporters' club, George Forster quickly becomes a magnet for people desperate to get the chance to go to Wembley. 'Tickets for the game were at an absolute premium,' he remembers. 'I was inundated with requests. I was lucky enough to get two tickets, one for me and one for my wife, as we were both season ticket holders.' But, all over the area, come tales of people missing out.

The town's excellent evening paper, the *Sunderland Echo*, launches a mini-campaign. Journalist Dave Bowman recalls that the paper did its best to ensure that tickets went to deserving causes. He says, 'As news of Wearside cup fever spread around the country via newspapers and quirky little TV features, some people who had acquired tickets via their county FA, referees' association or football club decided to forward them on to "real" Sunderland supporters who were finding the tickets impossible to buy.

'So a number of non-committed fans from around Britain asked the *Echo* to find a "good home" for the tickets – usually requesting that they went to, for example, a retired miner, deprived children or simply a lifelong fan who had been unable to get their hands on a ticket from the club's paltry allocation.

'We are not talking huge numbers here, but about ten to 15 tickets passed through the old *Echo* office adjacent to the Wear Bridge – and all of them went to the deserving fans the donors intended them to go to. Contacting the lucky recipients was like being the man from Littlewoods who rang to say you had won a fortune on the pools!'

Jeanette Coyle's dad, Bill, got a ticket due to his season ticket and, as a member of staff, Jeanette was given the chance to buy one. 'It cost £1,' she remembers, 'and I was also invited to travel to Wembley on the League Liner with other officials and members of staff. At the last minute, I was given two extra tickets allowing my two sisters, Trish and Fiona, to join us. My mam would watch it on telly with my nana.'

Aptly, Ray Leonard's unwavering support for many years will be rewarded. An old friend of his dad's knows someone who has been given a corporate ticket, but who has no interest in going. 'YES!' is Ray's considered response to this news. 'It was for the Leeds end,' he says, 'but we'd worry about that later.' Sadly, Barbara was to miss out on the great day.

So the build-up for the 1973 FA Cup Final begins. George Forster recalls it was a hectic time with the phone constantly ringing. One night, after a long day dealing with enquiry after enquiry from expectant, desperate fans, George sits at home deep in thought, looking out into his back garden. He is thinking of Clarke, of Lorimer, of Jones and Gray and whether Richie Pitt, Ron Guthrie, Dave Watson and Dick Malone can handle them. How can Mick Horswill and Bobby Kerr possibly cope with Billy Bremner and Johnny Giles? And will Halom, Hughes, Porterfield and Tueart get any change out of Madeley, Cherry, Reaney and Hunter?

As the sun sets, George is still looking out. He has convinced himself that his beloved team cannot and will not win the FA Cup. He just does not think it is possible. 'I simply could not see us doing anything at all against Leeds,' he says. 'They were a mighty squad – one of the best in the land. They were a team of internationals and we had none.' But, in time-honoured, some would say clichéd fashion, George was determined to enjoy the day.

The week before the final, Bobby Charlton plays his last game for Manchester United and everyone is lining up to pay tribute to him. His final appearance is at Stamford Bridge against Chelsea, a match the Londoners win 1-0. A Billy Hughes goal gives Sunderland a 1-0 win over Blackpool, after which the Sunderland squad sets off from Roker Park for Selsdon Park, Surrey, where they will be staying for the week, taking in a rather inconvenient away match at Orient on the Monday night. The squad are all dressed in new blue blazers and matching trousers with the blazers bearing the club badge on the breast pocket and the motif 'Wembley 1973'.

Leeds's only injury worry for the final is left-back Trevor Cherry, who is ordered to rest for three days after suffering concussion in the side's game against Southampton following a collision with Joe Kirkup. There is also an injury worry for Sunderland's Dennis Tueart who has to leave the field against Blackpool, but he thinks he will be okay.

Leeds are in a no-win situation. Everyone expects them to beat Sunderland handsomely, yet no one, apart from their own devotees, wants them to do so. Carole Parkhouse, our Leeds friend from 1970 and 1972, recalls this time clearly. She says, 'Everything had gone to plan and I had been looking forward to a re-run with Arsenal. Somehow, I knew Sunderland was going to be difficult and I had a bad feeling about it.

'We had a bad relationship with Sunderland, which went back many years and the whole country was against us and supporting them. But then I pulled myself together and remembered that we were talking about "Super" Leeds and, just because Arsenal had been dumb enough to lose to Sunderland, it didn't mean we should too.'

Wisely, Bob Stokoe fields a weakened side at Brisbane Road and gives starts to reserve goalkeeper Trevor Swinburne, left-back Joe Bolton, who wears the number 11 shirt, midfielder Mick McGiven and David Young, who scores in a 1-1 draw. Tueart is rested, as are two key men: Jim Montgomery and Ian Porterfield.

The town of Sunderland goes absolutely cup mad with red and white scarves, flags and ribbons everywhere. Workers at Hepworth's clothing factory decorate the shop floor, the canteen and rest areas with pictures and cards wishing the team well. Exiled fans have been making frantic arrangements to get home. George Green, based in Lima, Peru, flew in as soon as Sunderland beat Arsenal, but can't get a ticket. Brian Lipton and his son, Philip, arrive from their home near Vancouver in Canada – but they do have tickets for the match.

For 86-year-old John Hodgson, it will be the third time he has seen Sunderland in the FA Cup Final. He was among a record crowd of 120,081 at Crystal Palace in 1913 to see his beloved team lose to a 75th-minute goal by Aston Villa's right-half Tommy Barber, and then again in 1937 when goals from Bob Gurney, Raich Carter and Eddie Burbanks secured a 3-1 victory over Preston.

Wembley official Mr DMW Griffiths appeals to Sunderland fans with standing tickets to get to Wembley early and move to the front of the terracing.

Shops and businesses are getting in the mood. Popular sports shop Joseph's, in Union Street, is doing a roaring trade in Sunderland scarfs, hats, pennants and badges and Leeds and

Sunderland Subbuteo teams have also been selling like the proverbial hot cakes.

Sunderland Car Sales, based at the Barnes roundabout on the Durham Road, offers £100 to any player who scores a goal or saves a penalty against Leeds. Sunderland Shipbuilders goes one further and gives £100 to every squad member, with a promise of an additional £50 if they bring home the cup. The company says it is a 'thank you' to the team for bringing prestige to the region and providing such a morale boost to the firm's 9,000 employees.

The company has also taken over the town's Odeon cinema for a special big live showing of the match on a 30-foot screen. One of only two special machines in the country will relay the pictures to the cinema. The other machine will be used to beam pictures to a screen at the Top Rank Suite, where shipyard workers from Austin and Pickersgill will be watching the game.

For those who can't get to Wembley or a big screen, the priority is to watch the game on a colour TV. Companies like Tates, in Crowtree Road, are doing brisk business as people use the cup final as an opportunity to ditch the old black and white telly and buy or rent a colour set. People in Sunderland already with a colour set suddenly find their popularity soaring, as friends and neighbours clamour for a seat in their living room.

There is controversy when the landlord of the Forrester's Arms in Washington announces he is operating a 'no women' policy for a special screening of the final on the pub's colour television for 30 regulars. 'I want to repay them for their custom,' he says.

But what everybody wants, of course, is an actual match ticket. Thousands of devotees and Roker regulars can't get one, but will still travel to London to try to buy one at an inflated price. Supporters' club transport organiser John Tennick says at least 100 fans without tickets have booked on to official trains and coaches in the hope of landing one in the capital. 'They are dedicated supporters who will pay almost anything to see Sunderland's match of a lifetime,' he says.

Two days before the final, beaten semi-finalist Bill McGarry, boss of Wolves, stirs things up with an extraordinary attack on Leeds. He says, 'Don Revie can sort through his mail a hundred times on cup final morning and he won't find a "good luck" message from me. I want Bob Stokoe and his Sunderland side to win at Wembley – and I don't mind saying so.

'After Leeds beat us at Maine Road I deliberately avoided Don Revie. People expected me to do the polite thing and say "well done" to him. I couldn't. They are words that would have stuck in my throat. I was one of their greatest admirers. Not any more. They've changed. They are the "Great Untouchables". They like to dish it out, but they holler "murder" when they get a bit of stick back.'

It is an inflammatory article which spices things up nicely. Leeds, meanwhile, are saying all the right things. Interviewed by the national press, left-back Trevor Cherry says, 'If people think we're robots, I can assure them we aren't. And we're human enough to know that Sunderland might be Second Division but they are cup finalists and that means treating them as equals.'

But it would be foolish to suggest that Leeds – and the nation – are expecting anything less than a comprehensive victory for the men in white.

However, Britain loves an underdog and much of the media build-up focuses on Sunderland's fervent supporters. On the Thursday before the match, BBC1 screens a 30-minute documentary titled *Sunderland's Pride and Passion*, and includes interviews with the town's mayor, Cllr Leslie Watson, the town clerk Mr JJ Gardner, as well as Bob Stokoe and the players. Makers Peter Batty and Harold Williamson describe the programme as 'a splendid change from the usual unemployment or drift south story that seems to be Sunderland's lot on TV'.

The Sunderland squad make the trip up from their Surrey base to Wembley to inspect the pitch. A few express disappointment with the state of the famous turf but Stokoe says, 'The man who cannot knock a ball around here will never knock a ball around anywhere.' To which striker Billy Hughes adds, 'In this setting, even the greyhounds won't catch me.'

Thursday's *Daily Mirror* talks to some children of the players who will feature at Wembley. There is four-year-old Neil Reaney, son of Paul, Mick Jones's son, Mark, three, and Louise and David Guthrie, whose dad, Ron, will play at number three for Sunderland at Wembley.

But the last word goes to Ian Porterfield's little cherubs. Four-year-old Steve says, 'I'm going to watch Daddy on telly and wear my smashing new Sunderland scarf,' while his little sister, Caroline, says, 'I cried because Daddy went away to football. When he comes back he'll give me a bike for my birthday.'

It is Friday 4 May 1973 and, in the offices of the *Sunderland Echo*, sports desk sub-editor Dave Bowman sits, pencil in mouth, thinking up three different headlines to cover all eventualities the next day. It throws up some technical challenges for the newspaper, as Dave explains, 'What most people don't realise is that because of the archaic "hot metal" newspaper production system at the time, the main "white on black" line for the matchday *Echo* had to be sent to the composing room the day before.'

So Dave comes up with three headlines, starting with the one he thinks will, reluctantly, have to be used. He pens a simple 'HARD LUCK LADS!' Then, in the event of extra time, he comes up with 'EXTRA AGONY AT WEMBLEY'. Then, with a huge grin on his face, he crafts his final screamer, 'THEY'VE DONE IT!'

Just penning the line makes Dave, an ardent Sunderland fan, feel great. The three headlines are sent, each waiting to be slotted on to Saturday's front page. No one really expects the last headline to be needed though. It is a last-minute contingency.

As the great and highly-respected Bobby Moore writes in the *Daily Mirror*, 'The sight of Peter Lorimer saluting himself with that familiar two-handed clap above his head is something I'm sure Wembley will witness. Lorimer is one of football's most devastating strikers and just one reason why I feel Sunderland can't beat Leeds.'

The FA announces that Leeds will get the first choice of dressing room. And it is their fans who will be populating the tunnel end, meaning the first roar the Sunderland players hear will emanate from the throats of Yorkshiremen and women.

The annual battle for FA Cup Final viewing figures is in full swing. The hottest property in world sport at the moment is 17-year-old gymnast Olga Korbut who is visiting with the Soviet Union gymnastic team. Adored by the British public, she has been signed up to appear on *Cup Final Grandstand*. The BBC hopes her presence will help win the increasingly fierce ratings war between the corporation and ITV.

But ITV is hoping a couple of novelties of its own will draw in extra viewers. One of its young cameramen, Barry Morel, will spend eight hours – with just a 15-minute break during the wrestling – 150 feet above the ground, in a special *World of Sport* sky-high camera to give viewers a panoramic view of Wembley. ITV will also start its coverage 45 minutes before the BBC to try to capture viewers early and keep them, though it will be up against an early showing of a Laurel and Hardy show on the BBC. But ITV's trump card is a special camera on board the Sunderland team coach as it travels to Wembley from the team's hotel.

On BBC1 on Friday night, David Coleman interviews both managers. Also on the box are *Top of the Pops*, *Star Trek* and *The Good Old Days*. Over on ITV, viewers can tune in to *Hawaii Five-O*, *The Sky's The Limit* with Hughie Green and, at 10.30pm, *Who'll Win the Cup*, where Brian Moore, Jimmy Hill and a panel of experts try to predict tomorrow's outcome. Still, no one can foresee a Sunderland win.

And now the mighty exodus from the north-east to the capital begins, with Wearsiders in their thousands arriving by car, plane, coach and train. Twenty coaches leave Park Lane bus station just after midnight, forming part of the biggest fleet of coaches ever run by United Northern Companies. At the same time, 25 supporters' club coaches pull away from Dundas Street, just around the corner from Roker Park. George Forster and his wife are in charge of one of the coaches. 'It was a huge convoy,' he recalls, 'all bedecked in red and white streamers, team pictures and banners. My advice to the travelling supporters was to get their heads down as it would be a very tiring day.'

Fourteen special trains, carrying a total of 7,000 Sunderland fans, start to leave the town's station. The first arrives at London's King's Cross just after 3am and British Rail area manager James Carling says, 'To look at them, you would think Sunderland has already won the cup. I don't know what it will be like if they do. They'll just go mad.'

Another 20 coaches leave Park Lane at 6.30am to head to Wembley. The atmosphere is amazing. They are revelling in the role of underdog and there is a massive cheer when they see a banner draped from one of the bridges over the A1, presumably by a Leeds fan, or maybe a cheeky Newcastle supporter, which reads, 'Can but try, Sunderland.'

Two Viscount charter planes, each carrying about 60 supporters, leave Newcastle airport and British Rail's special League Liner, carrying members of the supporters' association, including Jeanette Coyle, sets off from the station at 7.10am. The town has never known anything like it.

Just as the second fleet of coaches is leaving Sunderland, the first convoy is arriving in London at around 7am and the cafes around Waterloo station, where the coaches are parked, are already swamped with Sunderland fans.

In the Saturday morning papers, Leeds boss Don Revie responds to mounting criticism of the way his side play. 'If we are as bad as everyone says we are, we should be going to jail, not Wembley,' he counters. He also stresses that his side are not underestimating the threat Sunderland pose and says, 'It will be a very close game.'

Bob Stokoe says, 'Leeds are a great side – but not unbeatable. Nobody gave us a chance against Manchester City or Arsenal. The difference this time is that everyone wants us to win.'

It is true. Neutrals everywhere are rooting for the men in red, white and black. But no one thinks they will win.

Meanwhile Wembley officials say they are planning to wage 'all-out war' on ticket touts. 'Our aim is to smash the touts, they can feel safe nowhere,' says one, as ticketless fans from both sides descend on the stadium. Privately, the police and officials fear outbreaks of violence if fans buy forgeries. 'We do not want a rough-house, and if people are conned by forged tickets, that is what could happen,' the unnamed official says.

It is late morning and the Coyle family – Bill and his three daughters, Jeanette, Trish and Fiona – arrive in the capital. 'It was drenched with rain,' remembers Jeanette, 'not unlike our last outing at Hillsborough. It seemed like the nation had taken us to their hearts and people were shouting and wishing us luck as we walked along. Though we were the underdogs we really felt this would be our day. We bought tea and ate the sandwiches mam had provided and started our walk up Wembley Way. I was wearing black trousers, a yellow jacket with black lapels and yellow platform shoes, which did not provide much protection from the rain!'

Ray and Barbara Leonard are staying with Ray's parents in Uxbridge, just a few stations from Wembley. While there, they watch the television build-up. Eddie Gray, who had given David Webb the run-around at Wembley three years earlier, is fully expected to make life difficult for Sunderland's wiry right-back Dick Malone. 'Dick was an entertainer,' says Ray, 'and had something of a cult following on Wearside, but he wasn't the most mobile of defenders.'

The Sunderland players are pictured in their hotel and seem unbelievably relaxed and jocular. Billy Hughes has a laughing box, they are cracking jokes and taking the mickey out of one another. Perhaps they are a bit *too* relaxed.

George and his wife visit some elderly relatives in Earls Court and then catch the Tube to Wembley. He says, 'We witnessed the huge crowds coming up Wembley Way, noisy, colourful and happy. There was no trouble.' In his mind's eye, George can still see both teams' coaches arriving at Wembley, followed by the coaches carrying their wives and relatives. The tension is growing. The rain continues to pour down.

Ray catches the Tube to Wembley and, overcoming his natural shyness, starts trying to exchange his Leeds end ticket for one in the right end. Within minutes he succeeds and enters the ground. 'The old Wembley was getting a bit decrepit, but it was still very impressive,' remembers Ray. 'There was plenty of room, and I enjoyed the pre-match entertainment, which included a gymnastics display by Olga Korbut, and a 10,000 metre race round the perimeter track featuring David Bedford going for some record or other.'

Jeanette recalls, 'As Wembley filled up the sight was amazing and it seemed there were twice as many Sunderland as Leeds supporters. We were, as ever, in fine voice. We were riding on the crest of a wave. Frankie Vaughan led the community singing and I feel we did him proud. Then came the hymn "Abide With Me". It was so emotional and difficult to get to the end. It made the hairs stand up on the back of your neck.'

George says, 'My wife and I had good seats, not too far from the centre of the main stand. It was almost a perfect view. It seemed as though our supporters outnumbered theirs and were much more vociferous.'

Two fans – Lawrence Wheatley and John Robinson – both of Silkworth, are attracting lots of attention with their two massive top hats with pictures of black cats, players and good luck messages. Every Sunderland fan seems to be smiling.

By comparison, the Leeds fans seem strangely subdued. Do they sense something is not quite right? Carole Parkhouse has travelled to Wembley in a minibus and remembers seeing an amazing home-made banner at Leicester Forest service station on the M1. It was a huge painting, depicting Billy Bremner on his team-mates' shoulders the previous year, holding the cup, with the wording, 'Hello, hello, we're back again!' 'It was magic,' says Carole, 'and I'd love to see it again.'

After wearing all black for the 1972 final, this time Carole has decided to push the boat out and invest in a new outfit which will get her noticed. She says, 'I bought a new pair of blue trousers – proper Oxford bags – a white top and a yellow jumper, the ones with short sleeves – very fashionable!'

Like the previous year, the Leeds fans are in the tunnel end again with Carole in the lower terracing, block C12. 'We thought this was our lucky end,' says Carole, wryly.

A TV reporter grabs Bob Stokoe for a quick word on the pitch. He is already fast becoming THE story of this FA Cup Final. There he stands in his trademark grey trilby hat and fawn overcoat. Gesturing behind him, to the hordes of Sunderland fans, he says, in his broadest Geordie accent, 'We've got some people up there who're gonna drive us on all afternoon. And we're going to take a lot of beating. We're going to die out there.'

On the BBC, John Motson gets a quick word with Dennis Tueart who, like the Sunderland fans, can't stop grinning. 'You seem very relaxed,' says Motson. 'Is there anything wrong with that?' says Tueart, happily. 'No, not at all,' replies Motty.

All over the UK people are settling down to watch the match with mates or family members. The roads and shops are noticeably quieter. The FA Cup Final is always special, but this one has caught the imagination more than most. Cans of beer are cracked open, packets of crisps demolished, biscuits devoured.

And finally the talking is over. Out come the teams headed by Revie and Stokoe. The former wearing his lucky blue suit, the latter breaking with tradition and eschewing the lounge suit traditionally favoured by cup final managers and emerging from the famous tunnel wearing a specially-commissioned bright red FA Cup Final tracksuit, which probably has some of the old duffers of the FA tutting with disapproval.

The two managers – who faced each other as players in the 1955 FA Cup Final, Revie for Manchester City and Stokoe for Newcastle – look pally and chat amiably as they enter the famous arena. Up in the stands the Sunderland fans still can't quite believe what they are witnessing.

Behind the managers are the captains, Billy Bremner and Bobby Kerr. And here is a corker for the stattos. At 5ft 4.5ins and 5ft 4ins respectively, they are the shortest opposing FA Cup Final skippers ever.

On ITV, commentator Brian Moore says, 'Sunderland are massive underdogs but Leeds know, despite what the forecasters might say, it won't be easy for them out there.'

As the players line up for the national anthem, all you can hear is a repeated low dirge of 'Sun-der-LUND, Sun-der-LUND'. On the terraces the camera pans in on a flag, which reads, 'Stokoe's Stars. Wembley 1973'.

Both sides are wearing tracksuit tops with their names on the back. The teams break and then Leeds, to the delight of their own fans, and the disdain of those from Sunderland, perform the now-familiar routine, where they form a line and slowly turn 360 degrees, waving to their supporters in the process.

This move appears to have an adverse affect as it sparks a mass rendition of 'Ha'way the lads', followed by 'The Blaydon Races', from the Sunderland fans. In response the Leeds fans give a spirited 'United [clap, clap, clap], United [clap, clap, clap]'. A banner carrying the popular slogan 'Norman bites yer legs' is seen for the first time.

Bremner looks deadly serious and gives the minimum amount of eye contact when he shakes hands with Kerr, who seems to have spent the last two weeks grinning and laughing. Referee Ken Burns, of Stourbridge, places the bright orange ball on the centre spot and, after what seems like weeks of hype, we are under way and immediately players of both sides start slipping on the greasy Wembley turf. The opening exchanges are cagey.

Then, with barely a minute played, the lanky, afro-haired Sunderland left-half, Richie Pitt, commits an atrocious foul on the classy Allan Clarke. Easily as bad as anything perpetrated at the infamous Chelsea–Leeds final of three years earlier, it would today probably result in an instant sending-off. But referee Burns shows leniency and just gives Pitt a ticking off and some finger-wagging. It is an important moment and even the Sunderland fans concede it was a particularly poor challenge.

Ray Leonard still remembers it, 'It was a "welcome to Wembley" tackle which would probably be a straight red card these days. The referee gave Leeds a free kick and Clarke was surprisingly subdued after that.'

George Forster recalls its significance too, 'It was a horrendous tackle which, in my opinion, completely changed the course of the game as, after it, Clarke seemed to keep well away from his usual position and hang about on the wing.'

Viewed many years later, Pitt's tackle doesn't look any better. Co-commentating with Brian Moore for ITV is Jimmy Hill, who says, 'This was a tackle for me, which, in any normal match, would have resulted in a name-take. It was really late, no question about it.'

The game goes on. Behind the goal, the Leeds fans are shuffling awkwardly. Carole Parkhouse says, 'Right from the start it just didn't feel right. After Allan Clarke was fouled and they got away with it, I thought to myself, "It's going to be one of those days." You know those feelings?'

Something is in the air. The Sunderland fans feel it, the Leeds fans feel it. At the *Sunderland Echo*'s printing works, reels of pink victory paper are already on the presses, which are ready to roll.

Back at Wembley, Pitt is unrepentant and follows up his vicious tackle with another foul on Clarke. Then Trevor Cherry slightly redresses the balance when he scythes down the skilful Billy Hughes. Leeds's forays are rare and when they do find some space, Watson is there to repel them.

As the game progresses, the Wearsiders grow in confidence, with Porterfield looking cool and composed in midfield. The men in red and white fashion a couple of half-chances too – Hughes is only denied by frantic covering from Cherry and Horswill goes close with a drive from 20 yards.

The rain continues to beat down. A TV camera pans in on Revie. He is sitting on the bench with a light blue towel wrapped tightly around his head. He looks like a shepherd in a junior school nativity play, or maybe the Virgin Mary before her visit from the Angel Gabriel. He seems suitably glum. Hunched up with David Harvey's tracksuit top over his knees for added warmth, this is not an image he will thank the cameraman for capturing.

The niggly challenges continue. This time Bremner fouls Porterfield, putting a hole in his sock. The two Scotsmen exchange words. 'He was hoping for a reaction from Porterfield, but it didn't work,' says George Forster. 'Many years later Ian told me that he patted Bremner on the head saying, "You won't win it that way, Billy."'

Sunderland are more than holding their own, but still nobody in the world can have predicted what was going to happen next. It is one of the most famous moments in FA Cup history.

A promising move by Sunderland ends disappointingly when Kerr over-hits a chip into the box. But, taking no chances with the wet ball, Harvey tips it over the bar for a corner that Hughes takes.

He hits it sweetly in a way that only quality players can. It is a deep, searching ball. Watson, Madeley and Bremner all go up for it and all miss it. Instead the ball travels through to Halom. It hits his thigh. He has mis-controlled and it is bouncing around in no-man's-land. Time seems to stand still. It falls to the left-pegged Porterfield, who controls the bouncing ball on his chest, swivels and from eight yards out, smashes it with his 'wrong' right foot into the roof of the net. He has kept it down beautifully. A nation gasps.

Porterfield's face is a picture. He looks around, almost as in disbelief, a massive smile across his face, head switching from left to right to make eye contact with one of his team-mates, as if to gauge their reaction and confirm that what he thinks has just happened *has* actually happened. Sure enough Guthrie hugs him tight, and Tueart and Horswill join the throng before the latter breaks free and leaps up and down, punching the air repeatedly.

The players' disbelief is mirrored on the terraces. Ray Leonard says, 'When that ball hit the net, just below where I was standing, I'll swear there was a moment of silence, a moment of stunned disbelief, before the ground erupted with the roar to end all roars. We all jumped around and shouted our heads off. We'd just seen Sunderland score in an FA Cup Final.'

'We just went beserk,' remembers George Forster. 'It was 31 minutes and 31 seconds, though most record books say 32 minutes. I just remember saying I wish it could be the last minute of the match because I just could not see us holding out. The tension was almost unbearable.'

'We were in a dream,' recalls Jeanette, 'the place just erupted. We couldn't believe it especially as "Porter" was a left-footed player and he scored with his right foot.'

Observing the Sunderland fans going doolally on the terraces, Brian Moore says, 'Just look at them. After all the thin years with so little success, how can you deny them an afternoon like this?' In the living rooms, pubs, clubs and cinemas of Wearside, chaos reigns as Sunderland followers dance, sing and whoop with joy.

At half-time Sunderland lead 1-0. One can only guess what is said by Revie to his team of stars. The teams emerge for the second half with the band passing them back down the tunnel, somewhat incongruously playing 'I'm Getting Married in the Morning'.

Leeds come out with all guns blazing. Now one of the best teams in Europe have the upper hand. The Wearsiders are clinging on. Then comes what is perhaps the defining incident of the match, and a moment almost as famous as Porterfield's goal.

With 65 minutes played, Leeds right-back Reaney floats a ball into the area. It eludes everyone. But ghosting in at the far post – Martin Peters style – is left-back Trevor Cherry who produces a fine diving header to Montgomery's left. The keeper saves well, but only succeeds in diverting the ball directly into the path of the man with the hardest shot in football, Peter Lorimer.

This is the inevitable moment which the watching millions knew would happen. Lorimer is five yards out, the goal is open. He goes for placement. It is a routine finish. But, in an act that has the nation rubbing its eyes in disbelief, Montgomery flings himself at the ball, gets both hands to it and, completing a miraculous double-save, somehow deflects it on to the underside of the crossbar. No one can quite comprehend what has just happened, least of all Brian Moore who virtually screams, 'And a goal! No! My goodness, I thought Lorimer had got that one.'

Cherry is still lying on the ground and, rather feebly it has to be said, tries to flick the ball back into the net with his studs. He fails and then starts to beat the ground with the palm of his hand in frustration when he realises that Leeds have not scored. It is a remarkable few seconds of true FA Cup Final drama.

Behind the goal, Ray Leonard is open-mouthed with amazement, 'My reaction to Montgomery's first save from Cherry's header was "Oh, great save. What bad luck that they've scored anyway" because the ball had rebounded straight to Lorimer, who had the hardest shot in football, and was only a few feet from the goal line.

'I was right in line with the shot, and I probably flinched as he hit it cleanly, and my mind had already registered the feeling of disappointed inevitability. Then it slowly sank in that he hadn't scored. Monty had sprung up from lying on the ground facing the other way, to twist around and get an arm to deflect the ball on to the bar, with Malone completing the clearance. People talk about Gordon Banks against Pele, but this was the best save of all time. Even Don Revie said so.'

Jeanette says that time stood still at this point and that, after this famous save, some Sunderland fans were forced to leave the stands because they could simply no longer stand the tension.

Still Leeds probe. Reaney and Cherry hurl themselves forward to add width to the assault. But it seems every cross and pass is intercepted by the imperious Watson, who is having the game of his life.

As the game enters the last ten minutes, the noise from the Sunderland fans is incessant and growing louder. 'These were not cheers at individual incidents,' explains Ray, 'but a general outpouring of emotion. Almost a loud wail as we willed the referee to blow his whistle.'

Jeanette says, 'I remember Dad shouting to the team to keep trying to play because we could score another goal.'

And Mr Coyle is almost proved right, because in the dying seconds Vic Halom bundles David Harvey and the ball, Nat Lofthouse-style, into the net. But a foul is given.

As the clock ticks down the old stadium resounds with the noise of the Sunderland fans giving an impressive, heartfelt rendition of 'You'll Never Walk Alone', combined with shrill whistles as they beg for the end of the game. The tension is palpable.

Then, suddenly, impossibly, referee Burns raises his whistle to his mouth, lifts his left arm skywards and blows for the end of the game. To the utter astonishment of everyone in the stadium and millions watching live on television Sunderland have won the FA Cup.

Barely has Burns finished blowing the whistle than Bob Stokoe is on to the pitch and suddenly he is off, bringing to mind an epic Grand National run just a month earlier. Stokoe is galloping like the eventual winner Red Rum, bearing down on the unfortunate Crisp on the home straight. Stokoe's fawn mac is flapping, belt waving, trilby balancing precariously on his head, arms outstretched.

'Where's he going?' cries Brian Moore. We soon find out. 'To Jimmy Montgomery. The goalkeeper whose punching and saving, saved the day for Sunderland.'

Montgomery and Stokoe embrace like long-lost brothers. Guthrie, Kerr and a fan join in. Kerr, looking like a cheeky schoolboy, and still grinning that grin, then removes Stokoe's trilby and puts it on his own head. 'The most surprising result that Wembley has probably seen in its 50 years of FA Cup Finals,' proclaims Moore.

The Sunderland fans are singing, dancing and embracing on the terraces. 'We could hardly believe what was happening,' says Jeanette. 'It was just like a fairytale, a dream come true. A man next to us was sobbing and dad had to tell him to pull himself together or he would miss the presentation.'

George Forster and his wife were also crying, 'The tears were streaming down my cheeks and I was almost choking with emotion,' he says.

Ray adds, 'We just hugged, shouted and shed tears.'

Back in Sunderland the party is starting. People are dancing in the streets, car horns are sounding, strangers hugging. No one has seen anything like it. The *Echo*'s presses start to roll. The printers and compositors are dancing jubilantly. Dave Bowman's 'THEY'VE DONE IT!' headline screams from thousands of copies of the special pink paper which races along the presses.

Soon, a triumphant fanfare of car horns starts in the town. As soon as Burns blew his whistle, doors throughout Wearside burst open and neighbours who were previously only on nodding terms dance together and sing in the streets like lifelong friends. Shop assistants – mostly girls and women – leave their counters to join the party and two long lines of them dance up and down in Market Square, cheered on by young lads from the first level of the shopping precinct.

Meanwhile, back at Wembley, Stokoe lifts up Bobby Kerr – his 'Little General' – while photographers clamour for a picture. Behind him the Sunderland thousands belt out the famous 'Ey-aye-addio, we've won the cup' number. And then, with millions of viewers still open-mouthed with shock, Kerr and his team begin climbing the famous steps to receive the cup from Her Royal Highness The Duchess of Kent. Kerr, sporting massive hair, a massive moustache and, of course, a massive grin, kisses the trophy and then raises it aloft.

Watching from the stand, Jeanette is in dreamland, 'When Bobby lifted that cup it was just an indescribable moment in time. To somehow make the day complete, the rain stopped and the sun came through. One for the history books that we were very privileged to be part of. We couldn't wait to ring mam.'

'After the "Little General" held the cup aloft,' says Ray, 'most people stayed on the terraces for a while, trying to take in what had happened.'

Spare a thought for Carole Parkhouse and the Leeds fans. 'I was devastated at the end,' says Carole. 'The players came round the pitch in a very despondent manner and I was crying, although I was really trying not to because, to be honest, I didn't think they deserved it. They hadn't played well.'

Anyone who has witnessed their team win a famous victory – though admittedly few will ever be lucky enough to experience what those Sunderland fans did in May 1973 – will know that the minutes after euphoria are weird, as the body and brain come to terms with what has happened and struggle to readjust to normality, such as the logistics of getting home, meeting up with friends and so on.

In a dreamlike reverie, Ray meets up with Barbara and his mum and dad at a pub near Wembley, where the light and bitter and Double Diamond is already flowing freely. Ray says, 'Barbara said watching the lads on TV had been like seeing her own children.'

The Sunderland fans dance and sing up Olympic Way. Some make their way back to King's Cross to begin a wonderful journey home, others head for central London.

Eyes wet with joy, George Forster and his wife leave the stadium and meet up with their friends from the London branch of the supporters' club and then go to a club in Harlesden. 'It was simply a night of joyous celebration,' says George. 'It was very late when they drove us back to Midland Road to board our coach home. We were drained after so much singing and celebrating and so most people settled down to sleep and we arrived back in Sunderland at about 6am on Sunday.'

Jeanette, meanwhile, has been rubbing shoulders with the stars. While the rest of her family caught the train back to Sunderland, she jumped into a taxi to celebrate the victory in style in London, guest, no less, of Billy Hughes and his wife Linda, at the winners' banquet at the plush Park Lane Hotel. Oh, and in the meantime, she telephoned Rod Stewart to share the good news with him.

'It's true!' she says. 'On the way back I stopped off at the Grosvenor Park hotel, where the team were staying overnight. While having a celebratory glass with Linda and Billy, we phoned Rod Stewart to tell him the good news. Thinking back, it's hard to believe I did that, but I did!'

The girl who began selling Bovril to football fans from a tea bar at Roker Park was now drinking champagne and chatting on the phone to a rock superstar. That is what happens when you win the FA Cup.

Jeanette remembers that evening with delight, 'Billy Hughes had his laughing box with him and that somehow set the tone for an evening of joy.' But there is one thing she recalls with a slight grimace, 'I have to confess that I wore a black and white dress to the Sunderland winners' banquet. I have never been allowed to forget that and I have never worn a black and white dress since!

'That evening was a fairytale. Champagne was flowing like there was no tomorrow. Brian Connolly, the lead singer from The Sweet was there and so were Alan Price and Georgie Fame. Suzi Quatro was performing too, and I remember she flounced off the stage in a huff because we wouldn't listen to her. We just wanted to dance and enjoy the moment.'

Wherever they were in the UK, or abroad, the Sunderland fans partied hard. Their team had pulled off one of the greatest FA Cup Final shocks of all time.

℘ ℘ ℘

The morning after the night before. There are sore heads and dry throats all over Wearside and a glorious, warm feeling of having achieved the impossible. Ray Leonard wakes with a smile and prepares to head back up north. He remembers,

'All the way up the motorway on that Sunday, there were red and white scarves fluttering from car windows. I couldn't wait to go into school on Monday. The Newcastle fans would be very quiet.'

While the delirious Sunderland fans flood back to Wearside, the players have to stay in London because, rather inconveniently, they must travel to South Wales for a league game against Cardiff on Monday evening. In the *Daily Mirror* there is a poignant picture of Billy Hughes bidding farewell to his wife Linda as they go their separate ways. So the wives and girlfriends head home, entrusted with the famous FA Cup itself. And, now, Jeanette Coyle will actually get her hands on it. She ensures it is in a position where any driver finding his or her self behind their coach, will see it.

'We put the cup on the back window of the coach and, as I was the only one with a scarf, we hung it between the handles. I still have that scarf and wear it to all the matches to this day,' she says.

Throughout football, Sunderland's glorious victory is greeted with delight and further enhances the FA Cup as the greatest domestic knockout competition in the world. For Leeds, it is more like a post-mortem. Writing in Monday's *Daily Mirror*, moustachioed columnist Frank McGhee is harshly critical of the performances of the usually outstanding Eddie Gray and Peter Lorimer. But, aptly, he finishes his article with the words, 'For me, the real stars of the day wore red and white – and despite how they gave everything, I don't mean the Sunderland players. The hordes who follow them, lift them and love them are the real reason I remember this game.'

On Monday night, at Ninian Park, Sunderland and Bob Stokoe receive a rapturous ovation from the Cardiff players and supporters. The Cardiff side form a guard of honour and applaud the Sunderland players on to the pitch, while Stokoe is clapped and cheered all the way to his seat in the dug-out. Sunderland's extraordinary victory has touched everyone in the game.

The team get a point at Cardiff thanks to Vic Halom equalising Bobby Woodruff's first-half goal in a result that ensures the Bluebirds' survival in the Second Division. For the Sunderland players it is not quite the end of the season but, as the team make the long journey back from Glamorgan to the north-east, it is light-the-cigar time. They know what awaits them.

Nobody quite knows how many people were there on the Tuesday to welcome the team back to Sunderland and the surrounding area. Jeanette simply recalls a sea of red and white gathered at Scotch Corner for the team coach to pass and start the 12-mile victory parade on the open-top bus. 'It started at Carrville,' says Jeanette, 'and it was just amazing.'

Up the Durham Road it went, Vine Place, Crowtree Road, Holmeside, Fawcett Street, North Bridge Street, Gladstone Street… At one local hospital, patients stood wrapped in blankets at windows to greet the triumphant players.

Alan Mitchell was a police officer on duty that day and in an ideal position to see at first-hand the incredible scenes. 'I was PC 1737 in Durham Constabulary and my daily duty was driving "panda cars" in the West area of Sunderland,' he says. 'However, for the homecoming event, I was put on a static foot position in Gladstone Street, next to rows of terraced houses, on the procession. The arrival time of the coach got more and more delayed due to the massive build-up of people and the crowds were very excited. My instructions were to remain at the location to ensure crowd safety but, as the coach passed, to then run alongside it until it reached Roker Park.

'I remember the excitement and atmosphere building as the coach approached and the noise of people cheering and applauding and waving at the bus. As the bus drew level and then passed me, I joined other officers and jogged alongside it until it got to Roker Park. I then went into the stadium to patrol the perimeter track while the team ran around the pitch parading the FA Cup to the crowds on the terraces.'

Bob Stokoe went on to the Roker Park pitch from where, his voice cracking with emotion, he told the fans, 'Royalty couldn't have got a reception like we got tonight.'

The following night, Sunderland lost 3-0 at home to already-promoted QPR and there was some crowd disorder, which needed the intervention of Stokoe. It is a minor stain on a quite magical period for football – and especially for Sunderland – when the true magic of the FA Cup which had, in previous seasons, seen amazing results at places like Colchester and Hereford, spread past the earlier rounds into the final at Wembley itself.

Jeanette remembers that it was simply an extraordinary time to be a Sunderland fan and the celebrations lasted well into the summer. 'The days after the final were incredible with parties galore,' she says, 'and celebrations which seemed to last for months.' It will take a long time but, eventually, the Sunderland fans would be able to put some perspective on the magical events of the first five months of 1973, otherwise that most depressing of years for the UK. For Jeanette, Ray and George, FA Cup victory was perfect and joyous reward for following the team all over the country during the previous seasons.

George is now 87 years old. He remains an active member of the Sunderland AFC Supporters' Association and is a highly popular and legendary figure on Wearside.

Dave Bowman, who wrote the 'THEY'VE DONE IT!' headline, is today editor of *Co-operative News*, the official journal of the UK Co-operative movement, and has worked as a sub-editor for many national newspapers since leaving the *Sunderland Echo*.

Three years after that epic match, Ray and Barbara Leonard flew to Canada to visit Barbara's mother, who had retired to a cabin on Kootenay Lake, in south-east British Columbia.

'We fell in love with the place,' says Ray. 'It took until 1986 to find out that Barbara could qualify for Canadian citizenship and we moved out then. We have a half-share in that same cabin and spend our summers there.'

Ray, a rookie teacher when Sunderland won the cup, taught chemistry in Prince Rupert on the north coast of British Columbia and was at the same school for 23 years. He is still Sunderland-mad. He says, 'I'm always up to watch or listen to the Sunderland games – the 3pm live games are on at 7am here. Barbara doesn't usually get up until half-time, but listens to the sound of my feet thumping on the sofa if we score.'

Ray is also a musician. 'I never tried to make it professionally, but am still active in several genres. A few years before emigrating I also took up running and I went on to run for Canada four times in the World 100km Challenge between 1997 and 2002. I've been back to the Stadium of Light for a few games. I have to say that, for all the changes that were made after the Hillsborough disaster – and many of them were overdue – the change to all-seater stadia took something away from the atmosphere of big games.

'Part of my heart will always be back on the Roker Park terraces, shouting myself hoarse and red in the face at a big cup tie. It's unlikely that we'll ever win the FA Cup again and even if we did, it could never be the same, because the big clubs now see the competition as an irritating diversion from their quest for European success and the big money.

'The fifth of May 1973 was the best day of my life and I feel very privileged to have been part of the Roker Roar that day.'

Looking back to those heady days, Jeanette says, 'It was a young team, many of whom had risen through the Sunderland ranks. They had a tough route to Wembley but, with great team spirit, they beat the mighty Leeds, whose players were all internationals. "Porter" and "Monty" were of course heroes on the day, but Dave Watson was superb throughout the whole cup run, not only in defence, but scoring some crucial goals that took us through the earlier rounds.'

For Jeanette, her team's stunning Wembley victory was the sweetest revenge possible for the hugely controversial events at Hull six years earlier. It was a case, perhaps, of what goes around, comes around.

Jeanette Coyle is now Jeanette Sutton and has lived in a leafy Birmingham suburb for the past 33 years with her husband Michael, a Spurs fan, and their two daughters, Amy and Gemma. 'The girls were brought up to follow Sunderland,' says Jeanette, 'and we have had some wonderful moments together following our team. Amy and Gemma are still great Sunderland supporters but due to their jobs [Amy is a doctor and Gemma a solicitor] cannot get to as many games now. I still get to the matches with my sisters and their children, who are all part of the red and white army, and I am secretary of the Heart of England branch of the supporters' association.'

May 1973 was a truly magical time for Jeanette and has provided glorious memories, which she treasures to this day. Memories sparked by her beloved football team and happy days spent with her father, Bill.

Bill died on 8 May 2011 and Jeanette says, 'It's difficult not to be able to hold those strong hands of my dad's or see his beautiful smile and talk over the match with him. My mam still sits in her chair and listens to the match on the radio but now puts my dad's photo on the coffee table beside her so he's part of the scene. I am still devoted to my beloved dad even in death and as my sister Fiona said, "However painful living with his loss is, the pain is far outweighed by living in the memory of his love – long may we serve his memory."'

Bill Coyle was a man who touched many people's lives. At his funeral, Jeanette read a tribute from close family friend Bernie Fagan who borrowed a verse from the great American essayist Ralph Waldo Emerson.

'To laugh often and love much; to win the respect of intelligent people and the affection of children; to earn the approbation of honest citizens and endure the betrayal of false friends…to find the best in others…to have played and laughed with enthusiasm and sung with exultation…to know even one life has breathed easier because you have lived…this is to have succeeded.'

He added, 'Billy was indeed a very successful man.'

'IT'S LIKE A RELIGION TO US'

Liverpool v Newcastle United

Saturday 4 May 1974

'YOU have to be a Geordie to understand what the cup means in these parts. It means glory, glamour, excitement and, above all, it is instant.' – Jackie Milburn.

'We went to Wembley Stadium. Was on the fourth of May.

'Nineteen hundred and seventy four on a lovely summer's day.

'We taught the Scousers how to sing, we taught them how to sup.

'The only thing we didn't dooooooooooooo,

'Was win the f***ing cup!' – To the tune of 'The Blaydon Races', unknown singer in a pub in Shakespeare Street, Newcastle city centre, summer 2003.

In 1974 Derek Thornton was, to all intents and purposes, a completely normal 12-year-old lad growing up in strike-torn, inflation-ridden Britain. His hobbies were playing Top Trumps, Subbuteo and collecting FKS soccer stars stickers. His favourite bands were Slade and Wizzard and he watched *Thunderbirds*, *On the Buses* and *Crackerjack*. He occasionally made Airfix models and, like a lot of the lads at his school, wore a luminous watch.

But young Derek also possessed an odd character trait, one his family despaired of. If he was told about a big event in advance then, as sure as night follows day, Derek would get so worked up that he became ill. The bigger the event, the more ill Derek became. Derek lapsing into sudden bouts of sickness ruined more special occasions than the Thornton family care to remember. Birthday parties, holidays and family gatherings would all get regularly thrown into turmoil by Derek's phantom maladies.

As Derek says, 'I had this terrible and greatly unwanted reputation in my family for ruining many a good day out. I never quite figured out how this happened but, believe me, it did, as my three older sisters never tired of telling me and indeed, one still takes great delight in telling me.'

However, the TV programmes, the bands, the hobbies and the games were a mere sideshow. The overwhelmingly, most important thing in Derek Thornton's young life was Newcastle United Football Club and they had an absolutely massive event coming up.

Derek, like his dad, was Newcastle through and through. In 1974, his bedroom walls were plastered with pictures of Malcolm Macdonald, John Tudor, Willie McFaul and Terry McDermott. He had grown up with tales of Jackie Milburn, Jimmy Scoular and the Chilean, George Robledo. Slowly, but surely, he was beginning to understand what it meant to follow Newcastle United and 1974 would prove to be the defining year in a lifetime of supporting this unique football team.

Four decades on, Derek says, 'I experienced Newcastle's 1974 cup run as only a 12-year-old, starry-eyed schoolboy could. My memories of each and every game are etched clearly in my mind.'

Mike Paxton, meanwhile, is a few years older than Derek. In 1974, he was a student in Leeds, and today remembers that May not so much for the events at Wembley – indeed many

Toon fans pressed the 'delete' button on them long ago – but for an extraordinary incident involving a London taxi on cup final night, which we will come to later.

Few clubs are as closely associated with the FA Cup as Newcastle United. Theirs is a special relationship, based largely on a superb run of success in the early 1950s when they became the first club in the 20th century to win the cup twice in succession, triumphing in 1951 and 1952, and then again in 1955, when they beat Manchester City 3-1 with a goal by Milburn after 45 seconds. This was their sixth cup win in ten attempts and had earned them a deserved reputation as *the* cup team in the latter part of the century.

Many young Newcastle fans growing up in the 1950s and 60s were acutely aware of this tradition, frequently regaled with tales of cup glory by mums, dads and grandparents and – as though by osmosis – inculcated with the pride and passion of a club which, even to outsiders, has always been more than just one part of the great north-east city. In many ways it quite simply defines it.

Mike Paxton was part of this generation. Born in Newcastle General in September 1953, he spent the first few years of his life in the Northumberland village of Seahouses, which he describes wryly as 'the Blackpool of north Northumberland'.

He says, 'My mother was from Bedlington and my granddad was a miner and a big football fan. His favourite goal was Jackie's first-minute opener at Wembley in 1955; only he missed it, because he'd bent down to light his pipe! He was a bit special because he is the only person I have heard of who had a season ticket for both Newcastle and Sunderland. He went alternate weeks.'

This granddad first took Mike, aged eight, to St James' Park on Boxing Day 1961 to see the side lose 4-3 to Middlesbrough. Mike still has some memories of St James' Park in the 1960s. He says, 'I remember a 5-0 win over Northampton in December 1964 and sitting on the cinder track at the Gallowgate End, watching big Wyn Davies smacking the bar a couple of times for

Bolton in April 1965. There were 60,000 in that day. I remember once getting in the ground at 12.30pm for a 3pm kick-off – they are spoiled these days.'

The cup victories of the 1950s created an expectation on Tyneside which has, probably, been the proverbial albatross ever since. Cup success never translated to the league and Newcastle were relegated in 1960/61, returning to the top flight as Second Division champions in 1964/65. But they continued to tread water.

Terry Paddison, a regular during this period, says despite the mediocre league form, there was already an expectation – almost a demand – from the fans that the team should be winning trophies on a reasonably regular basis.

They avoided relegation by one place in 1966/67. Next, something remarkable happened. The team improved and finished a creditable tenth in the league in 1967/68 and then, through an extraordinary set of circumstances and UEFA's ludicrous, outdated rules, qualified for the Inter-Cities Fairs Cup.

The competition was designed to be contested by teams hailing from European cities which had held trade fairs, but the complex qualifying criteria saw Newcastle slip in the back door in the fourth English qualifying place. But this massive slice of luck coincided with a team beginning to gel, as Terry explains, 'By now, we had a really good team. It was a solid, settled defence comprising Willie McFaul, David Craig, Ollie Burton and Bobby Moncur. A hard-working midfield with the likes of Tommy Gibb, Per Arentoft and Jackie Simpson and two great strikers in the shape of Wyn Davies and Bryan "Pop" Robson.'

The men in black and white grasped the opportunity with both hands and brushed aside Feyenoord, Sporting Lisbon, Real Zaragoza, Vitoria Setubal and then, in a notorious semi-final marred by crowd violence, Rangers, on their way to the final. They then completed an unexpected triumph by beating Ujpest Dozsa 6-2 over two legs to lift the trophy.

Once again, like those 1950s FA Cup wins, it looked like being the springboard for domestic honours, which the fans demanded. And, once again, it didn't happen. Terry says, 'In the early 1970s we did okay, always knocking on the door without really doing anything.' But manager Joe Harvey had at least brought some pride back to the club as Terry recalls, 'The man was a legend. He is the kind of person we would cry out for in later years. Someone to come in, drop anchor, and stabilise the club.'

Apart from Leeds, the only other club that resented Sunderland winning the 1973 FA Cup were Newcastle and, by the time 1973/74 started, Newcastle fans were desperate for some fresh glory of their own to stop the crowing of the Sunderland supporters. The players responded and Newcastle began the league campaign brilliantly.

Despite injuries to key players like Malcolm Macdonald, Tony Green, John Tudor and Irving Nattrass, by early November, the Magpies were second in the league. The only side doing better than them were Leeds, who were looking pretty much invincible. 'It's a great feeling,' said manager Harvey at the time. 'The trick is to stay there, but at least we don't have to worry about relegation.'

Newcastle season ticket holder Andy Griffin remembers, 'We laughed at the time, but three months later I think we'd only won two more games and relegation had become a definite possibility.' No such worries for Liverpool, who were a team on the cusp of becoming one of the most successful sides of the 20th century, ready to assume Leeds's crown. Spearheaded by the prolific strike partnership of Kevin Keegan and John Toshack, the goalkeeping excellence of Ray Clemence, the all-action dynamism of Emlyn Hughes and a rock-solid, largely settled defence consisting of Chris Lawler, Alec Lindsay, Tommy Smith and Larry Lloyd, they claimed the 1972/73 championship from Arsenal by three points.

Seven of the men who lost the 1971 FA Cup Final were still in the team and desperately wanted to lift the trophy to exorcise those ghosts.

So did their hordes of fans. Chris Wood, who was devastated after losing at Wembley in 1971, says, 'Just as players who have been on the losing side in a cup final talk in post-match interviews about their determination to go back as soon as possible and win, so do supporters.'

In December 1973 Liverpool had the First Division championship trophy proudly displayed in the Anfield boardroom cabinet. They looked like surrendering it to Leeds, so they desperately wanted the FA Cup there to replace it.

When the draw for the third round is made and Newcastle are drawn against Isthmian League side Hendon, there is probably not a single Toon fan who doesn't think back to the shocking events at Hereford two years earlier. Surely, there can be no repeat of the Edgar Street horror show, can there? Liverpool get handed what looks like a breeze. Doncaster Rovers, bottom of the Fourth Division, must go to Anfield. They have no chance. Doncaster fans spend Christmas 1973 wondering how their side can avoid a massacre. The ties are played on Saturday 5 January.

The UK is still in a mess. MPs are called back early from their Christmas holidays to debate the industrial crisis, which is engulfing the country. Every which way you look there are problems. Another miners' strike is looming over pay; there is deadlock in a rail dispute, which is causing massive disruption to services; and the Government is failing to meet its target figure for saving electricity, despite the imposition of a three-day week. With Edward Heath's Conservative Government punch drunk and reeling on the ropes, there is increased speculation that an early general election is on the cards.

Against this backdrop, the third round ties get under way, with a floodlight ban in place, to save fuel and send out a clear message to the public. At 6/1, Leeds are favourites to win the cup, Liverpool 7/1 and Newcastle 14/1, but many pundits believe Leicester and Everton are also in with a shout.

Hendon arrive at St James' Park and soon the Newcastle fans are again tearing their hair out in frustration. Their side struggle from the off. Though Pat Howard heads United in front five minutes from the break, the Isthmian League side fight back and equalise midway through the second period with a goal from Rodney Haider. After the game, Hendon boss Jimmy Quail is scathing of Newcastle's performance, saying their lack of physical effort was the reason his side were able to earn a draw – the sides will meet again at Watford in a Wednesday daytime kick-off.

Incredibly, Liverpool also fail to beat Doncaster, where there's more than a hint of *Billy's Boots* going on. Readers of *Scorcher and Score* know that Billy Dane becomes a footballing genius when he wears a pair of boots, which used to belong to a legendary striker called Jimmy 'Dead Shot' Keen.

Eighteen-year-old Rovers striker Brendan O'Callaghan also owns a pair of lucky boots – in fact Doncaster have never lost when he wears them. So, when he leaves them behind at his Doncaster lodgings, his landlady Gladys Norbury hops on a coach to Liverpool to deliver the lucky boots in person. It works. Doncaster play brilliantly and O'Callaghan scores in a 2-2 draw with Kevin Keegan – born at Armthorpe, just outside Doncaster – getting both Liverpool goals.

Now the energy crisis forces a new experiment – Sunday football. Four third-round ties – at Bolton, Bradford, Cambridge and Nottingham Forest – are played on Sunday, attracting more than 84,000 fans in total. This sparks calls for the Football League to stage league matches on Sundays. But the naturally conservative bigwigs of the game are cautious. League secretary Alan Hardaker says, 'I would want to see a lot more Sunday soccer in different parts of the country before I was convinced.'

Some 22,000 fans, including Chris Wood, cram into the normally sparse Belle Vue ground for the Tuesday visit of Liverpool. There is a brief stoppage when a dart is thrown from the crowd into the Doncaster goalmouth and then the home side tear into Liverpool, but goals from Steve Heighway and Peter Cormack knock the stuffing out of Rovers.

Meanwhile, a war of words breaks out between Newcastle boss Joe Harvey and midfielder Jimmy Smith as the post mortem into Saturday's dismal display against Hendon continues. Harvey says, 'Jimmy doesn't seem to want to play and I have no intention of playing him.'

Smith's form has nosedived since he was blamed for breaking the leg of Birmingham full-back Tony Want with a horror tackle in December. But Smith hits back and says, 'I always carry the can and I am sick of it. Whenever anything goes wrong the boss immediately drops me.'

Smith's case is hardly helped by Hendon's outspoken manager Quail, who adds his two pennorth, saying, 'I'm not really surprised Smith is out. He was one of several Newcastle men who didn't seem interested.'

The replay attracts 15,385 fans to Vicarage Road. Hendon play well but this time they are no match for United. Goals from Macdonald, Hibbitt, a McDermott penalty and John Tudor, earn a 4-0 victory for Newcastle and another winnable tie, at home to lowly Fourth Division side Scunthorpe United.

The energy crisis continues, the weather is still cold and a general election is looming. After being played constantly on the radio, Slade's 'Merry Xmas Everybody' is finally toppled from the top of the charts after a five-week reign. It's replaced by 'You Won't Find Another Fool Like Me' by the New Seekers, which is what Jimmy Smith could be forgiven for whistling to Joe Harvey.

The charts aren't great. Tight-trousered, bubble-permed falsetto Leo Sayer is right up there with 'The Show Must Go On'. Marie Osmond is also going for the top with the mawkish 'Paper Roses' and mean and moody Alvin Stardust is giving everyone the stare and a leather-gloved point with 'My Coo-Ca-Choo'. But look harder and there are a few decent numbers kicking around. Robert Knight's brilliant, northern soul-tinged 'Love on a Mountain Top' is heading for a top ten place, and Mott the Hoople's 'Roll Away the Stone' and Roxy Music's 'Street Life' bring some much-needed quality to the charts.

Round four is on Saturday 26 January. Now things are so bad that a two-day week is being considered. Energy supremo

Lord Carrington says that if the miners do carry out their threat to strike, coal supplies could become so scarce that electricity would have to be limited to essential services, such as hospitals and sewage disposal.

At least there is some light relief in the world. A charity Donkey Derby planned at Islington in North London is cancelled because of, wait for it, a shortage of donkeys. And in New Zealand, where the Commonwealth Games are currently taking place, two busty strippers brought in to pep up the nightlife in Christchurch have been given the cold shoulder. Only sailors from the Royal Yacht *Britannia* and a few team officials have visited the Pink Pussycat Club to see the charms of exotic dancers Black Pearl and Trixie. Striptease promoter Rainton Bastle admits he has made a 'big boob' in employing the two £105-a-week women.

At St James' Park, Scunthorpe play well and earn a deserved 1-1 draw but, four days later, the Newcastle fans make the trip down to the Old Show Ground and see their team secure a place in the last 16 for the first time in 13 years after a 3-0 win. Two goals from Malcolm Macdonald and an opener from Stewart Barrowclough are enough. After the game, a relieved Joe Harvey says, 'Now we have broken this 13-year jinx, I think we can go on to win at Wembley.'

Newcastle fans like Joe Blake, George Ackinlose and Alan Brabon are quietly starting to think this might be their year. But there are still some big names in the cup, including Leeds, who don't look like losing to anyone, in any competition. And first Newcastle have to get past West Bromwich Albion at The Hawthorns.

Fed up with the miners and their union flexing their muscles, Prime Minister Edward Heath announces a general election on 28 February, asking the electorate to decide who runs Britain – the Government or the miners? It is a risky strategy. Many members of the public growing accustomed to power cuts and fuel shortages would say the miners, obviously.

The car of the moment is the new Vauxhall Viva, which is leaving the showroom for £897. 'The right car, right now,' the ads say. 'Right when you buy it. Right when you drive it. Right when you sell it. 'If you want proof that a Viva is right for you, visit your Vauxhall dealer for a test drive. Right now.' Maybe a few Toon fans are driving Vivas when they travel to Staffordshire to meet West Bromwich Albion in round five.

And finally, those who travel are rewarded with a performance to be proud of. Even though West Brom have been playing well in the First Division they are blown away by United, who power to a brilliant 3-0 victory. The highlight of the match is a great display by Malcolm Macdonald, who scores one and makes another. He is having a terrific season.

Albion centre-half John Wile says afterwards, 'What a player. If you are two yards off him he has the speed and ability to use the space. If you stand on top of him, Newcastle knock the ball over your head.'

Macdonald's reputation is growing all the time. Some people think his ego is growing with it. Bearded goal-machine Bob Latchford has just left Birmingham for Everton for an eye-watering £350,000, prompting speculation as to how much would be needed to lure Macdonald away from the north-east.

In the first week of March, an old-fashioned 'moral panic' – the kind loved by sociologists and right-of-centre newspapers – sweeps the nation. Streaking – basically running naked in public places – becomes big news. Unfortunately the perpetrators are often skinny, bearded men protesting about something or other. But afterwards the only people protesting are innocent members of the public, forced to view the unedifying spectacle of Charles Manson lookalikes running nude at full pelt down crowded High Streets past Woolworths and Boots.

And now the shock of the FA Cup so far, which throws the competition wide open. After holding runaway First Division leaders Leeds to a draw at Ashton Gate, Bristol City do the unthinkable and win the replay 1-0 at fortress Elland Road. It is the result of the season. Liverpool, who have disposed of Carlisle and Ipswich, were all set to play Leeds but now have a preferable trip to the West Country.

And then Britain goes to the polls. Alas, it does nothing to alleviate the political chaos. Labour wins 301 seats, the Tories 297, meaning neither major party can command an overall majority. Edward Heath tells the Queen he will negotiate with Liberal leader Jeremy Thorpe to see if he can enlist his party's support.

While all this has been going on, Newcastle have been quietly preparing for their quarter-final tie v Second Division promotion-chasers Nottingham Forest. If the build-up was quiet, the match and its aftermath are explosive. It will be a controversial saga still talked about on Tyneside and Trentside to this day. Newcastle are hot favourites to progress to the semi-final for the first time since 1955 and their fans are packed into the ground, where the atmosphere is feverish and intimidating.

But Forest haven't read the script and, with 35 minutes to go, they lead 3-1. The Newcastle fans are at boiling point and, when referee Gordon Kew sends off United centre-half Pat Howard, it sparks mayhem. Hundreds of Newcastle fans storm from the terraces and charge the length of the pitch towards the Forest fans. Kew calls both sets of players off the pitch although, in truth, they haven't needed any prompting. Forest centre-forward Neil Martin says, 'It was like a cattle stampede. I've never been so frightened in my life.'

Play is delayed for eight minutes as police – heavily outnumbered – fight to restore order. Watching from the Gallowgate end, Keith Hudson says, 'The story goes that the beer bottles were flying and this bloke was dancing around trying to avoid getting hit. The bloke next to him says, "Divvent bother man – if ya name's on it, it'll get ye anyway." "Aye," the first guy replies, "trouble is my name's McEwan."'

Kew has a difficult decision to make. Should the game be restarted or abandoned? In the end, after lengthy consultations with police, he decides to restart it. The atmosphere in the ground is now more like an amphitheatre. The Forest players, perhaps understandably, are quaking. Newcastle come out like men possessed and, roared on by a frenzied crowd baying for blood, tear into Forest, who simply crumple.

Clearly disturbed by the invasion, they are caught like rabbits in the headlights and surrender their advantage. Terry McDermott converts a penalty, before a textbook diving header by John Tudor makes it 3-3 and then, when Bobby Moncur scores to make it 4-3, the roars around the ground could probably be heard at Roker Park.

Few there will ever forget the game. Andy Griffin was there and says, 'For sheer extremes of emotion, this game will never be improved upon. We Newcastle fans experienced supreme confidence at the outset, which turned very quickly to abject despair as the lower league opposition overran us. Then there was rage at the sending-off and revulsion at my fellow fans for the mayhem that followed.

'At that point, with the players in the dressing room, I was tempted to go home, but the ritual disappointment and humiliation is part of the masochistic tendency that comes with being a supporter of Newcastle United. I stayed, and three goals later we had won and the unforgettable high spirits that resulted were all the sweeter since they rose from the depths of despair. It might have happened yesterday as I can still vividly recall memories of that amazing fightback.'

Next day, millions of people watching *The Big Match* see for themselves the ugly scenes and hear the dramatic commentary from the sublime Hugh Johns. There is all-round condemnation in the media and the debate rages for days. Forest boss Allan Brown says, 'We want a fresh match. If the result is allowed to stand, it will be the biggest mockery football in this country has known.'

On Monday morning, 39 fans appear in court on charges of violent conduct and misbehaviour. One is accused of an attack on Forest centre-half Dave Serella who suffered a cut lip. Writing in Monday's *Daily Mirror*, Frank McGhee says, 'Newcastle should be slung out of the FA Cup semi-finals draw today and Nottingham Forest put in their place.'

Chelsea fan Steve Van Doorn with his son, Andrew, after winning the 1997 FA Cup. Steve attended the 1967 and 1970 FA Cup Finals with his older brother, Jeff.

Chelsea fan John Foley pictured with his Thai wife Ning and children Harry and Catherine Chelsea. John bunked school to attend the 1970 FA Cup Final replay and, back at school the next day, was caned for his trouble.

Derek Butt was originally a Manchester United fan but switched allegiance to win the heart of his future wife, Bernie, who was a dyed-in-the-wool Gooner.

Bernie and Derek Butt whose relationship flourished during Arsenal's never-to-be-forgotten double winning season of 1970-71.

The Double here we come. Young Gooners heading for Wembley before the 1971 FA Cup Final against Liverpool. Left to right: Steve King, Andrew Silver, Johnny Beslali and Dean Goodman.

Arsenal fan Dean Goodman pictured in 1969 when he was 15.

Dean Goodman today. Still living and breathing Arsenal.

A ticket for the 1971 FA Cup Final which saw Arsenal beat Liverpool 2-1 after extra time to clinch the league and cup double.

Phil Stubbs who has watched more than 2,000 Leeds games including his beloved side's 1972 FA Cup Final victory over Arsenal.

Leeds fanatic Carole Parkhouse with her partner Ashley. Carole was a 14-year-old schoolgirl at a convent school in Carshalton, Surrey when she attended the notorious 1970 FA Cup Final.

Lifelong Sunderland fan Jeanette Sutton (nee Coyle), second left, who attended the 1973 FA Cup Final, was delighted when she landed a job in the directors' lounge at Roker Park.

Jeanette Sutton, far left, has never lived down wearing a black and white dress to the function at the Park Lane Hotel after Sunderland's momentous 1973 FA Cup Final against Leeds. She is pictured with, centre, Sunderland's star midfielder Billy Hughes and his wife, Linda (second left). Jeanette says: 'Linda was wearing an Ossie Clark dress. I thought she looked super and, for all my infamous black and white dress, it went quite well with Linda's on the photos.'

Jeanette, aged 18, pictured in the players' lounge at Roker Park: 'It was more relaxed than the directors' lounge,' she says.

Sunderland-mad Bill Coyle and his daughter Jeanette Sutton pictured with the FA Cup at a memorial service for Bob Stokoe in May 2004: 'It was great to hold the Cup again after so long,' said Jeanette.

Bill and Jeanette at the Bob Stokoe memorial service in May 2004 where they represented Sunderland's Heart of England Supporters' Association.

Bill Coyle pictured with dog, Toby.

A statue of Bob Stokoe outside the Stadium of Light, celebrating his famous Wembley victory gallop.

PC Alan Mitchell, a Panda car driver in Sunderland in the early 1970s can remember the amazing scenes in the town (as was) after Cup Final victory.

George Forster, left, a legendary figure on Wearside and still chairman of the
Sunderland AFC Supporters' Association.

Young teacher and Sunderland fan Ray Leonard
proudly holding the FA Cup.

Ray Leonard and his wife,
Barbara. The couple moved to
British Columbia, Canada, in the
mid-1980s.

Ray Leonard pictured with legendary Sunderland goalkeeper Jim Montgomery, best-remembered for making THAT astonishing save to deny Leeds in the epic 1973 FA Cup Final.

1973 F.A.CUP WINNERS

GOLDEN JUBILEE OF
WEMBLEY STADIUM

SUNDERLAND

3p

F.A. CUP FINALISTS
WEMBLEY
5th MAY 1973

SUNDERLAND

SUNDERLAND A.F.C.
F.A. CUP FINAL 1973

Result
LEEDS UNITED 0 SUNDERLAND 1
(Ian Porterfield 32 mins.)

George W Forster (CHAIRMAN)

F.A. CUP

S.A.F.C.S.A.

Sunderland A.F.C.
Roker Park
Sunderland

A special First Day Cover produced to commemorate Sunderland's amazing win.

Sunderland fan, Ray Averre, 14, was pictured in the Sunderland Echo proudly displaying his cherished FA Cup Final ticket.

The Sunderland FA Cup squad recorded a special number called 'Sunderland All The Way' for the Final with local comedian Bobby Knoxall.

Liverpool fan Chris Wood, a veteran of the 1971, 1974 and 1977 FA Cup Finals pictured outside Anfield in May 1994, on the last day a match was played in front of the standing Kop.

Confusingly, this is not a West Ham fan celebrating the club's 1975 FA Cup win over Fulham, but Liverpool fan Chris Wood taking the opportunity to be photographed with the famous trophy.

Newcastle fan Frank Cozens leaving Bahrain on his quest to watch his beloved side in the 1974 FA Cup Final.

THE EMPIRE STADIUM, WEMBLEY

The Football Association
Challenge Cup
Competition

FINAL TIE

SAT., MAY 4, 1974
KICK-OFF 3 p.m.

TURNSTILES
B

ENTRANCE
30

ROW
29

SEAT
59

YOU ARE ADVISED TO TAKE UP
YOUR POSITION BY 2.30 p.m.

1. This ticket is not transferable.
2. This counterfoil must be retained
for at least 6 months.

CHAIRMAN
WEMBLEY STADIUM LTD

SOUTH TERRACE SEAT
£4.00

TO BE RETAINED   SEE PLAN AND CONDITIONS ON BACK

The precious ticket that Frank Cozens obtained just before the 1974 FA Cup Final kicked off. It all ended in tears for Frank and the legions of Toon fans who travelled to Wembley with such optimism.

Newcastle fan Ken Parkin travelled to the 1974 FA Cup Final on a coach from the Allerdene Estate in Gateshead. He is pictured, far right, outside Buckingham Palace on the morning of the match.

There's only one park that Newcastle fans travelling to London for the first time could be pictured in and that's St James's Park. Left to right, Kev Brown, Colin Parkin, Ken Parkin and, far right, Steve Williams wearing a butcher's coat which were popular in the 1970s.

Ken Parkin's bedroom bedecked with Newcastle colours ahead of the Cup Final.

Newcastle fan Geoff Buffey took great pride in decorating his Morris 1000 Traveller in readiness for the 1974 FA Cup Final.

West Ham fan Derek Hamersley who courageously fought cancer but died shortly before the 1975 FA Cup Final aged just 16.

Derek Hamersley, 1958-1975.

The Hamersley Hammers: Brothers, Peter and Derek, pictured at a wedding in 1969.

West Ham fan Peter Hamersley, who now lives in Australia. He writes so eloquently and touchingly about the brother he lost in 1975.

Fulham fan Mike Findley on the day he received his MBE. Mike, who was at the 1975 FA Cup Final, now suffers from Motor Neurone Disease (MND) and his charity, The Mike Findley MND Fund has, to date, raised more than £140,000.

Southampton fan Rob Innis, who now lives in Spain, looks back on Saints' terrific FA Cup Final triumph in 1976 and the following hot summer as a perfect time.

Southampton fan Peter Harris pictured with the great Denis Law. In 1976 Peter was a merchant seaman working on ships carrying oil from the Gulf back to Europe.

This prized ticket and its accompanying letter wishing fans an 'enjoyable outing' and a 'satisfactory result' was sent to Manchester United fans including Ian Brunton. It didn't work out like that for Ian and thousands of his fellow Reds.

The hottest ticket in town. A £2.50 standing ticket for the 1977 FA Cup Final.

In 1977, Ian Brunton received this rejection letter from Manchester United ahead of the epic Wembley showdown against arch-rivals Liverpool. Ian travelled down anyway in the hope of getting in.

A Liverpool v Manchester United FA Cup Final was deemed an aptly high-profile match between two of the game's most famous clubs during the Queen's Silver Jubilee Year.

Manchester United fan Mick Gorman who died from cancer in 2013: 'Manchester United lost one of their greatest supporters,' said his wife Rosemary.

The programme for the 1978 FA Cup Final between Arsenal and Ipswich Town.

Ipswich Town fan John Cross gets his picture taken with the FA Cup at Portman Road.

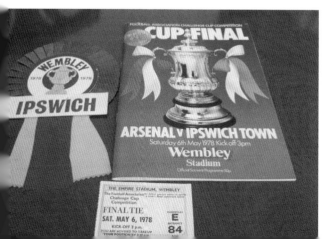

Ipswich fan John Cross paid £10 for a North Stand seat for the 1978 FA Cup Final. His ticket is pictured alongside a match programme and an Ipswich rosette.

Arsenal fan Emilio Zorlakki at last found Wembley joy after the dramatic 1979 FA Cup Final.

Arsenal fan Graham Stubbins. To this day he wonders if those amazing last five minutes of the 1979 FA Cup Final determined that he would devote a large part of his life to following the Gooners wherever they play.

Arsenal fan Gary Humphrey who can never forget the 1979 FA Cup Final.

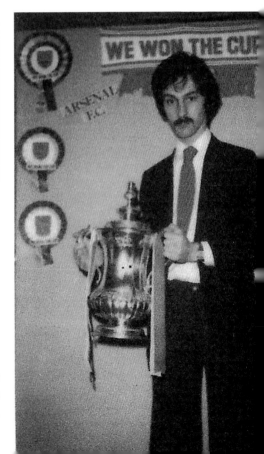

Arsenal fan Richard Davis with the Cup after Wembley glory in 1979.

The events at St James' Park are the talk of football. Everybody with even a passing interest in the game has an opinion. Some think the game should be simply replayed over 90 minutes at Newcastle. But there are many who feel the game should be replayed at a neutral venue with special preconditions. These are that Forest should start off with a 3-1 lead, Newcastle should have only ten men, and that the game should only last 33 minutes, because that was how long was left when the Geordie fans invaded. Newcastle argue that because Forest were prepared to restart the match and see it to a conclusion, the result should stand.

Eventually, a four-man FA commission decides to scrub the result at St James' Park and order a replay at neutral Goodison Park next Monday. FA secretary Ted Croker says, 'I think the decision has shown that we will not tolerate hooliganism. You can assume the committee felt the result was affected by the incidents and a dangerous precedent set.' Tyneside excepted, there is widespread approval for the decision.

The replay of the cup tie – rightly described as the most controversial of modern times – draws 40,685 fans to Goodison Park. Thirty police ring the pitch to ensure there is no encroachment. In the opening stages a four-foot metal rod and a bottle are thrown from the terraces but, thankfully, there is no repeat of the mayhem that marred the original match. The game ends goalless, but it was a great match.

The teams play for a third time three days later, again at Goodison Park. Still the controversy rages with Forest believing the game should be played at the City Ground, claiming it will be the third meeting between the sides but they are yet to play in front of their own fans. They have a point.

Finally, after nearly five hours, the saga is over. A 30th-minute goal from Macdonald is enough to take Newcastle through to the semi-final, but they have lost many friends and much goodwill in the process. It has also ignited an already fascinating competition, which, with Leeds out, is wide open.

But Liverpool look strong. They win 1-0 at Bristol City to book a place in the last four. After the match, City's captain

Ernie Hunt says, 'Liverpool are a better side than Leeds and they are the team anyone who wants to win the cup must beat.'

The Forest saga serves only to make football-mad Tyneside even more fervent. Demand for tickets for the semi-final at Hillsborough – where Newcastle will play Burnley – is huge. It will be a day still recalled with fondness by the thousands who were there. If the sixth round has shown a small proportion of Newcastle fans in a poor light, the semi demonstrates everything that is good about them.

For Derek Thornton, who travelled to Sheffield with his dad, the semi-final was a defining moment. 'It was at this point I realised just what travelling away to support Newcastle United was all about,' he says.

The open Kop end at the famous old ground is jam-packed with Geordies. To the millions watching on TV it is an extraordinary sight. Keith Hudson remembers a 'sea of black and white reaching up into the sky'. Mike Paxton adds, 'I think Hillsborough was the best moment for me – and thousands of other "Mags" of my generation – in my 50 years of support.'

After a slow start the team do the business, spearheaded by a clinical performance from Malcolm Macdonald who is again outstanding and scores two trademark goals in a 2-0 victory. The celebrations last long into the night. It has been 19 long years, but Newcastle are, at last, back at Wembley. And there they will meet Liverpool who, after a goalless draw at Old Trafford, beat Leicester 3-1 at Villa Park, including one of the goals of the season from Kevin Keegan, whose sublime finish following a delicious lob by Toshack leaves Peter Shilton with no chance. What a match is in prospect at Wembley.

Derek Thornton has been getting increasingly excited by Newcastle's cup run and, as yet, he has managed to stave off illness, although he swears he started to feel a bit odd after Supermac's second at Hillsborough. Even the prospect of *going* to Wembley gets Derek's pulse racing, his spine shivering and his head aching. But it doesn't really matter because Derek's dad has assured him that he won't be able to get tickets for the final, adding that it's a real shame because then Derek would *really* see what supporting a football club is all about.

But Derek is having none of it. 'I *had* to go,' he says. 'Hell, even though I was only 12 I'd have willingly walked down to London just to stand outside.' In actual fact, Derek has an inkling his dad might be kidding when he says he hasn't got tickets.

While his parents are downstairs watching *Nationwide*, Derek sneaks into their bedroom and quietly, yet efficiently, begins the hunt. It takes a good ten minutes of rummaging about in drawers, feeling under the bed and reaching up into cupboards before Derek finds what he is looking for. Two freshly-printed tickets to the 1974 FA Cup Final, one for him, one for his dad. He looks at them with a mixture of excitement, disbelief and awe. Then, suddenly, he starts to come over a bit strange.

He recalls, 'I found the tickets and then, almost immediately, I became ill – and I mean *really ill*. I was on my back in bed for the entire week leading up to the match, with the doctor identifying the problem as everything between a bad case of flu, bronchitis, tonsillitis, malaria etc.'

All over Tyneside, fans are desperate to get their hands on final tickets. The conversation is of nothing else. Ronnie Rutter, then 18, recalls queuing for 14 hours at Barrack Road to get his. Suffolk-based Geordie John Gateshill wins his in a draw organised through his FA-affiliated works team. George Ackinlose works at Drax power station in Selby, where just about everyone except him follows Leeds. George is the secretary of the power station's football team, which gets allocated a ticket by the FA. George's work-mates present it to him as the most worthy cause.

Liverpool fan Chris Wood secures one as a British Rail employee as the FA awards British Rail four tickets as a show of appreciation for transporting fans to and from Wembley on the day. But as Chris wryly says, 'Four tickets to one small department of British Rail, eh? No wonder people used to moan at the paltry allocation of tickets given to the finalists back then.'

Three days before the final a sensational soccer story breaks. Sir Alf Ramsey quits as England boss after 11 years at the helm. Ramsey, previously thought untouchable after steering England to World Cup glory eight years earlier, has been under increasing pressure following England's failure to qualify for this summer's tournament in West Germany. The FA is expected to look for a young manager with a 'tracksuit' image. Ipswich's Bobby Robson and Jackie Charlton of Middlesbrough are among the names being bandied around.

The Newcastle cup final squad travel south with the hopes of an entire city behind them. They arrive at their Surrey base. It is the same hotel used by Sunderland last year and has been recommended by Bob Stokoe, who is with the team, along with Jackie Milburn.

Through Wednesday and Thursday, with a smiling picture of Bobby Moncur looking down at him, 12-year-old Derek Thornton lies groaning in his bed, taking Disprin and milk of magnesia, while his loving mum keeps popping a thermometer in his mouth. He has a temperature and it doesn't look like he will be going to Wembley.

On Friday night, Derek hears the distinctive *It's a Knockout* theme tune come on the TV. It is the signal for him to flop out of bed in his paisley pyjamas and creep down to the bottom of the stairs from where he can hear his parents speaking in muffled tones. 'He's too ill to go,' says his mum to his dad. 'Aye, which means I canna go either,' says Mr Thornton. 'It's such a shame love,' says his wife, 'a reet shame.' 'Aye, we might have to wait years for another chance,' says Mr Thornton. 'Oh well.'

Derek hears the sadness in his father's voice as his words hang in the air. The moment has come. He says, 'At that point I burst through the door declaring that I'd never felt better in my whole life. I was raring to go and wouldn't miss the match for the world.'

Mr Thornton's face breaks into a broad grin and his wife simply bursts out laughing. Mr Thornton gets to his feet and goes to the sideboard. 'He reached in,' remembers Derek, 'and produced the match tickets, two brand new black and white scarves, two 1974 cup final rosettes and a black and white hat. Dad then issued the words "now get to bed and get some sleep or your mam won't let you go". Get some sleep? He had to be joking. Still, I was up them stairs and in to bed like lightning.'

Derek goes to sleep with a massive grin on his face and, just before falling into a deep slumber, hears his dad say to his mum that Derek will see for himself the true passion of the Newcastle fans. 'If he thought Hillsborough was special, this will be something else entirely,' says Mr Thornton.

Newcastle fans all over the globe have been caught up in the mayhem. Bahrain-based Frank Cozens has been watching the team's progress with growing excitement. He recalls, 'As we progressed through the rounds, I became convinced that we were going to win and that, come hell or high water, I would be there, even though my only prospect of obtaining a ticket would be from a tout.'

Frank books a late-night flight out of Bahrain on the Friday with a return on Sunday. He says, 'Friday is a day of rest in the Middle East and the normal practice for me was to spend the day at the British Club, eating, swimming and drinking, so it was a merry bunch that escorted me to the airport with me wearing my Newcastle shirt.'

Unbeknown to Frank, the flight's captain spots the famous black and white striped shirt and instructs check-in staff to upgrade him to first class. 'What a start,' says Frank. 'Despite me being pretty inebriated, the captain then spent half the flight talking to me about football in the first-class upper-deck lounge.'

Back on Tyneside the city is turning black and white. Supporter Joe Blake remembers going to great lengths to spell out Newcastle United with a letter per sheet of A4 paper, which he sticks to the bonnet of his dad's flashy Mark III Ford Cortina. The night before the game Joe stays at a friend's house in Cockfosters and then contrives to break his glasses. This is a problem. Joe's eyesight is so bad he makes Mr Magoo seem like a fighter pilot. Not what you want before a once-in-a-lifetime football match.

One man has dominated the build-up to the match. Malcolm Macdonald is idolised and revered on Tyneside. He is an old-fashioned goal machine, a worthy possessor of the famous Newcastle number nine shirt and in great form. He is also articulate, interesting and opinionated. The problem is, he can't keep his mouth shut and has a tendency to big up his own team and rubbish opponents.

Andy Griffin recalls how many Toon fans, though adoring him, wished he could put a sock in it occasionally. He says, 'He was never out of the tabloids and was quoted in the media saying how Liverpool were just a team of has-beens and that Newcastle would blow them away. Liverpool were only the reigning league champions and UEFA Cup champions and some of his comments were totally disrespectful.'

The Newcastle army is on the move. Mike Paxton's FA Cup Final adventure begins on Friday afternoon when he is picked up at Wetherby roundabout. With him are Gavin Turnbull, from Embleton, and three tough, hard-drinking fishermen from Boulmer, north Northumberland, called Ian McQueen and Albert and Main Stephenson. This lot are going to enjoy themselves. Wallets bulging with green pound notes, they are not just going for the football. They intend to drink some serious ale too.

Mike says, 'The fishermen had been going to the cup final for a few years and always met a guy in the same bar in Leicester Square and took him some fish and crabs.' Speaking of crabs, Mike decides the safest place for his cup final ticket is stuffed down the front of his super-fashionable blue Y-fronts. 'That way, anyone prepared to get my ticket would really get his or her money's worth,' he says.

The group arrives in London late on Friday afternoon. After handing over the fish and crabs and wetting their lips with four or five pints, the pals head for Trafalgar Square. There they find hundreds of Geordies milling around, draped on the base of Nelson's column or astride Landseer's famous lions.

Then, naturally, it was back up Charing Cross Road to Soho, currently at its seediest, where they get lucky. Mike remembers with a grin, 'We were in a pub and I went for a pee and there, neatly stacked around the back, were four or five crates of brown ale. Now, you can say what you like about Cockneys, but we thought it was a real nice gesture by the landlord to open what we presumed was a hospitality bar for the Geordies. It was a great night.'

The group, suitably lubricated, head back to their hotel in the small hours chanting 'Supermac' and drunkenly singing 'The Blaydon Races'.

Back in Newcastle, the mass exodus is under way. Ronnie Rutter, 18, spends cup final eve drinking with mates in the Stirling House pub in Bensham, in readiness to catch the midnight bus to London. Alan Brabon, 15, leaves Deneside Catholic Club in Jarrow at midnight and begins the long coach journey to London. Also travelling by coach is 19-year-old Keith Hudson and his little sister, Kath, 11.

Keith recalls, 'Kath had got a ticket at the last minute. So as not to be with the rowdy supporters, me mam insisted we went down overnight on the service bus and we arrived in London at about 7am.'

John Newton and three mates drive down on Friday and spend the evening in a pub car park. He says, 'We were woken up by a copper at 3am who wondered what the hell we were up to. We told him we were here to see the lads win the cup. He wished us well and left us alone, despite our insistence that he arrest the one whose feet absolutely stank!'

Dawn breaks on cup final day. Derek Thornton's mum enters her son's room and pops a thermometer in his mouth. Miraculously, her son's temperature has returned to normal. 'Get yourself dressed, pet,' says his mum, 'you're going to Wembley.' Derek leaps out of bed, gets kitted out in his black and white clobber and sprints downstairs, jumping the final four steps. He feels as fit as a fiddle. His dad assures him he will remember this day for the rest of his life. Father and son, clad head to foot in black and white, make their way to Newcastle

Central, which looks like a mobile zebra crossing with thousands of Toon fans milling around.

Derek's dad greets a fellow supporter, then says hello to a whole family. Then he shakes hands with another man and ruffles the head of the man's son. In fact, he seems to know everyone at the station. Derek looks quizzically at his father. Is he some sort of celebrity? Has he been hiding something from us? Young Derek comes to the conclusion he must know them all through work. But it's the same on the train.

Derek says, 'It amazed me. He talked to everyone, and everyone talked to him and me as well. All of them seemed to pat me on the head while uttering the same words, "Alreet there sonna, mind you're ganna hey one helluva day, mind. Ye'll remember thi day for the rest of ya life sonna".'

'Best fans in the world, these, sonna,' says Derek's dad, with a friendly wink, ruffling his hair.

The turquoise diesel engine pulls the blue and white inter-city carriages to the capital. In every coach there is at least one cassette recorder playing the team's tune 'Ha'way the Lads'. Everyone – literally everyone – is dressed in black and white. Long hair, flares, platform shoes, plastic bowler hats, smoking fags or pipes and sporting wispy moustaches. Newcastle have always attracted a large number of female supporters.

Two songs directly related to the two clubs and their respective cities are in the charts, 'Liverpool Lou' by Scaffold and Alan Price's 'Jarrow Song', with its memorable opening line, 'My name is Geordie McIntyre,' and chorus, 'Come on Follow the Geordie boys'. Both get plenty of airing on the day.

Back in Cockfosters, short-sighted Toon fan Joe Blake is feeling more like Joe 90 and, just like Gerry Anderson's nine-year-old 'Most Special Agent' Joe McClaine, desperately needs some special glasses. The biggest day in his football-supporting career looks like being ruined because he won't actually be able to see further than the end of his nose. He stumbles out of bed, squints unattractively and fumbles around trying to get his bearings. He needs some specs and fast.

He remembers, 'We headed down to Great Portland Street where there seemed to be a lot of opticians. They hunted out the back to see if they could find an old second-hand pair that would do for the day.' The optician eventually digs out an old pair. They are not exactly in the style of Dame Edna Everage but nor are they a pair Joe would have chosen. Still, beggars can't be choosers. But he is still embarrassed about them and decides not to wear them until he absolutely has to.

Fans are pouring into the capital. Some are at Wembley as early as 9am. There are hordes of people trying to buy tickets. One of them is John Archer, a 17-year-old Newcastle fan serving in the Royal Navy at Portsmouth. He has £30 in his pocket that he has saved since the semi-final. He spends hours frantically trying to buy a ticket from anyone willing to sell. Except no one is selling. It is that kind of occasion. Thousands of people are disappointed. Tony Mallon recalls one ticketless Toon fan heading back disconsolately to King's Cross, muttering, 'It's bin a lang way ti come for a ham sandwich.'

The scarcity of tickets causes plenty of anger and it's the touts who bear the brunt of the fans' frustrations – of both sides. John Doyle remembers a group of Newcastle and Liverpool fans joining forces to politely 'persuade' a tout to sell a couple of tickets at face value while a couple of policemen turn a blind eye.

London is awash with black and white and red. The distinctive accents and dialects of Tyneside and Merseyside are everywhere. All the talk is of Macdonald and Tudor, or Keegan and Toshack. Deep in the financial centre of the capital, members of the London branch of the Liverpool Supporters' Club are gathering at their regular haunt, The Three Lords, in the City of London, where the guv'nor has opened up early to enable the Reds to watch the pre-match build-up. They watch the teams being interviewed in their hotels and then being followed to Wembley.

Chris Wood says, 'I seem to remember Bill Shankly making a remark about Joe Harvey looking tired or worried, or something like that. Maybe Shanks really did sense that or perhaps he was using his well-known psychology to unsettle the Newcastle squad and their manager.'

Young Derek Thornton and his father have now arrived in London and head straight for a working men's club. They enter and it happens again. Derek's dad appears to know everyone. This is even more mystifying for Derek because many of these people speak with Cockney accents, which suggests to the young lad that his father's reputation has stretched even further than the north-east.

Once again, everybody is keen to ruffle Derek's hair and tell him that he'll remember this day for the rest of his life. But still Derek can't fathom out why his dad knows everyone. Is he famous? Has he been leading some sort of double-life? He just keeps telling Derek the Newcastle fans are 'special' and to take everything in. 'Because ye'll remember this day for the rest of your life, sonna,' he repeats like a mantra.

Finally Derek and his dad arrive at Wembley. For the wide-eyed 12-year-old, it is well worth the wait. He recalls, 'Jesus Christ man – what a sight! I loved it instantly – the twin towers, walking up Wembley Way – absolutely magical.' The youngster does his best to take it all in.

There is loads going on. A huge football match between Liverpool and Newcastle fans – it looks about 100-a-side. Newcastle fan Andrew Sanderson with a two-foot wide rosette, Geordies and Scousers sharing vodka, drinking from those ubiquitous plastic bowler hats, dozens of fans climbing up Wembley's back walls and getting into the stadium through holes in the top.

Fans are pouring through the turnstiles. Not all of them have tickets. They are helped, as usual, by a few 'bent' turnstile operators willing to take a back-hander. John Doyle says, 'A load of ticketless Newcastle fans bribed a gate man and then dozens of fans got in using the same couple of ticket stubs.'

The atmosphere is building. At 2pm there is a marching display by the Band of the Royal Marines. The banners are flying, 'Jesus Saves but Supermac gets the rebounds' is the one getting most laughs among the Toon fans.

Like 1971, the bulk of Liverpool's support is packed at the east end – the tunnel end – of the stadium. Chris Wood is among them and says, 'There seemed to be more spectators in the bay than was safe and there was a bit of a crush.'

It is 2.15pm. The pre-match entertainment has been getting increasingly off-the-wall and, once again, the FA doesn't disappoint. This time, in its wisdom, it has decided to put on a 3,000-metre race and gathers a decent field, including top distance runner and Geordie Brendan Foster who, at 26, is becoming a highly popular figure and the undoubted star of UK athletics, having just won silver in the 5,000 metres in the Commonwealth Games.

He is also a massive Newcastle United fan and his vest is, naturally, black and white. During the race, the Geordie fans will him on singing, 'Foster is a Geordie, Foster is a Geordie, la la la la. La la la la.' Some Liverpool fans are repeating the tune word for word. Except they swap 'Geordie' for an alternative word.

As Foster crosses the line in first place he whips off his top and throws it to the fans in true gladiatorial style to show his allegiance to the Toon, earning a huge ovation from the fans in black and white. But Foster's victory is the first and last time the Geordies will have anything to cheer about. 'What was to follow is still a painful memory,' says Andy Griffin.

Frank Cozens, tired and jet-lagged after his flight from Bahrain, is prowling around the outskirts of the stadium on the hunt for a ticket. But nobody has one. Surely he hasn't come all this way to watch the game on TV? He is getting desperate.

Twenty minutes to kick-off. David Coleman, with the trademark urgency suggesting he is reporting from Vietnam, not Wembley, announces to the millions watching on BBC TV that the community singing will be led by 'professional entertainer' Bruce Forsyth. Before anyone has a chance to properly digest this, Forsyth gallops on to the pitch, revelling in the spotlight. He is wearing a classic mid-1970s checked sports jacket and red corduroy trousers. His hair looks bushy and in need of a cut though, in fairness, viewed through jaundiced eyes, 40 years later, everyone in the stadium looks like their hair could do with a cut!

A raised podium has been placed on the pitch for Bruce to stand on and lead the singing and he heads towards it. So far, so good. Suddenly he is tossed a ball and then, to the delight of the crowd, he starts pegging it towards the Liverpool end, kicking it with surprising skill as he goes. Behind the mic, Coleman is giggling and chortling like a schoolboy.

Bruce gets near the goal and then half-connects with a right-footed shot which trickles along the ground before nestling in the bottom-left corner of the net. The Scousers are killing themselves. Suddenly they give a rousing rendition of 'Nice One Brucie, nice one son, nice one Brucie, let's have another one' (to the tune of 'Nice One Cyril').

Forsyth trots back and finally ascends the podium. He probably should have left the hi-jinks there, quit while he was ahead, and got on with the singing, but he is an attention-loving entertainer and can't.

Appearing to completely misjudge the make-up of a football crowd he yells, 'Anyone here from Liverpool?' There is a muffled grunt of assent from the Liverpool end. Turning to his right he then shouts, 'Anyone here from Newcastle?' A few embarrassed Geordies confirm that there are indeed a few present. He then calls out, 'Anyone here from Luton?' It's barely a gag at all really and is met with virtual silence and 100,000 people willing him to exit stage left, preferably pursued by a bear. Finally, the band strikes up 'Abide With Me'.

The sound of the famous old hymn is the signal for panic for those still outside hunting for a ticket. Frank Cozens – who has flown in especially from Bahrain remember – is one of them. It is now 2.50pm and he's standing on the junction of Empire Way and Stadium Way. His eyes are darting in every direction looking for a possible outlet. He is prepared to pay way over the odds.

Suddenly he spots two people emerging from a pub. Instinct tells him this could be the break he is looking for. Frank approaches them and lays it on thick, giving a real sob story about flying in from the Middle East, about how he has supported Newcastle all his life. His instincts prove right. There is a ticket going. With minutes to spare Frank offers £10, which is accepted. The fact it is in the Liverpool section doesn't matter. Frank is in by the skin of his teeth.

In the tunnel, the teams are waiting. Newcastle boss Joe Harvey towers above Bill Shankly, who has opted for a lurid cerise pink shirt. Harvey is wearing a suit that he has bought from Malcolm Macdonald's clothes boutique in Newcastle's Newgate precinct and is concerned that it might be too trendy for him. Out they come. Newcastle's cup final tracksuit tops are blue with a yellow trim. Newcastle goalkeeper McFaul guffaws at something and waves to someone in the crowd. It will be the last time he smiles for a few hours.

For Harvey, this is the proudest day of his managerial career, a day he has waited years for. He has freely admitted in the press that his life's ambition is being fulfilled. Skipper of the side in the glorious FA Cup wins of 1951 and 1952, coach in 1955, this is a natural progression.

He says, 'From the moment I got the manager's job 12 years ago, I have wanted to lead out a Newcastle team at Wembley.' He has also made a pledge to the fans, 'The north-east loves cup-fighting sides. Sunderland proved it last season. This time it is Newcastle's turn, and we are not going to let down our wonderful Geordie supporters. I want to hear "Blaydon Races" and "Ha'way the Lads" ring out as never before. If the Geordies win the vocal battle on the terraces, Newcastle will do their stuff on the field.' The fans will more than keep their side of the bargain. The players won't.

Twenty-four hours ago Derek Thornton was in bed with a thermometer in his mouth. Now he is at Wembley, opposite the Royal Box, watching his beloved team. He is now accustomed to his dad talking to everyone they meet and, though he still finds it odd, no longer feels the need to comment. 'As the teams came out, dad had to keep hold of me. I swear I was that excited I would have run down on the pitch given half a chance,' he says, looking back.

The Newcastle players look mean and moody; McDermott, Howard, Cassidy and particularly the surly, gum-chewing. Macdonald. He looks really up for it. He has a look which says 'I am in a clinical mood and I am going to score.' Now the camera swings left on to a bunch of smiling women. Brian Moore reveals who they are, 'The Newcastle wives are there. Gaily rosetted. They've chosen their dresses, they've chosen their outfits and most of them look to be – as you would expect – in black and white.'

Princess Anne, with her new husband Captain Mark Phillips trailing respectfully a step or two behind, strides on to the pitch to meet the players. Ian Callaghan wipes his mouth spectacularly with his right hand before shaking the Princess's hand. Thank God there was no swine flu about in those days. The Newcastle fans drown out a chorus of 'You'll Never Walk Alone' from the Liverpool fans. To the tune of Andrew Lloyd Webber's 'Jesus Christ Superstar', the Toon fans are singing 'Supermac, Superstar, How many goals have you scored so far?'

The atmosphere is reaching a crescendo. The mood on the terraces, for the most part, is good. The shared humour, industrial history and riverside locations of each city create a shared empathy. But Andy Griffin notices something new, 'When we Newcastle fans yelled "New-cass-ell" the Reds punctuated this with "shit" and when the cry of "Liv-er-pool" went up, the Mags echoed the pauses with the same response. It was the first time I had heard "collective" swearing on the terraces and, although it seems prudish by today's standards, I felt then that it was an unwelcome development.'

Joe Blake has held off putting on his replacement glasses but, now, as the players line up for the start, he self-consciously puts them on. Later he will wish he hadn't because it would have been preferable for him *not* to see the fare his beloved team is about to dish up.

Now the Toon fans are backing Macdonald's strike partner John Tudor with a deep, primeval chant of 'Tudor! Tudor! Tudor! Tudor!' But soon it's back to their favourite chant, 'Supermac! Supermac! [Clap, clap, clap]'. The Liverpool fans are being totally drowned out.

The blue tracksuit tops come off and Brian Moore expresses satisfaction that Newcastle are wearing a kit where you can see the numbers. 'Newcastle have two styles of kit,' says Moore. 'One is very difficult to see the numbers, which is very important for everyone in Wembley today. But the numbers today are as clear as a pikestaff.'

The game kicks off and the Newcastle support is amazing, they are outsinging the Scousers. A rousing rendition of 'The Blaydon Races' raises the hairs on the back of the neck. Emotions among the black and white half of Wembley are running high. They are bursting with pride.

Derek Thornton is so excited, he fails to see the way the game is actually going. He says, 'As the game progressed we were playing better and better, our defence was solid, we were controlling midfield and it was only a matter of time before "Supermac" scored (ah ha'way man, I was only 12). It was a few years later before I actually realised just how badly we played on the day.'

Macdonald, so effective in the semi-final, has been totally anonymous. His pre-match boasts are starting to look embarrassing. At half-time the Newcastle fans are ashen-faced, appalled at their team's performance. Nobody knows how it is still goalless. They console themselves that they cannot possibly play any worse. But they do.

Andy Griffin says, 'Our best creative player Jimmy Smith never even got a touch of the ball, nor, like nine of the other black and whites, did he seem to want to participate. On this, the biggest stage, with Newcastle fans bursting with pride and anticipation, there was only one team that cared.'

In the second half, Liverpool decide to stop messing around and wrap things up. Hard-done-by after a perfectly good, brilliantly taken goal by Alec Lindsay is ruled out, Liverpool drive forward. It is only a matter of time. 'And Shanks's army, this Liverpool side, swarming forward,' says David Coleman, as though he is describing a military operation.

A low cross from Tommy Smith takes a slight deflection. It evades Hall and falls to Keegan on the edge of the box. He controls it, flicks it up, then turns and smashes it with his right foot. McFaul gets a hand to the rising ball but it flies in the top corner. Keegan has executed it brilliantly.

Coleman says nothing for a few seconds as we watch Keegan leaping about before jumping into the waiting arms of John Toshack, his partner-in-crime. Then Coleman intones with something you can only assume he has been saving up for this moment. 'Goals pay the rent,' he says obliquely, 'and Keegan does his share.'

Suddenly there is a mental image of Keegan slobbing about in a dingy bedsit surrounded by empty cans of Long Life bitter and Chinese takeaway cartons, with a Rigsby-type landlord, in a dirty cardigan, demanding his rent.

The goal silences the Geordies. The Scousers are going mad. The camera pans to a man who looks like he should have been a roadie for Gerry and the Pacemakers – all sideburns and National Health specs. He is going crazy. Now there is only going to be one team that wins it.

The cameras catch Shankly and Bob Paisley giving some strange hand signals. 'And now the instructions come from the bench,' says Coleman. Perched uncomfortably, right next to them, is Joe Harvey, who looks like he wishes the ground would swallow him up. Whatever the two Liverpool bosses are signalling works because another goal soon follows. Clemence punts long. Toshack flicks on brilliantly into the path of Heighway who has made his way in from the left flank. The Irishman takes the ball in his stride beautifully and then slots a neat shot across McFaul and into the net for two.

Heighway leaps up with joy and is submerged by his team-mates. In the foreground, Jimmy Smith looks on helplessly, perfectly summing up his team's plight. They are done for. Paisley is on his feet. Shankly is pointing to someone up in the stands. Joe Harvey, who now has a fag on the go, takes a long, hard drag.

Three years previously, against Arsenal, Chris Wood had been dumbstruck when Steve Heighway had scored, sensing, correctly, that Liverpool would struggle to hold on. This time he has no such inhibitions and leaps up and down with the rest of the Liverpudlians who know they are on their way to cup victory.

Though Newcastle are 2-0 down and a beaten side, their fans still sing. John Newton remembers a rousing rendition of 'The Blaydon Races' apparently being led by a ventriloquist's dummy, decked out from head to toe in a little Newcastle United shirt with scarf and cap.

Macdonald, so brilliant in the earlier rounds, has barely had a kick. A new chorus of 'Supermac, Superstar, How many goals have you scored so far?' echoes around Wembley. Except, this time it is the mocking Liverpool fans who are singing it. Finally, with the game already lost, Macdonald gets a half-chance, but he screws his shot wide. Then, an even better chance. A great ball over the top of the defence from Cassidy gives the sideburned striker the kind of opportunity he usually thrives on.

He takes it on his chest and prepares to unleash a left-footed thunderbolt. But, just as he does so, the ball takes a vicious bobble, and Macdonald balloons it high and wide. As a metaphor for Newcastle's afternoon, it is perfect. It is the cue for a drunken-looking, though harmless Liverpool fan to run on to the pitch with his arms aloft. It's his team's day.

In no mood for charity, Liverpool come again. They are out-classing Newcastle in every department. 'And the place seems to be swarming with red shirts,' says Coleman.

Liverpool keep pressing forward. It is relentless. The ball is with Lindsay, who plays a little pass with the outside of his foot to Keegan in the left-wing position. He checks, cuts inside and then plays a gorgeous cross-field ball to Tommy Smith who, with echoes of the Leeds showboating against Southampton two years earlier, cushions it first-time into the path of Hall.

Smith goes for the return and gets it. It is too easy. Smith plays an obvious one-two with Heighway and is now at the byline. Newcastle make a rather pathetic appeal for offside. Smith crosses low and hard, three Newcastle defenders fail to clear the ball and it reaches Keegan who is lurking at the back post. It nearly passes him but he juts a foot out and turns it in for 3-0. 'Keegan's second,' says Coleman, 'and Newcastle were undressed. They were absolutely stripped naked.'

As the third goal goes in it is too much for Newcastle fan Keith Hudson, who finds some space on the terrace, sits down and starts sobbing. 'I just sobbed me heart out,' he recalls. 'Our Kath was saying, "Don't be so soft" but it was alright for her because she had a crush on Keegan to take the edge off the defeat.'

Another fan, George Ackinlose, says, 'Supermac and the rest of the team played like they'd never played before – literally! They were absolutely hopeless. Every one of them. They seemed totally overawed by the occasion and Liverpool walked all over them. It wasn't even capitulation. It was treason.'

The game is up for Newcastle and Liverpool are toying with them. There is a feeling that if Liverpool had really turned it on, it could have been a cricket score. Newcastle have been that bad. But something peculiar is afoot. Their fans are still singing. They are saying something, something more than the mere words of their songs and chants can convey. The subtext is that however bad our side is, *we* are Newcastle. This is *our* team. You – the 11 players that are currently wearing *our* shirt – will, at some point, head to pastures new. We will not. We are here forever. We are Newcastle till we die.

Derek Thornton looks around him, his eyes wet with tears. Slowly, he is starting to understand. He is beginning to comprehend all those slightly cryptic things his dad has been saying about Newcastle fans and what makes them unique. Derek says, 'A chorus of "You'll Never Walk Alone" started and quickly built up into a crescendo of noise. But it was not the Scousers. It was us. The entire end of the ground was an absolute sea of black and white. This is still one of the most wonderful sights I have ever seen.'

On the field, those in black and white have made a mockery of the shirt. Off it, they have displayed loyalty, pride and passion. This is the moment. The penny is dropping for Derek. This is what his dad has been hinting at. Mr Thornton knows it too. He turns to look at his young lad.

Derek sees tears in his dad's eyes. Their eyes meet for a second. 'There you go sonna,' says Mr Thornton, haltingly, sweeping his arm across the ocean of black and white. His voice cracks with emotion, 'That's it. That's what supporting Newcastle is all about – the best supporters in the world.'

Emlyn Hughes is mobbed as he ascends the steps to collect the cup from Her Royal Highness Princess Anne. It is the cue for the Newcastle fans to take a sharp intake of breath and dig deep in their souls for one final show of support. As Hughes, with his trademark beaming smile, raises the cup aloft, all that can be heard is the Geordies, to the tune of 'Cwm Rhondda' or 'Bread of Heaven', singing 'Newcastle. Newcastle. We'll support you ever more. We'll support you ever more!'

Thousands of them, like 17-year-old merchant seaman John Archer, have tears streaming down their faces as they switch their song to 'Ha'way the lads! Ha'way the lads!'

But it is Liverpool's cup and, at the tunnel end, Chris Wood looks on, holding back tears of joy as Hughes presents the cup to the Kop. Then up go Newcastle with the words of 'The Blaydon Races' ringing around Wembley.

Newcastle fan Peter Lawson recalls a symbolic moment. As the men in black and white sheepishly receive their losers' medals Andrew Graham and his father look on with tears rolling down their cheeks. In front of them is a friendly Scouser, who turns round to commiserate with the two men he has heard singing their hearts out for the entire match.

Peter says, 'In a broad Liverpudlian accent he pipes up, "Come 'ed lads, it's only a game"'.

This is not the right thing to say. 'Without missing a beat,' says Peter, 'Andrew's father looked at the man and said simply, "It might be a game to you, but it's like a religion to us"'. The Scouser politely nods and turns away to leave the father and son to grieve in peace.

But before we get too sentimental, let's not lose sight of what a shocking performance this has been by Newcastle – nothing short of an insult to their hordes of adoring fans. After the game, manager Joe Harvey says he is 'ashamed' of the performance.

For Andy Griffin the game remains a watershed in more than 50 years of supporting the team. His testimony speaks volumes. He says, 'I had supported Newcastle all my life since my dad first sat me and my brother on the low wall at the Gallowgate End, to the left of the goal. Now, at 30, I was still a loyal and hopeful fan. The 1974 cup final was a turning point. I didn't deserve the humiliation and hurt that I experienced that day. I'm not a bad loser, but I do believe it is possible to be a good loser.

'In other words clubs and individuals can lose with honour, they can "go down fighting". But, in 1974 we were a spineless side and I was so bitterly disappointed, that immediately after the final whistle, I put my scarf out of sight in my pocket and the rosette in the nearest bin. I did not want to be associated with that team.'

Liverpool fan Chris Wood felt completely the opposite and swelled with pride as he watched the men in red parading the cup. He says, 'I had a wonderful view of the players and the cup. I can still see Bill Shankly applauding the Liverpool fans and waving a red flag above his head before disappearing down the tunnel.'

The Newcastle fans leave the ground. Joe Blake takes his dodgy glasses off for the last time. How is he feeling? 'Utter despair for the rest of my weekend/year/life,' he says.

Ronnie Rutter, 18, sits on the steps at Wembley, holds his head in his hands and sobs. Phil Carmichael leaves Wembley with his dad. He remembers, 'We all trooped out, dejected and stunned, trying to understand what we'd seen. It was unbelievable.'

Andrew Sanderson, now appalled and embarrassed by the two-foot wide rosette he had worn with such pride earlier, is too upset even to go back to King's Cross. He says, 'I just wandered around Wembley, going round and round the stadium for the best part of an hour, trying to come to terms with having been beaten and wanting to kill Kevin Keegan.'

Derek Thornton and his dad return to the working men's club. Derek now hardly notices at all that his dad is stopped on several occasions by Liverpool fans, who all seem to know him.

He says, 'They were all keen to tell us that "the best team won, but the best fans lost". Even at my young age I was acutely aware of what they meant, and they were right.'

Derek was now looking at his dad in a new light. Football-wise it had been a terrible day but Derek felt a warmth towards his father that he had never experienced before.

Thousands of fans head back to King's Cross or Euston and prepare to head home. Others head for the bright lights of the West End. After all, the night is young.

Back at their central London hotel, Mike Paxton and the fishermen sit in the tiny bar sinking a few post-match beers and cursing their team's woeful showing. A jukebox is playing an unusual new single by a Californian group called Sparks, titled 'This Town Ain't Big Enough For Both Of Us'.

Mike and his mates are deep in conversation. To those not from the north-east their words are difficult to decipher – rather like Russell Mael's juddery, falsetto enunciation on the Sparks song – but even an alien would be able to tell that they are displeased with what they have just witnessed.

They then pledge to do what any group of self-respecting lads would after seeing their beloved team get humiliated in front of the world. They embark on getting as much ale down their necks as is humanly possible. They retire to their respective rooms, change into their finest clobber – flares, wide-collared cheesecloth shirts and platform shoes – and ring for a cab, which soon turns up driven by a young, loquacious Cockney with the unlikely name of Tommy Thomas, who doesn't endear himself to the Toon fans with his opening gambit, 'Hard lines today lads, but you were crap.' 'Aye, we know lad,' says one of the fishermen.

They tell Tommy where they want to go but the rookie cabbie gets hopelessly lost. Embarrassed by his poor 'knowledge' he offers to buy them a beer. The Geordies are not above accepting a beer from a young Cockney cabbie and nod. They find a boozer and soon Tommy is knocking back the lager and sharing his wisdom. 'What you shoulda done lads,' between gulps, 'is taken Keegan out early. You shoulda done him good and proper. Do what that lanky Sunderland geezer did last year to Clarkey.'

One of the fishermen silently slides another pint of lager in the young Cockney's direction. It is a fair assumption to make that Tommy has never been drinking with a group of fishermen from Northumberland and the pace they set is too much for him. Before long the poor cabbie is in no fit state to drive the famous Hackney carriage. Mike says, 'Now we had a problem but, for some reason, Gavin pipes up and says "Give me the keys, I've always fancied driving one of these."'

Elsewhere in London, the Liverpool fans are, naturally, cock-a-hoop, flooding the pubs of the West End and singing their famous anthem, 'Walk On, Walk On, with hope in your heart, and you'll ne-verrrrr walk, a-ha-lone. You'll ne-ver walk alone.'

Chris Wood enjoys a few celebratory beers eulogising with fellow Liverpudlians about their team's performance. He heads back to The Three Lords where the party is in full swing. Before he even enters he can hear, 'We won the cup, we won the cup, ee-aye-addio, we won the cup,' and 'one Kevin Keegan, there's only one Kevin Keegan'. At 10pm the landlord, Jimmy, invites as many people as possible upstairs to watch *Match of the Day*, where they joyously relive the massacre. 'None of us wanted the evening to end,' says Chris.

Tommy is now giggling like a seven-year-old girl in the back of his cab, slurring his words and, between imparting pearls of wisdom about how Terry McDermott should have taken out Steve Heighway and Bobby Moncur should have mortally wounded John Toshack, attempting to give directions. After about five minutes they spot a man – with all the tell-tale hallmarks of a tourist – flagging them down. Tommy finds this highly amusing. 'Let's pick the b*****d up and fleece him,' he slurs.

Gavin says, 'What, pick him up, I can't, I mean… Oh, alright then.' Mike says, 'The door opens and the guy has a strange expression on his face and says "I'm from New Zealand, is that okay?"' A million weak jokes about kiwis, sheep and women with testicles flit through everyone's minds, but they tell him to hop in. He wants to go to the Strand Hotel. Very posh.

Mike says, 'The New Zealand guy had just arrived from the Far East and started handing out these exotic cigars to us all from a snazzy box. It was very much like an explorer giving strange goods to the wild natives. We got to his hotel which was a bit upmarket.'

Unaware that he has just been driven not by a licensed, fully-qualified taxi driver, but by a half-cut football fan who has just witnessed the final of the most famous sporting competition in the world, the Kiwi, none the wiser, hands over four pounds.

Tommy remains slumped in the back of the taxi, occasionally bursting out in roars of laughter and slurring, 'Eh lads, you were rubbish weren't you? That Malcolm Macdonald. 'e was b******s. Ha ha ha!'

The Geordies are starting to simmer. Desperate to recover his London street cred after messing up earlier, Tommy announces to the Geordies there is a great place he knows in the East End, famous for selling a special drink, which will really sort the men out from the boys. The fishermen are nudging one another. Gav, several sheets to the wind remember, points the taxi east and heads out through Aldgate until they end up in a working men's club in deepest Canning Town.

All the way Tommy has been harping on about this drink, which the club is famous for. Mike says, 'He kept going on about it, saying nobody has been able to drink more than a couple of pints without passing out because it's so potent and we had to be careful. We entered the club and, as you can imagine, everyone was giving us very odd looks.'

They are at least heartened by the fact that many of the people in the club are wearing black. Not much white admittedly, but plenty of black. Black hair especially. It feels like Alice Cooper or Gene Simmons of Kiss is going to walk in at any moment.

The Geordie boys can't quite put their finger on it but they are all feeling distinctly uncomfortable. It is only when one of them needs a leak that the reason becomes clear.

The toilets are down in a dark and dingy cellar but, as Mike recalls, 'The whole place was full of coffins with their lids off. There must have been 20 or 30, all empty thankfully.'

Back upstairs, Tommy staggers through men with black clothes and powder-white faces to the bar and orders the drink which is called a 'Stingo' cider and turns out to be half beer, half cider.

Tommy smiles to himself thinking how this will get a real reaction from the men from the north-east. He wobbles back with the drinks and says, 'Here you go. There's a real drink for you.' The fishermen are used to drinking sessions where ten pints of strong ale is regarded as an hors d'oeuvre. One of them peers at the strange brew, looks distinctly unimpressed, takes a swig and says, 'Bloody Norah – it's a f*****g shandy!'

All the while the trains carrying despondent Geordies are travelling back up north. The mood is very different from the hope, optimism and expectation of ten hours earlier. 'A great day out ruined by a football match,' is how John Whiteoak describes it.

Earlier in the day the cassette recorders had been merrily belting out 'The Blaydon Races'. John says, 'But by now the batteries had run down, and the speed of the music was suitably funereal.'

The trains pull in to Newcastle Central and out step the black and white faithful. John says, 'As we left the Central station some wag (there's always one isn't there) shouted "Ha'waay the lasses!" Nobody argued.'

To add insult to injury, George Ackinlose has a nightmare journey home. He says, 'I was still in shock over such an abysmal performance and the long walks, no food, no drink and no joy of any kind. What should have been an exciting day turned out to be a horrific nightmare and put me off going to Wembley, ever again, to see any kind of match.'

Even the fishermen are now starting to feel the vague effects of alcohol and, after their Stingo experience, they head back into central London. Tommy is now like a clumsy octopus, slipping and sliding all over the place, belching and hiccupping and attempting to say things like, 'You fackin' Geordie boysh can really hold, hic, your drink, you barshtads. Yer fackin' team's rubbish though. Ha ha ha.' He launches into a song, which has the Newcastle fans sighing, 'Supermac, Superstar. Wears frilly knickers and a see-frew bra. Ha ha ha.'

The mood though in the capital is largely convivial with only sporadic and low-key outbreaks of the kind of violence that is prevalent at the time. John Doyle recalls, 'We spent the evening in the West End. There were about 100 Geordies and Scousers drinking in the same pub. There was no trouble whatsoever except when everyone joined together to see off a crowd of London skinheads who had duffed up a young lad outside. My friends and I met a few of those Scousers for a drink at every Newcastle–Liverpool game for years after.'

The black taxi containing the five Geordies and a p****d London driver heads back into town and they find another dodgy boozer in Soho (in truth, in mid-1970s London, all the boozers in Soho are dodgy).

More ale is consumed. The men are now seeing the world through a filmy, swirly haze. A haze where Malcolm Macdonald races past Emlyn Hughes and fires in the winner, where Jim Smith wins every tackle against Peter Cormack and Bobby Moncur snuffs out the threat of Kevin Keegan. It is clearly time to head home. Unfortunately, nobody is in a remotely fit state to drive.

Mike is deemed the most sober, or the most reliable, so he perches uneasily behind the wheel. Tommy is now virtually comatose, save for the occasional giggle and belch. From Soho, Mike steers the vehicle past Leicester Square and then on to Piccadilly Circus where the bright, iridescent neon adverts for Coca-Cola, Schweppes tonic water and Cinzano Bianco burn sharply into their eyes.

Mike says that 'at a conservative estimate' they drove round Eros about ten times, with Gavin and Albert each taking turns behind the wheel. Maybe the bright lights re-invigorate poor Tommy because he suddenly comes alive, starts hanging out of the window offering a swig from his bottle of brown ale to some coppers who are probably too stunned to apprehend the driver or drivers of the cab.

With Tommy slurring instructions from the back, Mike is directed down a one-way street. But a squad car has seen them. This is it, their luck has run out. Drunk in charge of a public vehicle. Mike is looking at six months at least. Not only has he seen his beloved Newcastle shamed in one of the highest profile domestic football matches in the world, he is now going to do some bird in Wandsworth, Brixton or Wormwood Scrubs for his trouble.

It is make or break time. He says, 'The copper was now right behind me. I did a sharp left, he went straight on and amazingly we lost him.' Somehow – Lord knows how – they get back to their hotel where they all look at each other and think, 'Did any of that actually happen?'

Perhaps only Newcastle fans could turn out in such numbers to welcome their team back after such a non-performance. But Andy Griffin did not want to be part of it and looked on aghast as he watched the television and read the regional papers. 'I could not believe it,' he says. 'Thousands turned out to welcome their "heroes". It was an astonishing display of loyalty. I personally could not have faced them again and had no desire to join in.

'The players were apparently moved to tears by the warmth of the reception. Supermac promised that he would do better and "win a trophy for these fans". He never did, no one has, although Kevin Keegan, the best player on the pitch in 1974, has come closest.'

For Andrew Sanderson, the massacre of May 1974 burned inside his soul – and kept on burning. 'It took ten years before I could forgive Liverpool for what they had done to my dreams,' he says. 'Even now, occasionally beating Liverpool has a special feeling for me.'

Andrew lives in Spennymoor, County Durham. The retired general practitioner lives with his wife and they have two children and four grandchildren. He says: 'My favourite player of all time is hard but putting aside some of the greats like Milburn, Bobby Mitchell, Wyn "The Leap" Davies, "Pop" Robson, Tony Green, Alan Shearer, Les Ferdinand, etc, the winner is Peter Beardsley. Skill, balance, dribbling, goal scoring, work ethic. He had it all.'

For Liverpool fan Chris Wood, his team's victory on that humid afternoon in May 1974 was all about eradicating the pain he had experienced three years earlier against Arsenal. He says, 'It was one of the biggest thrills of my life and, four decades later, it remains so. I knew what it was like to lose in the final. Now I knew what it felt like to win. The contrast was enormous then and it still is today.'

Try as he might, Mike Paxton can never forget 4 May 1974. He now lives in Norway, having moved there in 1978 with the girl who is still his wife. And his marriage with Newcastle has survived too, listening to the BBC World Service or, in the days before the internet, watching Teletext. 'Newcastle has always been there throughout my entire life, through the ups and downs,' he says. 'It's just like a member of my family.'

For Derek Thornton, the events of that day were significant for two major reasons. Firstly, they sealed for life his love for Newcastle United Football Club. He says, 'That day, the noise from the Geordies just blew me away. I was a part of it, but I wanted more. The people we met that day were right. I *would* remember the day for the rest of my life and I never tire of reliving it to anyone willing to listen.'

Secondly, 4 May 1974 was the day a father and son cemented their relationship. Derek smiles when he remembers his dad meeting and greeting everyone that day like a celebrity, talking to Scousers, Geordies and Cockneys alike. But how did he know them all? Why did he strike up so many conversations? Why was he friends with *everyone*?

The answer is, he wasn't. He didn't know any of them, not a single person. But something special had made conversation and fleeting friendship possible. That something special was the FA Cup Final. Derek says, 'It can only be summed up as camaraderie. A feeling of really belonging to something so special, a feeling which only true football folk will be able to understand.'

Derek now lives in Rosewood Park, Gateshead, just a stone's throw from his roots in Lobley Hill where he was born and was living in 1974. After leaving school in 1977, Derek gained an electrical apprenticeship with Swan Hunter Shipbuilders, staying there until 1993. He then worked as a student adviser at Newcastle College until 2001 when he joined Gateshead Council, where he remains today, managing a team of staff working with vulnerable children. Derek has two children, aged 26 and 27, and is married for the second time.

He says, 'My love for Newcastle United still burns strong, going back to those early days as a five-year-old being taken to St James' Park two hours before kick-off, so I could stand right at the front. Since I was first deemed old enough to go on my own (with my mates) aged 13, I have missed the grand total of three home matches (including league, cup, friendlies/testimonials) and as I approach my 53rd birthday that's three games missed in the last 40 years. Not too bad a record I suppose and I still enjoy the odd away match just for good measure.

'My first favourite player was Malcolm Macdonald, who had a perfect mixture of speed and power with a thunderous left foot. More recently, Mr Shearer has to be right up there for sheer goalscoring ability. However my favourite player has to come down to a choice of two: Gazza was simply brilliant. From the moment he made his debut, you could just tell he was special. He was a world-class footballer, no doubt about it, but his inner demons? Aaargh they ruined the player just as they ruined the man, which sadly resulted in him achieving but a fraction of what he could have.

'Then there is Peter Beardsley who was an absolutely magnificent footballer. He had wonderful vision, was an exquisite passer of the ball, the scorer of some truly world-class goals and yet totally selfless on the pitch (and off it apparently). Beardsley made so many other players look good, while always demonstrating a fantastic work ethic so, if pushed, my favourite player is Peter Beardsley.'

Finally, Derek's dad died in 1992 so father and son were never able to see their beloved team win at Wembley. But Derek has nothing but magical memories of the romantic old place.

He says, 'I've returned to Wembley several times since and I loved every single visit. We may have lost the lot and in reality the old place may well have been an absolute hole. But not to me. To me it was a magical place, a place where my love for my club was truly sealed and a place where I probably felt closer to my dad than at any other time in my life.'

LOVIN' YOU

West Ham United v Fulham
Saturday 3 May 1975

I N May 1975, the sweet soul singer Minnie Riperton, who was to die tragically young aged just 31, was riding high in the charts with the achingly-beautiful 'Lovin' You'. It is a song that has always had a very special meaning for the Hamersley family of East London.

Claret and blue blood first began to pump through lifelong West Ham fanatic Peter Hamersley's veins in the autumn of 1963. In the weeks leading up to his eighth birthday, Stepney-born Peter had started to play and watch the beautiful game. He followed his big brother Billy's lead in choosing West Ham – a natural choice for anyone growing up on the borders of Essex and East London.

'What a bonus that we should win the FA Cup in my first season, followed by the European Cup Winners' Cup, and then have such an influence on England's World Cup win in 1966,' says Peter. 'This was the West Ham team of Bobby Moore, Geoff Hurst and Martin Peters – the era of Ron Greenwood and the forging of the "Academy of Football" legend.'

But this was also the club's zenith and, after the successes of the mid-1960s, a barren period followed, with the low point, arguably, a humiliating defeat at Blackpool in the third round of the FA Cup in January 1971.

Peter recalls, 'By the 1974/75 season, the halcyon days had long gone and West Ham were a club and a team in transition. After some close encounters with relegation, Johnny Lyall had taken over team affairs, Trevor Brooking had taken over from Martin Peters, and no one had replaced Hurst. Even Bobby Moore had gone to Fulham to see out his days.'

Another season of struggle or mediocrity beckoned until some unlikely signings in the form of Billy Jennings, Keith Robson and Alan Taylor, coupled with experienced old lags like Bobby Gould, brought about a sudden change. Peter recalls, 'A 6-0 League Cup win over Tranmere was quickly followed by a 6-2 win against Leicester, a 3-0 win over Birmingham and a 5-3 victory at Burnley. We showed we had some potential as we moved up the league that season.'

By this time Peter was living in East Ham with his family, including his younger brother Derek. The family home was less than 800 metres from West Ham's Upton Park ground but Peter had stopped going to Saturday home games because he had started his own senior football career, which meant he could only attend midweek evening games. However, an injury soon put paid to that.

He says, 'In October 1974, I suffered a broken leg and couldn't play football for a year but I could still get over to the Boleyn Ground to stand and watch – plaster, crutches an' all. I was fortunate in this regard because I lived just a few streets away from the ground and getting to games to stand in the South Bank was not too bad.'

However, in November 1974, the lives of Peter's family were to change forever. He says, 'We found out that a lump on my younger brother Derek's shoulder was actually a malignant tumour and we were told he would have a year, at most, to live. At 16, Derek had his whole life in front of him. He was a lovely kid. He stood over six feet tall, but was a soft-hearted gentle giant really. He was, however, a very competitive all-round sportsman. He was a footballer at heart but had also represented his school at rugby and did some fencing. A local youth club,

Hartley, had entered him for the Duke of Edinburgh's award. But his main sporting love, like all of us, was West Ham.

'Although we decided to keep his illness from him, it wouldn't have taken him much to work it out for himself really. Treatment was pretty basic in those days and, initially, consisted of a large laser, burning the shoulder cancer on a weekly basis. This was a very painful process and resulted in a large burn that needed dressing and changing all the time.'

The laser treatment was reasonably successful however, and, by Christmas, the lump was gone. But the cancer was still inside Derek's bloodstream and would come up somewhere else soon.

The FA Cup third round draw sent West Ham to The Dell to meet Southampton. They took the lead thanks to a 25-yard free kick from left-back Frank Lampard and were 2-0 up at half-time after a brave header from Bobby Gould. Saints came back strongly in the second half, but a solid defensive display by the Hammers – with Kevin Lock outstanding – kept them at bay. Mike Channon pulled one back for Southampton from the penalty spot, but West Ham held firm. They were on their way.

'In the fourth round we were paired with Third Division Swindon at home,' says Peter. 'Lower league teams were often difficult for West Ham and we didn't really fancy our chances much after they came to Upton Park and held us to a draw. I stayed at home and listened to the replay second half commentary on the radio. We were one down at half-time and expecting the worst to be honest. But a Brooking-inspired comeback resulted in a 2-1 away win and an air of optimism began to creep in – especially as we now faced a home fifth round tie with QPR.'

Upton Park was packed for the QPR match, played on a waterlogged pitch on 15 February. Rangers took a deserved 25th-minute lead through right-back Dave Clement and, even when Pat Holland equalised seven minutes later, Rangers still looked the likelier winners. It was a magnificent tie, with man of the match Kevin Lock again outstanding, and was decided when Keith Robson headed home a sliced Billy Jennings shot to send the Hammers through.

After the game, all the praise was for Lock's performance. Trevor Brooking said, 'Early in his career Kevin was compared to Bobby Moore. Now he is a star in his own right.'

Peter says that at this stage, excitement was really starting to grow in East London. He and his brothers Billy and Derek were starting to think of Wembley. 'In all fairness, the QPR game should have been postponed,' he says.

'The pitch was waterlogged near the players' tunnel and, whenever play was near there, it became farcical. The groundsmen were still working on the pitch as the players warmed up, and they continued all through the interval too. But the atmosphere inside the Boleyn was really special and from this point on, we thought we had a real chance. If you could pinpoint a moment in time when cup fever set in, then this was it.

'Meanwhile Derek was beginning to show signs of change. He became short of breath easily and was gradually losing fitness.'

In the sixth round West Ham had to make the short trip to Highbury to meet Arsenal. Once again, it poured down and the pitch looked like a muddy battlefield. Peter says, 'This was a difficult tie that we were expected to lose. I went to the game with Billy and Derek and we failed to get in at the Clock End, where most of the West Ham fans were gathered. Looking back, this was a bit of a blessing because it would have been hard to stand on the large terrace with all the pushing and shoving.

'We managed to get in the lower main stand, which, in those days, was below pitch level. This awkward view was similar to the West Stand at Upton Park and meant that pitch markings were barely visible. I remember we were down by the corner flag near the Clock End and were entertained pre-match by the police band and singing sergeant they had at the Gunners back then.'

The Highbury game marked the emergence of a previously unknown player who, from this point, would have a huge influence on the 1975 FA Cup competition.

West Ham supremos Ron Greenwood and John Lyall believed Arsenal lacked pace at the back and, the day before the match, a squad of 14 names went up on the noticeboard at West Ham's Chadwell Heath training ground. Among them was 21-year-old Alan Taylor, a £40,000 buy from Rochdale the previous November. Lyall and Greenwood selected him to expose the Gunnners' lack of pace.

That Highbury cup tie on 8 March 1975 was a classic. Late winter, early spring, a packed house, muddy conditions, local rivals and two passionate sets of fans. The teams went at each other from the start but it was the Hammers – wearing all white, with claret and blue trim – who struck first.

And it was Taylor who got it after the Arsenal defence got into a terrible mix-up. A massive kick from goalkeeper Mervyn Day wreaked havoc in the Arsenal defence and after both Peter Simpson and Terry Mancini failed to deal with it, Keith Robson played the ball into the Arsenal box.

It looked like a straightforward collect for Arsenal keeper Jimmy Rimmer, but the ball stopped in a puddle and left Rimmer in no-man's-land. 'And the mud has beaten them all!' screamed David Coleman with trademark urgency. It allowed Graham Paddon to steal in and cross to Taylor, who scored from close range before swinging on the net.

There was a massive surge of fans down the North Bank terracing behind the goal where Taylor had just scored and clearly there were more than a few West Ham invaders on the North Bank that day.

One minute after the interval, the Hammers fans packed into Highbury went wild for a second time. Billy Bonds found Taylor on the right wing. He played a first-time ball to Brooking. A wonderful piece of skill took Brooking past Peter Storey and he played a delightful ball into the path of Taylor, who was haring towards goal in the inside-right channel.

Taylor controlled it beautifully with his left foot and then struck it crisply with his right. The greasy ball skidded past Rimmer and went in off the post in front of the Clock End. It was a great goal. 'Two-nil,' said Coleman, definitively. Taylor, shirt caked with wet mud, wheeled away, arms aloft. He could barely believe it and was submerged by his team-mates.

Arsenal were a beaten side. A decade, which began so gloriously for them, was fast becoming one to forget.

Peter and his brothers were overjoyed by West Ham's quarter-final victory in the Highbury quagmire, but the illness was beginning to take its toll on Derek.

Peter says, 'By the time of the Arsenal game, the cancer had shown up on x-rays of Derek's lung and he was sometimes noticeably short of breath. He was trying to live life as normal but this was interrupted by weekly treks across London to Hammersmith Hospital. Once again, treatment was limited to a laser, now directed at the lung. However, this could not penetrate deeply enough without causing other damage. It still left severe burns resulting in pain and limited movement. Incredibly, Derek had gone to Highbury and stood in that big crowd.'

It seemed as though West Ham's FA Cup run was giving Derek his own incentive to fight the illness.

It had been a fascinating year in the cup with giant-killing and shocks from the off. Southern League Wimbledon stunned the nation when they won at First Division Burnley and then held the mighty Leeds to a replay, before succumbing to a single deflected goal.

Then the big boys began to knock each other out. Ipswich beat Liverpool, Leeds beat Derby and then Ipswich beat Leeds. It meant the cup was there for the taking, although the smart money was on Ipswich, who West Ham would play in the semi-final. The other semi paired Fulham with Birmingham City. Now, all four clubs had a real scent of glory.

Cup fever gripped the East End and Essex. It was the talk of the pubs in Upminster, Stratford and Dagenham. Could the

Hammers do it? Peter remembers, 'Thousands of us queued from 6am on a Sunday morning to get tickets for the semi-final at Villa Park. Our league form had fallen away as it became obvious to everyone that the team was concentrating on the cup. I went to most games in those days with my mate Gary Dawkins who lived in the same street.

'We went together to the semi-final, leaving East Ham early on that cold April Saturday morning to make the trip up to the Midlands on Lacey's coaches. Claret and blue was everywhere you looked along the route.'

West Ham had to do without Keith Robson who wasn't able to shake off a nagging thigh injury. The Hammers coaches arrived at Villa Park and Peter says, 'We were disappointed to be given the small Witton Lane stand, as we had twice as many fans as Ipswich and they were only able to half fill the massive Holte End facing us.'

It was not a great game and finished goalless. Peter says, 'We travelled back to London in a blizzard as heavy snow fell over southern England that night. On this coach trip, a song came on the radio that struck a chord deep within me. The opening words were "It all seems like a dream, that voice, to me now." I mis-heard the word "voice" as "boy" at the time and it immediately made me think of Derek. The song stuck with me. It was an obscure Motown recording called "Child of Love" by Caston & Majors – but it was to remind me of the events of 1975 forever.'

The next morning Peter, along with thousands of other Hammers fans, had to get to Upton Park for 6am to queue for replay tickets. Demand was huge for the midweek replay at Stamford Bridge and, as usual, the touts moved in. The ticket offices at Upton Park were due to open at 9.45am but, much to the anger of arriving fans, touts were already milling around with handfuls of tickets.

The fact that a person could buy up to four tickets each probably helped the touts. It also helped Peter though because he was able to secure tickets for himself, his brothers, and his dad, Bill senior.

Now Derek's condition began to deteriorate, as Peter remembers. He says, 'Not long before the replay at Stamford Bridge, Derek had started to physically weaken. Just walking up the stairs at home could take him half an hour to recover. This meant half an hour of taking short panting breaths because he was surviving on one lung and could not breathe deeply. He had visibly lost weight too, but he had a determination about him and he just kept going.'

Peter continues, 'The weather hadn't improved much by the Wednesday as we travelled across London to Stamford Bridge for the replay. I went, as normal, with Gary, but this time in his old Hillman Estate car. The roads were so busy we couldn't even get close to Chelsea and had to park the car along the Embankment and walk the last two miles or so. We found ourselves in the open end once more as the Ipswich fans were given the Shed. It was cold, and snow fell through the game and soaked us all.'

But the Hammers fans massed behind the goal would be warmed by events on the pitch. And, once again, it was that man Taylor who did the damage.

Ipswich were still fuming over a couple of controversial decisions by Treorchy referee Clive Thomas when Taylor struck in the 29th minute. Graham Paddon's free kick gave Bobby Gould the chance to send Brooking away on the left. The idol of the Boleyn crossed to the far post where Taylor, virtually on the line, headed powerfully into the net.

A minute from half-time Town got a deserved equaliser following a mistake by Billy Jennings, who attempted a wild clearance of Mick Lambert's low corner, but succeeded only in slicing the ball over his own head and into the net.

Ipswich then poured forward and it looked like there could only be one winner, but they hadn't bargained on Taylor. With just eight minutes left on the clock Paddon drove in a free kick from the left and the long-haired Lancastrian Taylor fired in a right-footed shot past Laurie Sivell and into the net. It was enough to clinch the match and send West Ham to the FA Cup Final.

Peter says, 'I can still vividly remember the feeling as the final whistle blew and I realised we were going to Wembley. I can never forget that feeling – because it was also mixed with thoughts of Derek. I was concerned if he was okay, what with the weather and all. He was with Bill and my dad so I knew he was in good hands, but I was worried as the weather closed in and wondered how he could have stood on those terraces that night.'

It wasn't long before Peter learned that Derek had not seen the game. 'When I got home I found that Derek was in a bad way and had not been able to go in,' he says. 'They had travelled across London like me and had to park some distance from the ground. Although the walk really weakened him, he had pushed on, gasping for breath. But, by the time they reached the ground, Derek was panting heavily and could hardly stand. They decided it was best not to go in. They were literally at the entrance – but he could not carry on.

'By now, it was almost kick-off and my dad offered the three tickets to some other fans outside. Some low-life, who could see why they were giving away the tickets, complained about paying face value and I think my old man then just gave them to a policeman to give away.

'They faced quite a journey to get home, but somehow they managed it. After Derek recovered his breath, he waited with Billy until my dad came back with the car. They were outside the ground and could hear the noise from within. I know that the joy of winning the semi-final was felt equally by Derek – even though he had not made it into the ground. The date was 9 April 1975.'

It was now that the East End and parts of Essex went FA Cup mad. In the pubs on the Barking Road – such as the Boleyn, the Central, the Abbey Arms and the Denmark Arms – the talk was of one thing: this was West Ham's year. The shops on High Street North, stretching up from East Ham through to Manor Park and Forest Gate, were festooned with claret and blue. Windows in houses from Canning Town to Southend-on-Sea were filled with good wishes and displays of allegiance.

No one really cared that the Hammers' league form had slumped. They beat Carlisle on 1 February (when all four Hamersley males sat together in the West Stand for the last time) and Burnley on 15 March but, apart from that, couldn't buy a win. They lost at home to Newcastle, Chelsea and Coventry and the goals dried up.

The players had clearly taken their eye off the ball. It was the FA Cup they were after. And, naturally, everybody wanted to be there. Exiled East-Enders, who had dispersed to the likes of Basildon, Harlow and Leigh-on-Sea, suddenly re-emerged and pledged their undying love for the club. The scramble for tickets for the final against Fulham was going to be messy.

Peter recalls, 'It was now that West Ham revealed one of their legendary pieces of myopia, as they announced their ticketing scheme for the cup final. It was to be decided by vouchers handed out at a home league game to anyone going through the turnstiles – including away supporters! No recognition was given to anyone who had seen any cup games that season. And so it was, that someone like me, who had been to five cup games and most league games, was unlucky enough to get the wrong voucher on the day and face missing out on a final ticket.' But fate and sorrow were about to intervene.

At the time, Minnie Riperton's beautiful song 'Lovin' You' was receiving extensive airplay on the radio as it rose to number two in the British charts. Gentle, heartfelt and emotional, it is a song that Peter and his family would come to always associate with Derek.

Peter says, 'Even now, I still find it hard to talk about the events of April 1975. After six months of fighting lung cancer, my 16-year-old brother Derek (God bless) died on 22 April. His dying wish had been to see West Ham win at Wembley. I felt it was my mission to be there for him that day.'

Suddenly, events began to change in a most extraordinary way, shaped by one of the game's true gentlemen and a West Ham legend.

Peter explains, 'I was really mixed up emotionally. When Derek died, I cried for two days but then held it all inside and have barely cried ever since. We brought him home and he was lying in our front room. At the same time, West Ham were in the cup final. Everywhere you went, people were talking about the game, but I was holding my emotions deep within me. Only people strongly associated with the game would understand my feelings at the time.

'Derek's loss ran deep in me, and always has. But I would have gladly given up anything for him to have survived long enough to go the final himself. I knew he would have wanted me to go there for him but, having missed out on a ticket, it looked like it was not to be.

'Then, the night before Derek's funeral, the consequences of a strange coincidence came to the fore. My mate Gary Dawkins's mum had a good friend who worked at Trevor Brooking's plastic binding factory on the Romford Road. She had heard about Derek's sad passing and about how I didn't have a ticket to the final and, somehow, the word had got back to Trevor. If ever football had a gentleman, it was, and still is Sir Trevor Brooking.

'As we walked to the last home league game of the season, Gary revealed a secret that was burning within him. He told me Trevor Brooking was coming to my house later that week and he was going to personally give me a ticket for the final. Gary didn't want to spoil my surprise – but he just could not contain himself. And sure enough, a couple of days after, Trevor Brooking knocked on my front door at about six o'clock in the evening.

'As sad a time as it was, it was also totally unreal that one of my greatest ever heroes should come into my house, sit down and have a cup of my mum's tea. He was so nice, understanding and easy to talk to. We chatted about the final and the players and how well Bobby Gould had taken the decision to be sub. Then he gave me the ticket and I got him to sign the back of it before he left. Amazing.'

At Wembley, West Ham's opponents would be Fulham and, for 30-year-old postman Mike Findley it was a reward for following the men from Craven Cottage for 20 years. He remembers, 'My love affair with Fulham started in 1955 when I was ten when a mate's dad took us and some friends to see our first ever professional match at Craven Cottage. It was Saturday 24 August and we saw Fulham beat Blackburn 3-0. Apart from watching a very exciting football match, I really felt at home inside such a unique ground with the old-fashioned cottage in the corner and situated right on the banks of the Thames.

'Although Fulham was considered an old-fashioned club, I enjoyed watching some of the greatest players in the history of the game, including the maestro Johnny Haynes, Bobby Robson, George Cohen, Alan Mullery, George Best, Rodney Marsh and Bobby Moore, as well as Jimmy Hill who, as leader of the players' union, helped make Haynes the first £100-a-week footballer. Every season we looked forward to the FA Cup and hoped Fulham could one season get to Wembley.'

The side's journey to the cup final was epic, taking 11 matches to reach Wembley. Three games were needed to see off Hull City in round three and then four games to eliminate Nottingham Forest in round four. 'We were then drawn against Everton and actually won 2-1, which we never thought would happen,' says Mike.

Carlisle were despatched in the quarter-final and then a late, scrambled John Mitchell goal gave Fulham an extra-time winner against Birmingham at Maine Road in the semi-final replay after the sides had drawn 1-1 at Hillsborough.

'After we beat Birmingham, I'd never seen so many people with tears in their eyes around me at a football match,' says Mike. 'It was a dream come true to reach Wembley.'

FA Cup Final day, 3 May 1975, dawned and Peter and Gary Dawkins left East Ham at about 11am to make the journey to Wembley. Peter remembers, 'We were totally decked out in claret and blue. We both wore West Ham shirts (which was not common at games in those days). I also had on light blue trousers, a West Ham scarf, a claret and blue flat cap and a large West Ham rosette with the cup on it.

'We travelled by Tube and got there at about 12.30pm. Getting off at Wembley station was a fantastic feeling – knowing that you were going to your first cup final and it was West Ham that the rest of the country would be watching. It was also the first time I'd ever been to Wembley.

'There were thousands of us wearing claret and blue on the train and all down Wembley Way. Though we were playing Fulham you wouldn't have believed there was another team there. I can only remember the West Ham fans and the mass of claret and blue.

'We made our way from the station and got in the big queues outside the famous ground. It was a lovely warm day, my scarf and hat were hot, but not coming off. My ticket was actually for a different section from Gary's and we set about trying to find someone willing to swap tickets so we could be together.

'It turned out that the only way we could do this was for me to swap my ticket – even though it was the one signed by Trevor Brooking. I was reluctant to do this and took the name and address of the bloke I swapped with and gave him my details.

'It was on a shake and a promise that he would mail it back to me after the game. Thinking back now, I find it incredible that I did this in good faith and cannot thank whoever it was enough for keeping his word and uniting me with the ticket again – to keep forever.

'The FA Cup Final is a wonderful occasion. We made the most of it by getting in the ground about two hours beforehand and joining in the singing all through. How wonderful it was to be a part of the amazing "Bubbles" we sang that day.'

Yet throughout the day, Peter could not forget Derek for a single moment. He says, 'In amidst the 100,000 people there and the euphoria with it, I noticed a square light shining on the bottom of the electronic scoreboard at the Fulham end of the ground.

'This square was out of place and shouldn't have been lit up, because it was not part of the team names or score. I took this light as being a sign that Derek was there and watching – and that it was going to be our lucky omen.'

As the two sides emerge, Peter and Gary join in a rousing chorus of "I'm Forever Blowing Bubbles". All eyes are on former West Ham and England legend Bobby Moore, making his 47th appearance at Wembley and now wearing the white of Fulham.

It is a game of few chances and, at half-time, is goalless. A couple of enforced errors make the difference, though. First, Fulham right-back John Cutbush passes the ball directly to Pat Holland on the left wing. Holland cuts inside and rolls a three-yard ball perfectly into the path of Billy Jennings, advancing in the inside-left channel.

First-time, Jennings whips in a low curling left-footed cross/shot which bounces awkwardly in front of Fulham goalkeeper Mellor. The blond-haired former Burnley man can only parry the vicious ball into the path of man of the moment Alan Taylor. From six yards, Taylor cracks a low shot goalwards, which travels right through Mellor's legs and into the net. It is 1-0 and Taylor performs his familiar goal celebration, wheeling away to the right, arms aloft. Peter and Gary dance with delight.

Soon it is two and again Mellor and Taylor are involved. This time, Holland finds Graham Paddon, who unleashes a fierce shot from the left side of the penalty box. Sprawling to his left, Mellor fails to gather the ball and, lurking around the six-yard box, Taylor is there to lift the rebound, from three yards out, into the roof of the net.

Both goals are scored directly under the electronic scoreboard at the Fulham end of the ground and Peter feels sure Derek has been quietly watching over proceedings.

Taylor's third brace in consecutive rounds is enough to win the FA Cup for West Ham and, when skipper Billy Bonds ascends the famous steps to receive the cup from His Royal Highness The Duke of Kent, it is a special moment for every claret and blue fan, but especially for Peter, who says, 'When the final whistle blew it was the signal that we had won the cup – I had won the cup, Derek had won the cup.

'I stood on the Wembley terrace, arms aloft as Billy Bonds held the cup to us – and thought of nothing except my brother, Derek, and how much he would have wanted to see this.

'We left Wembley and, by the time we reached the East End, it was alive with celebrations. I can never forget the scene around the Boleyn pub that night as we drove around the block again and again tooting horns all the way – thousands were out climbing all vantage points as they drank and celebrated.

'The party went on all night and into the next morning, when hundreds of thousands lined the streets to welcome the team and the cup home.'

Peter knew that, somewhere, his beloved younger brother, Derek, was watching and smiling his big, beaming smile, taking delight in West Ham's cup win.

There is a heart-warming postscript to this story, albeit one born out of further sadness for Peter and his family.

Back in 1975, Peter's father Bill asked him to write some suitable words for Derek's headstone, saying that he wanted the cup final score inscribed on it. Peter recalls, 'I was 19 at the time and emotionally upset. I wrote a few simple lines and finished with the score, but a few months later I stood in front of Derek's grave and was overcome with shame at what I had written. I couldn't change these words and they remained uneasy for me as the years passed.'

In the early 1980s, Peter went on what he describes as the 'holiday of a lifetime' in Australia, including three months in Perth. He loved it so much that he promised himself that if he ever married and had children, this was where he would like to bring them up. When he met his future wife, Gail, in Corfu, it turned out her parents had connections in Perth and it all fell into place.

Following the birth of their first daughter Janine in 1987, they decided it was time to up and go. They settled in Perth, had another daughter, Laura, in 1991 and have stayed there ever since.

Speaking at the start of 2010 Peter said, 'Over the last few years my mum, Jean, had become very ill and bedridden following a fall in 2002. My sisters, Pat and Carol, looked after her night and day. Last year things took a turn for the worse and, sadly, my mum passed away on Easter Sunday, 12 April 2009.

'For many years, mum's wish had been to be buried with Derek, so this is what we planned. It was a very sad time and my sisters were devastated, even though they had been relieved of the 24-hour-a-day burden they had been carrying.'

In 1975, Derek had died on 22 April and Peter and his family tried their best to avoid having their mum's funeral on the same date.

Peter says, 'The funeral was finally arranged for 21 April and, due to the grief everyone was experiencing, this seemed the best solution but, as the time got nearer, we all began to wish we had made it the same day.

'The nearer we came to the funeral, the more I realised it was all fated. It was just surreal and coincidental and I told my eldest daughter Janine, who travelled back to England for the funeral with me, all about it. Everyone became convinced that it was all meant to be.

'Over the years, I have struggled to come to terms with Derek's passing. It has never been something I could just casually mention. It has always been deep within me. However, with my mum's passing at this time of the year and the fact she was being buried with Derek, it somehow allowed me to face the reality. My mum was gone, but Derek was now with her forever. It sort of all made some sense.

'Then, there was the stone and the words. I hated what I'd written in 1975 and this was the chance to have it removed and replaced with something a bit more fitting. But Billy, Pat and Carol didn't want any of it to change and, by the time we left London, it was still this way.

'Eventually, over time, we chose a new headstone and suitable words for my mum, but the strong consensus was to leave Derek's words exactly how I had written them as a 19-year-old, emotionally upset kid.

'I thought about this for a long time. It was so strange that I should try to face up to my inner thoughts and tell Derek's story for the first time in this book. I had never really been able to sit and talk at length about it but, then, events happened that brought everything out in the open to be faced.

'I began to see things from a different view. I started to think that Derek would be chuffed at having the 1975 cup final score on his headstone. He might appreciate me having written them for him. I think, also, something I had written has been cast in stone for 35 years and would be renewed on an even stronger piece of granite, possibly to be around for a couple of hundred years more.

'The day after mum's funeral was 22 April and Derek's anniversary. It is a sad day that I normally spend in some solace. But, now, I actually felt happy in the knowledge that my mum was with my brother and, whether you believe in the afterlife or not, it doesn't matter for they are still together, whichever way you look at it. On that morning, sitting with my daughter Janine, "Lovin' You" by Minnie Riperton suddenly came on the radio. It's hardly ever played in Australia and it was the first time I had heard it in years. Janine looked at me and neither of us could believe the coincidence. It was just so fated.'

Peter still follows the Hammers avidly from Australia, managing to see almost every game live on TV, and runs the West Ham supporters' club in Perth. He has written several articles on West Ham and football history in general – mostly on the Knees Up Mother Brown website. He is also a keen genealogist.

For as long as he lives, Peter will never forget the events of April and May 1975, neither his dear younger brother nor West Ham's FA Cup win. As he says, 'The glory of that win can never be taken away. Many involved in the story have since gone, including the old stadium itself. Some of the players and managers have also sadly passed away. But I still have some of my tickets from the cup run, plus my scarf and the cap that I wore.'

Peter's prize possession, however, remains the signed ticket that he was personally given by a true gentleman named Trevor Brooking. That, and the treasured memories of a much-loved and much-missed brother. As Peter says, 'For every day that I live, a thought of Derek is always with me.'

In memory of Derek Charles Hamersley (1958-1975)

'Although our lives are now apart
'You'll always be there in our heart.
'What you said finally came true
'It was Fulham 0, West Ham 2.'

In a further postscript, Fulham fan Mike Findley moved from South London to Teesside in 1978, the year he married Judith. In June 2005, he was diagnosed with Motor Neurone Disease (MND). That September, along with family and friends, Mike set up the Mike Findley MND Fund. In 2008, he was elected Mayor of Redcar and Cleveland and, in 2010, he was awarded the MBE in the Queen's New Year Honours List.

By March 2014, the fund had raised a supremely impressive £141,589. For more details, visit www.mikefindleymndfund.com.

SAINTS AND DEVILS

Southampton v Manchester United

Saturday 1 May 1976

ON a supertanker, laden with 360,000 tons of crude oil, making its slow but steady way southwards from the Persian Gulf, a man has his ear pressed tightly against a radio tuned to the BBC World Service. The crackly reception is just sufficient to tell the man the news he is desperate to hear – that his beloved football team have, that afternoon, secured a 1-0 away victory at Valley Parade, home of Bradford City, in the sixth round of the FA Cup and are now, magically, in the semi-final.

It is 6 March 1976 and Peter Harris is a merchant seaman, employed as a navigating officer on one of the enormous vessels carrying oil from the Gulf back to Europe.

The immensity of these ships means they are too large to pass through the Suez Canal. Instead, they must take the long, slow route south, round the Cape of Good Hope and back up to Europe. It is a lonely, six-and-a-half-week trip and news from home is scarce. Peter is 35, married with two children, and a fanatic of Southampton Football Club. He has been following from afar – with growing exhilaration, and no little frustration – his team's incredible cup run.

Away from home for periods of up to four and a half months, he relies on cuttings from the *Southern Daily Echo* and the regular sports show on the BBC World Service for his information. How he wishes he was back home.

While helping to load up the huge ships with hundreds of thousands of tons of crude oil in places like Ras Tanura in Saudi Arabia, Mena Al Ahmadi in Kuwait or Kharg Island in Iran, Peter also has half a mind on the fairytale that is developing back in Hampshire. And that afternoon, in March 1976, Peter's heart was firmly in West Yorkshire, where a great goal from Jim McCalliog secured victory.

That night, back in England, millions of *Match of the Day* viewers see Peter Osgood flick a free kick up for the Scot to ram a volley past Downsborough in the Bantams' goal. There were only 14,195 fans at Valley Parade – the lowest attendance for a quarter-final since the war. How Peter would have loved to have increased that number by one.

Peter first started following the Saints in 1966, while working as a police officer in Fareham. It was a great time to start supporting them, indeed a great time to get into football. This was the era of Terry Paine, Martin Chivers and Ron Davies and a free-scoring team, managed by Ted Bates.

Southampton had just won promotion to the First Division for the first time in the club's history, just before England's legendary World Cup victory. Prior to becoming a police officer, Peter was actually a football virgin. But, at Fareham nick, everyone was talking about it.

'I kept hearing my colleagues talking about going to football,' Peter says. 'The station was divided 50-50 between Southampton and Portsmouth and so I used to alternate between The Dell and Fratton Park.'

But, with a young family to support, money was tight and eventually Peter's wife, Gillian, politely suggested that he chose one or the other. What to do? The Saints or Pompey? The Dell or Fratton Park? 'When the Saints Go Marching In' or the 'Pompey Chimes'? Peter is unsure what finally swung it. No matter. The choice was made. PC Peter Harris, aged 26, became a Saint for life.

Once the decision was made, there was no turning back and Peter, almost overnight, became a huge fan, barely missing a game for eight years. His heroes were the likes of Scots Jimmy Gabriel, Hugh Fisher and curly-haired keeper Eric Martin, defenders Joe Kirkup, John McGrath and Dennis Hollywood and former Wiltshire County youth player Mick Channon. The Dell became Peter's second home.

Around this time, 15-year-old Rob Innis also started following the Saints, albeit by default. He says, 'I was born and raised in Worthing, West Sussex, and I only became a Saints fan because my uncle and his mates went to The Dell. This was because Brighton and Pompey were in a lower division at the time. Also, they did not want the aggro associated with the London teams. My early heroes were Mick Channon and Ron Davies.'

Ah, The Dell. What a much-missed venue. It possessed the best and worst characteristics of English football grounds. Compact, cramped and woefully inadequate in terms of facilities, it was also atmospheric, idiosyncratic and brimming with character. Back in the seventies, the quaint old ground was known for its so-called 'chocolate boxes', platforms of terracing above the old Milton Road End.

They were unique in that they were uncovered upper tiers of terracing. The Dell also had bench seats in the paddocks of both main stands, and a players' tunnel which was, unusually, situated at the south end of the ground, something rarely seen at any stadium.

During 1975/76, Southampton enjoyed a reasonably successful season in the Second Division, finally finishing sixth, but it was a season plagued by inconsistency. Highly effective at home, it was their away form that let them down. A five-match winning run in December briefly took them into fourth place and raised hopes of promotion, but their form slumped alarmingly in the spring and they fell off the pace. However, their fans were more than compensated by a storybook FA Cup run which began at a cold Dell on Saturday 3 January with the visit of Aston Villa.

Watching from the terraces that day was Exeter University student Pete Woods. Born just outside Southampton, Pete started going to The Dell in the early 1960s with his father and had been an ever-present ever since. Pete, like the vast majority of Saints fans in the crowd, was not expecting anything special in this cup run. All the supporters really wanted was promotion back to the First Division.

With just minutes left on the clock some fans were already heading for the exits. They trailed 1-0 to a 64th-minute goal scored by Andy Gray. Saints were heading out at the first hurdle. Then, with the Villa fans starting their victory celebrations, Saints left-back David Peach crossed. Substitute Pat Earles touched the ball to Mick Channon, who laid it back to Hugh Fisher, one of those pros who the word 'stalwart' is almost made for. From 12 yards Fisher shot with his 'wrong' left foot past a gaggle of players and past keeper John Burridge to snatch a draw.

Four days later the team travelled to Villa Park for the replay and secured an impressive 2-1 victory, with two goals from Jim McCalliog, one in extra time. Blackpool were then beaten 3-1 at home in round four. On Valentine's Day, the Saints went to West Bromwich Albion and an equaliser from Bobby Stokes clinched a 1-1 draw. In the replay, in front of 27,614 fans under the glare of The Dell's floodlights, Southampton produced their finest performance of the whole season and won 4-0, including a hat-trick from Channon.

The victory at Bradford followed and Peter Harris was, like thousands of Saints fans, totally caught up in the emotion. 'Somehow, watching it all from afar, made it even more exciting,' he recalls.

While Peter Harris, Rob Innis and Pete Woods were regulars at The Dell, so Ian Brunton and Pete Darby were at Old Trafford. The 16-year-olds, though not known to one another, were both Stretford Enders throughout the 1970s. Ian's reason for following Manchester United was straightforward. He says, 'My dad was a Red and it was just natural that I would follow suit. I started going to the odd game with friends in 1970 when I was ten and then, from 1972 onwards, I went to every game.'

In spring 1976 Ian was just about to leave school and United had become his life. He didn't have a season ticket, but never missed a home game and went to 90 per cent of away games too. Pete, meanwhile, played for a pub side in which some of the older lads were regulars at Old Trafford, so he started going along with them. He was quickly hooked. In 1975 Pete left school and started work as a sheet metal worker, with most of his wages spent on following United.

After the humiliation of relegation in 1973/74, United bounced back brilliantly and, at the start of 1976, were playing a superb brand of attacking football. On five separate occasions during 1975/76 they topped the league. Nine players made more than 30 league appearances that season. In goal, Alex Stepney remained one of the best custodians in the country. Scottish defenders Stuart Houston and the elegant Martin Buchan were both ever-present and Brian Greenhoff missed just two games.

But it was up front and in midfield that United really excelled. Steve Coppell, Sammy McIlroy, Stuart Pearson, Lou Macari and Gerry Daly were all intelligent, attack-minded players who knew where the back of the net was. And in November 1975, manager Tommy Docherty had paid £70,000 to Millwall for an exciting young left-winger called Gordon Hill, saying, 'He is the last piece of the jigsaw in my team-building.'

While Docherty had moulded a genuinely exciting side who, on their day, were a match for anyone, reporters and the media were becoming just as interested in the exploits of the United fans. In the mid-1970s they enjoyed huge away support. And with that, came trouble.

Throughout 1975/76 the papers were full of stories about United fans going on the rampage in some town or city. A frequent 'fall back' story on the TV news was to show nervous shopkeepers pulling up their shutters before the arrival of

United. It was all grossly unfair on the thousands of loyal and law-abiding United fans, but hooliganism and how to eradicate it was on everyone's lips at the time.

To the frustration of legendary Old Trafford luminaries like Sir Matt Busby and Bobby Charlton, the mere mention of the words 'Manchester United', was more likely to conjure up an image of rampaging, long-haired fans in flared-trousers and denim jackets than the skills of Stuart Pearson, Sammy McIlroy and Gordon Hill.

United's followers had become the pariahs of the football world. And with some justification, it has to be said. A small section of their supporters had regularly wreaked havoc all over the country during the 1974/75 season, which United spent in the Second Division. And there was more trouble the following season too.

In August 1975, London-based United fans returning from a match at Stoke caused havoc on their train journey back to London, when about 100 of them stormed the buffet car and ransacked the stock room of spirits and beer. Then, in October, there was a serious incident at Upton Park when United faced West Ham. A combination of overcrowding and fighting – involving fans from both clubs – resulted in hundreds of fans spilling on to the pitch and referee Peter Reeves was forced to take the players back to the safety of the dressing rooms.

United pushed Liverpool and QPR all the way for the title but a shock home defeat to Stoke, three games from the finishing line put paid to their ambitions, and they eventually finished third. Narrowly missing out on the championship made them even more determined to get their hands on the FA Cup for the fourth time and the first since 1963.

Their cup journey was not straightforward. They trailed 1-0 at Oxford United's Manor Ground in round three, before two penalties from Gerry Daly saw them through. *Match of the Day* viewers watched goals from Alex Forsyth, Hill and McIlroy defeat Peterborough 3-1 at Old Trafford and then Leicester were beaten 2-1 at Filbert Street, taking United to a quarter-final meeting with Wolves.

A 1-1 draw at Old Trafford saw the teams reconvene under the floodlights at Molineux for a terrific, old-fashioned cup tie. Classic goals from Steve Kindon and John Richards put Wolves two up, but United dug deep and goals from Pearson, Brian Greenhoff and, in extra time, McIlroy, booked United's place in the semis. Throughout the competition, the heavyweights had been knocking each other out, paving the way for Third Division Crystal Palace to join United, Southampton and the reigning league champions, Derby County, in the last four.

The purists want a United v Derby final, while the romantics are praying that either the Saints or Palace make it. The latter get their wish when the semi-final pairs Southampton and the Selhurst Park side, guaranteeing that one of them will be at Wembley and that United and Derby must meet in the battle of the giants in the other tie. The Saints fans are ecstatic. Suddenly, from absolutely nowhere, they have a chance of going to Wembley.

Now things were really starting to stir in Hampshire and cup fever begins to spread. News of the draw quickly reaches Peter Harris who had, by now, realised with delight that he would be back in the UK 12 days before the final. Not that he thinks he has a cat in hell's chance of getting a ticket.

The semi-final between United and Derby is probably – in terms of the stature of the participating teams – the biggest semi-final clash for several years. Only the Leeds v Manchester United match of 1970 or the following season's all-Merseyside affair came anywhere close to it. Perhaps tempting fate, United boss Docherty was extensively quoted in the papers in the week leading up to the game. With typical mischief he remarked, 'This is the first time the cup final will be played at Hillsborough. The other semi-final is a bit of a joke, really.'

Maybe he had a point, but this is the FA Cup and you have to beat whoever the draw throws at you. The United v Derby game was one of the biggest domestic football matches of the

1970s and the famous old Sheffield ground was rocking on the day. Derby were a fine side who, managed by 1967 FA Cup-winning captain Dave Mackay, had won the league in 1974/75, having done so in 1971/72 under the legendary Brian Clough and Peter Taylor partnership. Like United, they were capable of scoring goals from many different sources.

Some 55,000 fans travelled to Hillsborough for the match, with most of the Derby fans positioned on the Kop and the United fans in the Leppings Lane end, which is a mass of scarves and banners. In truth, United fans were everywhere, with large pockets of them jostling alongside the Derby fans on the Kop.

They are treated to a fine match settled by two goals from Gordon Hill. The first, after 12 minutes, is classic United, a brilliant, counter-attacking goal after a stray pass from Roger Davies puts United in possession. A long, flat pass from Brian Greenhoff finds Hill, who lays it off beautifully first-time to Gerry Daly. He takes his time before playing it back to Hill, who curls a sublime, left-footed shot from the edge of the area past Graham Moseley in the Derby goal. The United fans go wild. Behind the mic, Barry Davies exclaims, 'And that confident, cocky youngster from London's Millwall has put Manchester United in front.'

Then, with six minutes left, United win a free kick five yards outside the box. Hill steps up and, again with his left foot, strikes the ball cleanly. It takes a deflection from the Derby wall and sails past Moseley to put the game out of sight. 'And there's the happiest Londoner that ever went to Manchester!' cries Davies, once again referring to Hill's roots, as the goalscorer is submerged by team-mates. United are going to Wembley.

The other semi-final, so cruelly belittled by Tommy Docherty, is at Stamford Bridge. One man dominates the build-up. Malcolm Allison is one of the few people in football who is capable of attracting more headlines than Tommy Docherty. Outspoken, affable and with a dry wit, the media – especially the tabloids – love him. He has shamelessly courted publicity throughout the Palace run, donning a spectacular fedora hat, wearing a chunky sheepskin coat and smoking his trademark cigar.

Most famously of all, for some inexplicable reason, he invited glamour model and soft porn actress Fiona Richmond to Selhurst Park where she was pictured in the bath with the team. It had started to resemble a circus.

Not that Southampton minded. Allison's domination of the papers helped take the pressure off them. But there was still a hot-house atmosphere with a cup final place up for grabs. In the week before the game, Saints manager Lawrie McMenemy decided to take his squad to Frinton-on-Sea on the Essex coast to get away from it all. It almost worked.

McMenemy blew his top when three of his players, including his captain Peter Rodrigues, stumbled across a private function, sipped a bit of ale but, most importantly, arrived back after the curfew that McMenemy had imposed. The next morning, McMenemy gathered the squad together and looking directly at Rodrigues and the other two players – Jim McCalliog and Jim Steele – said, 'If we lose on Saturday, I will blame you three.'

The day before the semi-final Allison makes a bold – some might say rash – prediction, 'We will win 3-0. Lose? I have never even considered it. Why should I worry about something that can't happen?'

Saints fan Rob Innis travelled to Stamford Bridge with his sister and, looking back, he admits to a few nerves. Maybe Allison's mind games were having some effect? 'Though Palace were in the Third Division, they were still serious opposition and a win was by no means a foregone conclusion,' he says. Rob and his sister were seated in the famous three-tiered East Stand. 'This was quite a big deal for us,' he remembers. 'Although I was 21 and my sister was a bit older we had not been to many away grounds and so to go to Stamford Bridge – home of the famous Shed – was quite a thing.'

Allison continued to attract headlines right up to kick-off, famously holding up his fingers to the Palace fans on the pitch to indicate the predicted margin of victory. In the dressing room before the game, all the Southampton players were thinking is how much they'd like to see him eat his words. It wasn't a classic by any means – all that mattered was winning. As the game entered its closing stages, it looked like being a 0-0 draw. Then, on 74 minutes, a speculative, low, long-range drive from Paul Gilchrist, which probably should have been saved by Palace keeper Paul Hammond, put the Saints one up. Then, five minutes later, a controversial penalty was converted by David Peach to make the game safe and take Southampton to Wembley. 'We were in the final!' says Rob Innis. 'Now the excitement would really kick in.'

Thousands of miles away, Peter Harris, aboard a ship called the *London Pride*, punched the air when the news filtered through on BBC World Service. Immediately, colleagues on the supertanker started ribbing him about how United would thrash Southampton, but that it would be a nice day out for the team and the fans. Peter laughed. But, inside, he just wanted a ticket to *have* that nice day out.

That night, before *Match of the Day*, which featured the United v Derby game, millions of viewers tune in to the Eurovision Song Contest, live from The Hague. It is won by the UK, who are represented by Brotherhood of Man, whose two-girls-two-guys line-up mirrors that of Abba, whose 1974 winner 'Waterloo' raised the bar for Eurovision entries. Not that Brotherhood's cloying 'Save Your Kisses For Me' comes anywhere close. It is cruelly, yet accurately, derided as 'music for ten-year-olds'.

The musical scene in the UK is in dire straits, which might explain why the record stays at number one for six weeks. This period is a musical nadir. Populist glam rock – never a radical force at the best of times (the brilliant Slade excluded) – is dribbling to a lame conclusion. Bowie – sublime in the first half of the decade – is in a period of musical inactivity and, the last great hope, Roxy Music, have split. 'Save Your Kisses For Me' is finally displaced by one of Abba's lesser numbers, the Latin-tinged 'Fernando'. Waiting in the wings to take its place at the summit is J.J. Barrie's mawkish country and western-flavoured 'No Charge' – which is given heavy airplay by Capital Radio's Dave Cash, as is, perhaps even more disturbingly, 'Combine Harvester (Brand New Key)', a humorous take on a song written by American singer/songwriter Melanie in 1972.

For some reason 'Combine Harvester', by West Country novelty trio The Wurzels, briefly captures the imagination of Brits in those hot, early summer days and, for a couple of weeks or so, has a nation going round saying, 'Oooo… Aarrr, Oooo… Aarrr, Oooo… Aarrr' in a terrible West Country accent.

This will eventually be picked up by fans of urban-based football clubs, who will sing it as a term of derision at any club based in the shires, which to most of these geographically deficient individuals – especially Londoners – will include Reading, Colchester, Ipswich and Gillingham, let alone the Bristols, Plymouths and Norwiches of this world. It will usually be followed by a chant suggesting that said followers are partial to the company of ovine livestock.

So Southampton are in the final and now the media spotlight is firmly on them. On the way back from Stamford Bridge, the team stop in a pub called The Winning Post in Twickenham, which is crammed with Saints fans and where the atmosphere is apparently superb. It is a long night, which continues back in Southampton. And McCalliog and Steele – this time accompanied by Peter Osgood – are in McMenemy's bad books yet again, as their celebrations go on too long for the former guardsman's liking.

Without them, Saints beat arch-enemies Portsmouth 1-0 in a league match. David Peach is booked and may miss the final. Consecutive home wins against Blackpool and Charlton follow. Southampton are bang in form and the city is going cup-mad.

All the talk in the city is about tickets. In a move to give genuine Saints fans the best chance of going to Wembley, the first tickets will be sold to those fans who can produce counterfoils of the semi-final match or the Bradford quarter-final. Ten days before Wembley, there is a special Meet the Saints night at the city's popular nightclub and entertainment venue, the Top Rank Suite in Bannister Road, where the team sign autographs for fans.

If that is not enough of a draw there's a late bar and 'dancing to Dave Griffiths' – and all this for just 65p. If you don't fancy this you can always go to the City's Guildhall, where Carry On stalwart Charles Hawtrey is starring in *Snow White and the Seven Dwarfs*, though what role Hawtrey has is anyone's guess.

Bass, the brewers, announce they are presenting wives and girlfriends of Saints players with special blue and yellow suits to match the colours the team will wear at Wembley. A presentation of the suits takes place at the Heathfield Toby Inn, Fareham. The Ford motor company then announces that if a Southampton player scores a hat-trick in the cup final they will be given the best car in the Ford range, a £4,500 Granada Ghia automatic saloon. The offer is made following a request from the Sports and Social Club of the Ford works at Swaythling.

A letter is sent to the *Southern Evening Echo* from RA Hammond, the branch correspondence secretary of shop workers' union, USDAW. Mr Hammond says that because so few people will be out shopping on the afternoon of the match, retail outlets in Southampton should close. He says, 'As this is the first time the Saints have reached Wembley, my branch ask all retail employers to respond to the occasion and show their support by enabling their staff to cheer on the Saints.'

Meanwhile, Jim Callaghan becomes the UK's new Prime Minister, after defeating Michael Foot by 176 to 137 in the final vote for the job. The leadership contest follows a surprise announcement three weeks earlier by Harold Wilson, in a move that stuns and baffles the political world. Some say Wilson is mentally and physically exhausted. Cynics say he has decided to get out before some balloon he knows about bursts. Across the Atlantic, the world's most notorious recluse Howard Hughes dies on a plane taking him to hospital after suffering a stroke. He was 70.

Weather forecasters start predicting a long, dry spell and there are fears of a drought. There could be water rationing unless there is more rain. Many areas are already facing hosepipe bans. In the *Daily Mirror*, columnist Frank McGhee – himself a Manchester United supporter – provokes fury when he says that it should be made more difficult for United fans to get tickets to prevent their notorious hooligan following from ruining the cup final.

Merchant seaman and Saints fan Peter Harris is now back home from the Middle East and desperate for a ticket. He starts to ring round his mates and anyone he knows to see if there is one available, but it is to no avail. 'My wife wrote to Southampton and explained my predicament, i.e. that I'd been a supporter for many years, but had been at sea and couldn't get to games,' he says. 'Basically, she was told "no chance". It was devastating to think I was going to miss the biggest game in the club's history.'

Meanwhile, Rob Innis gets lucky. He is not a season ticket holder at The Dell at the time, but an uncle who Rob regularly goes to home matches with is given a ticket by a retired referee, who has been given one by the FA for services rendered. Rob's uncle passes the ticket on to him. What a result for Rob. He is Wembley-bound.

There is a week to go. As a queue of Saints fans waits patiently outside The Dell to claim their Wembley tickets, a four-minute drama unfolds. A man stretches his hand into a hatch from which cup final tickets are being allocated and snatches in the region of 100 of them. But he is spotted by the driver of the coach waiting to take the Southampton reserve team to Chelsea, who notes the number of the getaway car. Police are radioed and four men from the Reading area are soon arrested.

Later that day, Southampton Ladies show the men how it is done and win the Mitre Cup – the women's equivalent of the FA Cup – by beating QPR 2-1 after extra time at Bedford. While they are doing this, the men of Southampton FC secure a 1-0 victory over Hull City at The Dell, with a goal brilliantly made by Peter Osgood and despatched beautifully by a certain

Bobby Stokes, who would no doubt have scoffed if someone had suggested that the score and the scorer at Wembley in a week's time would be the same.

Especially as Stokes is on the transfer list and, in December, turned down a move to his home-town club, Portsmouth, in an exchange deal for Pompey's Paul Went.

Back in the First Division, Manchester United lose 2-1 at Leicester City and, after the game, attacking midfielder Lou Macari more or less admits that the team were operating at half pace. 'If we'd needed to win here to take the league championship we would have won alright,' he says. It is United's second consecutive league defeat. But, when manager Tommy Docherty is asked if he thinks the team will recapture form in time for the final, he replies, 'With class like ours, you never lose your rhythm.' Confident words indeed from 'The Doc'.

So cup final week begins. Manchester United are not just favourites to win – they are expected to win handsomely. In fact, even usually moderate individuals like Bobby Charlton seem to be getting carried away.

Interviewed on the Monday before the game, Charlton picks up where Docherty left off and says, 'It would not surprise me to see United running around the stadium having beaten Southampton by six goals. I am confident they will win by at least three goals and feel it could well be six. They are so talented, so rich in enthusiasm, confidence and energy, that the result could be an entry for the record books as the biggest winning margin of all time in the FA Cup Final.' Not much to live up to there then.

Alongside the interview is a picture of left-back Stuart Houston in muscle-man pose, as if to demonstrate the might that United possess all the way through the team.

In contrast, Saints manager Lawrie McMenemy – rapidly earning a reputation as a likeable and highly-quotable Geordie – is pictured, somewhat bizarrely, wearing an Arab head-dress sent to him for good luck by a fan from Abu Dhabi. Meanwhile, the only L. McMenemy in the Southampton phone book has been fielding calls from all over the world from fans desperate to get tickets. Except this is the wrong man.

Leo McMenemy, who is in the marine, sand and gravel business, says he has been besieged with calls. But he gets his reward after sympathetic Saints officials arrange a meeting with the real Mr McMenemy, who gives him two precious tickets for his trouble.

The whole ticketing issue is causing all sorts of ructions in Southampton. Some fans claim to have been cheated by unscheduled sales of tickets from The Dell. There are also rumours that the club have disposed of some tickets to outsiders, with stories doing the rounds that some travel agencies have been offering tickets marked 'Southampton FC' to European football fans.

Saints secretary Keith Honey is adamant that the club have tried to be unscrupulously fair but, on police advice, did make some tickets available ahead of schedule. Supt George Jones, of Southampton Central sub-division, confirmed that he asked for sales to go ahead because of the huge queues developing on Milton Road. He says, 'My concern was for the welfare of local residents and general hygiene, because there were no adequate toilet facilities.' It leaves hundreds of fans bitterly disappointed and some threatening legal action. This is what happens when cup fever hits a city.

All week the press are predicting crowd trouble at the match and several pubs around Wembley announce that they will stay closed until Saturday evening, fearing United fans will go on the rampage. The Rev Derek Goodman, of Eastwood, Nottinghamshire, says he was knocked unconscious by United fans after the Leicester game and calls for emergency legislation to save Saints fans, 'should they be unlucky enough to beat Manchester United'.

The Southampton team is announced and there is big relief for Paul Gilchrist, whose name appeared as substitute when the cup final programmes were printed. Gilchrist – a United fan as a boy – will start, with Hugh Fisher on the bench. The side to play United will be Turner, Rodrigues, Blyth, Steele, Peach, Holmes, McCalliog, Gilchrist, Channon, Osgood and Stokes. The team will stay at the same Surrey hotel that accommodated the Sunderland cup-winning side three years earlier. Is this an omen?

The *Southern Evening Echo* canvasses the opinions of fans in the city and finds, perhaps surprisingly, the majority of those asked think Saints will win. East Stand season ticket holder Linda Savage, of Highfield, says, 'We will win because we have the more experienced team and United are out of form.' Eric Goddard, 18, of Eastleigh, predicts a 2-0 win for Southampton. 'But it's going to be tough,' he says, 'now that United are out of the championship race they have a greater incentive to play better.'

And Gordon Whelan, guv'nor of The Running Horse pub predicts a 3-0 win for Southampton, with one goal a David Peach penalty, which Channon's speed will earn.

While most Saints fans are foaming at the mouth with excitement, Peter Harris is as miserable as sin. He is sitting at home in a state of despondency, barely able to look at the *Southern Evening Echo*, knowing that he is going to miss out on the greatest day in his beloved club's history. His wife Gillian is trying to console him when there is a knock at the front door. Peter is tempted to leave it, but Gillian insists he answers. He lumbers over to the door and opens it with the minimum level of enthusiasm possible.

It is an old friend, Martin Rogers, who Peter hasn't seen for a while. Martin says, 'Hello Peter. I didn't realise you were back.' 'Yes,' Peter replies, 'got back a week or two ago. In some ways, I wish I wasn't.'

Peter notices an odd look on his friend's face. His years of experience as a police officer tell him Martin is concealing something. 'I've got something for you,' says Martin. All these years on, Peter can still remember the moment and recalls, 'Martin's face broke out into a huge grin and then, from his pocket, he produced a cup final ticket. I just couldn't believe it.

To be honest, before Martin knocked on the door, completely out of the blue, I was feeling terrible and had given up.'

Peter's mood changes immediately. He shakes Martin warmly by the hand and hugs Gillian tightly. He is going to Wembley.

The dry spell continues and the weather is getting warmer. Last summer was long and hot and it was followed by an exceptionally dry winter. Britain is drying up and the weather forecasters' predictions of another long, hot summer look like coming true. A cartoon character called 'Waterhog' is introduced to drive home the message that water is precious and must not be wasted. Sales of shorts, T-shirts and flip-flops are rising. It looks like being hot at Wembley.

As further evidence that Southampton has gone absolutely cup-mad, an astonishing 30,000 people descend on the city's main sports centre for a special pre-final *It's a Knockout*, which will be screened on *Grandstand* on Saturday. Also there are Radio One disc jockeys Tony Blackburn and Dave Lee Travis, Lesley Judd and Peter Purves of *Blue Peter* and, somewhat randomly, Noel Cantwell.

The massive crowd includes a sprinkling of United fans who have travelled down for the occasion and they threaten to seriously damage their fans' street cred by trying to kick off. Several of the naughty lads clamber over fences and break down barriers to enter the arena, disrupting games and bringing the TV recording of the event to a halt. They are clearly not very interested in games such as 'Hooping to Win' and 'Wobbly Walk', which are compered by Stuart Hall and Eddie Waring and refereed by Arthur Ellis. By all accounts, it is a good event, although Eunice Maurin of Sholing writes a letter to the *Echo*, expressing her disappointment that the team themselves did not put in a brief appearance.

Now there is another ticketing story for the tabloids to lap up. Father Seamus Gillooly, given two tickets by Lawrie McMenemy, falls foul of FA regulations when he raffles them to raise money for his church in Thatcham, Berkshire. The papers are full of match talk with both managers very much in the limelight. One man, John Brew of Clacton-on-Sea, Essex, even pens a 'clerihew' – a four-line, whimsical, biographical poem. It goes:

'Lawrie McMenemy
'Is nobody's enemy
'He's not at all trembly
'About All Saints Day at Wembley.'

To which comes the reply:

'Tommy Docherty
'Is not a bit crotchety
'He knows the Saints are all sinners
'And the Reds will be winners!'

In fact, McMenemy's stock is rising all the time. Constantly in demand for interviews, he is winning admirers for his good-natured, composed air. A few big clubs are starting to sniff around him, and not just in the UK. Ajax are thought to be looking closely at him and there is talk that he might be in line for the vacant Arsenal job.

Another man who the press are taking a close interest in is Terry Venables, coach at beaten semi-finalists Crystal Palace. He has ambitions to manage at a higher level, with Arsenal, Spurs and QPR all thought to be interested in luring him across London. Palace manager Malcolm Allison says, 'Terry is an extremely talented young man and I wouldn't want to stand in his way.'

It is announced that, win or lose, the Saints will take a 19-mile tour of the city on the Sunday, setting off from The Dell at 3pm before meeting up with the Southampton band outside the Odeon cinema and arriving at the Civic Centre for drinks with the mayor at 4.15pm. One man who is really looking forward to this is Eddie Maton, a lifelong Saints supporter, who will have the honour of driving the open-top bus through the streets. Eddie's name was pulled out of the hat in a draw held by the city council's transport department. And Eddie, who claims to be an expert at predicting the outcome of top sports matches, believes Saints will win 2-1.

There is disappointment for patients when Wembley bureaucrats say that hospital radio broadcasters can't come to Wembley, as there is not enough room. Because of the ban, nine hospitals in the Southampton and Winchester area relax their rules on allowing portable radios and TV sets in the wards, but the Hospital Broadcasters' Associations say patients will be 'distressed' not to have the personal touch from their regular commentators.

It is Friday 30 April. The must-see film, which is just hitting the screens, is the Watergate-inspired *All The President's Men*, starring Robert Redford and Dustin Hoffman, who play *Washington Post* investigative reporters Bob Woodward and Carl Bernstein. Showbiz is mourning the death of another Carry On star, Sid James, who died on stage on Monday.

In the *Daily Mirror*, reporter Nigel Clarke writes that United, though red-hot favourites, can be beaten. Clarke, with impressive prescience, believes that, if Southampton bypass United's midfield with long balls to Channon and Osgood, they have a chance. Also, if Saints can force the ball infield by closing down United's full-backs Forsyth and Houston, luring Greenhoff and Buchan forward in the process, it can free up Channon.

It is possible that Southampton's Second Division status could work in their favour. Lawrie McMenemy points out that United haven't had a lot of time to do their homework on them and Tommy Docherty concedes, 'We rarely see them on television and we're obviously more aware of teams in our own division.' But the Doc remains upbeat and highly confident. United's flying wingers Coppell and Hill are expected to be simply too good for Saints' full-backs, Peach and Rodrigues.

Friday's *Daily Mirror* runs its annual cup final 'soccerscope', which includes mini-portraits of all the players in the next day's starting line-ups. The paper feels that Southampton's 'surprise element' does not extend much beyond their three most accomplished players – Channon, Osgood and McCalliog. They, plus Peter Rodrigues, are all pictured with their shirts off, posing for the camera and demonstrating the muscle they will need to overcome United.

Little or no attention has been given to Saints' number 11, Bobby Stokes, who is given this billing, 'Feeds off chances made by Mike Channon and Peter Osgood. No genuine status, but the sort of player who could come good in a Cup Final.'

Both teams are making the traditional pre-match pitch inspection, simultaneously. They are not supposed to be at Wembley at the same time, but the Saints' coach was delayed and the team late, meaning the players come virtually face-to-face 24 hours before the big game.

There is a late injury scare for Southampton when it is revealed that defender Jim Steele has been playing with a broken hand sustained in a practice match. He knocks it again on Friday morning, but says he will play against United.

Meanwhile, thousands of Manchester United fans – far more than actually have tickets – are knocking off work at lunchtime and starting to head south by road and rail. Hundreds are expected to hitch-hike through the night. The trains and motorways are crammed with United fans.

By late afternoon, the pubs around Euston station are buzzing. All the talk is about tickets and how to get them. Stories are circulating that tickets bought from touts for £10 are now changing hands for an unbelievable £90. But, with 24 hours to go until kick-off, even a lot of the touts are heading out of town. One tells reporters, 'For one thing, most of us haven't got any tickets left and, anyway, we don't want to be around for any trouble.'

At university in Exeter, Southampton fan Pete Woods is just finishing his lectures. In truth his mind has barely been on his studies for weeks, such is the excitement he feels about his beloved team being at Wembley. In a dream he makes his way to Exeter railway station and heads home to Southampton. 'Is this really happening?' he asks himself.

That night, on the box, there's the *Freddie Starr Show*, *Sale of the Century* and *Starsky and Hutch*, while at 10.30pm on ITV experts discuss tomorrow's match on *Who'll Win The Cup?* Finding someone who thinks Southampton will win is not easy. Most bookmakers are so confident of a United victory they are offering odds as high as 5/1 *against* a Southampton win. It bewilders racehorse owner Mick Channon, who says, 'There are only two runners in this race and there will never be a better chance for anyone who isn't a United fan to beat the bookies.'

The *Echo*'s headline on FA Cup Final eve is 'SAINTS TUNED TO A PEAK' and reporter Bob Brunskell writes, 'The ballyhoo, the intricate build-up and the anxious waiting are almost over. Saints tuned to a mental and physical peak by manager Lawrie McMenemy are set to do battle with the Red Devils of Manchester United in tomorrow's FA Cup Final at Wembley. Although tagged the underdogs against the most respected and feared club side in England, Saints go into the biggest showpiece of British sport with anything but an inferiority complex.'

Saints fans go to bed still pinching themselves that tomorrow they watch their team in the FA Cup Final. United fans hit the sack fully expecting that, this time tomorrow, they will be the cup holders.

Dawn breaks on Saturday. It is a hot day. From the top of Southampton's famous Bargate, boys from King Edward VI School herald the dawn by singing 'When the Saints Go Marching In'. There are no public schoolboys singing songs in Manchester, just thousands of denim-clad, mostly lads, leaving their houses in Salford, Urmston and Ashton-under-Lyne, and countless other parts of the UK where their support is already spreading.

In Stalybridge, Pete Darby's mum is doing what any good mum does – ensuring her lad has plenty of food for the coach journey. She opens a packet of Sunblest white bread, makes him a nice round of sandwiches and puts them in a sealed plastic bag for him.

Pete says, 'I had an older mate called Brian who was 29. Brian assured my mum that he would look after me and she waved me off in his safe hands.'

No sooner are they around the corner and out of mum's sight then a can of bitter is thrust into the 16-year-old's hands. 'Six or seven cans later and I'm well drunk,' remembers Pete. 'We'd only been on the coach 90 minutes and weren't even at Birmingham.'

Ian Brunton's coach is setting off from Manchester and there is plenty of booze aboard this too. The atmosphere is raucous. 'Our coach left Piccadilly Gardens at about 8am,' remembers Ian, 'and was full of the usual football fans of the time, young, loud and already on the beer. Most of us wore denim jackets covered in sew-on badges. I had no food but sneaked two bottles of Newcastle Brown ale on to the coach.

'I was terrified of losing my ticket and must have taken it out of my pocket to look at it every few minutes. Although we were hot favourites, I was so excited about going to Wembley I realised I had not actually thought about the game that much. But I know I never gave the thought of losing a second's thought.'

A couple of hours after the bulk of the United fans have left, the happy yellow and blue exodus from Southampton starts. There are no nerves for them – just laughter and enjoyment. One of the coaches stops at Southampton Register Office on its journey to allow ardent Saints fans Jane Radford and Neil Self to tie the knot.

Pete Woods and his father have decided to get on the road early and it soon becomes clear that thousands of other Saints fans have had the same idea. Pete recalls, 'We pulled in to Fleet Services on the M3 at about 9am to discover a car park that was practically full and hundreds of Southampton fans clad in yellow and blue.'

The M3 was virtually gridlocked as Saints fans made their way up to the capital. Pete and his father arrive at about 11am, having crawled all the way along the motorway to the north circular.

While Rob Innis travels up alone from Worthing, Peter Harris and Martin Rogers meet at Park Gate on the A27 where the shops are all bedecked in Southampton colours. Peter says, 'There was a bread shop and all the girls who worked there were wearing yellow and blue. We travelled up to Wembley in a minibus alongside members of Nick Holmes's family, whom Martin was friends with.

'Another thing I clearly remember is seeing a coach with a banner which said, "Yellow and Blue versus Manchester Who?" The banner will later be seen on television by millions. It isn't the best banner on view, however. That honour goes to another displayed by the Southampton fans which reads, 'Channon strikes more often than British Leyland'.

It won't be long before Saturday morning TV will change forever with the introduction of *The Multi-Coloured Swap Shop*. But this morning it's a classic pre-*Swap Shop* line-up with BBC showing *Ragtime*, *Marine Boy*, and *Champion the Wonder Horse*. Later that morning comes *Zorro* and *Bugs Bunny*, who might well have asked the timely question, 'What's up, Doc?'

But the ultra-confident United manager has little to concern him on this bright warm morning as his side wakes at their team's hotel. The Doc is not shouting it from the rooftops, but he expects to win. That expectation is the one thing that Southampton have in their favour. Experienced campaigner Peter Osgood, a cup winner six years earlier, speaks for the whole squad when he says, 'Never in my life have I been so relaxed before a game. I just know I'm going to do well.'

Now the vehicles are approaching Wembley. United fan Ian Brunton recalls a huge procession of vehicles, including an ambulance fully decked out in United colours. It was at this point that Ian's nerves started to jangle. 'The closer we got, the more nervous I became,' he says. 'My stomach was in knots although everyone else around me seemed very confident.'

The police have mounted a massive operation for the match. It is not just the fearsome reputation of United fans. It is the far more sinister and genuinely life-threatening possibility of action by IRA terrorists who recently targeted the Ideal Home Exhibition. Police leave is cancelled. Trains, buses and stations are all being heavily patrolled. Saturday's *Southern Evening Echo* hits the streets before the result is known, but tells its readers of some trouble perpetrated by United fans, which sounds like rather small beer in comparison with later crowd violence.

Based on Wembley Way, reporter Peter East writes that a milkman had all his bottles stolen by United fans, three windows were broken in a shopping precinct and the windows and doors of a pub smashed as United fans tried to break into an off-licence. But East balances his report, quoting 41-year-old miner and United fan John McCormack, of Macclesfield, who says, 'We are not all idiots. A lot of us have just come down here for a good day out and to see our team win.'

However, there is no doubt that many Southampton fans do have at the back of their mind slight apprehension about being caught in the wrong place, at the wrong time by some of United's less welcoming fans. This includes Pete Woods, who has now reached Wembley.

He says, 'From our car park we realised we would have to walk around the ground and through the United fans. Even though we tried to be as inconspicuous as possible we were confronted by a group of about six United supporters. I immediately thought, "Oh dear, I'm not sure I like the look of this", but they held out their hands to shake ours saying, "Enjoy the day, may the best team win". They obviously thought it would be them, but it was a nice gesture nonetheless.'

Rob Innis is also now at the ground and waiting, with thousands of others in the hot sunshine, for the gates to open. 'I realised I was in a standing section which had mostly United fans in it,' he remembers. 'Luckily, I found a United fan who had the reverse problem. I clearly remember being wary of getting a forgery and held on to my ticket while looking closely at his. I remember thinking, "Ye, of little faith", but I wasn't going to have a northerner putting one over me!'

Rob is dressed in classic mid-1970s gear. In keeping with the fact Saints will play in yellow, he has on a bright yellow shirt with a big floppy collar, a pair of flares, a blue denim jacket and a huge pair of platform shoes in which he hides his exchanged ticket to ensure it isn't stolen. 'The gates opened and I went in straight away to find a stanchion to stand against,' says Rob.

Pete Woods also enters the stadium early, although he says this was to avoid being pestered for tickets, as there were thousands of people milling around outside – mostly United fans – clamouring for them. He says, 'We could have made a lot of money, but there was no way we were going to sell. I found a good spot in the upper tier of the stand, quite close to the TV cameras that were on a platform above the players' tunnel.'

The coach carrying Ian Brunton and the other United fans is now pulling into Wembley. This is a moment Ian had waited years for, but his initial reaction is one of disappointment. He says, 'As we approached Wembley I thought how dirty and scruffy the whole area looked. It was not at all how I had pictured the home of football. We parked and made our way to the United end to try and meet some friends, but we never did find them because the number of people who were there without a ticket was huge.'

If Ian had been disappointed with his first glimpse of the stadium, then his first sight of Wembley Way compensated for it. He says, 'I was just amazed at the human tide approaching the ground. We stood at the top and it looked so good that we wanted to make the walk up Wembley Way as well, even though it meant fighting the tide to reach the bottom of it. We did and I was very impressed and proud as Punch to be finally part of the Red Army at Wembley.'

But Ian and his friend are also concerned about the sheer numbers of United fans milling around and felt there were simply too many to all get in. He says, 'We had both been to many games where gates had been knocked down by ticketless fans and the last thing we wanted was to get turned away by a police blockade.' Hundreds, perhaps thousands, of United fans are on Wembley Way offering up to £25 for a match ticket or devising schemes to somehow get in.

Most Southampton fans are now safely in the ground and ready to greet the players when they walk on to the pitch on their arrival at the ground. Their fawn-coloured suits make them look like some dodgy cabaret act.

Pete Woods remembers the moment well, 'There was a look of astonishment on Bobby Stokes's face when he walked up the tunnel to an enormous cheer and looked round at the sea of yellow and blue. Then Lawrie McMenemy strode out of the tunnel as if he owned the place, waving to everyone. I discovered I was standing next to a referee who, as a thank-you for many years of service, had been given his ticket by the Cornish FA!'

Shortly after 2pm, as the BBC is showing the Goal of the Season competition – which goes to a brilliantly-crafted goal scored on the opening day of the campaign by Gerry Francis for QPR against Liverpool – the Southampton sections are virtually full and their supporters in fine voice.

Yet while this is going on, outside, at the United end of the stadium, there are some disturbing scenes. Ian Brunton recalls, 'As we got near our turnstile, I can only describe it as absolute chaos. People were trying to jump over turnstiles, knock down gates, anything at all to get in. Frankly, I was terrified.'

Ian saw some fans have their tickets snatched from their grasp as they got close to the turnstile, a sight that saddened him. He says, 'I had absolutely no intention of taking mine out of my pocket until I was physically in the turnstile itself. The turnstile I entered was operated by a man who had a plastic bag full of money he had taken off fans willing to bribe their way in.

He looked a little disappointed when I gave him a ticket rather than a fiver!' Ian is in. The time for talking is over.

There is a hum of anticipation. The weather is getting hotter. Nobody knows how much beer has been drunk but the stench of alcohol is clinging to both sets of fans. The teams emerge, both wearing natty Admiral tracksuits, all tightly zipped up, apart from Mike Channon who has his open in a way that looks slightly rebellious, and probably is. Saints are led out by skipper Peter Rodrigues, who sports an impressive moustache, giving him something of the Mexican bandit look. All he needs is a poncho and a sombrero and he could be in a Sergio Leone film.

The teams are presented to the Duke of Edinburgh. Of the two sides, it is Southampton who appear more relaxed, doing exercises, laughing and joking and giving thumbs-up signs to friends and relatives in the crowd. Then the national anthem, sung impressively by both sets of supporters. 'Well, I've never heard the national anthem sung with more gusto than that Brian,' says co-commentator Jack Charlton.

For United fan Ian Brunton, this is the moment he has waited for. He says, 'Being part of that crowd inside the ground was the stuff my dreams were made of. I had seen loads of cup finals on TV but being there in person was completely different. There were so many flags being waved that at times our view of the pitch was completely cut off.'

But, once again, Ian found certain elements of Wembley a huge let-down. He recalls, 'I thought the ground itself was a total disgrace. There was urine flowing down the terraces and the staircases to the upper levels. The facilities were non-existent. I thought it was one of the worst grounds I had ever been in.'

The TV cameras pan in on United's Gordon Hill, whose bouffant hairstyle looks suitably blow-dried for the occasion. 'He's only been to Wembley once before,' says Brian Moore, 'and that was to watch a speedway competition.'

If Rodrigues's moustache is impressive, Hill's effort is anything but. He looks like a fifth-former trying to impress his mates by not shaving for a few days. Then we get a closer look at Channon, who is making his own facial hair statement with a dense pair of mutton chop sideburns. But they're all trumped by Saints midfielder Nick Holmes who has, gulp, an actual *beard* – a full-face rug. He resembles something between Kenny Rogers, Grizzly Adams and Benny from Abba. Treorchy referee Clive Thomas blows his whistle for the start of the game in a most impressive way, swinging his body and waving his arm forward to let battle commence and we are under way.

As usual, it is an edgy start and showing most nerves is Saints goalkeeper Ian Turner who, just hours earlier on national TV has, perhaps unwisely, admitted to being apprehensive. For the first time ever, his mother Evelyn is watching her son in action and he makes a couple of fumbles as United try to make an early breakthrough. It is just the start United wanted and Southampton didn't.

Watching from the stands, Pete Woods fears the worst. He says, 'The opening minutes seemed to be pretty much one-way traffic towards our goal with a number of chances dealt with – sometimes none too convincingly – by our keeper Ian Turner. I remember thinking "Oh dear, we're going to get hammered".'

In truth, it is a fairly dull opening punctuated by frequent offsides at both ends. 'If anything's going to ruin this cup final, it's this,' says Jack Charlton, with that familiar north-east brogue, 'because at the moment these tactics are stifling all the good attacking intentions.'

Both sides are adopting the offside trap. Soon, inevitably, someone is going to get it wrong and it is the Saints defence who make the first misjudgement. It is Hill who springs the trap, latching on to a ball lobbed over by Stuart Pearson. The young Londoner bears down on Turner. He just gets to the ball first but can't get enough purchase on it and Turner is able to parry away. It's the first real chance of the game.

Ian Brunton is watching at the other end of the ground, quietly pleased at United's opening. But it is not easy to follow the game. He recalls, 'I was about two-thirds of the way up. It was jam-packed and very uncomfortable. The steps were so shallow that I had to stand on tiptoes to see over the heads in front. And the heat was unbelievable. I think it was about 80 degrees. Quite a few fans fainted due to the heat.'

After 20 minutes, apart from Hill's half-chance, neither side have done very much, which will have pleased McMenemy more than Docherty. The Saints fans chant 'Ossie, Ossie, Ossie, Ossie' after Osgood does a bit of tidying-up in defence. The same chants intensify shortly afterwards when, at the other end, Osgood gets between two United defenders, but heads over from 15 yards. The team in yellow are growing in confidence. The Southampton fans are clearly delighted to see they are not being overawed and keep their chants going. Soon, there's the first really rousing rendition of 'When the Saints Go Marching In'.

Behind the mic, Moore is moved to comment. 'Significantly, there is not quite so much noise coming from the United supporters at the moment,' he says. It is because their team aren't really doing enough to excite them. It is a strangely low-key performance by United, lacking their usual verve.

Down the right, Coppell is his typical energetic self and keeps probing, but blond-haired left-back David Peach is, contrary to many pre-match predictions, handling him well. A third of the way through the game, Brian Moore says, 'We've had the half an hour which we said we'd need for Southampton to get through and so far there's been no disasters for the underdogs.'

Then, suddenly, almost out of nothing, they fashion a great chance. McCalliog receives the ball midway inside his own half. He moves forward, looks up, then plays a ball over the United defence who are, unusually, caught square. Before anyone can blink, Channon is in on goal. But he makes a hash of his shot and Stepney, narrowing the angle well, saves with his left foot. It is a glorious chance and the Southampton fans could be forgiven for wondering if such a clear-cut opportunity would present itself again.

At half-time it is goalless, much to the relief of Rob Innis, crammed in among the Southampton fans. He says, 'I was glad we got to half-time at 0-0, as of course we were frightened of being slaughtered. We seemed to be doing okay, but I expected that to change in the second half and for United to go into top gear.'

As the teams come out, it's the Southampton fans who are in better voice and another chorus of 'When the Saints Go Marching In' can be heard around the stadium.

The game restarts, but still United can't find their rhythm and Jack Charlton says, 'You get a feeling about this United side that, unless they score soon, a little bit of their confidence could go.' The cameras go to the hordes of Southampton fans, who are bouncing up and down and outsinging their Mancunian counterparts. 'I think that tells its own story,' says Brian Moore.

It can still go either way. On the hour, Saints skipper Rodrigues takes a knock and is concussed for several minutes and still groggy when United win a corner, which Hill takes. It is an inswinger which is met beautifully at the near post by Stuart Pearson. He swivels his head and flicks the ball across the face of the goal to the far post where McIlroy is lurking. It is moving fast and McIlroy has to lean back slightly to get his head to it. He does, but only succeeds in heading it on to the crossbar. It is one of those moments that induces conflicting emotions in fans of both sides. United start to think it's not going to be their day. Behind the goal United fan Ian Brunton is starting to fear the worst, 'The longer the game went on, the more I thought it was going to go against us.'

The United scarves and flags – waving with such fervour during the first half – are beginning to droop slightly. The songs from their fans are starting to dry up and are being replaced with a confused silence, as they struggle to come to terms with why their side is not putting the Saints to the sword. In stark contrast Southampton fans can now sniff a glorious opportunity. Pete Woods is starting to dream the impossible and dares to say, or at least whisper, to his companions, 'I think we can win this.'

Hill, who was expected to have such an influence on the game, is replaced by McCreery as Docherty goes for the win. Hill, so brilliant in the semi-final against Derby, has been largely anonymous and later says, 'I could have torn off my shirt and thrown it down in anger – not because I got pulled off, but because I played so badly.'

But McCreery can't alter the course of the game much. Southampton continue to hold firm with Steele, especially, having a blinder. In attack, they are starting to fashion more chances and, after a decent effort from Bobby Stokes, which goes just over the bar, Southampton still have belief.

We enter the last ten minutes. The game is on a knife-edge, which is reflected in the growing urgency in Brian Moore's voice. 'Still no goals here as we reach nine minutes to go,' he says. On the terraces, the Southampton fans, delighted to be in this position, are doing all the singing. Perhaps they sense something special. There is real tension in the air.

New father Mel Blyth fouls McCreery and, from the ensuing free kick, Brian Greenhoff tries a wildly ambitious shot from some 40 yards which poses Turner no problems at all. It is a goal kick to Southampton and a natural break in play. The crowd and players relax briefly. There is no hint that another famous cup moment is about to happen.

Turner, short, curly hair, very slightly protruding teeth, with his sleeves rolled halfway up his arms, produces a massive goal kick. It is like a long-distance rugby union penalty. An aerial challenge is inconclusive and the ball falls to Channon who, with his mind ever alert, lays it off first-time into the path of Jim McCalliog. The talented Scot quickly glances up and then, sniffing a chance to catch the United rearguard out, lobs a beautiful, defence-splitting pass over Buchan into the path of Stokes, who has found some space. His immediate body language suggests he thinks he might be offside.

On the BBC, David Coleman, voice quickening with growing urgency, tells the listening millions he is not. It is still only half a chance but Stokes manages to adjust his body into a position where he is in control of the situation. Pete Woods, Peter Harris, Rob Innis and 20,000 Southampton fans freeze, open-mouthed. Stokes has a crucial decision to make. Should he shoot first-time or should he make sure he has full control of the ball and then try to hit the target?

Out of the corner of his eye, he spies Stepney. He is covering the goal. But, just maybe, Stokes has a few inches to aim at. As the ball reaches its perfect height, Stokes shoots with his left foot, deliberately angling his effort as far away from Stepney as he can while still hitting the target. The little man has judged it perfectly. The shot has just enough power and direction to evade Stepney in the only part of the goal he is unable to cover.

'One nil,' intones Coleman, disbelievingly. It is a route-one goal but also a tribute to quick, first-time football. Stokes turns away in delight, arms aloft and with a cheeky, gap-toothed smile, reminiscent of the Artful Dodger in *Oliver*. First to him is the bearded Holmes, followed by Peach, Steele and Channon. McCalliog, meanwhile, appears to be saying something to Steve Coppell.

Pete Woods remembers, 'The goal seemed to happen in slow motion. When we saw the ball nestle in the net it was the cue for absolute pandemonium. The referee from Cornwall was knocked over in the excitement and I remember simultaneously trying to help him up, while leaping in the air.'

'Southampton go mad!' screams Coleman as the camera pans to the cavorting Saints fans and then turns to their bench. Kitmen, reserves and physios are dancing around, red-tracksuited backroom staff hugging and kissing in a fashion most unbecoming of middle-aged men. There is utter mayhem among the Saints fans for a good couple of minutes. No one cares about the heat any more.

Peter Harris says, 'It was simply an unbelievable moment.' Rob Innis recalls, 'It was completely out of the blue. For a split second I could not believe it, then the Saints fans erupted just hugging whoever they were closest too, cheering and laughing, I am sure the upper terraces actually moved a bit! There were some United fans in our section and I sensed a bit of aggro going on but it was too tight for much to happen.' 'It was offside!' protests Ian Brunton, vainly.

The camera turns its focus on McMenemy, who is wearing a fetching yellow shirt with paisley tie. He is sitting in an odd way – very upright with his hands on his knees – maybe the guardsman in him coming through – but the effect is of a manager posing for his team's pre-season photograph, not of a manager who is five minutes away from winning an FA Cup Final in exceptional circumstances.

For as long as they live, those Saints fans at Wembley and watching on telly, will never experience time moving so slowly again. 'An absolute eternity,' says Pete Woods. 'It dragged on for ages,' recalls Rob Innis. 'The longest seven minutes of my life,' confirms Peter Harris.

United go all out for the equaliser, but the Hampshire side hold firm. And then, to the delight of the Saints fans and, it has to be said, most neutrals (apart from Pompey fans), Clive Thomas blows his whistle for the last time and the unthinkable has happened. Southampton have beaten Manchester United and are the new holders of the FA Cup.

Back in Southampton, the presses at the *Southern Evening Echo* start rolling. Soon a special edition of the paper will hit the streets with a picture of the FA Cup accompanied by a simple headline, 'IT'S OURS'.

The Saints fans are in shock, as Rob explains, 'We were gradually starting to realise that we had achieved what 90 minutes before had seemed impossible. It was just unbelievable, an amazing feeling of overwhelming jubilation and relief. It was brilliant to have actually been there witnessing and experiencing the emotion.'

There are incredible scenes, not least a bizarre spot of rather dubious-looking wrestling between goalkeeper Ian Turner and left-back David Peach, who roll around on the ground hugging one another. But they can be forgiven because Southampton's achievement is a magnificent one. McMenemy goes straight up to Stokes and says to him, 'You're off the list!' Rob remembers, 'It was just incredible. We'd done it! The Man U fans seemed in a daze.'

On the pitch, United centre-back Brian Greenhoff sits with tears streaming down his cheeks while all around him can be heard the chants of the Southampton fans, 'We won the cup, we won the cup. Ee-aye-addio, we won the cup!'

And now it's time to get that cup. Up they go, fighting their way through the delighted backslapping and hair ruffling of their fans. Her Majesty The Queen, resplendent in a blue get-up and matching hat, which looks like a tea-cosy, presents the cup to Rodrigues who, watched by Prime Minister Jim Callaghan, raises it above his head as the yellow and blue ribbons flutter slightly in the gentle breeze. Goalkeeper Turner carries down the cup's base and Osgood puts the lid on his head. Turner picks out his mother in the crowd and holds up his medal. 'I'm giving it to her,' he says later.

Then the lap of honour, round the athletics track and down below the electronic scoreboard, which confirms the result. 'Congratulations Southampton 1976 FA Cup Winners' it says. 'Hard Luck Manchester United'.

The fans start leaving the great old stadium. United's reputation has gone before them and some sections of the media had predicted trouble if they lost, as Ian Brunton recalls, 'The press had been writing stories for a while about United fans wrecking Wembley if the result went against us. But they were completely wrong, as I never saw a single act of vandalism or violence after the game.'

There are a few Southampton fans who would not agree with this and there were certainly some flashpoints, but not the widespread disorder that was feared.

The fact is, most United fans are simply too shocked to misbehave.

United fan Jim Smith recalls, 'Nobody ever anticipated for one moment that we were going to lose the game. One of my mates saw me at the Tube station after the match and he really thought I was going to jump in front of a train. We were so confident after beating Derby in the semi-final and, against Southampton, I just could not imagine anything but a win. It was my first Wembley final and I have never felt so depressed in my life.'

Pete Darby's intake of bitter on that hot May afternoon means he can recall little of the day's events but he does remember leaving the ground bitterly disappointed and saying, 'We'll be back.'

Pete Woods, Rob Innis and Peter Harris all make their way out of Wembley. They are equally shocked, but in a delighted, ecstatic way. Pete remembers, 'We walked back to our car and joined the traffic crawl away from Wembley. After a few minutes we found ourselves alongside a large chauffeur-driven car containing a familiar face. It was Don Revie, who had been working for the BBC at the game. He was still in full television make-up and I remember that he looked very orange.

'Eventually, we reached the M3 and joined the returning procession of yellow-and-blue clad vehicles. All along the route, people were filling the motorway bridges to wave to the cars. In those days, the M3 did not go all the way to Southampton – there was a section of dual carriageway around Winchester – and, as usual, we got stuck at the infamous Hockley traffic lights. But instead of quietly seething about the delay, as was the norm, with all the car windows open, due to the heat, we all struck up a few choruses of "When the Saints Go Marching In".'

Peter also recalls a memorable journey home. He says, 'Oh, it was absolutely fabulous. Coming back along the A27, all the bridges were lined with people who had hung up flags and banners. In the more rural areas that we passed, many farms had put signs up on their driveways and entrances saying things like "Well done to the Saints". It was just marvellous!'

Rob says he was in a dreamlike state and the journey back to Victoria station for the train ride back to Worthing is a blur. For United, the loss is hard to take. The coach carrying Ian Brunton back to Manchester is not a happy place to be and light years away from the expectant journey south 12 hours earlier.

'It was a very quiet affair and seemed to take forever,' he recalls. 'My dad met me in Manchester town centre and he told me I was trudging along dragging a flag behind me, which I had bought outside the ground. He thought I was on the verge of tears. I told him that was it. Never again would I ever get to see United in a cup final. Never again would I see a successful cup run.' Fortunately for Ian, he will be proved very, very wrong.

At around 7.30pm, the FA Cup Final special trains start arriving back at Southampton Central station, where the fans get a tumultuous welcome. Car horns are blaring, people are dancing in the road and street vendors are doing a roaring trade in flags and scarves. There has been hardly any time for much real analysis of the game, but general consensus among Saints fans is that their man of the match is the young Scottish defender Jim Steele.

Boss McMenemy certainly thinks so. He has occasionally been irritated by Steele's love of the champagne lifestyle attached to footballers but, on this occasion, can forgive him. McMenemy says, 'Jim is typical of a Scottish player being caught up in the trappings of top level football…the money, glamour and hangers-on. But today, he was great. He is young enough to get into the Scottish side as long as he concentrates on the football and keeps a level head.'

The night goes on. The Southampton players attend a celebratory function at the Talk of the Town nightclub, on the junction of Charing Cross Road and Leicester Square. It's a good night but, like Sunderland three years earlier, many players would secretly have liked to be back in their home city. At the club, Jimmy Hill interviews several players, with popular match-winner Stokes getting most of the attention and plenty of affectionate ribbing from his team-mates.

Pete Woods recalls getting home to Exeter and waiting for *Match of the Day* to start so that he could watch it all over again. Then, after *Cannon*, starring William Conrad, and the news, Barry Stoller's familiar theme tune starts up and a nation can relive the day's wonderful events.

Back home in Worthing, Rob Innis remembers, 'We all gathered at my uncle's house to watch the TV and relive the moment. It was a big party with neighbours and other family members suddenly becoming football fans.' Saints fans everywhere are partying into the night, still coming to terms with what their side have achieved.

Back in London, their heroes are knackered and emotionally drained and finally get to bed. David Peach sleeps with his victory medal under his pillow. What a day to be associated with Southampton Football Club. In their excellent book, *Tie a Yellow Ribbon – How the Saints Won The Cup*, Tim Manns and David Bull say that some fans described the celebrations in Southampton and the surrounding area the next day as 'wilder than VE Day'.

The coach carrying the players back to Hampshire is greeted with ecstatic waves virtually from the off. By Basingstoke, the crowds are starting to build on the bridges and, by Eastleigh, there are fans and well-wishers on the streets.

At Swaythling, just outside the city centre, thousands of people are gathered outside the Ford factory on Wide Lane, home of the famous Ford Transit van. It is an unscheduled stop but, apparently, word has reached McMenemy that if they didn't pass the plant then mass-absenteeism would likely follow!

Two men climb a parked crane to get a better view of the bus. Two girls ride on horseback to meet the bus. One horse has the word 'Super' painted on it and the other the word 'Saints'. All over the city there are people sleeping off the effects of last night's revelry. The city has never seen anything like it.

The coach reaches The Dell, where the traditional open-top bus awaits to take them on a tour of the city. An estimated 200,000 people are gathered. Pete Woods is among them. He is determined to see the team and the cup before he goes back to university. 'So many people had turned out,' he says, 'that the tour took far longer than expected and I was beginning to think that I wouldn't be able to see the players before I returned to Exeter. But, finally, the bus came into view and I was able to give them a wave before sprinting down the hill to catch the train with minutes to spare.'

Eventually, the bus reaches the city's Guildhall where the players fight their way through the ecstatic crowd. Peter Harris still gets a shiver down his spine when he recalls seeing the team emerge, in twos and threes, on to the small Guildhall balcony.

'It was just amazing,' he remembers, with a lump in his throat. The Mayor of Southampton, Cllr Elinor Pugh, gives goalscoring hero Bobby Stokes a £1,000 'Golden Boot' trophy. Stokes also gets a new Ford car (even though he can't drive yet) and the whole club is given the freedom of the city.

As his train sped back to Exeter, Pete Woods was finally able to reflect on the most amazing weekend of his life. His face keeps breaking out into a smile. He remembers, 'When I got back, I went straight to the university bar, where I was greeted by a huge cheer from my friends. I had managed to convert most of them into Southampton supporters for the weekend.'

Pint after pint is thrust into Pete's hand. What a weekend for the young student! Come Monday, the celebrations show no sign of slowing down. The cargo liner *Southampton Castle* arrives at the city's port from South Africa, a flag saying 'Well Done Saints' flying from it.

There is also the small matter of Mick Channon's testimonial to attend to at The Dell. It is the perfect excuse for more festivity. All 6,000 stand seats are sold by midday. By early afternoon, queues are starting to form outside the ground and the traffic is virtually at a standstill. There are just under 30,000 fans packed into the stadium – many of them regulars deprived of the Wembley experience by the usual ticket policy.

Southampton wear their yellow kit again and Channon is applauded on to the field by his team-mates. Channon does a lone salute to the ground before the team performs a lap of honour holding the FA Cup aloft. The game, against league runners-up QPR, finishes 2-2, with Saturday's hero Stokes netting both Saints goals.

Southampton's glorious fairytale cup win was the first event of a summer still remembered for a wonderful period of hot, rain-free sunshine. Pallid-fleshed Brits, with pot bellies or bodies like pipe cleaners, nurtured on cloudy skies and drizzle, were suddenly exposed to an incredible spell of blue skies and sun, sun, sun. Somehow, it didn't seem to matter that the country was in a mess, the West Indies would slaughter England at cricket – despite Tony Greig saying they would be made to 'grovel' – and the Notting Hill Carnival would explode into violence as racial tensions simmered. Just the mere mention of the year is enough to bring a smile to Saints fans everywhere.

Pete Woods, the former Exeter University student, took early retirement from his job as a project manager with a large multi-national IT company in 2008. He lives with his wife, Karen, in Chandlers Ford, between Southampton and Winchester. He says, 'I spend my time cycling, gardening, travelling, watching sport and going to the theatre. I still support the Saints and attend some home games at St Mary's, usually with my 20-year-old daughter Samantha, who is studying law at Oxford University and is another lifelong Saints fan. Sadly, my father, who I was at Wembley with in 1976, died in June 2009.'

Peter Harris now lives just north of Aberdeen, where he keeps a trunk-load of Southampton memorabilia, including programmes and 'Pinkies'. He has a son and daughter from his first marriage and one stepdaughter and three stepsons from his second marriage. Between the two marriages, Peter has ten grandchildren and two great-grandchildren. Two of his grandsons are ball boys at Balmoor, home of Peterhead FC, where Peter now watches every home match.

He says, 'I haven't been able to get to St Mary's as every time I've gone south to visit my mother, the matches have been sell-outs. However, I never miss a "Pinkie" and I have a history of the Saints which I am constantly updating. My favourite ever Saint is a tough one as they've changed so much over the years. In the 60s it was Terry Paine, the 70s Mick Channon and then of course there is Matt Le Tissier and Ron Davies. I'll go for Terry Paine but it's a close call.'

The years pass but Peter will never forget that joyous day in May 1976 and he says, 'I still relive the match every so often.

I have the video of the game and it still sends shivers down my spine when I watch it now. I also have my shirt, hat and scarf from that final and, of course, my mirror, mug, record and video. I also have a mouse a friend made for me with a scarf, hat and badges which used to go to all the matches with me. I still give him a tickle before every game.'

Rob Innis moved to Spain in 2000 and is now a freelance writer, whose e-book *Spain Exposed* was published in 2012. He is an aficionado on Spanish football, and remains an avid Saint. The memories are still strong approaching 40 years on, of a great time to be alive. 'It was a very hot year,' he says. 'It was my first year in my own flat and life was perfect. The year the old misfits, the ale-house brawlers, lifted the FA Cup.'

LOVE THY NEIGHBOUR

Manchester United
v Liverpool

Saturday 21 May 1977

IN June 1968, life was sweet for Mick Gorman. He was 20 years old and the star player in his university football team. He had a girlfriend coveted by just about every bloke on the campus. He was the right age, at the right time. More importantly, the team he had followed and adored since boyhood had just been crowned European champions. What Mick would have given to be part of that Manchester United team that brushed aside Benfica on that glorious May night at Wembley. Though an extremely capable footballer, Mick didn't quite have what it takes to get to the top.

Mick was born in Collyhurst, just a couple of miles north of Manchester city centre, the eldest of eight children. His father, Tommy, was a porter in the biggest market in Manchester. Tommy, a Catholic, was raised in the United stronghold of Newton Heath. He was a massive United fan and one of the first lessons he taught his eldest son was about the football team he was going to support. And this, as Mick explains, was non-negotiable.

'From my very earliest days, I was a United fan – there was simply no alternative,' he says. 'You hear stories from that period of people watching United one week and City the next. Well, not in our house you didn't. My dad made sure the right choice was made and City, who in the 1950s were a bit of a force in their own confused sort of way, were immediately identified as the enemy. Living through the Munich tragedy just reinforced my love for United. All my childhood heroes had been taken away and I lived to play football. If only I could replace my heroes – but I wasn't good enough.'

While City were considered the real rivals of United in the Gorman household, the attitude towards Liverpool was somewhat different – at least in footballing terms. According to Mick, while there was geographical and industrial rivalry between the two cities, it was yet to manifest itself in footballing terms. He says, 'From what I can remember, in those days, Liverpool were fairly anonymous. They were only famous because Matt Busby once played for them. But I never liked them, especially because I remember going there with my dad for a cup match and someone stole my bobble hat.'

Some historians suggest the bitter rivalry between the two football clubs, which still exists today, grew out of economic factors beginning in the 19th century, when the two cities vied for industrial supremacy in the north-west. Manchester was world-famous for its manufacturing while Liverpool had for centuries been a major city due to its port. Yet many think the hostility really started when the Manchester Ship Canal was completed in 1894. This gave Manchester direct access to the sea and meant ships could bypass Liverpool completely. The loss in jobs understandably created bitterness on Merseyside.

On the other hand, the canal was a source of immense pride in Manchester, evidenced by the fact that both United and City have a ship on their respective badges, representing it. Still, says Mick, it took many years for the rivalry to emerge in footballing terms, with United tending to look down on the club 30 miles down the East Lancs Road. But, if Liverpool were an irrelevance to United in the 1950s, the appointment of a new manager in the last month of the decade was to change that.

When Bill Shankly took charge at Anfield, Liverpool were also-rans in the Second Division. The club were paupers feeding at the table of other clubs like United, Wolves and Spurs. But things were about to change. Slowly, but surely, Shankly and his backroom staff Joe Fagan, Reuben Bennett and Bob Paisley, began to turn things around. Promotion to the First Division in 1961/62 was followed by an impressive top ten finish in their first season, during which time Anfield began to build a reputation as an intimidating, daunting ground for away fans and teams.

Then, in 1963/64, at the height of Beatlemania – which, much to Manchester's disdain also turned world spotlight on the city – Liverpool won the championship itself, taking it off Everton in the process and leaving, of all clubs, United in second place. For United, Liverpool were no longer a small club somewhere near the Irish Sea, they were a fully-fledged, out-and-out rival, a team to be beaten and dominated and put back in their place.

For five years in the 1960s, United and Liverpool battled it out to be England's number one team, just like they had battled 100 years previously to be the most prosperous industrial city. United won the title back from Liverpool in 1964/65, while Liverpool won the FA Cup. Liverpool grabbed the title again in 1965/66, before United reclaimed it in 1966/67. The die was cast. Two brilliant sides, two great cities, desperate to get one over the other.

Then, in 1968, United raised the bar in spectacular fashion, winning the big one. Before a frenzied crowd on a hot evening in May, they brushed aside Eusebio's Benfica 4-1 to win the European Cup. Liverpool could only look on in envy. It was as though, at that point, United had won the battle of the northern giants. Their team was sublime – Best, Law, Charlton, Kidd and Crerand. It looked as though United would go on to dominate English football for many years to come.

Born in 1948, Mick was exactly the right age to enjoy the 1960s. It was, he remembered, a brilliant time to grow up and a brilliant time to support United. And despite all the undoubted distractions, Mick still managed to pass three A-Levels and win a place at university.

'Come 1970,' he says, 'I had lived through a magical decade. Culturally and artistically, the world had been turned upside down. United had won the cup, the league twice and the European Cup. Could things get any better?'

It was a wonderful time to go to university and be young and, as we have seen, Mick enjoyed all the trappings of university life. There was just one nagging problem. Out of all the universities Mick could have found himself at, the one he ended up at was... Liverpool. 'Yes, I was at university in the very heart of enemy territory' says Mick. 'I didn't know it then, but things were going to get a lot, lot worse.'

Mick's footballing prowess earned him heightened status and a place in the university first team. He was popular, had a pretty girlfriend called Chris and had a whale of a time. Overall, he loved being a student. But something prevented Mick from reaching nirvana. Too many Scousers.

As Mick says, 'Liverpool University always had more "home" students than any other in England and, in those days, there were also loads of "plastic Scousers" drawn to the city by the pull of the Beatles and the misplaced belief that it was the centre of the music universe. Every Scouser was a natural-born comedian. A cultural myth was being played out in front of my very eyes and I didn't like it one little bit.'

However, it was more than just an intrinsic dislike of the city of Liverpool that started to irk Mick and thousands of other United followers.

After the memorable European Cup win – which had looked so much like the precursor to domestic domination – United went into rapid decline. Suddenly they weren't challenging for the championship any more and could only watch helplessly as Everton, Arsenal, Leeds and, especially, Liverpool asserted themselves. United hit rock bottom in December 1972 when, after a 5-0 drubbing at Crystal Palace, Frank O'Farrell was relieved of his duties. With United fighting relegation and their bitter rivals Liverpool heading for the First Division championship, the Scotland manager Tommy Docherty took over the Old Trafford hot-seat.

He managed to stave off relegation but, the following year, the ultimate ignominy did come when United went down, just as Liverpool were on the cusp of domestic supremacy. United had gone from European champions to the Second Division in six years. As Mick explains, 'Now Liverpool were in the ascendant it was suddenly extremely tough being a United fan.'

Wisely, the United board kept faith with the Doc and the fans loved everything about him.

Mick says, 'The Doc was the wind of change that we needed. He was brash, iconoclastic, had an edge and, most of all – after a whirlwind of player changes – got United playing with pace and pride and we absolutely loved it.'

After hitting rock bottom, United are suddenly on the up. They win the Second Division title in 1974/75 and then, in 1975/76, finish an impressive third in the First Division. Then came the disastrous defeat to Southampton in the 1976 FA Cup Final. That match had been United's chance to exorcise the demons that had haunted them for the first half of the decade.

Defeat had hurt. They had found themselves in a similar position to Leeds three years earlier. They were the slain giant and neutrals didn't care one iota. Nobody spared a thought for the United fans, who left Wembley weeping, while the Saints were rightly lauded by all and sundry. But that's what happens when you're a big club.

Mick was 28 on that hot day in May 1976 and remembers, 'My lasting memory of that day was one of devastation of the fans around me. Grown people crying quietly at the end of the match and there was total silence on the Tube away from Wembley. I had that feeling that we would never get to Wembley again. But then, shortly after, Tommy Docherty had stood outside Manchester Town Hall and said, "We'll be back next year" and everybody cheered.'

Of course, to rub salt in their wounds, Liverpool won the league title again. Try as they might, United could not seem to get one over them any more.

The 1976/77 season starts in the middle of searing heat, towards the end of the hottest summer in living memory. But any hopes that the sunshine might improve the humour of those fans bent on causing trouble prove totally without foundation.

On the August Bank Holiday Saturday there is a fearsome punch-up on the pitch at the Baseball Ground at the end of a brilliant 0-0 draw between Derby and Manchester United. At the final whistle, hundreds of fans of both sides surge on to the pitch and police fight for 15 minutes to contain the kicking, punching mob. Twenty people, including three police officers, are taken to hospital and 65 are treated on the pitch for their injuries. Police make 16 arrests. News programmes screen the terrifying images, which show real, drunken violence with punches and kicks landing, causing genuine injuries. The mayhem prompts Derby to consider fencing fans in.

United fan Ian Brunton, who was so devastated after the 1976 cup final defeat, was there and says, 'There had been loads of trouble on the way to the ground, and it seemed as though all the local residents had come out to have a go at us. Lots of missiles were flying about from both sides. Inside the ground, we were penned in and I ended up near the fence separating both sets of supporters. Every kind of object was being thrown across the divide including batteries, coins, bottles and even bits of terracing.

'We got a free kick just outside the area and as I was waiting for it to be taken, out of the corner of my eye, I could see something heading my way. Instead of ducking, as I would usually do, I swayed backwards. Big mistake! The missile followed me and smacked me flush on the top of my head. Like most people I had long hair then and I could feel liquid running through my hair and down my forehead, which I assumed would be blood. I put my hand to my head and looked, fearing the worst. My hand was covered in a thick brown liquid.

'I put my hand to my nose and sniffed gently. A crisp bag full of brown sauce had hit me and my long hair was matted with the stuff. As it dried, my hair stuck at all angles and I looked like a punk rocker. As you can imagine, I got lots of sympathy and helpful comments from my mates.'

Humour aside, the fighting alarmed everyone who witnessed it. Even Derby's manager Dave Mackay, one of the hardest men in football, admits he was petrified by what he witnessed, telling reporters, 'No matter how tough you are, you must be terrified when this sort of thing is going on.'

A visibly shocked Tommy Docherty believes corporal punishment is the only way to stop the hooligans. He says, 'These people should be locked up and birched – they are idiots.' It is the start of a season where crowd violence is hardly ever out of the newspapers.

United make an indifferent start to the season. They are plagued by inconsistency. Despite this, Docherty is frequently quoted as saying that he has complete faith in his side. The prevailing feeling therefore is that there will be no more major signings. But then, in November, Stoke striker Jimmy Greenhoff suddenly becomes available. The Potters don't want to sell him, but have crippling financial problems and need the money. The Doc has admired him for a long time and pays Stoke £100,000 for his services. It turns out to be an inspired signing.

It is not just football violence that is causing concern – there is another issue raising its head, which promises to be an even greater threat to the establishment. The papers start covering 'punk rock' at the start of December 1976. In an article in the *Daily Mirror*, reporter Lesley Ebbetts writes, 'A new teenage craze is rearing its head. And it's not a pretty sight. This is the punk rock scene. And punk rock people don't want to be pretty. They reckon they are appealing only if they seem appalling.'

To demonstrate the point, two 18-year-old London punks are shown. Both have safety pins through their nostrils. One has a chain running from his nose to his ear lobe and a dog's collar. The other sports earrings and has a star painted over one eye.

That same night a band called the Sex Pistols – hailed as the leaders of the new cult – appear on Thames TV's family tea-time show with various hangers-on. Goaded on by interviewer Bill Grundy they issue a tirade of four-letter words. Nothing remotely like it has ever been seen or heard before and there is a huge reaction. Thames bosses immediately carpet Grundy and furious members of the public jam the switchboards. For the next few months, punk rock and all its 'evils' will rarely be out of the media.

As the year ends, Liverpool are top of the league but United are floundering in 15th place – not what the Doc ordered. It is looking like the FA Cup is their only hope of silverware. A home tie against Walsall in round three gives them the chance to make a decent start.

The Queen's Jubilee Year begins with Johnny Mathis at the top of the charts with 'When a Child Is Born (Soleado)'. It is the gentle, acceptable face of pop music. At the other end of the scale, the Sex Pistols continue to cause huge offence. As they check into a KLM flight to take them from Heathrow Airport to Amsterdam they allegedly swear, spit and vomit, which takes some doing. A KLM ground hostess says, 'They are the most revolting people I have ever seen.' It is the final straw for their record company EMI, which pull the plug on their contract, worth a reputed £40,000.

Back in England, the third round of the FA Cup is played on Saturday 8 January. Favourites Liverpool face last season's beaten semi-finalists Crystal Palace at Anfield and surprisingly are taken back to Selhurst Park where, in front of 43,000, they win 3-2. Despite their league position, the bookies have United as third-favourites for the cup and a solitary goal from Gordon Hill is enough to beat Walsall.

A new car goes on sale. It is the Vauxhall Viva 1300GLS which, so the adverts boast, has a 'breathtaking' array of features including; velour cloth trim interior, pile carpeting, continental front door armrests, dipping rear view mirror, two-speed wipers with flick wipe, heated rear mirror, cigar lighter and illuminated heater controls. Retailing at a mere £2,416, it is the new must-have car of 1977.

Britain shivers in late January and the pitch at Old Trafford for the fourth-round tie against QPR is like an ice rink. Most people are surprised when referee Ken Burns says the game goes ahead but, when players with the poise and balance of Rangers' Stan Bowles keep falling over, you know the pitch is unfit. It is a lottery with both sets of players appearing to have an unspoken agreement not to go clattering into one another and risk causing a serious injury. Once again, United triumph 1-0 with a Lou Macari goal the decider.

Liverpool sail through to the fifth round. They brush aside Carlisle United 3-0 with John Toshack, back in action after a three-match absence, superb. Carlisle, still hurting from a 6-0 defeat in the league to Southampton, are outclassed and their manager, Bobby Moncur, says, 'It was their sheer class which told.'

Come February, it is business as usual at British Leyland. Some 3,000 strike rebels have brought the car empire to the brink of total shutdown meaning 45,000 people could lose their jobs. Prime Minister Callaghan warns the firm that if strikes continue, it will get no more money from the Government.

The UK charts are dominated by smoochy ballads like Leo Sayer's 'When I Need You' and David Soul's 'Don't Give Up On Us' or disco hits like Heatwave's 'Boogie Nights' and 'Car Wash' by Rose Royce. And, if you want to listen to your favourite record, then you might like to shell out £329 for the latest Hitachi music centre which comes with belt-driven turntable, Dolby cassette deck, and four-waveband VHF stereo tuner with six pre-select stations.

Back in the FA Cup, at The Dell, Ted MacDougall gets the winner as Southampton beat Nottingham Forest 2-1. It sets up a classic cup tie as the Saints will play host to Manchester United in a repeat of last year's final. From the moment the draw is announced there is concern that United's notorious hooligan element will be looking to exact revenge for the events of May 1976.

Massive publicity surrounds the match on 26 February where a 30,000 capacity crowd is expected. Southampton quickly issue a warning to fans not to buy black market tickets amid rumours that £1 terrace tickets are selling for up to £20. More than 300 police and dogs are likely to be drafted in for the game to 'look after' thousands of ticketless United fans, who are expected to travel to Hampshire for the game. Saints boss Lawrie McMenemy says, 'We don't want trouble and hope there won't be any, but there are hot-heads on both sides.'

However, McMenemy's hopes prove futile. Though the game is a thriller there is trouble before, during and after the match. Southampton include only five players who triumphed at Wembley nine months earlier. And it is one of those players – Mick Channon – who earns the plaudits. Dropped three weeks earlier by England, Channon has a point to prove and plays superbly although he can't quite do enough to earn Saints a win as the game finishes 2-2.

But it is overshadowed by crowd trouble and, three weeks later, becomes the focus of a House of Commons speech by Southampton Labour MP Bryan Gould, who says it is time to stop talking about crowd trouble and take concrete measures to prevent it.

Liverpool make sure of their place in the last eight with a win over Oldham who, despite playing brilliantly at Anfield, lose 3-1. The United v Southampton replay is scheduled for 9 March at Old Trafford but, such is the reputation of the United hooligans that only just over 3,000 Saints fans will travel with thousands apparently deciding it is too risky.

Certainly that's the view of Lawrie McMenemy, who tells reporters, 'We've sold only 3,000 out of 5,000 seats and just 300 terrace tickets – people are obviously too scared to stand.'

Those who do travel witness a bruising encounter, which is dominated from the off by the home side. An early goal from Jimmy Greenhoff settles United's nerves and they could have – and probably should have – wrapped it up by the interval. But, three minutes before half-time, ref Clive Thomas rules that

Martin Buchan has fouled Saints' rising star Steve Williams in the box and left-back David Peach smashes home the resulting penalty.

In the second half, Greenhoff restores United's lead before one of Saints' Wembley stars, Jim Steele is sent off by Thomas for 'persistent misconduct'. It is the end of the road for Saints and they bow out. Manager McMenemy says after the game, 'We have held the cup with dignity and we hope we gave it up in the same way.'

The following weekend, hooliganism once again dominates the news. There is major violence outside Ninian Park with thugs brandishing flick-knives and a 24-year-old Cardiff fan nearly dies when he is stabbed through a lung after being surrounded by eight Chelsea fans. There is also trouble in the streets around the Baseball Ground where six police officers are hurt when rival fans fight with bricks and bottles after the match between Derby County and Birmingham City. And, in London, 39 fans are arrested after the League Cup Final at Wembley between Everton and Aston Villa. Violence at football is a talking point all over the country.

Meanwhile, Liverpool draw FC Zurich in the semi-finals of the European Cup and talk of them doing the treble of league, FA Cup and European Cup intensifies. It is really looking possible now and Joe Coral bookies are offering generous-seeming odds of 25/1. But skipper Emlyn Hughes is strongly advising any punter who fancies a flutter not to bother. 'Keep your money in your pocket. It can't be done,' he says. The problem, according to Hughes, is not the cup matches – it's the constant grind of league fixtures that present the biggest obstacle. He says, 'There are simply too many league games. Every one of the matches is a crunch. Success for Liverpool has meant that most of us are being asked to play 70 games a season.'

The FA Cup is getting increasingly interesting with an extremely strong-looking last eight. At Goodison Park, Everton face Derby, while just across Stanley Park, Middlesbrough visit Anfield. Wolves play Leeds at Molineux and United face Aston

Villa at Old Trafford. The ties take place on a blustery spring day.

At Old Trafford there is an early scare for the home side. Villa, stricken with injuries and a patched-up side, take a shock lead after just two minutes. A brilliant shot by Brian Little flies in past Alex Stepney. Then youngsters Gordon Cowans and Charlie Young take control and, for a time, it looks like Villa might cause an upset. But United dig deep and a lively performance from the irrepressible and seemingly ubiquitous Lou Macari, epitomises what this team are about. They equalise when Scottish left-back Stewart Houston blasts home a free kick and then Macari notches the winner 15 minutes from time. United march on.

After the game, Docherty is in a positive frame of mind and, perhaps a little prematurely, tells reporters, 'I've been invited out to dinner in London on cup final eve, but I've already told the fellow that I can't leave the team before such an important match.'

Pens poised, the gentlemen of the press know a gag is not far behind. The Doc doesn't disappoint, 'Mind you, I've also told him that if the lads are going to play like they did at Wembley last season, we might as well all go along and enjoy his hospitality.'

Yet underneath the wisecracking exterior, lies a steely, ambitious manager and he concludes with the words, 'This is a better team than the one that lost to Southampton. Better, because it is more experienced.'

They are a team who are also winning plaudits for the fast-flowing, ball-to-feet way that they perform. The crowd love it and so do the directors. They meet shortly to discuss a new contract for the Doc and it's expected to be both lengthy and lucrative in recognition of the job he has done.

Meanwhile, down the East Lancs Road at Liverpool, there is talk of a new star in the making. He is a gangly 20-year-old local lad with flame-coloured hair, freckles and piercing eyes whose name is David Fairclough. It is a stroke of brilliance from him that changes the course of the sixth round tie at Anfield against Middlesbrough. Just past the hour, Fairclough collects the ball and unleashes a superb left-footed shot from 30 yards and sets Liverpool on course for a 2-0 victory. After the game, all the talk is about Fairclough. Veteran Boro striker Alf Wood pays him an astonishing compliment when he says, 'He may still have a lot to learn, but he does certain things that even Jimmy Greaves or Bobby Charlton wouldn't contemplate.'

In the other quarter-final matches, Everton beat Derby 2-0 and Leeds win 1-0 at Wolves. It sets up a delicious semi-final draw: Liverpool, United, Everton and Leeds. Whichever way the balls come out of the hat, it would mean two tasty ties. As it is, the draw creates a Merseyside derby and pits United against their old adversaries, Leeds. Mick Gorman could always recall listening to the semi-final draw and the excitement he felt when United were drawn with Leeds, 'Though we were both mid-table, drawing Leeds seemed massive at the time. And it was back to Hillsborough where we had destroyed Derby 12 months earlier.'

Before that comes a notorious visit to Carrow Road where United's fans riot again. After United go down 2-1 – their first defeat in 12 matches – their hooligan followers get to work. They begin to dismantle the stand they are in, ripping boards and asbestos from the roof and hurling them at police and Norwich fans. One fan, filmed by TV cameras, somehow manages to clamber on top of the stand before crashing through the flimsy structure. It is a miracle he is not killed and not just because of the fall itself. He is placed on a stretcher and then has to flee for his life when angry Norwich fans try to get to him. It is mayhem again and probably worse than events at The Dell.

Several stabbings are reported, cars overturned and fires started. A 20-minute film of the events at Norwich is screened on BBC's early evening news magazine programme *Nationwide* on Monday, bringing the subject to an even wider audience. It seems everyone has an opinion, but no one has a realistic remedy.

Now it is the turn of outspoken Norwich manager John Bond to offer his opinion. He says, 'This has gone on long enough and it's time the authorities did something to crush it.' Always guaranteed to give reporters a few decent paragraphs, Bond goes on, 'One idea might be to put these people in "hooligan compounds" every Saturday afternoon. They should be herded together, preferably in a public place. That way they could be held up to ridicule and exposed for what they are – mindless morons with no regard for other people's property or well-being.' The Doc meanwhile falls back on his usual 'bring back the birch' refrain.

Ian Brunton, part of the notorious United following at this time, has this take on events, 'Up to my late teens I lived in the Manchester suburb of Collyhurst, which was as rough as hell. I then lived in Moston for 30 years. In both areas, you either sank or swam and it was an absolute "must" to look after yourself and never back down from a confrontation. If you did, there would be a queue the day after of people wanting to have a go at you.

'Fighting was so common that it became an acceptable part of a lot of people's lives, although thankfully not mine. When I started going to United away games, fighting at football was an everyday occurrence. I knew if I went to a game I would either see trouble or, if I was unlucky, get involved.'

Ian continues, 'I decided that I would rather be in a large group of older lads than go on my own and get attacked so I used to get the train with the Collyhurst Reds, a motley crew who would get involved in any trouble going on or start it themselves. I never directly wanted to get into any of that but I also knew that I was safer with them than without them. If we went to, say, Newcastle away, I knew that we would have to fight our way out of the train station and, after the game, fight our way back in.

'There was no way I was going to achieve that on my own as a 15- or 16-year-old so my options were either "don't go" – which was not a real option – or go with a group of nutters. As I became accepted in the group, I made it clear I wouldn't get involved unless we were attacked which, sadly, happened a lot. As a complete paradox, I admit that I took huge pride in going to places and taking over and even more so, if the home supporters put up a fight.

'I have spent my entire life trying to figure out why I thought that way, as I am not a violent man. I have yet to think of a reason! I can honestly say I have never attacked an opposition supporter just for the hell of it, but I have to admit to often being involved in fighting in the late 1970s and early 80s.'

Tony Ryan, another fan who regularly followed United away in the mid- and late 1970s, says, 'I was only in my teens then and it was great to feel part of a large crowd fuelled with adrenalin and drink. I have to say that I quite admired the larger group but wasn't a fighter at all. I just liked the buzz of the crowd that took over places due to the numbers and I usually felt safer in the larger groups rather than smaller ones.'

The hooliganism debate refuses to go away and, inevitably, the Government gets dragged into it, including Home Secretary Merlyn Rees. High-level talks take place between FA officials and Sports Minister Denis Howell, who is expecting a grilling in Parliament about what football is doing to put its house in order.

While this debate is raging, Liverpool are preparing for the first leg of their European Cup semi-final in Zurich and spring a surprise by calling up another youngster who has been knocking on the door of the first-team squad. Sammy Lee is 18, pint-sized and Liverpool born and bred, and is drafted in because veteran winger Ian Callaghan has a heel injury.

It is a game Liverpool win easily, 3-1, and now their path into the final seems assured. No matter how hard they try, they can't escape talk of the treble. But they are being pushed hard in the league by Ipswich, who go top of the table, after beating Coventry 2-1 at Portman Road.

Meanwhile, United have an absurdly busy April ahead of them. Not only do they have the small matter of the semi-final against Leeds, including the Norwich match, they must play eight league matches in the month, covering thousands of miles in the process. Sports Minister Howell says United followers will be banned from away games as soon as possible. Bristol City, on the other hand, don't wait for an official ruling. They decide there and then to ban United fans from the match at Ashton Gate on 7 May.

It is late April and, at Lord's, a promising 21-year-old all-rounder called Ian Botham scores an unbeaten half-century for MCC against Middlesex. There is talk that the Somerset youngster might be drafted into the full England team for this summer's Ashes series.

All over the UK communities are drawing up plans to hold street parties in honour of the Queen's Silver Jubilee. Time was when neighbours could simply gather in the street and celebrate a Jubilee or Coronation – but not any more. This is the 1970s and residents are being advised to make it 'official' by applying to their council to have their street shut to traffic on the day. And to do this, you'll need to appoint a party organiser or secretary who'll have to fill in a special form.

The council will then make sure that the police, the Post Office and the emergency services all know. Then notices have to be displayed clearly warning that a party is in progress. As one reporter writes, 'Because, after all, you don't want a juggernaut ploughing through your jelly or brown ale.'

One of the most popular ideas people have been coming up with is to roast an ox at their street party. Joseph Barren, president of that august body The Old English Ox Roasters, who has been roasting oxen for 35 years, says so many people have approached him for advice that he is suggesting they roast a lamb instead. He says, 'Roasting an ox is a job for professionals. And when I think that a body of beef, which once cost £45 now costs between £300 and £350, well, better ruin a lamb than an ox, I say.'

While the nation ponders whether to roast a lamb or an ox at its Jubilee street party, Liverpool prepare to meet their Merseyside neighbours Everton in a repeat of the 1971 semi. The chances of Liverpool doing the treble no longer seem so far-fetched and the bookies are starting to look on nervously. William Hill are now offering no more than 11/2 and say they might have to cough up in the region of £50,000 if Liverpool do it. Fewer and fewer punters are starting to bet against it, such is the masterful way the men from Anfield are playing. Emlyn Hughes himself is having second thoughts, saying, 'I know I said a month ago that I didn't think the treble was on. It wouldn't be wrong to say I've changed my mind.'

So, now we know, Liverpool are going hammer and tongs for all three – and think they can do it. So does a fortune-teller called Mr X, who uses a 'magic pot' to help him make predictions. Mr X says they are going to do it. 'And I've never known him to be wrong,' adds Hughes.

On the day of the Leeds v Manchester United semi-final, all the pubs around Hillsborough and large numbers in Sheffield city centre are shut as fans of these two massive, great clubs descend. Many shops have pulled their shutters up, content to forego a day's takings rather than risk having their businesses ruined. It is grossly unfair on the law-abiding fans but such has been the panic surrounding football violence during the last few months that it is inevitable.

The ground is rocking on the day and United tear into Leeds, taking the game by the scruff of the neck, roared on by their fans. And they get their reward with two quick goals from Jimmy Greenhoff and Steve Coppell. In truth, Leeds can't cope with United's fluent attacking moves with Pearson outstanding up front, Macari dynamic in midfield and Buchan his usual ice-cool self at the back.

Leeds barely turn up and, apart from picking the ball out of the net in the 67th minute, Alex Stepney hardly touches the ball. United are simply too good for Leeds and the final score of 2-1 flatters the Yorkshiremen. The Doc is ecstatic, 'We are back at Wembley in the final because we earned it and deserved it. And, this time, we are not going to let ourselves down.'

After beating Leeds, United fan Mick Gorman knew where he felt most of the credit should lie. 'The Doc had delivered,' he said. 'After suffering the ignominy of relegation and watching Liverpool rise inexorably to be the number one side, it was special to get to Wembley again. Wembley finals were always special.'

There is major controversy in the other semi-final at Maine Road between Liverpool and Everton. With the clock ticking down and the scores at 2-2, substitute Bryan Hamilton slots the ball home. It looks like the winning goal for the Blues, but referee Clive Thomas rules it out for offside. Millions watching that night on *Match of the Day* see for themselves that the goal should have stood. It would have meant Everton going to the FA Cup Final for the first time since 1968.

But it is not to be and, the following Wednesday, Liverpool make no mistake, brushing their opponents aside 3-0 with goals from Phil Neal (penalty), Jimmy Case and Ray Kennedy. Now the bookies are getting really twitchy as the elusive treble begins to look ever more possible.

The intrinsically conservative FA is delighted that, in the Queen's Silver Jubilee Year, two greats of the modern game will contest the FA Cup Final. In fact, most people are drooling at the prospect. Most people, that is, except the two sets of supporters. Liverpool fan Chris Wood articulates this perfectly, 'If this was the "dream final" that the media wanted, it was certainly the "final from hell" as far as I was concerned and I suspect that many Liverpool and United supporters of the time would share my view. The rivalry between the two clubs was now becoming so intense that the results seemed to be even more important than the long-standing rivalry with the "other" clubs in the respective cities.'

Tickets for the United end are ludicrously hard to come by. Even those fans who have been to 42 league matches are not guaranteed a ticket – you also need to prove you have been to some reserve games as well. And plenty of fans can. Ian Brunton, who has spent the last 12 months trying to expunge the Southampton defeat from his system, decides to travel to Wembley without a ticket.

'I'd been to every home game that season, but knew that was unlikely to be enough,' he says. 'I applied anyway and, as I expected, was unsuccessful. But I wasn't too bothered as, the previous year, I had seen thousands get in without a ticket and was sure it would be the same again.'

Liverpool fan Chris Wood doesn't have a problem, recalling, 'I was in my fourth year as a season ticket holder and qualified that way. My standing tickets in both 1971 and 1974 had cost just £1 each, so no inflationary increases during those three years. But my ticket in 1977 was £2.50. This was around the time when the ticket prices started to rise every year.'

On 3 May, United have to travel to Anfield for a midweek match which Liverpool win 1-0 thanks to a goal by Kevin Keegan. It is a game recalled for all the wrong reasons by United fan Tony Ryan, who says, 'I was living in Crewe at the time and was travelling back on the train with a group of Cockney Reds who were really raucous and were scaring the life out of a bunch of Scousers in the same carriage.

'The United fans graffitied the carriage while all the Scousers sat quietly trying to ignore what was going on. I got off at Crewe, but didn't realise that the Scousers had also got off and a group of about six of them gave me a real kicking on the station front. I ended up with a broken nose.'

As the countdown to the final gathers pace, the papers continue to devote large numbers of column inches to stories of hooliganism. Two weeks before the final, United travel to the West Country to face struggling Bristol City, who have banned all away fans from Ashton Gate. Robins secretary Tony Rance says, 'We don't want anyone to come here to follow Manchester United. I don't care if they come from London, Manchester, Bristol or New York. They haven't got a cat in hell's chance of getting in without a ticket.'

All five divisions of Avon Police have their leave cancelled and special patrols are put on throughout the Bristol area to hunt down any United fans attempting to travel under the radar. And plenty do, including Ian Brunton, who remembers, 'We went down to Bristol anyway assuming that we could force the gates open and get in without much effort. There were probably a couple of thousand Reds with the same idea and, as the police feared a riot, they opened the gates and let us in, putting us in the empty away section. From Bristol's point of view, it was a disaster as every single one of us got in.'

It is a 1-1 draw with more crowd trouble before and after the game. But the main concern for United is a serious injury to left-back Stewart Houston, who fractures a leg and will miss the final, creating an unexpected opportunity for 19-year-old Arthur Albiston.

On 10 May, barring a virtual mathematical impossibility, Liverpool make sure of the First Division championship with a 0-0 draw at Coventry and will be crowned champions at their home game with West Ham on Saturday. But it is a lacklustre display at Highfield Road and some people think the Mersey machine is running out of steam at the crucial moment.

Then there is a furore when the FA announces that, should the FA Cup Final end in a draw, a replay will be played, somewhat bizarrely, on the evening of Monday 27 June, claiming it is the first available date. Both sides slam the decision with Liverpool boss Bob Paisley saying, 'Only people who have never played the game could come up with something like this. It's outrageous and ridiculous. I'd rather settle it at Wembley with penalties.'

Docherty agrees, saying, 'The idea of playing on 27 June just isn't on.' Then, in a suggestion which no doubt has the FA blazers choking on their lobster thermidores, he adds, 'Let's play it the following Saturday – 28 May – because, let's face it, the Home Internationals are a bit of a joke.'

Ever since his beating at the hands of Liverpool fans on the forecourt of Crewe station, United fan Tony Ryan has been in severe discomfort. He sits with a black eye and a broken nose as a doctor examines him closely, 'We're going to have to straighten your nose,' the doctor says. 'We'll need to operate. There's a slot on Friday 20 May, which we'll fit you into. You'll need to stay in a few days to recuperate of course.' 'Great,' thinks Tony. 'The day before the cup final.' His heart sinks as he realises he won't be at Wembley.

On the Monday before the cup final, United, whose league form has slumped alarmingly, travel to West Ham for a game which the Hammers must win to ensure their First Division survival. Three of United's expected Wembley side are spectators. Alex Stepney has a cold and a bruised ankle and is replaced by Paddy Roche. Sammy McIlroy has 16 disciplinary points and Docherty wants to make sure he can play at Wembley while striker Stuart Pearson has a groin strain.

But during the game, which West Ham win 4-2, Trevor Brooking falls with his full weight on Martin Buchan's knee. The following day the highly influential Buchan is seen by reporters hobbling around United's Surrey hotel, deep in consultation with physio Laurie Brown. His condition is a real worry for the Doc and United.

As Buchan fights for fitness, a quite extraordinary seven days begins for Liverpool. With the First Division championship trophy safely back at Anfield, the club are heading towards a unique treble of league championship, FA Cup and European Cup. Whatever happens on Saturday at Wembley they must dust themselves down before travelling to Rome, where they will face West German champions Borussia Moenchengladbach.

But there is no doubt they will be casting all other competitions to one side when they face United in football's showpiece occasion. Under the clever headline 'TREBLE RUM AND CHASER' a picture appears of Emlyn Hughes training on the sand at Southport behind three-times Grand National winner Red Rum. 'Emlyn' says the caption, 'has two more fences to clear to achieve his own treble.'

United, meanwhile, are indulging in training of a rather different kind. Never one to do things the predictable way, Docherty enlists the services of a 'glamour troupe' called Popmobility, a group of young, attractive women who specialise in keeping fit to music, to put his United team through their paces. Quite how this exercise is intended to help United cope with the likes of Terry McDermott, Jimmy Case and Tommy Smith is unclear, but the players seem to like it.

In Wednesday's papers, Gordon Hill is pictured with three of the young ladies, with a slightly knowing grin. Also in the picture is Stuart Pearson who, rather incongruously, is holding a half-drunk pint of bitter. It's a very '1970s' picture.

The referee for Saturday's final is 47-year-old Bob Matthewson, a former Bolton Wanderers squad player. Matthewson says, 'With two teams like Liverpool and Manchester United it could be the most exciting final and full of the best football for years. But as a referee I can't afford to stand and admire. I have to look at everyone objectively and ensure the rules of the game are being obeyed.'

Matthewson is surely hoping for no repeat of August 1974, when he had to send off Billy Bremner and Kevin Keegan in the infamous Charity Shield match, but he will be acutely aware that there are plenty of players on both sides who can be euphemistically described as 'not being shy in coming forward' and prepared to put a boot in, should it be necessary.

On the Thursday before the big day there is great news for United fans as Buchan is cleared to play. And Buchan gets a double dose of cheer. He is also rewarded with a new three-year contract. At the same time, veteran keeper Alex Stepney is awarded a one-year deal. He says, 'This cup final could well be my last big game and I shall be out to show I can still do it at the highest level.'

With just over 24 hours to go before the match, United fan Tony Ryan is wheeled into an operating theatre to have his hooter straightened. All he can think of is that he should, at this precise moment, be travelling to Wembley, not lying in a hospital with a steely-eyed surgeon hovering above him. As the anaesthetist does his stuff, Tony Ryan curses his luck. Such were his injuries and the date of the operation that he hasn't even bothered to get a ticket.

He is feeling no better when he comes round after the operation and sees a mate beaming above him. 'How are you feeling Tony?' says his friend, still smiling. 'What do you think?' says Tony, morosely. Saying nothing, Tony's friend reaches into his pocket and pulls something out. Despite being ordered to lie still, Tony springs up and grabs the small piece of paper, which his friend is now waving in front of him.

He recalls, 'Somehow, he had managed to get me a ticket. He had paid £15 for it – more than three times the face value – although that sounds remarkably cheap now.' To say the ticket is the best cure imaginable is an understatement.

Two white-coated doctors with stethoscopes hanging round their necks are doing the rounds of the wards. Finally they reach Tony. 'Ah, Mr Ryan, hopefully you'll be fit enough to be able to watch your beloved Manchester United in the cup final on the television tomorrow,' says the more senior of the two. Tony's words tumbled out, 'Well, actually doctor, my friend here has got me a ticket for the actual game so I was rather hoping that I could leave tonight and…'

'A ticket?' says one of the doctors, laughing derisively. 'A ticket for the actual game? You've just undergone a major operation Mr Ryan, under general anaesthetic. The body needs time to recover. The last thing you need is to be in the middle of a heaving crowd. We need to keep you in over the weekend.'

Tony looked despairingly at the solemn-faced medical men and then turned quickly to his mate whose facial expression was saying, 'Tony, how can you possibly miss this game? Come on Tony, it's no contest.' The doctors knew any protests were futile. 'You are making a grave mistake Mr Ryan,' said the older doctor. Tony doesn't think so. This is the FA Cup Final we are talking about. Against Liverpool. Nothing was going to keep him away. Not even an operation. He recalls, 'I signed myself out and assured the doctors that I wouldn't be doing anything daft the following day – and they eventually, reluctantly, let me go.'

On Friday night's 'Sportswide' (a special sports slot within *Nationwide*) both teams' strengths are assessed. Stamina could be a factor. There is a feeling that United might have a chance if wingers Coppell and Hill are prepared to have a go at Liverpool full-backs Joey Jones and Phil Neal, who were recently given a hard time in a league game by QPR wide-men Don Givens and Dave Thomas.

On the flip-side, United are perceived as having weaknesses in the air and Stepney has gained an unwanted reputation as being reluctant to come for crosses. United's bustling schemer Lou Macari and Liverpool's brilliant, roaming attacking midfielder Ray Kennedy could both stamp their respective marks on the game. Otherwise, it is just another typical Friday night on the box. There is *It's a Knockout* at 8pm with a three-way contest between Surrey Heath, Windsor and Maidenhead and Basingtoke, while on BBC2, Penelope Keith is one of the special guests on *Call My Bluff*.

Liverpool fans go to bed that night, no doubt thinking about the words of their skipper Emlyn Hughes. For the last few months, he has been constantly asked to rate Liverpool's chances of winning the treble. Now, on cup final eve, he offers this assessment, 'If we beat United to add the cup to the league then we'll go on to complete the treble. But defeat will make it very difficult for us to go on and beat Moenchengladbach in Rome on Wednesday. After we lost to Arsenal in 1971 it was a killer and took me a couple of months to get over it, never mind four days.'

This is the motivation that Hughes believes will power Liverpool on to do the treble and he concludes, 'No team, surely, has ever had a greater incentive to win the cup. We're playing at Wembley for two trophies.'

%, %, %,

The sun rises on cup final morning and it looks like being a warm one, which is hardly surprising as we are closer to June than April. The red exodus from the north-west is in full flow.

Train after train pulls out of Lime Street or Piccadilly. Both sets of fans are buoyant. On one of the special trains is

Ian Brunton. He hasn't missed a single first-team game at Old Trafford since 1972. He and his mates are desperate to see United halt Liverpool in their tracks.

'Although the press thought differently, we were confident we could stop them,' he says. It is only 6am, but there is already the distinctive sound of beer cans being fizzed open. By Crewe, Ian and his mates are already on their third can. By Stafford they are up to six. It is going to be a long day.

The southbound motorways are alive with cars sounding their horns. Scarves bearing either the famous Liver Bird or the trident-holding red devil flying from what seems like every other car. Though punk has been dominating the news, the charts are still dominated by radio-friendly, mainstream sounds: Deniece Williams's 'Free', Kenny Rogers's 'Lucille' and Elkie Brooks's 'Pearl's a Singer' are the songs being played on the radios of the Wembley-bound cars and coaches.

As the United fans travelled south, many of them were in thoughtful mood as Mick Gorman explains, 'For United fans of my age, in our late 20s and early 30s, there was the distant memory of the Babes being reduced to ten men and a passenger, by what in modern terms could only be described as an assault by Aston Villa's Peter McParland on our keeper Ray Wood and us consequently losing what should have been the double.

'Twelve months later a "rough house" Bolton side beat a scratch United side. Yes, there had been the moment in the sun when Leicester were beaten in 1963, but Wembley had no favourites and I went more in hope than anticipation. After all Liverpool had already won the league and the European Cup beckoned for them – European football was what United dreamt about!'

All over the country, televisions are being switched on. BBC1 viewers can watch *Chigley*, *Robinson Crusoe*, *Daffy Duck*, *Zorro* and a Laurel and Hardy programme before the cup final coverage starts at 11.30am. On ITV, it is *Saturday Scene*, presented by Sally James, which contains programmes including *Junior Police Five*, *Clapperboard* and *Space Club 1999*.

ITV's cup final coverage starts at noon, hosted by anchorman Dickie Davies. ITV hopes the pundits it has assembled – Jack Charlton, Mick Channon and Malcolm Macdonald – will lure viewers away from the BBC, whose coverage is fronted by Mr Clean-Cut himself, Frank Bough.

Mick Gorman had made his way to Wembley with a university mate called Ian. 'A Blackpool Scouser,' says Mick, 'and he was feeling pretty smug when we left each other to go into the ground, saying all those things you don't mean like "all the best", "enjoy the game". What you really mean is, "I hope we thrash you and the score is something great like 5-0".'

Mick's dad, Tommy, who explained to his son all those years ago that United were the only team to follow, is also at Wembley.

It is 1.15pm and at Wembley, the festivities begin with a half-hour performance by the Massed Bands of the HM Royal Marines, led by the Marines' principal director of music, Lt Colonel Paul Neville. Outside the ground, the atmosphere is extremely tense.

Liverpool fan Chris Wood, a veteran of 1971 and 1974, says it is the most nervous he has ever felt before a match of any description. He recalls, 'I knew that, apart from a European final, this was likely to be the biggest and most important club match I would ever see live. I wanted to put my nerves to one side to enjoy the spectacle, but I couldn't.' One thing quickly becomes apparent to Chris and the other Liverpool fans – they are going to be outnumbered by United. 'It was very clear,' he says, 'that even though United had had a pretty barren decade, this had done nothing to halt the rise of their fan base.'

Coach after coach pulls in to the car park. United fan Pete Darby recalls a light-hearted confrontation with some Liverpool followers carrying a placard depicting Tommy Docherty as a skeleton and the line, 'That shave was too close, Doc' – basically a p**s-take of an ad campaign for the new double-bladed Gillette GII being fronted at the time by the Doc.

Like their previous two finals in the same decade, Liverpool's supporters are at the east (tunnel) end of the stadium.

The terraces are filling rapidly. Those in the stadium are served some more bizarre fare, this time in the shape of the Wonderwings Display Team, described in the programme as 'aeronautical acrobatics' but, to you and I, model aircraft flying. First British team members Pete Tindall and John Newnham show us how it is done, before a special aerial battle between British champion Mick Lewis and runner-up Richard Wilkens – who are flying 'for' Liverpool – and Manchester United, who are represented by European champion Richard Evans and British team member John Hammersley. Nobody present at the match can quite recall this event at all, let alone who won it.

Liverpool fan Chris Wood takes his place behind the goal at the tunnel end. His nerves are jangling. Like thousands alongside him, he will be travelling to Rome in a few days' time but, for now, he is only thinking of this game. He, like all the other Liverpool fans, is desperate to beat United.

In the official matchday programme, FA secretary Ted Croker says, 'If we were setting out to "stage manage" a cup final fit to celebrate the Silver Jubilee Year, we would have needed to look no further than today's contestants.'

No sooner has the crowd recovered its breath after the excitement of the Wonderwings than it is the turn of the Royal Air Force Police Dog Demonstration Team to take to the famous turf to entertain the crowd. Once the dogs have done their stuff, the Junior Parachute Regiment treats the crowd to a display of gymnastics.

Thousands of fans are still outside. Ian Brunton and his ticketless mates have somehow made their way to the ground and are thinking how to get in. The obvious thing is to simply leap over the turnstile. The problem is, this manoeuvre requires a level of agility beyond the capability of someone who has consumed 12 cans of bitter. 'I had drunk myself into a stupor,' says Ian, 'and simply wasn't capable of jumping over a turnstile. I had also spent all my money so a bribe was out of the question too. As the kick-off got nearer, I began to realise what a fool I had been and I had blown my chances of seeing the game.'

But fellow United supporter Mick Gorman was now safely in the stadium. He remembered the Old Wembley with some ambivalence. 'It was a magical place, but it was also a tip,' he says. 'The views were terrible and, with the greyhound track and the low sloping terraces, the view was atrocious. So having a ticket in the lower west was not the greatest view in the house – but at least I was in the right end. My ticket cost £2.50 and the programme 50p. But the noise was intense and the colour of the occasion with flags and homemade banners was what made the occasion so special.'

Just behind Mick was a banner that was getting plenty of laughs from the United fans. It read, 'I'd rather be a Muppet than a Scouser'. Another referred to United's potent strike force and, with a further reference to that Gillette ad, says, 'Jim and Stu – the new 1-2'.

At 2.45pm, with thousands of fans still outside without tickets, Lt Colonel Neville raises his baton and the Royal Marines Band starts to play 'Abide With Me', accompanied by the Derek Taverner Singers. Opinion was always divided on the relevance of 'Abide With Me', but, for Mick it sent a shiver down his spine and brought a lump to his throat. For him, it conjured up the period immediately after Munich. 'It somehow managed to link sadness and hope,' he says. The singing of 'Abide With Me' sparks panic outside the ground, as those without tickets know they are running out of time. A hum of expectancy can be heard from within the stadium. It means the players are in the tunnel.

It is a hot day, not a cloud in the sky. The sunniest FA Cup Final since 1971, warm, but not as humid and sweaty as 1976. The teams leave the tunnel, proudly preceded by ball boys from the Leicestershire and Rutland FA. Both sides look relaxed. This is moustache city. They are everywhere – Stepney, McDermott, Heighway, Johnson and Smith. The Rod Stewart 'feather cut' is also much in evidence. Jimmy Case pulls a silly face as he passes the camera. The teams get a rapturous welcome. They are true heavyweights of the game with huge support not just within these shores, but also all over the world.

The managers, Bob Paisley and Tommy Docherty, lead the players up the pitch past adverts for Bush colour TVs, Dulux Paints and Chessington Zoo, at that time one of the major attractions in southern England. ITV commentator Brian Moore supplies one of those stats which mic men keep up their sleeves, just waiting for the apposite moment. He tells us that referee Bob Matthewson is the sixth member of the Bolton Referees' Society to be granted a final. 'That's a tremendous achievement for those referees up in Bolton. Well done,' says Moore.

Outside the stadium, Ian Brunton finally accepts that he is not going to get in. In desperation he asks a technician in one of the fenced-off TV vans if he can come in and watch the game on a monitor. 'He agreed,' says Ian, 'but as he unlocked the gate to let me in, some other fans noticed and rushed towards the gate, which blew it.'

The players line up and are introduced to the Duke and Duchess of Kent. Then the national anthem is played. Outside the ground, hundreds of ticketless fans are gathered. The police move in and herd them all into an area behind the United end. Ian Brunton is among them and recalls being bemused that the noise of 100,000 people suddenly disappeared. 'I was amazed at how quiet it was,' he says. 'Even the loudest roar sounded like a whisper.'

In the stadium itself the preliminaries are over and the players take their positions. Liverpool are in a change strip of white shirts and black shorts. John Lennon, circa *Sgt Pepper*, doppelganger David Johnson touches the ball to a pre-bubble-permed Kevin Keegan and we are off.

It is a clash of the titans, two giants of the game and, in truth, in the first half both teams play like the lumbering giants you would see on *Jeux Sans Frontieres*. There is not much for the estimated 400 million people watching around the world to get excited about.

Ian, locked outside the ground in the pen underneath the United section, recalls, 'I remember one of the odd things about

Wembley was the fact that the stairwells had window shaped openings on them – presumably to let the smell of urine escape! It had dawned on a few United fans that we were outside and, every so often, they would come to an opening and let us know how the game was going.'

A cross/shot from Gordon Hill has Ray Clemence back-pedalling to tip the ball over for a corner and then Stuart Pearson has a half-chance which Clemence saves easily. For Liverpool, the influential Ray Kennedy, now a very different player from the 19-year-old from Arsenal's winning side, is looking the most likely to do something with his late, surging runs into dangerous areas.

Ian and the herd of United fans outside can only guess what the occasional, barely audible 'oohs' and 'aahs' emanating from the stadium mean. They are desperate for their informants to give them a signal but it is not until half-time that they give the neutral signal, which tells them it is goalless.

Neither side have been able to assert themselves sufficiently to alter the course of the game. If anything, Liverpool have probably shaded it and, as Mick Gorman recalls, the United fans were content, albeit slightly relieved. He says, 'We weren't really in the game at all and the first half passed by in a whirl and, to be honest, 0-0 seemed a good place to be.'

It looks like another one of those finals where a single goal might win it. It is tight and tense. The fans drinking their half-time pints discuss how their team might be able to unlock the opposing defence. Liverpool fans are marginally more satisfied. Their defence doesn't look like being breached. As the fans return to their seats or their spot on the terraces, they are willing one of their players to produce just one moment of magic that will be enough to win the game. That is all it will need. No one in the ground, however, can predict what will happen next.

With just five minutes of the second half played, the game explodes into life out of nothing. The ball is with Alex Stepney. The United keeper kicks long but it goes straight to Liverpool skipper Emlyn Hughes, who heads it back hard. The ball sails to Keegan in the centre circle, who leaps and twists his neck muscles to try to head it onwards. But he mis-times and, instead, his header goes slightly backwards, in the air, to Sammy McIlroy.

The head tennis continues as McIlroy nods the ball back into the Liverpool half towards Hughes. Hughes is suddenly caught in two minds and the ball bounces in front of him. It is a crucial error. His hesitation has allowed Jimmy Greenhoff to steal in and nod it forward.

Suddenly, the Liverpool defence are caught square and Pearson, though marked closely by Welsh left-back Joey Jones, has a sniff of a chance. Pearson heads it away from Jones and then, from 12 yards out and at a tight angle, fires a great shot under Clemence, who looks slow going down. It is a superb finish by the former Hull man and he celebrates in his distinctive way – a single clenched fist raised to the sky. It really is a well-taken goal, though a keeper of Clemence's quality should have done better with it. The deadlock is broken. First blood to United.

Behind the goal, Mick Gorman was going mad. 'It was a Pearson classic,' he says. 'One on one and you knew it would be a goal. Pearson was one of the Doc's great purchases. Inspired even. When United got relegated he just took the top scorer in the Second Division and said "Get those goals again and we'll be back in the top flight". He was right. After Pearson's goal, we were in dreamland.'

Outside the stadium, Ian and his mates can hear the muffled cheers and are pretty sure it is the United fans. But it is only when the delighted face of one of their informants appears through the stairwell aperture and raises his fist and mouths 'Pearson' that they know they can celebrate. In their little area, they dance and sing. Everyone agrees that one goal might be enough. The Liverpool fans are mute and angry. 'Ray Clemence should have done better with it,' is Chris Wood's stark assessment of the goal.

As the game restarts, the United fans are going mad, flags and banners waving. 'We shall not, we shall not be moved!' they bellow. They already think the cup is coming back to Old

Trafford for the first time since 1963 and they are bouncing up and down and singing. But they are woefully premature. This is a truly great Liverpool side and they hit back almost immediately.

Chris says, 'Because of my experience of seeing so many games at Anfield, I knew our support would often lift our team if we were behind or perhaps struggling in a game.'

So, though the United fans are in fine voice, the Kop digs deep and starts to will their side on. And it works.

There doesn't look to be a lot of danger for United when Terry McDermott finds Steve Heighway lurking on the left wing. The Eire international has few options so he nudges the ball back to McDermott, who slides it to Joey Jones, who is being hassled by the livewire Coppell. But Jones beats the Liverpudlian Coppell with a deft step inside. The obvious pass looks like one back to Heighway. Instead, Jones flights a long searching ball into United's box.

It is probably meant for Keegan but it's too high for him. Instead it sails to Case who is 15 yards out, with his back to goal. Three great touches with his right peg prove decisive. First, he controls it brilliantly on his thigh. Then, before the ball has bounced he takes another deft touch and, as he does so, swivels, before unleashing a brilliant rising drive past Stepney and into the net. It is a piece of real quality from Case and a smashing riposte from the Scousers who are delighted. 'Stepney prostrate. Liverpool celebrate,' says Brian Moore.

'It was a ferocious shot,' recalls Chris Wood. 'There was a split-second as our eyes followed the ball and then we watched it hit the back of the net before we realised for sure what had really happened.'

Liverpool fans, naturally, are totally delirious to have equalised so quickly. They are convinced that they will now go on to win the game. It is a goal that keeps their dreams of the treble alive. On the other hand, Case's equaliser has stunned the United fans into silence. They now fear that the famous Liverpool 'machine' will shift up a gear.

'It was like being woken from a dream,' says Mick Gorman. 'We United fans were now wondering if we'd be steamrollered out of it.'

Outside the stadium, the clump of United fans have suddenly stopped their dancing as news of Liverpool's equaliser filters through. Their informant at the window has a very different face on this time. He grimaces and gives them the thumbs-down sign and mouths 'Case'. United's joy has been fleeting. It has been a mere two minutes between Pearson's opener and Case's reply. As the game kicks off again, some sort of calm is expected. No chance. Before anyone can come to their senses, there is another goal. And what a crazy, flukey goal it is too.

Coppell and right-back Jimmy Nicholl exchange passes before the ginger-haired Ulsterman lofts a high ball into the inside-right channel. Somehow, the pint-sized Lou Macari leaps prodigiously, beats Emlyn Hughes in an aerial battle and flicks the ball into the Liverpool box, where Jimmy Greenhoff and Tommy Smith tussle for it.

In the midst of their skirmish, the ball runs free – straight into the path of Macari who, after winning the heading duel with Hughes, has turned and sprinted into the area. The ball is slightly wide for him to hit cleanly but he swings his right foot. His shot looks like it is going wide but, mysteriously, it seems to change direction in mid-air and, suddenly, to the astonishment of everyone in the stadium, spins goalwards.

Liverpool right-back Phil Neal reacts with horror and desperately tries to keep the ball out. But it is to no avail and it is in the net. No one can quite believe it, least of all Macari, who leaps high into Gordon Hill's arms. To all intents and purposes it looks like Macari's goal. Neither set of fans can quite take in what they have just seen.

Mick Gorman can't have been the only United fan thinking that Case's equaliser would be the catalyst for a Liverpool win, as that is what Liverpool usually did. 'I was still assuming this when we were back in front,' says Mick. Everyone still thinks it is Macari who has scored. Mick adds, 'Macari, the player who turned Liverpool down to come to United. How fitting would that be? Our end of the stadium just exploded and the celebrations began.'

Outside the stadium, confusion reigns. The United fans are pretty sure a third goal has gone in but have no idea which way it has gone. Ian Brunton says, 'Then, all of a sudden, our friend appeared and we immediately knew from the expression on his face that it was a United goal.' The informant mouths the word 'Macari' and the fans are jumping about again. 'One Lou Macari, there's only one Lou Macari, one Lou Ma-caaaa-ri. There's only one Lou Ma-caaaa-ri!'

Closer scrutiny of the goal, however, reveals something different. It takes the slow motion TV replay to unravel the mystery. It shows that Macari actually sliced the ball and it was heading wide. However, with incredible good luck for United, the ball has hit Jimmy Greenhoff somewhere between the chest and shoulder and spun goalwards. It remains one of the oddest – not to mention luckiest – goals ever scored in an FA Cup Final.

Mick says, 'Of course, there were no big screens in those days and no instant replays. So, it wasn't until I read the Sunday papers that I realised it had been a lucky bounce off Jimmy Greenhoff.'

Not that United care. They are in front again. Mick says, 'When everyone recovered their breath after that incredible five minutes we suddenly realised there was still half an hour to go and that our celebrations might have been a bit premature.'

Now Liverpool's treble looks in real danger. To this day, Chris Wood believes Liverpool uncharacteristically switched off after Case's dramatic equaliser and it was this loss of concentration that subsequently lost them the match and the treble.

He says, 'There's an old and oft-used adage that teams are at their most vulnerable when they have just scored, because they are caught up in the moment and lose their concentration and focus a little. High up on the terraces that day, I certainly felt this when United's second goal went in. As the players lined up for yet another restart I was already resigning myself to defeat because, though my heart was telling me we could come back again, my head was telling me something different.'

Perhaps Emlyn Hughes was right all along. All those matches against Turkish side Trabzonspor, St Etienne of France, Swiss outfit FC Zurich and the constant grind of the league are now beginning to take their toll.

Outside the United fans are desperate to get in to try to watch the closing minutes. If their team are going to defeat their mighty rivals and deprive them of the treble in the process, they want to witness it first-hand. Ian Brunton says, 'As the game wore on we wondered how early they would open the exit gates and if we would be able to rush in. The police knew what we were thinking and tried to move us away from the gates. Without causing any trouble, we tried to stay as close as we could, trying to guess which gate would open first.'

At about 4.30pm the group hears the locks being opened. This is their chance. Ian says, 'I was determined to make a dash for it as soon as I saw a gap and I'm sure everyone else thought exactly the same. As the gates opened we set off for the gap but then realised stewards were behind the gate trying to stop us. Once they saw how many were running towards them they simply stood aside and let us in.' Ian's patience has paid off. He is in.

The Liverpool fans are slowly resigning themselves to defeat and the loss of the treble. Though they are still singing their hearts out and 'You'll Never Walk Alone' is resounding around the stadium, their great team can't seem to unlock the United defence. They huff and puff but the closest they get is in the 88th minute when Keegan gets his head to a long Clemence punt. The ball falls to Kennedy, who brushes aside a tiring Brian Greenhoff before unleashing a terrific left-footed shot which scrapes the junction of post and bar as it fizzes over.

It is the last salvo. Referee Matthewson blows the final whistle. United have won and, in the process, shattered their arch-enemy's treble hopes which, with the warped psychology that any football fan will understand, probably gives greater pleasure than victory itself.

Mick Gorman is still able to savour that moment now and says, 'The delirium that greeted the final whistle is hard to put into words. In those days, Wembley finals were so special. No play-offs, paint pot trophies or all manner of other games. This was a one-off. You had to be there and you had to win. We had won this one and it couldn't have been against anyone nicer.'

Ian Brunton closes his eyes, raises both fists to the sky and simply says, 'Yeeeessssss!' This is the reward for watching every single home game since August 1972. Gordon Hill, who was taken off, charges on to the pitch, arms aloft. Stepney falls to his knees as though he has just met the Messiah. 'The team that came here and ate humble pie last year have come back to celebrate,' says Moore. For Tony Ryan, beating Liverpool is the greatest revenge of all for that beating he took outside Crewe station. His face is still sore but does he care? Not a bit.

The Liverpool fans are not hanging about. As the United players embrace on the pitch, they are heading for the exits, already turning their attention to Rome on Wednesday. But the defeat hurts badly, as Chris recalls, 'As Bob Matthewson blew the final whistle, the despair and tears of the Liverpool players on the pitch was matched by the desolate looks of the supporters around me on the terraces. Earlier, as I travelled to the stadium, I had made a decision that I would not hang around to watch United pick up the cup.

'I changed my mind, partly because I wanted to applaud the Liverpool players off the pitch as they returned to their dressing room. It was clear that very few Liverpool fans felt the same way as me. By the time the players had departed, the upper bay I had been standing in for the last three hours was almost empty.'

The defeated Liverpool players sit disconsolately in a tight huddle in the centre circle. Docherty congratulates them all. Ian Brunton fights back tears of joy as he sees the elegant Buchan leading his United side up to collect the cup and their medals. The Liverpool fans that have remained find their voices and the cry of 'Champions, champions!' can be heard above the cheers of the United fans. As Buchan reaches the top of the steps Brian Moore briefly turns into a fashion critic and comments on the 'spectacular tassel' on the Duchess of Kent's hat.

Ian says, 'When Martin Buchan lifted the cup the noise was such that I thought my ears would bleed. How that noise can't be heard outside is still a mystery to me.'

Now it is Liverpool's turn. Captain Hughes – always an emotional man – has a face twisted with tiredness and anguish as he collects his loser's medal. It is as though a season's worth of effort and exertion is etched into Hughes's face. 'It's not often you see that face without a great big broad grin on it,' says Moore. Liverpool embark on a tired, rather half-hearted lap of honour and then disappear down the tunnel. No doubt their minds, too, have turned to Wednesday.

As the United players perform their own lap of honour, the United fans break into a rousing version of 'Bread of Heaven'. 'Manchester United, Manchester United. We'll support you ever more,' they chant. Singing as loud as anyone is Mick Gorman, who says, 'Even in the closing stages of the game when Liverpool hit the woodwork it didn't seem that it was important or was going to change things. The cup was won. The Doc had delivered on his promise and the team had looked like a proper United team again. Two Wembley finals and finishing third and sixth since relegation. Now I felt things were getting back to normal, what Sir Matt and the Babes would have expected.'

On the pitch, the team play to the gallery. Stuart Pearson and Lou Macari place the famous trophy on the Doc's head. Docherty looks delighted. Nobody knows it, least of all the Doc himself, but this will be his last game in charge of United.

Finally the United fans start to make their way home. Ian Brunton is walking on air. He, and every United fan, fully appreciates the significance of this victory. As the joyous fans head up Wembley Way, a group of them start imitating the stunning opening bars to Stevie Wonder's 'Sir Duke', which is in the charts. 'We were all absolutely euphoric,' remembers Ian.

'We sang all the way back to the station and then as we waited on the platform for our train home.'

Meanwhile, Chris Wood and all the other Liverpool fans are in that private, silent place which follows defeat. Nowhere is this more apparent at times like these than on supporters' club coaches. As Chris climbs aboard his he sees sadness etched on the faces of fans who have travelled the length and breadth of not just England but Europe too in support of their team. And these fans are not used to losing.

'Many of my closest friends were on that coach,' says Chris. 'Some looked in worse shape than others but everyone, without exception, was pretty distressed. I tend to withdraw into myself after a defeat.' While the United fans celebrated, the song going through the heads of most Liverpool fans is that week's number one record. Rod Stewart has just hit the top with 'I Don't Want to Talk About It'.

The Liverpool coaches start to edge out of the huge Wembley car park. There is no quick getaway in these situations. You just have to be patient. And this gives ample opportunity for gloating rival fans to 'give it large'.

'We had to endure a lot of verbal abuse and gesturing from victorious United fans,' says Chris. But, magnanimously, he adds, 'I don't blame them for that. We would have done exactly the same if the situation had been reversed.'

Now it is time for the post-match interviews on ITV, which are conducted by Gerald Sinstadt, who is wearing glasses the size of dinner plates. First up is Brian Greenhoff. His Yorkshire accent is so strong it sounds like he has just walked off the set of *Kes*. He says he didn't care if they were underdogs, they just wanted to 'go out and play'. The United players are in a mischievous mood and take great delight in confusing Sinstadt as he tries to interview them. Sinstadt is like an incompetent shepherd trying to gather a flock of rebellious sheep as he tries to round up the players. The interview quickly descends into farce.

Sinstadt, 'What made the difference this year do you think?'

Macari, 'We scored two goals and they only scored one.'

Sinstadt, 'Here's David McCreery. David, did you manage to get involved in the game very much?'

McCreery, 'No.'

Sinstadt, 'Okay, here's Sammy McIlroy.'

And now there is an excruciating exchange with Tommy Docherty whose private life is already the subject of whispers.

Sinstadt, 'Now you left your wife, err, at home this year, Tommy. Is she going to be allowed to come next time?'

Doc, 'I thought you were going to say I left my wife for a minute.' Nervous shuffling from all present. 'I didn't leave her at home, actually. She did come down for the game. But she's been a jinx all along.'

Cue embarrassed giggling from Sinstadt. His huge glasses shake slightly as he laughs. He is the only commentator who employs a window cleaner to clean his glasses.

Though brief, it is an odd exchange between Sinstadt and Docherty, more for what isn't said, rather than what is. There is more to this than meets the eye. And we won't have too long to find out what it is.

The fans disperse into the night. It is a glorious summer evening – a night for drinking lager. The United fans hit the capital, crowding into the pubs around Euston or descending on Trafalgar Square, before celebrating in Leicester Square or Covent Garden. Liverpool fans drink as well, but in a very different frame of mind. Make no mistake, they wanted that treble.

Chris Wood recalls meeting a friend on London Bridge station, 'He was proudly and defiantly wearing his Liverpool colours,' says Chris. 'We tried to talk about the game, but it was really, really hard to do so, such was our disappointment. We talked more about what was just ahead than what had just happened. In just four days' time, both of us, along with 26,000 others who wore the Liver Bird on their hearts as well as their sleeves, would be inside another stadium for another cup final...and this time history would give us a happier ending.'

Mick Gorman and his mate Ian – the Blackpool Scouser – meet back up. Ian was very quiet, Mick, by his own admission, unbearable. Back at the pub in Farnham, the booze flows, as Mick remembers, 'The more the alcohol took effect, the more lucid I became about the virtues of United and how easy it had been to beat the Scousers. Ian and I have since lost touch. I don't think it was just that day, but it won't have helped.'

The trains heading back up north are rocking. Ian Brunton and his mates have got their drinking boots back on and are downing the cans again and singing every United song they know. For Tony Ryan, beating Liverpool was sweet revenge for the battering he received at Crewe. And there is a postscript to the tale, as Tony recalls, 'Not long after the incident, the local coppers came round to my house and interviewed me. They had managed to get a good description of one of the Scousers and chased him up.

'When they called to see him he wasn't about to cough to anything until the coppers told him that I was in a coma and might die! He then spilled the beans on who his mates were. Justice was served again, as one got a £200 fine while the ringleader got six months – result!'

But what of Tommy Docherty? On 20 June, one of the biggest football-related scandals of the decade breaks. It is the news that Docherty has fallen in love with Mary Brown, the wife of United physio Laurie Brown. It is sensational news and no one can quite believe it.

A hastily-convened press conference gives new meaning to the word bizarre. It takes place at the Brown family home in Mottram, near Manchester. As Docherty and Mary Brown sit on the sofa holding hands and declaring their undying love for one another, heartbroken Laurie Brown is upstairs, apparently unaware of the impromptu press conference.

Father-of-four Docherty says, 'I told my wife Agnes about our plans last Thursday and Mary told Laurie. Personally, I think Laurie and I can still work together.' The distraught physio, perhaps understandably, thinks differently. 'I've lost my wife, my job and my two smashing kids. I've not been sacked or anything but could you work with a boss who has taken your wife?' he says. In the event, it is immaterial. Docherty is accused of breach of contract and a moral code. The Doc, never one to hold back, says, 'I am the first manager to be sacked for falling in love.'

All these years on, fans like Ian Brunton and Tony Ryan still take pleasure from beating Liverpool in the 1977 FA Cup Final. Tony says, 'By comparison, the competition doesn't mean very much at all these days. But, in the 1970s, we didn't win much and going to Wembley was easily the biggest trip you could get. The intense feeling of beating Liverpool can probably best be summed up by the equal fear of losing to them. I was in Milan in 2007 when we lost 3-0 in the semi-final and therefore missed out on playing Liverpool in the final of the Champions League. Everyone I know consoled themselves with two things: firstly we wouldn't have to even consider the indignity of being beaten by them on the most important game of both clubs' history. Imagine losing in the final and thereafter being taunted by your most hated rivals as a result?

'The second issue was that every single United fan I know – and I'm not talking about hooligans at all here – agreed that it was better for all concerned that we didn't play each other in Athens, as English football clubs would definitely have been banned for a very long time. Everyone just knew that there would be serious fighting leading up to the game and absolute mayhem afterwards, irrespective of the score. It was commonly accepted by all the Liverpool fans I know as well.'

Mick Gorman worked as a teacher and a football coach in Bahrain before returning to the UK and ending up in the advertising world, including a spell as media director at Saatchi & Saatchi. He then worked as a freelance media consultant and retained a season ticket at Old Trafford. Mick owed his lifelong love of United to his father, Tommy, who also took great delight in the 1977 FA Cup Final victory.

But, sadly, that was to be Mr Gorman's last ever trip to Wembley. On 26 November 1977 he made another rare trip down to London to visit Mick, who was about to go travelling abroad. Tommy and Mick went to Loftus Road to see their beloved United play QPR but, tragically, during the game Mr Gorman suffered a massive heart attack and died. He was just 53, but died watching the club he loved and which had brought him so much pleasure.

Just before the publication of this book in 2014, I received this email from Mick's wife, Rosemary:

'Mick Gorman died from cancer on 18 May 2013, having fought the disease for exactly one year. He lived life right up until his death, displaying courage and fortitude all the way. His last visit to Old Trafford was on Monday 8 April to see the home derby. He made that trip on sheer willpower as he was extremely weak by then. We were told on 8 May, ironically the day it was announced that Sir Alex Ferguson was retiring, that there was no more treatment and it was a matter of time.

'I am utterly devastated but have so much to be thankful for and there are daily reminders of his passions in life. When I hear anything connected to United, I think of him and have to wonder what he would have said about United's performances under Moyes.

'I have lost the love of my life and United have lost one of their greatest supporters.'

SUITS YOU, SIR

Ipswich Town v Arsenal
Saturday 6 May 1978

WHAT is more interesting? The repeal of the corn laws or your beloved team being in the FA Cup Final for the first time in their history? Would you rather be grappling with the intricacies of Pythagoras's Theorem or trying to secure a ticket for the biggest game of football you are ever likely to see?

In April 1978, this was the tricky dilemma facing 16-year-old Paul Devine who, in a few weeks, would be sitting his O Levels at school in Ipswich. It is an unattractive prospect at the best of the times. When your team is about to play the biggest game in its history, exams become about as welcome as an uncastrated bull mastiff on heat at a WI craft fair.

While Paul, who saw his first Ipswich Town match in 1969, was half-heartedly boning up on the Peasants' Revolt and the difference between a spur and an escarpment, another Town fan, John Cross, was preparing for the big day. He intended to make the most of cup final day and decided to wear a suit for this once-in-a-lifetime experience.

John started supporting Town during that remarkable period for the club, the mid-1950s to the early 60s. Then, a certain Alf Ramsey took them on a fabulous journey which saw them winning the Third Division (South) in 1956/57, the

Second Division title in 1960/61 and then, the following year, to the astonishment and general delight of football, the First Division championship itself.

John says, 'For the first few years, my support was spasmodic, because I could only go to games when I was not playing myself. But, when I stopped playing, I became a regular, going to virtually every home game and then, in later years, away games too. I became a season ticket holder, a committee member of the local supporters' club and shareholder of the plc.' In other words, John Cross became Ipswich Town through and through.

Ramsey's stunning success did, of course, earn him the England job and World Cup glory. And, for a time, his shoes proved impossible to fill with his successor at Portman Road, the Newcastle legend Jackie Milburn, only lasting 16 months, during which time Town were relegated. Then came Bill McGarry, who won the Second Division title in 1968, before the following season taking the vacant manager's seat at Wolves. McGarry's departure opened the door for a man who would take Town to places they could only have dreamed of.

When Fulham sacked Bobby Robson, it looked like the usual scenario of a great player not being able to cut it as a manager. But Robson had something about him and, given the freedom to operate by the Ipswich board, started to build a new team. First he installed Surrey-born defender Mick Mills as skipper and, early in the decade, brought in talented youngsters like Geordie defender Kevin Beattie and Norfolk-born striker Trevor Whymark to mould a side that brought fresh success to Suffolk.

Between 1972/73 and 1976/77 they were remarkably consistent, finishing third twice, fourth twice and sixth once in the top flight. No episode of *The Big Match* during this period seemed complete without a breathless commentary from Anglia's football correspondent Gerry Harrison, describing goals flying in from Whymark, Brian Talbot or David Johnson, often crafted by Clive Woods, Bryan Hamilton or Mick Lambert.

Norwich aside, everybody seemed to love Ipswich. They were honest, unpretentious and entertaining. Portman Road was a terrific ground with a great atmosphere and Bobby Robson was popular everywhere. What the club needed – and deserved – was a major trophy to show for their efforts.

In stark comparison, considering the magical way the decade had begun for them, the 1970s had been a massive let-down for Arsenal. At precisely the time Ipswich's star was beginning to ascend, Arsenal's was beginning to wane. Double winners in 1971, cup finalists in 1972 and league runners-up in 1973, they looked set to battle it out with Liverpool and Leeds as the team of the decade.

But, by 1973/74, the ageing team was starting to break up, the rot was setting in and they finished tenth. They then went from bad to worse, finishing 16th in 1974/75 and one place lower the next year. It was a fall from grace almost as bad as Manchester United's.

Diane Betts, known as Di, was born in 1961, and even though she grew up in North London there was no tradition of supporting Arsenal in her family, as she explains, 'My dad was from South London and a Charlton fan and my mum, although she liked football, had no particular allegiance to any particular club.'

Maybe the natural club for Di to gravitate towards was Spurs. After all, they were the most successful club by far in the area in the 1960s. So why didn't Di support them? Simple, she didn't like their name. When Di was about six, a boy at her school asked her who she supported, Arsenal or Spurs? It was a closed question. There were no other alternatives. It simply wasn't conceivable in that part of London that anyone would even contemplate following another club.

'I didn't know what to say,' remembers Di. 'There was no other choice offered, it had to be one or the other. So I said Arsenal. I didn't like the sound of "Tottenham Hotspur". I thought the words sounded ugly, whereas "Arsenal" rolled off the tongue. It was as arbitrary as that. I had inadvertently committed myself to a lifetime of being an Arsenal fan. It could just as easily have been the other lot. Perish the thought!'

So a simple linguistic preference sealed Di's fate. Desperate to start watching some live football, Di began going to non-league Barnet, but while standing on the sparse terraces at Underhill, could only dream of one place. Highbury. It would take years of badgering her dad before he finally agreed to take her. When she did get there, she was absolutely smitten. The die was cast, or maybe the Di was cast... By the time 1977/78 came around, Di was a regular on the North Bank.

When the season began, no one was really expecting anyone other than Liverpool to lift the First Division title. Certainly hardly anyone was putting any money on Brian Clough's newly-promoted Nottingham Forest. Yet, boosted by the September arrival of Peter Shilton from Stoke, Forest stormed to the top of the table and stayed there virtually all season to complete a remarkable success. Ipswich, as usual, were expected to be there or thereabouts, but a lengthy injury list meant they never got going in the league and, come January, the FA Cup was their only hope.

From the outset, the 1977/78 FA Cup was branded the 'Year of the Minnows'. Six non-league clubs are still in the competition when the third round arrives. Ahead of Arsenal's third-round tie, full-back Pat Rice predicts that one of four teams will lift the cup: Nottingham Forest, Liverpool, Southampton or Spurs. He modestly declines to mention his own side, who travel to Bramall Lane to meet in-form Second Division side Sheffield United. But *Mirror* reporter Harry Miller does. He includes the Gunners in his last-four tip, the others being Derby, Wolves and Sunderland.

In the event, Arsenal play superbly at Bramall Lane and, incredibly, are 4-0 up inside 17 minutes, eventually running out 5-0 winners.

Meanwhile, Ipswich have an awkward-looking third round trip to Cardiff in a game that kicks off at the unusual time of 2.30pm. It is a wet day in South Wales and those hardy Town fans who do make the trip are 'welcomed' by some of Cardiff's somewhat notorious followers. Ipswich fan Colin Kriedewolf was there and he recalls the day, 'There was no proper segregation in the ground and midway through the second half, with the Town ahead, some Cardiff fans tried to get overly friendly and a few scuffles ensued, but it was a comfortable 2-0 win and we moved into the next round.'

In truth, most Town fans are thankful to get away from the ground in one piece. However, a notorious incident later on in the cup run will make the events at Ninian Park seem like a chimps' tea party in comparison. Arsenal and Ipswich both get home ties in the fourth round and both come through. The Gunners beat Wolves 2-1 and Town cruise through by beating Hartlepool 4-1.

It is February 1978. Anna Ford starts work as ITV's first woman newscaster. In America, Leon Spinks becomes the first professional boxer to beat Muhammad Ali for the world heavyweight boxing title and, in the UK, inflation falls to 9.9 per cent, the first time in nearly five years it has been in single figures. Abba continue their domination of the UK charts with 'Take a Chance on Me' riding high. ELO, whose double album *Out of the Blue* continues to be a massive seller, get close to the top spot with 'Mr Blue Sky'. Rose Royce is 'Wishing on a Star' and there's a first glimpse of a 19-year-old stunner and doctor's daughter from Welling in Kent, called Kate Bush, whose remarkable song 'Wuthering Heights' is looking a strong candidate to top the charts.

One film is dominating the cinema. John Travolta's portrayal of Tony Manero in *Saturday Night Fever* helps make disco the definitive dance style of the late 1970s and results in Travolta wannabes strutting their stuff in discos from Weymouth to Wallsend.

The fifth-round ties are played on Saturday 18 February with the south of England covered in snow. Arsenal brush aside Walsall 4-1, the highlight being a superb goal by Alan Sunderland, a recent £200,000 capture from Wolves. Ipswich fans are back down the M4 to Eastville, home of Bristol Rovers. The pitch is icy and treacherous but, for some reason, the referee decides the game should go ahead, despite the objections of a cavalcade of Bobbys – Bobby Robson, Rovers boss Bobby Campbell and their player/coach Bobby Gould who says, 'Players should be consulted on whether conditions are playable.'

The game is a lottery and Town are close to going out, with only a late equaliser from Robin Turner, his second goal, keeping their cup dream alive. But Town make no mistake in the replay and the Pirates are sent packing from Suffolk back to the West Country licking their wounds after a 3-0 defeat.

The competition is wide open and the last eight is interesting for its lack of big names. Arsenal and Ipswich are both drawn away to lower-league opposition. The Gunners have a long trip to Wrexham and Ipswich, much to their chagrin, must go to Millwall. It is an unenviable prospect for the Suffolk side. Fans of the South London team can scent a bit of cup glory themselves and are right up for the match.

The sixth-round game at The Den has gone down in footballing history as one of the worst cases of crowd disturbance in the seventies, which is saying something. Any away fans going to The Den knew it wouldn't be a walk in the park. Many didn't bother. Even the name of the road the ground was on, Cold Blow Lane, created a sense of desolation, fear and foreboding.

A BBC *Panorama* programme, screened in November 1977, had put the club's hooligans in the spotlight. Soon everyone in football was talking about 'F-Troop', the 'Halfway Line Mob' and, comically, 'Treatment', a group of thugs who – perhaps with a nod to *Clockwork Orange* – supposedly dressed up in surgical gowns and masks and meted out violence to those unfortunate enough to meet them. There would later be allegations that some of the programme's content had been fabricated, or at least contrived for the purposes of extra drama. Whatever the case, the events at The Den on 11 March 1978 are frighteningly real.

More than 6,000 Ipswich fans did make the trip to south-east London, but Colin Kriedewolf remembers, 'You wouldn't have known it for the atmosphere of fear and apprehension that seemed to pervade the stadium.'

Coaches carrying Ipswich fans were stoned before the match had even started and the atmosphere inside the ground was apparently venomous. General consensus is that it reached boiling point when a group of late-arriving Ipswich fans were herded into a part of the ground where the worst element of Millwall's supporters lurked. Colin says, 'I was part of that group which arrived late and was directed to the far corner of the ground in an area that was supposed to be reserved for Town fans, but clearly was not. As soon as I got in the ground I sensed something was wrong and made my way to the front of the stand, so as to give myself an "out" should something kick off.' And kick off it did.

Colin recalls, 'George Burley's opening goal was the signal for all hell to break loose, with missiles being rained on the Town fans in the seating section and fights breaking out in the standing area.'

Hundreds of Ipswich fans found themselves penned in as they were showered with bottles, tins and blocks of wood. One Ipswich fan, company director Alan McCusker, says, 'Children whimpered and women fainted.'

More than 200 Ipswich fans fled the stadium in fear when the trouble started. Eleven policemen were hurt, three of them seriously, as the mob turned its anger on anyone and anything. The game was held up for 18 minutes. Later, officers in the nearby stations of Lewisham and Deptford threatened to boycott the ground.

The fact that Ipswich annihilated Millwall 6-1, including a hat-trick from Paul Mariner, was almost forgotten. Post-match analysis focused on explosive comments made by the usually mild-mannered Bobby Robson who, according to newspaper reports, was subjected to some of the vilest personal abuse ever heard during a game. 'Get the flame-throwers out and burn the bastards,' was Robson's immediate reaction.

Town goalkeeper Paul Cooper says, 'When we went 2-0 up early in the second half, I was showered with coins and a broken glass from behind the goal, where all the trouble was.'

Although the Ipswich fans were ecstatic to be in the semi-final, no expressions of joy or jubilation were possible after the match, as Colin Kriedewolf says, 'Little was said about the game afterwards. Everyone just got out as quickly as they could and I found myself among Millwall fans, who were throwing missiles at the Town fans on the other side of the street. I just tried to keep my head down.

'All these years later it seems strange that I now live in Bermondsey, only about a mile from the New Den and a number of my friends are Millwall fans. We have discussed the events of 1978 many times and they very much saw it as defending their turf.'

At the time, the violence caused extreme consternation in the game. Football Association chairman Sir Harold Thompson called for Saturday afternoon detention centres for hooligans. Others called for The Den, and indeed the club as a whole, to be closed down for good.

Bobby Robson, now calmed down, said more reasonably, 'When people go to games with the sole intention of inflicting damage on human bodies, the only answer is not to play football in that part of the world.'

A lot of words are spoken, lots of well-intentioned ideas mooted. But nothing very much happens.

At least in North Wales, all the talk is about a classic FA Cup tie. Despite a great performance by Wrexham, Arsenal edge into the last four with a 3-2 win at the Racecourse Ground. But Arfon Griffiths's Third Division side win praise all round for their display, with Malcolm Macdonald saying, 'They should have no trouble getting promoted.' He is right and they do go up.

Now three teams are definitely in the hat for the semi-final: Ipswich will play West Brom at Highbury and Arsenal will meet the winners of a replay between Orient and Middlesbrough. This second semi-final is due to be played at Villa Park or

Hillsborough but, if Orient win, Arsenal are expected to demand that the game is also played in London – probably Stamford Bridge – to defuse potential trouble between Arsenal and Orient fans travelling to the game together.

The incidents at The Den are weighing heavily on people's minds. Arsenal secretary Ken Friar says, 'If Orient win, it is illogical to expect both sets of fans to travel out of London together. Chelsea and Arsenal's grounds are far enough apart for there not to be any trouble.'

Before the game against West Brom, Ipswich striker Paul Mariner says memories of the club's defeat by West Ham at the semi-final stage in 1975 are still raw with the Town players who played in that match, and that no further motivation is required.

He tells *Daily Mirror* reporter Jack Steggles, 'Skipper Mick Mills and the other survivors from the 1975 semi-final have still not really got over that defeat. It had a devastating effect on them. Their disappointment has got through to us and we are all determined to see it does not happen again.'

During the interview we also learn that Mariner and his schoolteacher wife, Alison, like to visit antique shops in their spare time. He is also a keen gardener and the accompanying picture shows Mariner busy with a spade in the garden of his Hadleigh home. 'On Saturday he plans to turn over West Bromwich…' the caption writer quips.

Arsenal's fears about the semi-final being played at Villa Park prove irrelevant. Orient win the replay and the FA bows to pressure and agrees that Arsenal and the O's will play at Stamford Bridge. Both matches will be played on Saturday 8 April.

Arsenal fan Di Betts makes the short trip to Stamford Bridge and has good reason to remember the game. She says, 'I was actually on the pitch when Arsenal scored. I didn't eat any breakfast that day, fainted on the terrace behind the goal and had to be passed over people and down to the front. I was then taken into the medical room underneath one of the stands. When I felt better, I was making my way back around the perimeter of the pitch and cut the corner a little bit just as we scored.'

Two goals from Malcolm Macdonald – both deflections – and a third from Graham Rix earn a 3-0 win for Arsenal and a trip to Wembley. Back at Arsenal's own ground, in the other semi, there is high drama. Colin Kriedewolf is one of thousands of Town fans packed into Highbury's Clock End. He says, 'If the quarter-final was disappointing because of the crowd trouble, the semi-final was just fantastic. The atmosphere was electric and there was a real feeling it was going to be our day.'

Ipswich win 3-1 but today, many people throughout the game still remember the occasion for the blood-soaked bandage worn by Albion skipper John Wile. Brian Talbot heads Ipswich into the lead after just eight minutes, but his clash of heads with Wile results in blood flow of a kind thankfully rarely seen on a football pitch. Talbot goes off, but Wile soldiers on and wins the sympathy of millions of *Match of the Day* viewers that evening.

Colin remembers, 'After John Wark scored our third goal, and we knew we were at Wembley for the first time, a cascade of emotions erupted around me. For a moment it seemed that time just stood still as the realisation hit us. I was rolling around on the floor among a sea of bodies hugging anyone who was there. Fantastic!'

So it is Arsenal v Ipswich Town, another unusual but very interesting-looking FA Cup Final. For Arsenal fans there is a feeling that their team are back where they belong. It is the ninth time they have made it to the FA Cup Final. But, for Ipswich, this is absolutely huge – it is their first time – and, quite simply, the town goes cup crazy.

At home in Felixstowe, 14-year-old Town fan and music prodigy Ken Dyer has all the necessary vouchers to qualify for a cup final ticket except one. Word goes out at Deben High School and eventually the missing voucher comes from an unlikely source. His music teacher, Mr Ellis, who is also a Portman Road regular, manages to get the voucher Ken needs. Ken gets his application in and a couple of days later the magical prize arrives at his house. 'There were whoops of ecstasy and lots of jealous people at school when the ticket arrived,' says Ken.

Sixteen-year-old Paul Devine, O Levels looming remember, has his mum to thank. 'I raced home from school,' he says, 'to find that mum had been successful in her mission to get me a ticket. Bless her; she had queued for five hours around the streets of Portman Road. I'd been to all the home games. Loads of fans had the vouchers from the Manchester United or Liverpool games, but not quite so many had them for the likes of Leicester and Middlesbrough.'

Jonathan Morley would be the first to admit that he hadn't been to those sorts of games. He lived in Highgate – Arsenal territory – but his mother was from Ipswich and his grandfather had died at an Ipswich match in 1964.

He says, 'For these reasons, supporting Town was in the blood and my first game was an FA Cup tie against Chester City in the mid-1970s. My dad managed to get a couple of tickets simply because, at the time, Wembley stadium was owned by the TV company Rediffusion and dad, being a TV director/ producer, managed to pull the necessary strings.'

By virtue of being a season ticket holder, John Cross automatically got a final ticket. He remembers, 'Immediately after the semi-final, I made up my mind to get the best possible seat at Wembley I could, regardless of the cost, and I duly obtained one. Befitting the occasion, I decided to wear a suit together with my club tie and club rosette.'

Arsenal fan Di Betts says, 'I sent my vouchers off with a cheque for £2.50 and hoped for the best. My ticket arrived in the post on Saturday 22 April. I know because I noted it rather excitedly in my diary. At the time I didn't realise how lucky I was to receive one. The following season I went to every single cup game, including all four replays against Sheffield Wednesday *and* had a full set of coupons, and I still didn't get a ticket for the final.'

※ ※ ※

It could only happen in Britain. Monday 1 May is May Day and, for the first time, it is an official Bank Holiday, meaning millions get a new day off. There is real excitement about this. A trip to the coast maybe, a picnic, or a leisurely drink in the garden of a country pub?

Not a chance. It buckets down. Incessant rainfall from dawn to dusk. Rows of deck chairs lined up expectantly in Britain's seaside towns lie idle. Ice cream vans are ignored. Britain's answer to Evel Knievel, Eddie Kidd, abandons an attempt to jump 25 cars at Beaulieu, Hampshire, because of the downpour.

The *Daily Mirror* comments wryly that it has been raining more or less constantly since September 1976 when Prime Minister Jim Callaghan called in Denis Howell to do something about the drought. 'It is time now for the Prime Minister to tell him to stop,' the paper says, 'before we are all drowned.'

All week long, the tabloids get the cup final players to dress up in silly costumes. The *Daily Mirror* runs a feature called 'My Wildest Dreams', in which players say what they would like to be if they weren't footballers. It conjures up some bizarre images and desires. Arsenal captain Pat Rice says, 'A traffic warden's job would be just the ticket.' Malcolm Macdonald would like to be a Formula One driver; Paul Mariner says with his name, he'd have to be an old-time, buccaneering sailor. Ipswich defenders Mick Mills and Kevin Beattie would like to be tough hombres starring in cowboy films.

Beattie says, 'In my dreams the saloon doors swing open and the whole place goes quiet when they see me standing there. I see myself as the hard man everyone respects – a tough, John Wayne type.'

Rather alarmingly, Arsenal's lanky ginger-haired centre half Willie Young is photographed pointing a syringe at the camera. He would like to be a surgeon. Most embarrassingly of all, Town midfielder Brian Talbot is pictured wearing a distinctly dodgy outfit and toe-curlingly awful leopard-skin boots. He dreams of being a pop star and his hero is a certain Gary Glitter.

All week long there is injury news coming out of the Ipswich camp with major concerns over both Beattie and his central defence partner Allan Hunter, the tough Ulsterman, as well as South African-born playmaker Colin Viljoen. But Arsenal have injury worries too with Liam Brady, Alan Sunderland and Graham Rix all carrying knocks.

The band Eruption are in the charts with 'I Can't Stand The Rain', and never was a song more apt. It continues to pour down, with risk of flooding in many areas. The relentless rain starts to take its toll on the Wembley pitch. On the Tuesday before the final, the Ipswich players train on the surface. Wembley groundsman John Gallacher is not amused and tells reporters, 'They were putting their heels in and making sliding tackles.'

Back in Ipswich Paul Devine is trying to turn his attention to *The Merchant of Venice*, *To Kill A Mockingbird* and wildlife poetry in preparation for his English literature O Level exam. But instead of Shakespeare, Harper Lee and Ted Hughes, all he can think of is Paul Mariner, Clive Woods and David Geddis, who is standing in for the injured Trevor Whymark. Before long he casts aside his Venn diagrams and periodic tables and concentrates on what really matters.

He gets caught up in the cup fervour which is sweeping the town. After all, what self-respecting football fan would really care about exams at a time like this? Today, still with a glint in his eye, Paul recalls the mood in Ipswich in those days leading up to the final. 'The build-up in the papers and at my school was just fantastic,' he says. 'The night before the match we headed to the once infamous underage watering hole in town – the Rose and Crown. The whole town centre was full of groups of lads getting p****d and singing footie songs, obviously "Wem-ber-ley" and anti-Norwich songs were the favourites. I can't remember ever feeling so much a part of "it" and, even now, I can still really feel the excitement of that distant evening.'

Life goes on. Punk rockers still strike fear into 'ordinary' members of the public and, in Kingston, Surrey, an estimated 200 punks go on the rampage smashing shop windows and fighting after a gig in the town.

Those staying in on that Friday night don't have a huge amount of choice on the box. At 8pm, there is *It's a Knockout*. For the first time in ten years, the competition comes from Northern Ireland and later on BBC1, there is *Petrocelli*, in which lawyer Tony Petrocelli is asked to defend a singing star mixed up in a murder. On ITV there is the traditional *Who'll Win the Cup?* hosted by Brian Moore and with special guests Kevin Keegan, Emlyn Hughes, Jack Charlton and the wounded soldier from the semi-final, John Wile.

As the Arsenal fans turn in for the evening, most of them are quietly confident that the FA Cup is coming back to Highbury. Their league form is good, much better in fact than Ipswich's, who are having their worst season in five years. But those fans would do well to read the *Daily Mirror*, which has given ratings out of ten for every player. Receiving a seven for Town is, arguably, the least well-known player in the two line-ups. Roger Osborne is described thus, 'Busy, and functions best on the wide right. Neat control. Gets in to support the strikers.' Arsenal, you have been warned.

※ ※ ※

As dawn breaks on Saturday, it is still pouring with rain and the Wembley pitch is sodden. Throughout the morning, a huge team of workers armed with spikes and garden forks attempts to drain away the excess water from the pitch. Wembley officials are hoping a new drainage system will cope and a spokesman says, 'The kick-off will be on time no matter what the weather brings.'

Most pundits think Arsenal will win, pointing to players like Liam Brady and Alan Hudson, both of whom can put their foot on the ball, dictate the pace of the game and play killer passes to the front three of Macdonald, Stapleton and Sunderland. The feeling is that Ipswich, without Viljoen pulling the strings in midfield, will be forced to hoof the ball long, which will make life comparatively easy for Arsenal's big central defenders Willie Young and David O'Leary.

But there is a huge boost for Ipswich with news that the inspirational Kevin Beattie will play. Skipper Mick Mills says,

'I've seen newspaper quotes from Malcolm Macdonald and Pat Rice that Kevin is the Ipswich driving force and a player to be feared. They are worried about Kevin and they have every reason to be. He is a great player.'

BBC1 kicks off at 9am with *Teddy Edward*, which is followed by a 25-minute show – now long forgotten – in which John Arlott and Fred Trueman 'talk cricket'. A special edition of the *Multi-Coloured Swap Shop* follows this. At 11.30am, the waiting is over and *Cup Final Grandstand* begins. It includes 'The Road to Wembley' and 'Cup Final Mastermind', with fans from the two sides' supporters' clubs answering questions on their teams.

The referee for today's match is 47-year-old gas service officer Derek Nippard, from Christchurch in Dorset. He is known in the game for doing everything to avoid sending a player off. In fact, he has only ever sent three players off in his whole career. Two of those were Francis Lee and Norman Hunter, following the infamous Baseball Ground incident of November 1975, when Hunter and Lee indulged in a fully-fledged, stand-up, bar-room brawl with flailing fists, bringing to mind the 1970s boxing game 'Raving Bonkers'.

The A12 is rammed with cars, minibuses, coaches and vans making their way down from Suffolk to Wembley. Blue and white scarves and flags are everywhere. In a beaten-up old Mini is Paul Devine, a school friend and three older lads. Paul says, 'I remember the cringe factor of my mum waving us off. I was wearing jeans, those horrible green and white tennis shoe type trainers and a blue puffa jacket with white slashes on the sleeves. To cap it all I had the 'away' silk scarf tied to my belt. I thought I looked the b******s!'

The old Mini, laden with the five teenagers, struggles along to Wembley with the older non-drivers drinking Colt 45 lager. Metaphorically tossing his French vocabulary exercise book out of the window, young Paul accepts the occasional offer of a sip of beer.

Ipswich will have 25,000 fans at Wembley, some sporting special blue and white haircuts, courtesy of a free offer from a local hairdresser. Ipswich centre-half Allan Hunter faces a last-minute fitness test to decide whether he plays, with youngster Russell Osman waiting to step in if required. Arsenal manager Terry Neill tells his players to forget Ipswich's injury woes and regard them all as fully fit. Playing down the fact his team are expected to win he says, 'There are no favourites in a cup final.'

BBC TV director Alec Weeks is preparing his squad of cameramen for the big match. They line up on the Wembley pitch for a publicity shot. There is a worrying amount of facial hair and it looks like a convention of David Bellamy doppelgangers. Weeks drives them hard and demands that each member of the hirsute coterie acquire instant recognition of players on the pitch to ensure they don't miss a trick.

Testing their prowess, he shows them shots of players from different angles. 'They get to know Pat Rice's thick neck and Malcolm Macdonald's bow-legged walk,' says Alec. 'They can pick out George Burley's baby face, Allan Hunter's strut or Roger Osborne's broken nose.' It is amazing they can see anything at all through those face rugs.

The Mini carrying Paul and his mates arrives at Wembley and parks in the famous huge car park. Paul soaks up the atmosphere and thinks how much better this is than learning the bones in the ear for his human biology exam.

He recalls the scene, 'There were loads of Ipswich fans sitting on the roofs and bonnets of their cars, munching and drinking. There were also what seemed like big laddish mobs of Arsenal fans strutting past. There was a bit of trouble, but it just seemed to be a quick flurry of swinging fists and it was over before it started. My first outstanding, yet inconsequential, memory of Wembley stadium itself was the amount of steps there were simply to reach our turnstile in the upper section of the tunnel end.'

As Paul and his mates wait to enter the turnstile they all turn around and look back down Wembley Way to see thousands and thousands of fans clad in red and blue and white. It is a fabulous sight and brings home to each of them precisely what they are about to experience.

Among the throng of fans is John Cross. He buys himself a blue and white rosette, which he pins carefully to his crisp, white shirt. He is on top of the world and looking forward to taking his place in one of the best seats in the house.

Fourteen-year-old Town fan Ken Dyer finds himself in a seated area, but would rather stand with his mates, so he clambers over three walls with railings to join them. In doing so he splits his trousers from the zip to the backside. 'This gave me some much needed ventilation on a sticky afternoon,' he says.

As the years pass many people tend to forget the finer details of their Wembley experience, but it seems most people can recall their first glimpse of the famous pitch. Paul certainly can and he says, 'My first ever recollection of the inside of a football ground was at Portman Road nine years earlier and I was astounded at just how green the pitch seemed. The same feeling was evoked when I first laid eyes on the Wembley turf and it was a surreal feeling. Move over Lord Percy from *Blackadder* who thought he'd discovered green!'

John feels into the breast pocket of his suit and pulls out, nestling among the silky lining, his expensive ticket. He feels a surge of pride and emotion as he shows it to the turnstile operator, who John is sure gives him a quick look of admiration when he realises where John is sitting. Taking a deep breath, John straightens his clobber one last time and, with a gulp of anticipation, enters the great old stadium and heads towards a steward to lead him to his seat.

He is almost beside himself with excitement. The steward ushers John in and points to where he will sit. His heart sinks. He feels there must be some mistake. His face drops, 'To my disappointment, I found I was sitting against the barrier between the seats and the terraces and I had a better view of the corner flag than the centre circle,' he says.

Arsenal fan Di Betts has a sketchy recollection of the day, but does recall one thing in particular. As the 1970s wore on, the DIY banners brought in by fans were becoming increasingly risqué and one catches Di's attention. She says, 'One detail I've never forgotten was a banner which read "Willie pisses on Gates", referring to our Willie Young and their Eric Gates. It would be interesting to see what would happen if someone did unfurl a banner like that today. They wouldn't be able to show "Willie pisses on Gates" on TV today, would they?'

Plenty of banners are shown on TV. Most Arsenal banners concern their midfield talisman. 'Brady sells more dummies than Mothercare' reads one; 'Brady carves up Woods' says another.

But the best banner, brought along by a group of Ipswich fans, refers to the ability of Town's left-winger Clive Woods to get the better of Arsenal right-back Pat Rice. 'Woods fries Rice' it states with wonderful economy.

Among the Arsenal fans stands 15-year-old Emilio Zorlakki and his Greek Cypriot father, Alex. Emilio recalls the bizarre pre-match entertainment of a competition between model aeroplanes representing both teams and a display by police dogs also wearing club colours. 'Arsenal won both contests,' says Emilio.

Any Arsenal fans packed behind the goal thinking this might be an omen are to be sadly mistaken. Other fans are clinging to another omen – Arsenal's choice of shirt. Emilio says, 'The club produced a replica of our yellow 1971 cup final kit, but I was surprised and disappointed that we were not wearing red.'

Much of the build-up to the game has focused on Ipswich's supposed rural sensibilities and stories have abounded about sleepy farmers, with only a passing interest in football, chugging to the capital aboard tractors. Indeed some sections of the media seemed to envisage the Ipswich support consisting of a bunch of village idiots, with gaps and straw in their teeth, leaping about on the terraces wearing smocks and clutching pitchforks, speaking in some kind of bucolic pidgin English.

On the day this ridiculous stereotype is completely blown out of the water, as Town fans knew it would be. Their support is passionate and rousing. As Paul Devine says, 'We completely outsang Arsenal. All that sleepy Suffolk crap is just that – crap!' And their side are about to give them something to sing about.

The teams come out into bright sunshine. Arsenal boss Terry Neill wears a jacket and trousers and Bobby Robson favours a lounge suit. They look like extras from *The Fall and Rise of Reginald Perrin*. Behind them come their teams, led by Pat Rice and Mick Mills. It is Umbro v Adidas.

It emerges that, somewhat surprisingly, Bobby Robson has identified Arsenal left-back and old Ulster warhorse Sammy Nelson as a threat. Apparently, Robson thinks if you stop Nelson coming forward then Arsenal will be neutered, their supply line severed. Geddis, Osborne and Burley all have a role to play here. But the general feeling – certainly among the Arsenal fans – is that the Gunners will still have too much for Town.

Derek Nippard blows his whistle and we are off. Though Ipswich are out of the traps quicker, Arsenal carve out the first opening when O'Leary moves forward but cracks his shot wide. The Arsenal fans like what they see, but this early attempt is about as good as it is going to get for the Londoners.

From this point on, Ipswich take the game by the scruff of the neck and proceed to annihilate their opponents, launching attack after attack. Their first chance falls to Mariner. A mistake by Willie Young gives Clive Woods acres of space on the right. He gets to the penalty box and then plays the ball square to Osborne, who is in a great position. Osborne fluffs it but the ball rolls on to Paul Mariner, who slides in and smashes it against the bar with Jennings beaten. It is the blue banners that are being waved with gusto. 'Mariner sinks Nelson', reads one nautical-themed effort.

Ipswich are all over Arsenal who haven't carved out a single chance, and once again Malcolm Macdonald is anonymous. The Gunners fans are mystified by what they are seeing from their team. All over the pitch, Ipswich are winning the individual battles. Woods is indeed frying Rice, Allan Hunter and Kevin Beattie are not giving Macdonald an inch. Brian Talbot is running the show in midfield where Arsenal's Liam Brady and Alan Hudson look curiously off the pace. Arsenal's fans are horrified by what they are watching. Half-time comes as a relief.

Emilio Zorlakki says, 'At half-time I asked my dad how we could possibly hold out in the second half and extra time to force a replay. Everyone around us was shocked about how badly we were playing. By contrast, Ipswich were playing like their lives depended on it and what was hard to take was that they were fitter, stronger and faster.'

Despite a rollicking from Terry Neill, Arsenal start the second half in much the same way and Ipswich continue to pile on the pressure. Arsenal's fans do their best to rouse the troops, singing a half-hearted version of the 'na, na, na na-na na' from 'Hey Jude'.

Then another song with Beatles connections, or at least John Lennon, is heard. They start to sing a song based on 'Give Peace A Chance', much to Emilio's dismay. 'This is what I always called the "kiss of death" song and one you should never sing, especially at Wembley. You know the one – "All we are saying is give us a goal". It's guaranteed to leave your team goalless.

'I knew our fate was sealed once we started singing this. But how do you try and persuade 25,000 fans not to sing it? This cursed chant was replaced many years later by "Sing your hearts out for the lads" – believe me, it's true.'

Emilio might just have something because, almost immediately, David O'Leary fails to deal with a long punt from Paul Cooper, which lets in Paul Mariner. Willie Young, who is not having his best game, makes a weak challenge and loses his footing, and looks like a thin stag scrabbling around on the floor.

Mariner slips the ball to John Wark in the inside-right position but his cleanly-hit shot smashes against the post with Jennings beaten. It deserves a goal. Ipswich's dominance is becoming almost laughable.

The players in blue keep pouring forward and creating chance after chance. Though the score remains goalless Arsenal are, in truth, being slaughtered. Then it is a case of 'déjà vu all over again' as Wark hits the same post, in the same place, with his same foot, from virtually the same position.

Paul Devine says, 'We really did outplay them, but I remember thinking it was not to be as the stalemate continued, with us missing chances galore or being denied by the woodwork. I started to think about a night match replay situation and all the hassle of re-applying for tickets.'

Emilio Zorlakki remembers, 'When they hit the woodwork for the third time, I remember squirming and thinking that we were embarrassing ourselves in front of the whole nation.'

Next, Clive Woods moves the ball back on to his right peg and arrows a beautiful cross into the Arsenal box. Steaming in is future Town boss George Burley, who produces a stunning bullet-header which Jennings deals with superbly.

While some Town fans are thinking it is going to be one of those days, Ken Dyer remains optimistic. He says, 'Defeat never came into the equation for me. Even when we kept hitting the woodwork, that amazing header by our future manager and an even more amazing save by Pat Jennings, we just kept going.'

Jennings's save gives pessimistic Emilio Zorlakki a fleeting glimmer of hope. He recalls, 'After that, just for a moment, I thought maybe we could prevail.' However, for Emilio and the Arsenal fans it is a forlorn hope because the richly deserved knockout punch is just around the corner.

Roger Osborne has been at Ipswich since 1973 but, though appreciated at Portman Road as a consistent if unspectacular clubman, he has never really won any acclaim outside his native Suffolk. His role at Wembley was expected to be as a destroyer, nullifying the attacking threat of Arsenal's muse and playmaker Liam Brady, and preventing Nelson's forays from defence.

With 13 minutes left on the clock, Ipswich attack yet again. Clive Woods – who is playing a blinder – switches wings again and makes a surge down the right. He finds the blond-haired rookie David Geddis, the pin-up boy of the Ipswich side. He is up against Nelson and it is no contest. Geddis skins him and moves towards the byline. He then crosses low and hard. Willie Young juts out a foot and it rebounds straight to Osborne who is ten yards out. He shoots first-time, not with any great venom, but with sufficient accuracy to beat Pat Jennings. Ipswich are ahead and no neutral can begrudge them that fact. Suffolk goes mad. You can hear the cheers in Bungay, Stowmarket and Felixstowe.

Behind the goal, at the other end, there is an explosion of colour and noise. Paul Devine says, 'Our end just erupted. These were the magical days of proper terracing when you could leap around and end up a dozen yards and a dozen steps from your original standing position. The "bopping" was awesome and seemed to go on for an age and I literally felt sick when it calmed down, through pure exertion and the effort of not falling over and getting trampled.'

Emilio Zorlakki buries his head in his hands. 'I heard my father say simply, "Had to be".' Mr Zorlakki was right. It did have to be. Ipswich have been superb on the day and Arsenal anything but. Now Town must hold on for the last 12 minutes.

After the goal Osborne is submerged by team-mates. It is all too much for the number seven who is overcome with emotion, faints with all the excitement and Lambert comes on to replace him.

Ken Dyer recalls, 'The next 13 minutes were the longest I've ever known. Brian Talbot, who we called Noddy, and David Geddis both had their socks around their ankles and we just prayed for the final whistle.'

As the Ipswich fans give a rousing rendition of 'You'll Never Walk Alone', Emilio feels the tears welling up in his eyes. He wills a couple of half-hearted efforts from Malcolm Macdonald and Graham Rix to go in, but it is clear that Arsenal are not going to score, and nor do they deserve to. With the Town fans frantically whistling for the game to end, referee Nippard finally raises his left arm and blows for the last time.

The cup is going up the A12 to Ipswich. And no neutral can possibly deny them the honour. They have outplayed the yellow-shirted Londoners. John Cross stands proudly in his suit, clapping and cheering. It is his proudest moment as an Ipswich fan. Ken Dyer describes the moment as 'magical'. Paul

Devine says, 'At the final whistle everyone was hugging, friends, strangers, anyone. Which lucky sod got to hug the blond girl with the tight, white, sleeveless t-shirt I wonder?'

Alex and Emilio Zorlakki stare vacantly and miserably at the cavorting Ipswich fans and players and have no answers. You can't say Arsenal have played badly because they didn't play at all. They have been totally off-colour, toothless, supine and effete. And this seems to have translated to the terraces because, throughout the game, the atmosphere among the usually passionate North Bank has been strangely subdued.

Di Betts is having what can only be described as an existential moment, feeling an acute sense of isolation and disconnection from what is really happening.

She says, 'At the final whistle, the mixture of disappointment and deflation that had been weighing on me, ever more heavily as the match wore on, was replaced by a sense of detachment, an emotionless void, only an awareness of how pointless and wrong it felt to be even there. Now that the occasion was, from this point onwards, nothing to do with me any more, nor any other Arsenal fan.'

On the pitch, Paul Mariner consoles David O'Leary who looks as if he is going to cry; Clive Woods, Brian Talbot and Mick Mills indulge in a three-way embrace; David Geddis runs to the touchline to hug Roger Osborne. The TV cameras show blue and white flags waving ecstatically and the smiling, almost disbelieving faces of the fans.

'And what a lovely journey they're going to have back to Suffolk tonight,' says Brian Moore.

Arsenal coach Don Howe stares impassively, chewing gum so fast that it looks like the Wrigley's spearmint in his mouth is red hot. 'Osborne takes the biscuit,' says another one of those wonderful punning banners in the crowd.

And then Mick Mills – affectionately known as Gladys – leads the team up. They look remarkably sprightly for a side who have just played in a cup final. A tubby Ipswich fan with a moustache, looking a bit like Tosh from *The Bill*, raises his arm rather too enthusiastically for Mills who, somewhat over-dramatically it has to be said, stops in his tracks, throws his head back and nearly nuts Clive Woods in the process.

Mills receives the trophy from Her Royal Highness Princess Alexandra, plants a kiss – on the trophy, not the Princess – and raises the cup aloft. Behind the Princess are two shadowy figures, applauding wildly and grinning broadly. They are already quite well known.

Watching from behind the goal is Ken Dyer who says, 'I couldn't see "Gladys" or the others going up the stairs to receive the cup, but I recall something shining with blue and white ribbons being thrust aloft followed by a deafening roar. That is something I will never forget.'

Paul Devine remembers, 'I still love it when you can see who the clowns of the dressing room are and those who are embarrassed by being caught in the headlights!'

For Emilio Zorlakki there is just sadness. He says, 'My dad didn't want to hang around and my last glimpse was of Mick Mills lifting the cup through my tear-stained eyes.'

The players go on their traditional lap of honour with Kevin Beattie wearing a blue and white Ipswich sun hat, rather like the one sported by the gormless 'middle' bear in Hanna and Barbera's *It's the Hair Bear Bunch*. Mick Mills dons some even more peculiar headgear – a floppy, light blue, full-brimmed hat, the kind of thing Margot Leadbetter might wear to do the garden in *The Good Life*.

John Cross gets up, straightens his club tie and gives his jacket a shake to ensure it's sitting nicely on his frame. He makes to leave the stadium. 'But then things began to move in ways I could never have expected,' he says.

The unmistakeable voice of Gerry Harrison can be heard summoning Town players for interview. Roger Osborne says he has so many relatives in the crowd that he has forgotten how many were there. John Wark says that, after hitting the post again, his team-mates said he should stop playing one-twos with the woodwork and Mills, swigging milk from a pint bottle, says Ipswich's fitness was the difference between the sides.

Beattie, the team's court jester, grins, gurns and gives the camera the thumbs-up, tells Harrison he has now achieved all his ambitions in the game: to play for England, to play at Carlisle with Ipswich and to play in an FA Cup Final. This is an interesting segment. By today's comparisons, the players seem so normal, so unaffected and down-to-earth. They could almost be workmates or neighbours.

By now Emilio and his father are trudging back to their car, with the chants and singing of the Ipswich fans ringing in their ears. 'Walking back down Wembley Way the inquest was already in full swing,' says Emilio. 'How could we play so badly? How could they let the fans down like that? Terry Neill and Pat Rice later revealed the extent of our injury list. It turns out that only David Price, Alan Hudson, Frank Stapleton and Graham Rix were not carrying some kind of injury on the day. I remember thinking, "Please God, let us come back next year and make up for this disappointment".'

John Cross is preparing to leave the stadium by way of an exit that comes out on a walkway bordering the famous Wembley Banqueting Hall where the great and the good congregate. Rather like the child with his nose pressed up against the toy shop window at Christmas, John decides to take a closer look.

He says, 'I saw many famous faces, including Sir Stanley Matthews, and I decided to get near to the entrance to the hall to try and spot a few more celebrities.' John marches up to the entrance to the hall. It is a bit like a starstruck autograph-hunter waiting by the stage door. At this point a well-to-do looking lady, who is leaving the hall, approaches him. To John's astonishment, the lady gives him a special pass and directs him inside. It is the suit that has done it – no doubt about it. Topped off with the tie, the suit is John's ticket to another world.

Feeling rather odd, John approaches one of those dreaded commissionaires who wield a disproportionate level of power and can either ruin your day or be the passport to paradise. In

John's case, it is the latter. He says, 'I showed my pass and, to my amazement, the commissionaire waved me through.'

Suddenly it is like something out of *Mr Benn*, the resident of 52 Festive Road, London, who, each day, visits his local fancy dress shop where he is met by a fez-wearing shopkeeper who arrives 'as if by magic' and escorts him to a changing room from which Mr Benn departs to another world of fantasy and adventure. But even Mr Benn's script-writers would have struggled to come up with this one.

As John walks through the door he is greeted by a drop-dead gorgeous waitress with a soft, lilting accent. She smiles radiantly and leads John to the biggest spread of mouth-watering food and drink he has ever seen in his life. 'This is turning into a seriously good day,' thinks John.

Deciding to do the decent thing, John fills his boots and piles his plate full of vol-au-vents, finely cut sandwiches and coronation chicken. As he turns another smiling waitress shimmies towards him and hands him a glass of champagne. 'If there's anything else you'd like at all, sir, just ask,' she says, smiling sweetly. Though he is a matter of yards away from the stalls selling greasy burgers, chips and hot dogs, John is in another world, a sort of parallel universe paradise.

The fans are streaming out of Wembley. For Arsenal supporters, the optimism they felt three hours earlier has evaporated. Di Betts is still feeling a bit John Paul Sartre, or maybe Albert Camus.

Digging deep into her memory, she says, 'I have a vague recollection of walking back down Wembley Way and wondering what on earth I could do now. That evening I ended up going for a drink with a friend who had no interest in football whatsoever. By this point, it was almost like the final had never happened at all, which is possibly why I remember so little of the detail. It isn't that the memory has faded in the 35-odd years since; I just think maybe I never bothered storing it!'

Understandably, Ipswich fans *have* stored their memories. Ken Dyer remembers getting back into the minibus and the radio being turned on. A voice, which will, in time, become arguably the most famous and instantly recognisable voice in Britain, and a staple for *Spitting Image* impersonators, is talking.

It is Margaret Thatcher, for she and husband Denis were those shadowy figures behind Princess Alexandra and Mick Mills when the cup was being presented. Bizarrely, Thatcher is giving her views on the game – how Osborne 'did a job' on Brady, how Hunter had Supermac 'in his pocket', and how 'Noddy' Talbot demonstrated a great 'engine'. Not really of course. But, what is true is that, when asked who was her man of the match, she replies 'Trevor Whymark'. Shame he wasn't playing.

Growing in confidence and becoming acclimatised to his new surroundings, John Cross mingles with the privileged few present in the hall. 'There's that bloke from the telly,' he thinks to himself. 'Is that Bernie Winters over there?' he ponders silently. 'No, can't be. There's no Snorbitz.'

'Now I'm sure I've seen that guy over there presenting *Top of the Pops*,' he muses as he looks at a man with a Hawaiian shirt and a bubble perm. In the background, Gerry Rafferty's 'Baker Street', a big hit in February, is playing quietly. 'Is that Robin Nedwell?' he thinks as he spies another actor-type, 'or Richard O'Sullivan?'

Another enchanting waitress comes and fills John's glass with champagne as a man who John is sure he has seen in a comedy like *Porridge*, *Citizen Smith* or *It Ain't Half Hot Mum*, chats amicably with another man who looks like he might have been in *Z-Cars* or presenting *Magpie*.

Meanwhile, the Ipswich convoy of cars, coaches, minibuses and trains is heading back to Suffolk, where the party to end all parties is waiting to greet them. Fourteen-year-old Ken Dyer gets a shiver down his spine remembering the events of that warm, early evening.

He says, 'The journey home was just epic. I remember we drove through loads of North London and Essex towns and villages that I'd never heard of. We saw hundreds of well-wishing fans, who were lining the route and standing outside their houses, cheering us. At the time, there was a famous ad on the telly for Kronenbourg lager in which the winners of a football match drink champagne and the losers – to their delight – get their hands on a pint of Kroney. I remember seeing a load of Arsenal fans singing, "We lost de cup. We lost de cup, ee-aye-addio, we lost de cup".'

By now, John Cross has left the Banqueting Hall and made his way down to the tunnel area. When he arrives he does a double-take as he sees a familiar figure. Hair still wet from his post-match shower, it is a certain Mick Mills. John says, 'Mick was showing his family his winner's medal.'

Then John Wark enters the room with his mum, then Brian Talbot emerges, and to John's delight, Bobby Robson leaves the dressing room with a huge grin on his face. He is joined by first-team coach Cyril Lea, who is clutching the trophy itself.

Open-mouthed, John approaches Bobby Robson and shakes him warmly by the hand. John wants to say so much. He wants to thank Robson for the fabulous work he has done at Ipswich, how he has made supporting Ipswich such a pleasurable experience, and tell him how respected and revered he is among the Portman Road faithful. But the words don't come and, before John knows it, the great man is away. Still, it is a handshake that John will treasure forever.

More and more of the Ipswich team appear. They are preparing to leave. John says, 'I wandered out briefly and saw the team board the coach to leave Wembley. The cup was displayed in the coach window for all to see. Another magic moment.'

He then heads back in and helps himself to some superior French cheese. John smiles to himself at the events of the last few hours. Shelling out for an expensive seat and wearing a smart suit has paid dividends. He won't forget 6 May 1978 for as long as he lives.

Paul Devine doesn't remember too many Gooners being around after the game, but clearly recalls the joy of the Ipswich fans, despite a horrendous queue to get out of the car park.

He says, 'People were singing, sounding their car horns and, from time to time, doing "moonies" to other carloads of girls or older, more sensible people and, in both cases, the "victims" pretended to be only slightly p****d off so as not to ruin the occasion.

'The journey back was spent listening to endless reports and interviews on the radio and talking about Europe. But it really hadn't sunk in until then that we had actually won the bloody trophy! Just on the outskirts of the London suburbs the traffic started crawling again and I remember a group of lads led by a lanky prat with punk hair nicking a couple of flags or scarves from a coach window as it crawled past. But then three older Town fans got out of their cars and chased them off.'

By early evening, many Arsenal fans are starting to accept defeat and are acknowledging that Ipswich had been by far the better team. Ken Banham, a veteran of the 1971 and 1972 finals, says, 'Ipswich played really well and, after the game we shook their fans' hands. It seemed like many of them were still in a state of shock.'

By 6pm, most Gooners were back in their regular boozers, downing pints and getting the match out of their systems. As Ken recalls, after the anger of their team's performance had subsided, a more charitable view took hold in the pubs of Finsbury Park, Stoke Newington and Islington. He says, 'As the night wore on and the beer began to sink in, the mood changed a bit and we all started to reflect on how well our team had done to get to Wembley at all. I can still hear my dad saying, "We will be back next season". How right he was.'

No one who was at Wembley will have cared that, on BBC1 tonight, is the lollipop-sucking, balding 'Who Loves Ya Baby' detective *Kojak*, played by Telly Savalas or, on the other side, some real high-class fare in the shape of *Celebrity Squares* and 'live from Norwich' the enduringly popular *Sale of the Century* presented by Nicholas Parsons. Win or lose, a cup final is not something you can get out of your system quickly.

While the Arsenal fans are getting quietly reflective, the convoy of vehicles carrying the cock-a-hoop, singing, chanting, whooping Town fans is approaching their home turf. Paul Devine says, 'The bridges spanning the A12 all had banners welcoming home the conquering troops. That felt great. We headed straight to Portman Road, where it appeared you could simply abandon your car and join the throng of celebrating fans.

'When I first saw the film *Fever Pitch* I really had goose bumps at the scene where Arsenal fans gathered outside Highbury when they won the league in that famous 2-0 win at Anfield, with virtually the last kick of the season. I was eventually dropped off a few houses away from home to avoid any "Mum" cringes.'

At around the same time Ken Dyer is arriving back at Bury St Edmunds, already reflecting on a day he will still be able to recall years later. Those Ipswich fans who have made it home did what every normal football fan would do in the same circumstances – watch a re-run on *Match of the Day*. And, it was now that the penny will drop for John Cross, watching from his armchair in Clacton-on-Sea, smiling to himself as he recalls the events of his day in his mind. He is in for another surprise.

He says, 'When I watched the highlights on TV, I spotted a face I recognised in the Royal Box.' It was the same distinguished looking lady who gave him a pass to enter the Banqueting Hall. 'I then realised that it was Lady Blanche Cobbold, the president of Ipswich Town Football Club,' he admits. 'Little did she know how her gesture had triggered so many marvellous moments for me thereafter – memories I shall always treasure.'

The party goes on long into the night. It is not just a victory for Ipswich, it is a victory for Suffolk. Sudbury, Lavenham, Bury St Edmunds, Woodbridge and the port of Felixstowe are full of revellers waving blue and white scarves and singing, 'One Bobby Robson, there's only one Bobby Robson.'

And, in the tiny village of Otley, sandwiched between Ashbocking Green, Gosbeck and Pettaugh, they have even more reason to celebrate. Roger Osborne, with one of those accents that could have won him a supporting role as a labourer in a period drama, is a son of Otley. You can bet more than a few glasses were raised in his name in the White Hart in Otley that night.

When you wake with a hangover, the initial reaction is a prolonged despondent groan. When you wake with a hangover after your team have won the FA Cup Final, the initial reaction is, by all accounts, a momentary despondent groan. Then you remember. Then your face creases into the wildest smile imaginable.

Then you say 'Yes!' or 'We did it!' Then your hangover disappears. Then you get up. Then you go and watch your team displaying that cup in your town, on your streets. For some fans, it could easily be a once-in-a-lifetime opportunity.

The next day, thousands greet the cup winners in the traditional, open-top bus ride through the town. At last the 'May Monsoon' is over and now the sun is shining.

Cup victory inevitably promotes the cause of the growing numbers of people who think Bobby Robson should get the England job. Maybe the conservative, traditional FA will like the symmetry of Robson, like Ramsey, being an Ipswich man and, therefore, a shoo-in for the job. Ron Greenwood is doing okay but, in an early example of 'succession planning' maybe Robson is being considered for a crack at bringing England international success during the 1980s.

Ipswich know they have a job on their hands to keep the avuncular Geordie. Town chairman Patrick Cobbold tells reporters he would like Robson to stay at the club for life, saying, 'Bobby has seven years to go on his contract. If he wants to stay for life with us, he can. We would be delighted. There is only one job we would release Bobby for. That is the England one. We would have to. It is like a royal command.'

So Ipswich start preparing for Europe and are also planning a concerted push for the First Division championship after coming close several times in the middle of the decade. There is talk that West Ham's brilliant midfielder Trevor Brooking could be a transfer target.

On the Monday, the Ipswich fans, with their faces still fixed in broad grins, return to work and school or whatever their daily routine is. Paul Devine makes a token effort to get to grips with calculus or the Luddites, but all he wants to do is talk football. And who can blame him?

Luckily, the whole school has been gripped with football fever and, even with the dreaded O Levels just a couple of weeks away, Saturday's match is the only subject on anyone's lips – even the teachers. Paul says, 'At school on Monday, nothing bar football was discussed in or outside the classroom. I remember our maths teacher – a real disciplinarian called Mr McGlaughlin – relaxing totally and, for once, not launching into any of that sine/cosine stuff at all but, instead, asking 5S who had been at the game and how the day had been. Huge cred and respect earned by him that day for sure.'

That was in Ipswich but, spare a thought for Jonathan Morley, the Town fan at school in Highgate, definite Arsenal territory. He recalls, 'As I entered the school, someone met me and told me to "leggit" as a load of Arsenal fans were going to get me. And, as predicted, I was chased off the school grounds by 30 meatheads and I didn't stop running until I made it home.'

Today, Ken Dyer, the young musician who went to Wembley thanks to his music teacher coming up trumps with the final voucher, is a music teacher himself, working in Nottingham and living in Grantham. Though he can't get to so many games, he is still mad on the Town. 'I taught (1990s player) David Johnson's daughter and son. His daughter gave me a signed photo of her godfather – a certain man by the name of Richard Wright. It even said, "To Mr Dyer"! I was made up for the next few hours!'

Get Ken on to the subject of the 1978 FA Cup win and his eyes light up and he relives the match in his mind, as he has done countless times since. He says, 'Super Paul Cooper reigning in our penalty area – wasn't he brilliant? Allan Hunter thumping the ball away, Kevin Beattie just hoiking anything and anyone that got in his way, Paul Mariner running and running, and we can't forget, "He's here, he's there, he's every f*****g where,

Johnny Wark, Johnny Wark!" Or my man of the match Clive Woods who, as the banners said, "fried Rice" all afternoon.

'The sixth of May 1978 is an experience etched in my memory, right up there with my wedding day and the births of my three children. I've still got the "We Won the Cup" record with Pete Barraclough saying, "And this must be a goal… it's a goal" and my video of the match that my son laughed at when I showed him as he said it looked really slow. What a day!'

John Cross, now 77, lives with his wife Carolyn in the village of Little Clacton in Essex. They have two adult sons. John was a civil servant working predominantly in the Social Security sector. He took early retirement in 1994 before taking a part-time job in the lottery office at Colchester United, accompanying the club on two visits to Wembley.

After retiring completely in 2003, he has continued to be a season ticket holder at Portman Road, plays some golf, but also indulges another sporting passion which is following Essex County Cricket Club. After much thought, John decided his favourite Ipswich player ever is Ray Crawford. 'A wonderful centre-forward and prolific goalscorer,' he says.

Paul Devine has doubtless forgotten all about calculus, trigonometry and periodic tables. Now Paul lives in Kent and works for Royal Mail. Through the ups and downs of supporting the club he has loved since that first glimpse of the Portman Road pitch in 1969, that glorious day will never be forgotten.

'However Ipswich are doing,' he says, 'memories of days such as 6 May 1978 keep me going footie-wise and I long for a similar memory which, as I have been telling my two sons since they were small, is only just around the corner…'

FIVE MINUTES OF MADNESS

Arsenal v
Manchester United
Saturday 12 May 1979

IKE thousands of Arsenal fans, Emilio Zorlakki and his father, Alex, traipsed out of Wembley after the Ipswich defeat feeling angry and bemused. How could their team have played so badly? When Zorlakki senior turned to his son after the match and said, 'We'll be back next year' it was more an attempt to quell the teenager's sadness, born more out of paternal love, than a genuine conviction. After that flaccid display, many Arsenal fans couldn't imagine their side getting to Wembley again for a long, long time. And maybe three FA Cup finals in a decade was sufficient anyway. Except Emilio craved cup glory.

The 16-year-old, from Wood Green, North London, had been to Highbury several times in the late 1960s, mainly to watch North London derby games, but didn't show any real interest in football until the captivating 1970 World Cup in Mexico.

He recalls, 'That tournament was just so exciting. I loved collecting those Esso football coins. After that I was smitten with football and my first proper season at Highbury was 1970/71. How lucky was that?'

But he had missed the 1971 and 1972 finals so, after Ipswich, he could have been forgiven for thinking he had missed the boat completely. Surely Arsenal couldn't get to four FA Cup finals in the space of one decade, could they?

The 1978/79 season kicks off with the sensational news that Spurs have signed not one, but two players from Argentina. Osvaldo Ardiles and Ricardo Villa make their debuts in a pre-season friendly at Antwerp, where Spurs win 3-1. The reaction to their arrival is mixed. While Tommy Docherty says Tottenham have pulled off a marvellous coup, the PFA believes it might be the thin end of the wedge and representative Cliff Lloyd says, 'I don't think we would stand for a big influx of Argentineans into this country.'

When Sheffield United sign 23-year-old Alex Sabella from River Plate, shortly after, PFA executive committee member Gordon Taylor makes a statement which foresees possible problems in the future. 'If the trickle of foreign players becomes a flow, it would be detrimental to our members. There could already be two players out of a job at Tottenham. There is also the wider issue of the possible effect on the future of English football,' he says.

Arsenal begin the season with a settled side, but start indifferently. Then, in the autumn, they hit form and embark on a ten-match unbeaten run, which culminates in a glorious 5-0 away win at Tottenham two days before Christmas. As the third round of the FA Cup approaches, Arsenal are in fine form and lie fourth in the table. But suddenly, without warning, the weather turns and creates one of the coldest New Years in living memory with snow, ice and Siberian winds bringing widespread chaos across the country. In some areas, temperatures plunge to a teeth-chattering -20 degrees.

Shoppers and motorists are warned to stop panic-buying as food store shelves are stripped bare and garage pumps emptied after striking petrol tanker crews and lorry drivers threaten Britain with more misery. It is a winter becoming dominated by industrial unrest and political turmoil.

The freezing weather decimates the third round and only three ties go ahead, equalling that of the notoriously bad winter of 1963. One of these is at Hillsborough where Arsenal face Jack Charlton's Sheffield Wednesday. In time-honoured fashion the tricky surface is expected to nullify Arsenal's greater skill levels and even the sides up though few could have predicted precisely how much so. Over the ensuing weeks, it proves almost impossible to prise the sides apart. A draw at Hillsborough is followed by another at Highbury. A third game at neutral Filbert Street ends 2-2 and two days later it is 3-3. The sides are sick of the sight of one another.

It is not until 22 January, after nine hours of football and five matches, that the outcome is decided. Arsenal win 2-0 at Filbert Street in front of 30,000 people, with goals from Steve Gatting and Frank Stapleton.

Emilio Zorlakki recalls the marathon cup tie well. He says, 'It was a magnificent five-match epic, worthy of the final itself. The competition should have been suspended there and then and both teams should have been allowed to share the cup, was my view at the time.'

A routine 2-0 victory over Notts County follows in round four, ensuring Arsenal are in the hat for the last 16. But, as Emilio and his dad traipse back home through the winter darkness, after a performance which boss Terry Neill describes as 'uninspired', Wembley seems a long way off. And it will seem even further away when the draw for round five is made.

Today Emilio looks back on this as 'a strange time'. He is studying hard for his O Levels, though his school, Wood Green Comprehensive, is shut due to the weather and he can vividly recall trudging through the snow to collect his homework from the local scout hut. And now his heart sinks when he hears the fifth-round draw on Radio Two.

Arsenal must travel to Nottingham Forest, the reigning league champions, who have not lost at the City Ground since April 1977, nearly two years ago. It looks like the end of the road for the Gunners and the end of Emilio's dreams of cup glory.

The freezing weather continues. The UK is in the middle of what will become known as the 'Winter of Discontent'. It is the last few months of a beleaguered, battered Labour Government, struggling to prevent the country sliding into total disarray.

Over this period, the public becomes used to seeing TV images of rats scurrying through piles of uncollected rubbish and pickets in donkey jackets huddled around braziers. It is more a case of which workers *aren't* on strike.

Amidst the doom and gloom comes a strange story from the West Midlands. A 43-year-old housewife called Jean Hingley claims three little green men with wings entered her house after parking their flying saucer on her back lawn. Declining the housewife's offer of a cup of coffee, they each drink a glass of water instead. Then the three invaders flee, stealing some mince pies as they leave. Jean tells reporters, 'People will say I'm daft, but I know what I saw. They had horrible waxy faces, like corpses.' West Midlands Police promise to investigate.

Back in the real world and the First Division, Liverpool are leaving all others trailing in their wake. Their only blips in an almost perfect season have been narrow away defeats at Everton, Arsenal and Bristol City. At Anfield they are virtually invincible. Even in London and the south-east, many young lads are starting to adopt Liverpool as their team of choice. They have become the side of the 1970s and Kevin Keegan – though now plying his trade in Hamburg – is the player of the decade. Only Manchester United can rival Liverpool for attracting widespread geographical support.

Graham Stubbins, an Arsenal fan from Rainham in Kent, remembers this period vividly and says, 'I was the only Arsenal supporter in my group of mates and the vast majority of lads I hung around with supported Liverpool. But I had something on all of them. Although they thoroughly enjoyed giving me constant grief about the relatively mediocre team I supported, deep down I knew there was an element of jealousy that I had a dad who actually took me to see my team regularly.

'Turning up to Wakeley Junior School on a Monday morning with my treasured programme and sometimes a new badge almost seemed to give me a kind of nine-year-old celebrity status.'

The fifth-round ties are due to be played on 17 February but, for the first time in the competition's history, the entire round is wiped out due to the weather. Bristol City manager Alan Dicks makes an appeal for the season to be extended into midsummer to save supporters risking their lives on treacherous roads. As City prepare to make a 160-mile trip across Salisbury Plain to face Southampton, Dicks asks, 'I don't see the point of playing games in these conditions just for the sake of it. Why should we expect our supporters to put their lives and limbs at risk?'

The eagerly awaited Forest–Arsenal tie is rescheduled for Monday 26 February. Forest take advantage of the school holidays and recruit hundreds of local youngsters to help clear the pitch. Back home in Kent, Graham Stubbins has been taking relentless stick from the other lads telling him that Arsenal are going to get thrashed at the City Ground and dumped out of the cup.

And few are betting against that. So, when Graham, Emilio and their dads tune into Radio Two to hear the distinctive voice of Peter Jones announcing the teams from a freezing Nottingham, none of them holds out much hope of getting a result.

Almost 36,000 fans cram in to the City Ground, 10,000 up on Forest's normal gate. Roared on by a passionate crowd, Forest tear into Arsenal. They annihilate them, attacking relentlessly from all areas of the pitch, which still has patches of snow on it. Arsenal have no answer to the onslaught.

The trouble is, Forest don't score. They come mightily close on several occasions but Lady Luck, said by envious fans of other clubs to be an Arsenal fan, is certainly smiling over the Gunners. A deflected free kick from John Robertson strikes the bar and then the same player hits the post. Pat Jennings makes save after save and Garry Birtles, John McGovern and Dave Needham all go close.

For Emilio, Graham and the thousands of Arsenal fans glued to their radios, the tension is almost unbearable. With 11 minutes to go, it is somehow still goalless. Arsenal have barely got out of their half. But then, in a rare foray into Forest territory, Alan Sunderland is harshly adjudged by referee Peter Willis to have have been fouled by Viv Anderson on the edge of the box.

It is Arsenal's one opportunity. Talisman Brady stands over the ball. He floats in a perfect free kick, just over Larry Lloyd. It is met by Frank Stapleton, lethal with his head from this distance, who leaps and, right in front of the Forest fans, guides the ball past Peter Shilton, who furiously collects it from the net and angrily punts it back out.

Back home, the Zorlakkis, the Stubbinses and Arsenal fans everywhere dance around their living rooms or their bedrooms at this stunning goal, which shocks the whole footballing nation. It is an archetypal smash-and-grab. It is the only goal of the game. Forest, against all the odds, are out of the FA Cup and Arsenal's extraordinary record in the competition during the 1970s continues. Terry Neill says after the game, 'I have to say that, if I was Brian Clough, I'd be feeling a bit upset about the way things went.'

Graham Stubbins can't wait to see his school pals the next day and wave his Arsenal scarf at them.

With Forest out of the way, the clubs left in now start to dream of Wembley. But nobody is looking much beyond Liverpool, who have powered past Burnley 3-0 in round five. Surely, this year, the double is theirs for the taking. The last eight includes Manchester United, who have brushed aside Chelsea, Fulham and Colchester to get there. Nearly 52,000 are at White Hart Lane to see Spurs and United draw 1-1 before goals from Joe Jordan and Sammy McIlroy earn the Reds a place in the semi-final.

Arsenal dispose of Southampton after a replay to make the semi-final for the fifth time in the decade. There they will face Wolves at Villa Park. The other semi is massive – United v Liverpool at Maine Road. Most pundits are expecting a repeat of the 1971 final. Arsenal book their Wembley ticket with a 2-0 win over Wolves with goals from Stapleton and, against his old club, the bubble-permed Alan Sunderland, whose reputation is growing. Now Arsenal have a chance to expunge the horrible Ipswich performance from their memories. Willie Young says after the Wolves game, 'We can never play as badly as that again.'

At home in Kent, Graham Stubbins is praying that he can get a ticket to Wembley. His dad went to Villa Park for the semi-final and Graham says, 'As I listened to dad's tales of a hair-raising trip back to Birmingham New Street, avoiding the bricks and bottles, after the Wolves win, I absolutely longed for him to come home from work one day with two tickets to the final.

'At school, the lads would ask me if I would be going pretty much every time we gathered. I would like to think that deep down it was so they could wallow in the glory that one of their mates was going to Wembley, but I couldn't help but feel at the time they just wanted to be able to take the mick if I wasn't successful in getting a ticket. Kids can be so cruel to one another.'

Meanwhile, United supporters gathered at Maine Road are feeling less than confident about their side's chances. United fanatic Ian Brunton remembers, 'My main memories of this time were that we had absolutely no chance at all of winning. We were so bad under Dave Sexton and so negative it was painful to watch us play. I can remember sitting in the pub before the Liverpool match with my friends and most of us thought we would get absolutely stuffed.'

Liverpool strut on to the field at Maine Road in superb form. Riding high at the top of the table, with Kenny Dalglish banging in the goals left, right and centre, no one expects anything but a Liverpool victory, especially because the Merseysiders want to exact revenge for 1977.

But United have other ideas and a fabulous match ensues. Largely forgotten now by neutrals, the clash of these two northern giants, both wearing their change strips, is a genuine classic. Watched by some legendary figures of both clubs – Sir Matt Busby, Bill Shankly, Denis Law and Bobby Charlton – the two footballing leviathans serve up a belter. Four great goals, a missed penalty, desperate goal line saves and three bookings – it has everything.

Ian Brunton says, 'As the game got under way, it looked as though we wouldn't get the hammering I expected, as we seemed to be matching them in all parts of the field. Just as my confidence was growing, they scored.'

And what a goal it is. Inevitably it is scored by Kenny Dalglish, reminiscent of Jimmy Greaves at his masterful best. It surely means Liverpool are going to Wembley. That is what everyone in the ground thinks including Ian, who says, 'As far as I was concerned, that was it, I thought it was imperative United scored first if we were to win, a thought shared by most around me.'

But then, that feisty, niggly centre-forward Joe Jordan does what he does best, getting among defenders and rising high in the box to nod the ball past Ray Clemence. Then Terry McDermott misses a dubiously awarded penalty, which seems to give United fresh impetus. And, on 66 minutes, to the disbelief and joy of the United fans, Brian Greenhoff puts them ahead.

'We just went wild,' says Ian, 'as we dreamed of a return to Wembley. But we also knew they would throw the kitchen sink at us.'

They do. This Liverpool side don't know how to lose and the team in yellow pour forward. Blame for both United goals could feasibly have been attributed to Alan Hansen, so there is some personal relief for the former Partick Thistle man when he side-foots home an equaliser eight minutes from time to ruin United's dream. It is the final goal in a thriller and means the teams must meet again on Wednesday at Goodison Park.

'As the final whistle went, I felt completely drained,' recalls Ian. 'I was shattered mentally and physically as though I had played in the game myself.' Sadly, yet predictably, violence follows. 'Fighting was breaking out everywhere,' says Ian. 'It was utter chaos.' Liverpool had to go to Manchester for the first semi-final. Quid pro quo. Now United must go to Liverpool. The replay will be at Goodison Park.

And now the Labour Government, lurching from crisis to crisis for some time, finally falls. Prime Minister Callaghan has only been managing to keep things going through a series of deals with minor parties and by means of the Lib–Lab pact. But now, the Government loses a vote on home rule and it is announced that a general election will take place on 3 May. Margaret Thatcher demands Parliament's quick dissolution. It looks almost certain that the country will have a Conservative Government again and a female leader for the first time.

Gloria Gaynor might be number one in the charts with 'I Will Survive' but Callaghan knows in his heart of hearts it is over. The Bee Gees' 'Tragedy' is more appropriate for him and his party and, as the fateful Commons sitting which decides his party's fate ends, a group of Labour MPs, led by Welsh left-winger Neil Kinnock, sings a defiant and emotional chorus of 'The Red Flag'.

Meanwhile, Manchester United travel to Goodison Park more in hope than expectation. In those days, you tended not to get more than one pop at teams of Liverpool's quality. Despite the draw at Maine Road, the United fans still have a downer on their team. 'The general opinion among us,' says Ian Brunton, 'was that bad teams don't get two chances to beat good teams. My own opinion was that we would get beaten by three or four goals.'

There is more trouble before the game with the less-pleasant element of Liverpool and Everton fans joining forces to pick off any United fans who stray into the wrong areas of the city.

The atmosphere is taut. The Liverpool fans have had their noses put out of joint by not disposing of United first time around. Now the Stretford End is on their manor and they are less than welcome.

Some 53,000 fans packed in to Goodison with the nation expecting the Liverpool 'machine' to mesh into gear and see off

United. But it doesn't work like that. United tear into Liverpool, with the little Scottish dynamo, Macari, outstanding. The United fans can barely believe what they are watching.

Ian Brunton says, 'Suddenly, we were playing the best football we'd played for months and my confidence was growing by the minute.'

It is only the brilliance of Ray Clemence that stops United from scoring. Then, 23 minutes from time, the unthinkable happens and United inflict the killer punch. Welshman Micky Thomas crosses and that wily blond-haired veteran, Jimmy Greenhoff, heads it home. The United fans are gasping for breath, 'Our sections of the ground simply erupted,' remembers Ian. Greenhoff, not for the first time, is United's saviour.

He is a player Ian recalls with great affection, 'I always count Jimmy Greenhoff as one of my favourite players ever. I love that type of unselfish, thoughtful player, and how he wasn't capped by England is a mystery. I used to marvel at his work off the ball, the runs he would make across the last line of defence, dragging defenders all over the place and leaving gaps for others to exploit and gain the glory. A fabulous player.

'The rest of the game seemed to last forever, but somehow we hung on for a famous victory. The celebrations in the stands and terraces will always stay with me.'

Liverpool, the side who never lose, have lost. And United are at Wembley for the third time in four seasons. After beating the invincibles, who will bet against them now?

At school in Kent, a justifiably smug Graham Stubbins charitably says nothing to the sheepish, glory-hunting Liverpool fans who suddenly have very little to say for themselves, although they give it a bit of 'We've won the league so who cares about the cup?' The truth is, everyone wants to win the FA Cup, and everyone wants to get to Wembley. It is still, by some considerable distance, the most important club football match in the country. And Liverpool fans are irked. Though they have had massive success during the 1970s, they have only won the cup once during the decade and should have done better.

On 3 May, Britain goes to the polls. It is a foregone conclusion. The Labour Government has imploded and the country
is in a sorry state. There is a sense that the unions are running
the country and nobody is in control. The electorate feels it is
time for a change. The public wants a firmer hand to steady
the ship.

The next day, a 53-year-old grocer's daughter from
Grantham, Lincolnshire, clad in a striking blue dress, emerges
from 10 Downing Street into the sunlight, paraphrasing St
Francis of Assisi and wittering on about finding harmony where
there is discord. Enter Margaret Thatcher.

Meanwhile, the touts start moving in. In a desperate bid
to outwit them and stamp on the black market, the FA draws
up stricter rules for the allocation of tickets. For the first time,
each club in the final is allowed to sell only 2,500, or ten per
cent of their share, to officials, players and directors. And each
person is limited to just 30 tickets. Like everyone in football,
the FA knows that the majority of tickets reaching the black
market come from players and officials, and so now everyone
who gets a ticket has to provide names and addresses of those
people they sell to.

But, whatever the FA does, tickets still get through. And
that is good news for middle-men, like Stan Flashman who says,
'If people want to call me a tout, that's up to them. I'm doing
nothing illegal; I'm doing people a good turn, getting them
things they want at a price they're willing to pay.'

Another tout – who prefers not to be named – says there
are 7,000 black market tickets being sold in Manchester alone.
Freely admitting that the vast majority of tickets which end up
in his hands come from people working in football, including
players, he says, 'There are some players who wouldn't walk
across the road to see United and Arsenal play, never mind travel
to Wembley so they're more than happy to sell.'

Back in Manchester, Ian Brunton doesn't want to repeat
the experience of 1977 and end up huddled beneath the stand,
so he gets his ticket application in early. He hasn't missed a

single home game and has been to loads of away games, so he is confident. In fact, he is sure he will get a ticket. So, when the postman walks up his drive clutching an interesting-looking envelope, Ian is convinced it is good news. The official Manchester United stationery is another good sign, so he tears open the envelope and starts to read with a massive grin on his face. It soon vanishes.

'It was a bombshell,' he says. 'I hadn't got a ticket. I had to read it several times for it to sink in. I just couldn't believe I wouldn't get a ticket again. I had missed out in 1977 but had expected that one in a way. But in 1979 crowds were down and I was certain I would get one.'

Ian was gutted. He worked in a bookie's in one of the rougher parts of Manchester and came into contact with several local 'characters'. He says, 'They were all telling me the same thing. "No problem, I will get you a ticket." Even though I had heard it all before I actually believed someone would get me one.'

But as the big day got closer, all the promises counted for nothing. No ticket was forthcoming. 'I had no chance,' Ian says, 'nor could I bribe a gateman, as it had all been tightened up and we were told no one would be on the take.' With a heavy heart, Ian made a decision. He recalls, 'Much as it hurt me to do so, this time I decided not to travel ticketless and stayed at home instead.'

The build-up starts. Arsenal players are accused of avarice after establishing a 'perks pool' and demanding an unreasonable fee for an official team picture. But they are defended by one of the true luminaries of the game. Former Manchester United boss Sir Matt Busby says, 'Footballers have a short life and I don't blame them for trying to get everything out of the game.' Speaking at a Sports Writers' Association lunch in London, Sir Matt believes the key figures at Wembley will be Jimmy Greenhoff and Liam Brady, who Sir Matt says is the most gifted player in England since George Best. 'Brady has skills which are above the ordinary,' he says.

Twelve-year-old Arsenal fan Colin Sibbard, of Pedbury, Bucks, writes to *Daily Mirror* reporter Frank McGhee, begging him to back Manchester United in tomorrow's final. 'I would like you to back Manchester United because you keep getting it wrong, but dad says at least you admit it,' he requests. 'I would like Arsenal to win so I don't get teased like I did last year.'

At Wakeley Junior School in Rainham, Kent, the Liverpool-supporting boys are in full flow, teasing Graham Stubbins mercilessly about how Arsenal have no chance. United will be too good for them, Arsenal will fail just like they did last year, they say. Graham remembers, 'As the big day got closer, the grief got worse and worse. The irony in how much these so-called Liverpool fans appeared to want United to win is incredible, given the hatred between the two clubs these days.'

At home in Wood Green, Emilio Zorlakki is getting in the mood and putting together his cup final 'kit'. First he goes out and buys a klaxon. Then he decides he needs a cup final banner. He thinks long and hard about what to write. Then it comes to him. He decides to take the opportunity to remind Arsenal's friends at White Hart Lane that they are at Wembley again and Spurs are not. So he gets to work. 'Spurs may have a Pratt, but we have a bigger Willie' he writes, uncertain whether ITV or BBC will consider it a tad risqué to be shown.

'There was an air of more determination to put things right this year,' remembers Emilio. 'We were also not hot favourites and were playing another giant who had ended Liverpool's double hopes. On ITV's *Who will win the Cup?* the majority of the pundits were tipping Man Utd. We'll see, I thought.'

Arsenal's centre-half David O'Leary echoes Willie Young's comments after the semi-final and says the Gunners' spineless display and deserved defeat in 1978 is their prime motivator this year. He tells the *Mirror*'s Harry Miller, 'Last year, we went back to Highbury to meet the fans and tour the area in an open-top bus. It was awful. We were empty-handed. We'd lost and we felt lost. We had let the supporters down and we knew it. I returned home, switched on the telly and saw Ipswich parading the cup in front of 100,000 fans. There is no way I want to experience that hollow feeling again.'

In Manchester, the last-minute scramble for tickets is in full swing. The word is that no one will get in without tickets this time. All across the city, people are trying to do deals, pull in favours. Everybody seems to have a friend of a friend of a friend who might be able to come up trumps. But they rarely do. False leads are followed up; people make promises they can't keep. 'Someone who drinks in my mate's pub works with Ashley Grimes's brother' and the like. In the end, it is all froth. Except sometimes, people get lucky.

United fan Ian Short is stunned when he hears he has won a raffle held by Wembley stewards after a Thursday night dog meeting. Out of the blue, he is going to the final.

Ian Brunton is at home glumly watching television, green with envy as the exodus from Manchester begins. Then the phone rings and Ian can barely believe what he hears. The voice at the other end of the phone is offering a train ticket and standing ticket for the game for £50, about ten times the face value. 'I couldn't believe my luck,' says Ian, 'and jumped at the chance.'

Train after train pulls out of Manchester Piccadilly, crammed with expectant United fans. Having cut it so fine and got a ticket at the last minute, Ian Brunton is probably the happiest person on the journey. The euphoria of beating Liverpool in the semi-final has evaporated, league form has slumped, and the United fans are in a pessimistic frame of mind, as Ian says, 'Chatting to others on the train, we came to the conclusion that as United were so poor, it was just a case of how many Arsenal would win by. I was sure we would lose. This was my fourth trip to Wembley to see United and I was yet to see us score a goal (1976 0-1, 1977 I didn't get in until all the goals had been scored, 1977 Charity Shield 0-0 and now the 1979 final) so I decided that I would be happy just to see us score, never mind win the cup.'

Ian Short, the lucky winner of the raffle at Wembley dogs, travels down and picks up his ticket from the house of the Wembley steward. 'The steward had left,' says Ian, 'but his wife told me that if I made my way to the Royal Box restaurant after the game he would be on the door and he would let me in.' Ian can hardly believe his luck.

'What a thrill,' he says, 'my first United cup final and I would be mixing with all the celebrities after the game. I put the ticket into a plastic bag and then taped it to my chest where it stayed until I reached the turnstiles.'

The Arsenal fans are preparing to make the much shorter trip to the twin towers. Emilio puts on his scarf, picks up his flag, his banner and klaxon and gets into the family car. His dad is banned from Wembley as he is considered a jinx! Emilio says, 'Dad drove us to the same spot near Brent Town Hall and said he would come back to collect us after the match.'

Much to the disgust of the Liverpool fans at his school, young Graham Stubbins's hopes of getting a ticket have come to nothing and he has to watch the match at a neighbour's house. The ribbing from the Liverpool fans continued in the park the night before the game. A pretend FA Cup Final has resulted in a 6-0 win for United, immediately followed by the imaginary sacking of Terry Neill and rotten fruit being thrown at the Arsenal players in front of Islington Town Hall.

Graham trudges home almost believing that Arsenal would lose after all, with the taunts and jibes of his mates ringing in his ears. 'You're going to lose the cup! You're going to lose the cup! And now you're gonna to believe us!'

The next morning Graham wakes and suddenly feels full of pride for the club he loves. Carefully, he gathers every scarf and ribbon he owns and – purely for his mates' benefit – hangs them from his bedroom window. Then he and his dad go to the neighbour's to watch the entire build-up.

Ken Banham, a veteran of 1971, 72 and 78, leaves for Wembley in a coach from the White House pub, opposite Clissold Park, deep in Arsenal territory. And everyone is looking at Ken, or rather at Ken's companions. 'I had two Page Three girls with me, who were really good friends and real Gooners too,' he says. 'We found a pub near Wembley stadium, which was mixed with both Mancs and Gooners. The Mancs could not believe their eyes when they saw the two girls who were wearing low-cut tops and miniskirts. One of the United fans said, "Now we know what they mean when they say lucky Arsenal"!'

Arsenal fan Gary Humphrey sets off by train from Haslemere in Surrey. Like many Gunners fans he is trying not to get too excited, remembering the massive low he felt after losing to Ipswich. Even so, Gary has felt sufficiently confident to call into his local bookie's. He places an ambitious bet. He puts £10 on Arsenal to win either 3-1 or 3-2, another £10 on Arsenal to be ahead at half-time and another on them being ahead at the end.

'Thirty pounds on bets,' he says, 'and obviously, if Arsenal failed this time, I would have even more reason to be fed up.'

When Gary reaches Wembley he savours the walk up Wembley Way and, as the ground moves into view, he feels his heart beat faster. 'Every time I went to the old Wembley, I got goose bumps as the famous twin towers came into view,' he says. 'You can build an arch a mile high, but it will never have the same historical meaning as those towers.'

Now the fans are on the terraces with the United fans to the right of the Royal Box and the Arsenal fans massed at the tunnel end. Emilio Zorlakki is in the upper tier, just above the tunnel itself, a great spot. 'What struck me this year was the kaleidoscope of colours at our end, especially of red and yellow,' says Emilio.

Gary Humphrey is also pleased with his position, right at the top of the terracing. 'I couldn't have chosen better,' he says. 'All around me were Arsenal fans from a South Wales supporters' club and boy, could they sing. I sang that day like I have never sung at any other game in my life.'

The model aeroplanes are back again as part of the pre-match entertainment to 'delight' the crowd. It is an uninteresting, dull contest, which United win to general indifference.

The teams come on the pitch for their traditional pre-match walkabout. Gunners skipper Pat Rice waves his arms up and down in the direction of the Arsenal fans, urging them to up the noise levels. And they do. They break into a rousing chorus of 'We won 5-0 at the Lane' to the tune of 'Those Were The Days', and 'Tottenham Hotspur, Tottenham Hotspur. Can you hear us on the box?' to the tune of 'Cwm Rhondda'. The banners are waving. One reads, 'We did it Howe way'. Another says, 'God Gave the World Jesus Christ. Now He Gives It Liam Brady'.

Opposite them, the United fans seem strangely subdued. Ian Brunton is in the right-hand corner and describes the view as appalling, but Ian Short, right behind the goal in which Charlie George, Stuart Pearson and Ian Porterfield have scored over the last few years, is happier. 'The ticket couldn't have been better,' he says. The atmosphere builds and now the United fans find their voice. A simple chant of, '[Clap-clap. Clap-clap-clap. Clap-clap-clap-clap] – GREENHOFF!'

The teams are in the tunnel. Terry Neill comes out wearing a slightly dodgy powder blue suit. Very 1979. Dave Sexton, on the other hand, has a sober jacket and tie and looks like a head of department at a Home Counties comprehensive. The two share a joke as they walk to their places. 'Come on you Reds,' sing the United fans.

His Royal Highness Prince Charles stands earnestly on the touchline waiting to be introduced, fiddling nervously with his hands. His presence calls to mind Mike Yarwood's impressions of him. Now the national anthem. The players look business-like but tense. They just want to get on with it. Preliminaries over, the pitch is cleared, the players break. Referee Ron Challis of Tonbridge, Kent, blows his whistle and we are off.

United know Brady is the danger man and, from the outset, it appears that both Lou Macari and Mickey Thomas have been charged with stopping him playing. They are watching his every move like hawks. Will Brady have the nous to escape their clutches?

Both sides hold back in the opening ten minutes, sizing each other up. No one seems able to put their foot on the ball and make anything happen. Long hopeful balls are made, or nothing sideways passes made to colleagues. It needs someone to step up to the plate and take responsibility. Someone does. That someone is Brady.

With only 12 minutes on the clock, the Irishman collects the ball just inside the United half. Nothing looks on. Macari and Thomas, like a couple of junkyard dogs hunting in a pair, close in on him and try to snuff out any creative intention. But Brady is too good for them and beats both of them with a combination of strength and skill. His movement has created an opening.

Brady then neatly lays the ball off to his compatriot Frank Stapleton in the right-wing position. Stapleton cuts inside and then, seeing a darting run by David Price in the inside-right channel, curls a lovely, incisive low pass into the United box. Price gets there a split-second ahead of Martin Buchan and prods it forward towards the byline.

Gary Bailey races out to collect but Price screws the ball to the edge of the six-yard box. Sensing danger, Coppell has raced back and nearly cuts out the ball but fails. Arriving at almost exactly the same time are Alan Sunderland and Brian Talbot and it is the latter who gets a foot to the ball and sweeps it into the net, past the vain attempts of Jimmy Nicholl. It is 1-0 to Arsenal and it is the earliest FA Cup Final goal since 1966.

In Kent, Graham Stubbins raises both hands skywards and says, 'Yeeeessssss!' and wonders what those Liverpool fans are thinking now. Back at Wembley, Emilio Zorlakki is dancing around and gives his klaxon a good squeeze. The Arsenal fans are raving about Brady and the United fans cursing their team for not dealing with him.

The goal wakes United up and they start to play, but they don't really trouble Pat Jennings. And, then, a minute before half-time, Arsenal get a second. Once again it is the skill and invention of Brady that carves it out. After a surging run, Talbot slips the ball to Brady, who is 45 yards out and, apparently, posing no danger for United.

But suddenly he accelerates, shrugs off the challenge of Arthur Albiston and then, with a shimmy, coolly beats Buchan on the edge of the area. Seemingly with all the time in the world, he takes stock, looks up and sees Stapleton unmarked on the edge of the six-yard box. With his right foot he floats a perfect cross to his fellow Irishman and Dubliner who, with a jerk of his neck muscles, heads the ball past a stationary Bailey. It is 2-0, half-time, and it looks like game over.

The Arsenal fans are in heaven. Gary Humphrey says, 'As the team went down the tunnel at half-time, they received rapturous applause. There was a real party atmosphere about the place.'

Back in Kent, Graham Stubbins considers running around the block and calling on one of the Liverpool supporters to see what they have to say for themselves but, perhaps wisely, he decides against it. Now he is convinced Arsenal are going to win, school on Monday seems quite a desirable prospect.

You can imagine the two team talks. Terry Neill's must have been of the 'Keep doing what you're doing but don't get complacent' variety while Dave Sexton, in his usual understated way, must have been saying, 'We've got nothing to lose now, let's go for broke. But for God's sake, try and stop Brady!'

As the teams emerge for the second half, there is a strange murmur from the ground. Perhaps the fans sense it is all over. Emilio Zorlakki just remembers wanting the second half to pass as quickly as possible. He says, 'Though we were 2-0 up, I was still on tenterhooks. I was hoping we could score a third goal to put the game to bed.'

United play better in the second half and come close a couple of times, but Jennings isn't really worried. The Arsenal fans are completely relaxed and, with the clock counting down nicely, they are preparing to celebrate. With 25 minutes to go, the main camera suddenly turns to Prince Charles. His chin is resting on his fist. He takes a sneaky look at his watch. He is bored. Maybe he wishes he was playing polo.

He is not alone in his mind drifting as the game is petering out and it appears to be Arsenal's cup. As Gary Humphrey recalls, 'Defensively, we were in control and really just playing out time, holding on to the lead we deserved. There was really no sign of any likely change in circumstances.'

In Kent, Graham, his dad and their neighbour, Eric, are almost in cruise control. 'Fancy some chips at the end of the match?' says Eric. 'I'll put the fat on now. We can celebrate winning the cup with a nice chip butty.'

There are five minutes to go and some United fans are already heading for the exits. Most of them have thrown in the towel and can't bear to watch and listen to the Londoners at the other end of the stadium, starting their party.

A rousing chorus of 'Good old Arsenal' is sung with gusto, followed by 'We shall not, we shall not be moved!' The yellow and blue ribbons are being prepared. It is not quite 1971 all over again, but it is certainly far better than 1972 and 78. It has been an average kind of game, a bit dull to be honest. But now, suddenly, it will explode and produce one of the most extraordinary five-minute periods in FA Cup history.

There are 86 minutes on the clock when Steve Coppell lifts a free kick in from the edge of the box. It eludes everyone and reaches Joe Jordan who plays the ball back into the middle of the penalty area. There it finds Gordon McQueen, who takes a first-time shot with his left foot, which keeps low and beats Jennings. It is a goal out of nothing and a consolation at best. United barely celebrate. But they are anxious to get going again.

Ian Brunton is pleased because he has finally seen United score in the FA Cup Final, though it's not really how he would have wanted it. But 2-1 does look a bit better than 2-0.

McQueen's goal, however, has had a strange effect on everyone connected with Arsenal. Suddenly they don't have their feet up, smoking a cigar. Watching at home, Graham Stubbins is beside himself, as only a nine-year-old can be. He says, 'After United pulled one back I was shaking with nerves. Both my dad and my neighbour, Eric, began stomping around the room making the usual negative comments such as, "That's it, we're gonna blow it", littered with the kind of expletives I was only used to hearing when actually attending games!'

Gary Humphrey says, 'Now it was as if Arsenal had changed places with a poor amateur side. Passes went astray and tackles were missed.' Decades on, Gary is still able to replay what happened next in slow motion in his mind.

Suddenly it is all United. It is as though Arsenal have caved in. United are surging forward and their fans sense something special might be happening. Suddenly they are roaring their team on. But how often will a team come back from 2-0 down with five minutes to go?

Hardly ever. Especially in an FA Cup Final. Yet United are suddenly full of belief and 100,000 pairs of eyes are glued to the action. An Arsenal clearance ricochets off Graham Rix into the path of Coppell. Coppell turns and plays a searching ball into the inside-right channel into which Belfast-born Sammy McIlroy has made a darting run.

There is a murmur of expectation from the United fans at the western end of the ground. McIlroy is tracked by David O'Leary, but McIlroy's sudden stop and turn leaves O'Leary on his backside. McIlroy is now in the area. There is a collective gasp from the Arsenal fans.

Sensing danger, substitute Steve Walford slides in, but McIlroy nudges it past him brilliantly with his right foot. Suddenly, McIlroy has a real chance. All that stands between him and the goal is fellow Ulsterman Pat Jennings. The huge keeper races out of his goal and flings himself to the ground, but McIlroy has managed to connect with his left foot and, to general disbelief, the ball rolls into the net.

The United players and fans go absolutely wild. Arsenal can't believe it. Nor can commentator Brian Moore. 'The Arsenal players were preparing their victory speeches and now they are absolutely dumbstruck,' he says. Co-commentator Brian Clough adds, 'Unbelievable. I'm delighted for them. They've earned it since three o'clock.'

Behind the goal in which United have just scored, their fans are writhing in disbelieving ecstasy. Ian Short says, 'After "Big Gordon" scored we had of course cheered, but it was more in hope than conviction. Then up strode "Super Sam" and we had equalised. We went absolutely berserk and were jumping up and down and hugging perfect strangers as if they were our long-lost family.'

Ian Brunton recalls, 'The scenes at our end were just chaotic as people tumbled down the terraces as we celebrated the most unexpected of comebacks.'

The Arsenal fans at the tunnel end are open-mouthed at what they have just seen and furious at their team for throwing away a two-goal cushion. Emilio Zorlakki remembers a 'cold shiver' after McIlroy's goal and being sent into a dreamlike trance by the cheers of the United fans.

Just below him, a small group of United fans are celebrating. Two men either side of Emilio slump to the ground. Both appear to be crying. Emilio wants to cry as well and momentarily lowers his head on to the crush barrier. He remembers, 'An old fella behind me said "Don't worry mate, we'll still win", patting me on the back as he said it.'

At home in Kent, Graham Stubbins can only think of the merciless ribbing he is going to get back at school. 'I felt like bursting into tears,' he says. 'But the disappointment and anger in my father and Eric's voices left me fearful that crying would just make it a lot worse!'

There are always strange little incidents that stay with people down the years and Graham remembers Eric lurching up from his armchair saying, 'I can't watch this any more. We have blown it. I'm going to start cooking those ****** chips!'

Gary Humphrey says, 'I looked down at the Arsenal team. They were dead on their feet and totally dispirited. Extra time would have seen only one winner and that was the boys from up north who were now scampering about like revitalised men.'

All around there is abject misery, anger and bitterness. The momentum is now firmly with United. Gary says, 'I sank down, sitting on the terraces with my head in my hands. I realised another defeat in the final was on the cards…a more complete picture of misery you couldn't see anywhere.'

As Gary's eyes start to well up and Arsenal prepare to kick off again, one of his new Welsh friends says, in an almost comedy accent, 'Don't worry, boyo, knowing the Arsenal they'll go up the other end and score now. They never do things the easy way, see.' Gary looks up and just about summons a weak smile. How can anyone be so optimistic, he thinks.

Thirty-five years later, Gary reflects on this brief exchange on the terraces. He says, 'Those two sentences often come into my mind when I see something relating to that epic final. The first sentence proved to be one of the greatest predictions of all time and the second more than adequately describes just about everything about the club I love so much, but have frequently been frustrated by down the years.'

It has been an extraordinary couple of minutes. Presumably, the teams will now settle for extra time. Everybody needs to catch their breath, including the players. But there is to be one final, incredible twist. And the catalyst for this most amazing drama is that man Brady.

The United fans are still singing and dancing and telling everyone they are going to win the cup when Arsenal gain possession on the left. Lurking, just feet inside United's half, is Brady. He has already made two goals and he digs deep for one final effort.

Dropping his shoulders he embarks on a run. Suddenly he picks up pace. The two guard dogs, Macari and Thomas, can see what he is doing but, again, he is too good for them and evades their challenges. He has travelled 20 yards and advanced coldly right into United's territory. As Buchan moves towards him to stop the run, Brady slides the ball enticingly to Graham Rix, out on the left wing. Brady has put it on a plate for the Yorkshireman who, first time, curls over a dangerous ball. It looks like Gary Bailey should claim it, but it is too high for him.

Now it is the United fans' jaws that are dropping. The ball also sails over Arthur Albiston, who is suddenly horrified when he realises that, lurking just behind him, is the permed-haired figure of Alan Sunderland. Sunderland stretches and gets his right foot to the ball and, astonishingly, unbelievably, directs the ball into the net.

Nobody can quite believe it. This is the drama to end all dramas. Sunderland clambers to his feet and starts sprinting away with Walford tugging at his shirt. Sunderland is totally lost in the moment. His eyes are closed, his head swaying from side to side. He is saying something, but it could be anything. It probably wouldn't be repeatable though.

United fan Ian Short remembers that he, like many other United fans, was still caught up in the emotion of McIlroy's equaliser. People all over the ground are having trouble computing what they have just witnessed. Ian says, 'We were dancing and singing when suddenly we heard this roar from the other end. We all thought, "Well, we've just scored so what the hell are they shouting about?"'

Soon the penny drops and Ian Brunton says, 'I know many Reds who still describe that moment as the worst they have ever experienced at a United game.'

One minute earlier, Gary Humphrey had been sitting on the terraces with his head in his hands. Now look at him. 'Absolute bedlam broke out all around me,' he says. 'I was ahead of everyone else as I had anticipated the net bulging. I was leaping about all over the place, with genuine tears of joy pouring down my cheeks and I noticed many other people around me had tears in their eyes as well.'

Among the mayhem, Gary feels a hand rapidly ruffling his hair and that same sing-song voice emanating from the Welsh valleys, 'See. I told you, boyo. That's Arsenal all over, see.' Emilio Zorlakki had been spellbound as Brady and Rix built the move. 'Then I was grabbing everyone in sight,' he says, 'total strangers who were hugging each other like long-lost relatives! The two men who had been crying just before had both missed the goal, but were celebrating like they'd seen it.'

Back in Kent, the chips are forgotten about. Nine-year-old Graham Stubbins is delighted and a little confused. He says, 'It was probably my first experience of total and utter football supporter carnage. Grown men leaping around like idiots. Me trying to join in without really knowing what to do, and Eric desperately trying to find a cloth to clean the fat from his kitchen walls and ceiling where he'd lobbed the chips all over the place in the excitement!'

There is still time for another heart-in-mouth moment for the Arsenal fans when Jordan heads goalwards, prompting a piercing shriek of fear from a woman standing behind Emilio, but it is too late. Ron Challis gives a piercing blow of his whistle. Arsenal have won the last final of the 1970s, a fitting finale to a dramatic decade of football.

There is great sportsmanship at the end between both sets of players and managers. They know they have served up something special. Dave Sexton, a fine gentleman and so modest in victory nine years earlier when boss of Chelsea, is equally gracious in defeat, warmly congratulating Terry Neill.

But United are clearly devastated. Sammy McIlroy, whose brilliant equaliser looked like taking the game into extra time, sits forlornly on the ground as his compatriot Pat Jennings consoles him and hauls him up to his feet. Gordon McQueen lies flat on his back, topless, clutching a yellow Arsenal shirt. Suddenly the lanky ginger-haired frame of fellow Scot Willie Young lollops over and, rather bizarrely, straddles the United centre-half, sitting on his midriff and then pulling McQueen's head up towards him. It is porn for people who like the sight of six-foot plus, correction fluid-white, scantily clad Scottish men, embracing. It looks a tad dodgy, it has to be said.

And now, skipper Pat Rice, the sole survivor from the 1971 team, is climbing the steps to receive the trophy. Just above the tunnel, Emilio Zorlakki wipes a tear from his eye as he watches the Ulsterman – Arsenal through and through – collect the cup. As he does so, Emilio thinks back 12 months to the tears he shed when his beloved team lost to Ipswich. He thinks back seven years to 1972 when, as a nine-year-old, he cried when Allan Clarke's header hit the back of the net and he thinks further back to the glorious year of 1971, when his father had left him standing at the school gates before the title triumph at White Hart Lane and then couldn't get tickets for the final. Memories, all washed away.

He says, 'This was the first time I had seen Arsenal lift a trophy and the euphoria was overwhelming. This was the moment I had been waiting for since I fell in love with Arsenal. I couldn't wait for Pat Rice to lift that trophy.'

Gary Humphrey also recalls seeing Rice in the bright late-afternoon sunshine and says, 'When your team has won the cup, you want the on-pitch celebrations to go on forever and after a finish and result like that I really wish it could have.'

Emilio recalls a lovely touch at the end of the game. As the United players headed off, the Arsenal fans at that end of the ground applauded them warmly before breaking into a chant of 'United! United!' He says, 'But soon we were screaming the names of all our players and the backroom staff, as Terry Neill was holding aloft Don Howe's arm. "One Liam Brady, there's only one Liam Brady!" He was the architect and the best midfield player in Europe. A year later he was gone.'

Gradually, the ground starts to empty. The match has clearly taken its toll on the supporters, who are emotionally drained. Arsenal fan Ken Smith, who saw his first Arsenal match in 1946, remembers the atmosphere walking back up Wembley Way was almost ghostly, because fans of both sides were still in a state of shock.

He says, 'Thousands of us – both sets of supporters – were walking across the bridge to the station. There was no real noise or chanting, only people walking silently in disbelief and shock at what they had just seen. The loudest noise came from the thousands of empty beer and drinks cans which were being kicked by people as they walked along.'

You would need a hard heart not to feel sorry for the United fans, who have been through the wringer and, in the end, left distraught.

Remember Ian Short? He was meant to have been a guest in the famous Royal Box restaurant. If United had won, it would have been the perfect thing to do. But the manner of United's defeat has put a different slant on everything.

'I just couldn't face it,' says Ian. 'I was completely devastated.' Ian simply left Wembley, headed to King's Cross and caught the first train home.

Ian Brunton merely recalls an extremely quiet and sombre journey back to Manchester.

Back home in Kent, the homemade chip cooking has been abandoned. The aptly-nicknamed 'Chippy' Brady put paid to that, so Graham Stubbins's dad says, 'Come on, let's go and buy some fish and chips.'

Graham says, 'Not that exciting you might think, but the car journey would take me past the football "arena" I mentioned earlier, a place where I knew, even though they definitely wouldn't tell me, my mates would already be re-enacting Alan Sunderland's last-minute winner and even more famous curly-haired celebration!

'As we approached, the tell-tale signs of a pile of bikes came into vision. Twirling my scarf out of the window, dad brilliantly obliged with a torrent of car horn sounds. The lads briefly stopped their own cup final and looked on open-mouthed. My moment. Nobody else's. All mine.'

In North London, the party is beginning as the fans relive the final five minutes over and over again. Back at the White House pub, the beers are flowing as those Gooners who haven't been at Wembley await the arrival of those who have, like Ken Banham and his Page Three girls.

'By 9pm,' says Ken, 'the cars were cruising down Green Lanes sounding their horns, flags and scarves flying, people hanging out of the windows. The singing went on until the early hours. We were all very, very drunk and very, very happy.'

There are hangovers from hell all over North London on Sunday morning, but every Arsenal fan wakes with a huge smile as he or she recalls the events of yesterday. Thousands attend the civic reception at Islington Town Hall. For Ken Banham and his mates it was then back to the White House to pick up where they had left off in the small hours. Ken describes a magical occasion.

He says, 'There was more drink and more songs. Whole families were there. Mums, wives, dads, granddads, babies dressed from head to toe in red and white. This is what supporting the Arsenal has always been about. My mum always had open house on match days and she always laid on food and drink. This time all the lads treated her and made her feel like a queen, which she was. Without her, our family could not have given the commitment that our family have given to this great club, this institution.'

For another Arsenal fan, there was still another moment to put the icing on the cake. In all the excitement of Saturday, Gary Humphrey had forgotten about the betting slip, which was still lodged in the pocket of his Levi jacket. It proved a nice little earner. 'When I handed it in on Monday morning I received £285 in return, which represented nearly four weeks' wages to me as a youngster,' he says.

United fan Ian Brunton doesn't go to home first-team matches at Old Trafford any more. After not missing a game at Old Trafford for 34 years – including friendlies – he was finally priced out. Initially, he switched his allegiance to the reserve and youth teams, going to every home and away reserve game, including overseas friendlies, and every home academy match and most aways.

But, by 2014, health problems were restricting Ian's visits, as he explains, 'I've gone from going to around 100 games a season to as few as 13 games last season and probably fewer still in 2013/14. I'm now restricted to youth home games and the occasional local away game. I went to Huddersfield last week for an FA Youth Cup game and that's the furthest I've been in about 18 months. I cannot begin to describe how much I miss going to watch my beloved team but I realise its just a matter of time until I have to give it up altogether.' Ian's passion for the club he loves still burns and he keeps busy by writing for the excellent *United We Stand* fanzine and a couple of other websites.

Today, those Arsenal fans who were at the 1979 FA Cup Final still get a warm, tingly feeling when they look back and recall a truly special event. Graham Stubbins is in his mid-40s now, and wonders if during those final five minutes was the exact moment when he decided he was going to dedicate almost his entire spare time to following Arsenal all over the UK and Europe. Getting briefly Proustian, he ponders, 'It's the search for more moments like 1979 I suppose.'

Alan Sunderland's winning goal is still etched as visibly on Gary Humphrey's mind as it was all those years ago, on that sun-drenched afternoon. He can still see Brady bursting forward, determined not to be a Wembley loser. He says, 'It remains one of the greatest possible achievements for a fan. To see your team win the FA Cup is just fantastic. To do it in such dramatic circumstances was just overwhelming.

'No matter how long I live, that day will always be extra special to me as it was the first time I had actually been in the stadium when Arsenal had lifted a trophy – a truly momentous occasion; 1979 was a wonderful year for me both as an individual and as a supporter of Arsenal. On a personal basis I met and got engaged to a gorgeous girl, Jeanette, who I later married.'

Life has been tough for Gary since that wonderful Arsenal victory 35 years ago. Unable to work since 2006 due to ill health, his love for the Arsenal still burns strong. He is still married to Jeanette and they have two sons, Tom and Liam. Gary says, 'Tom has now joined the staff at Arsenal helping with the stadium tours and the museum. I am very envious of him and Liam still goes to games when he can. We also have two daughters. Vicky lives just outside Newcastle with a family of Toon fans and Kerry is recently married to a Liverpool season ticket holder.'

Despite his personal difficulties, Gary still prides himself on a huge collection of Arsenal memorabilia. 'If it is Arsenal-related, I want it,' he says.

Emilio Zorlakki, now 52, says, 'I didn't realise how much the 1979 FA Cup Final win was to mean. A few weeks later, my family were evicted from our home because of a contractual cock-up. We had to leave all my familiar surroundings and friends and move to a run-down council flat. I was about to sit my O Level exams.

'In normal circumstances, I would have found this period in my life very hard to deal with and would probably have suffered depression, which is something I've had to contend with in adult life. Yet this cup triumph was my salvation!'

Emilio, who now works as a local government officer for the London Borough of Haringey, has been a season ticket holder for 35 years and goes to every game, home and away.

He says, 'I have seen all our subsequent triumphs and count myself particularly lucky to have been at Anfield on 26 May 1989. I was a regular steward on the Arsenal Travel Club for almost 25 years and still steward on the odd trip once in a while. I'm a bit of an Arsenal historian and get quite a number of people calling me asking if I know the answer to some obscure question. I have some just as knowledgeable friends who take part in a number of Arsenal or football quizzes too.

'My remaining wish is to see Arsenal win the European Champions League to finally complete the club's trophy collection and satisfy my last Arsenal ambition.'

Writing just before Arsenal prepared to face Wigan in the 2014 FA Cup semi-final, Emilio says, 'Following Arsenal today, I try and be cautious and realistic about our prospects, especially against the very wealthy clubs. It's true what they say, "It's the hope that kills you"! Nevertheless, in spite of my craving for European success, I'm happy to temporarily sacrifice that ambition in the hope that we could win any piece of bleedin' silverware!'